MINISTER'S ANNUAL

MINISTER'S ANNUAL
PREACHING IN 1987

Compiled and Edited by
Jim & Doris Morentz

ABINGDON PRESS
NASHVILLE

Minister's Annual

Copyright © 1986 by Abingdon Press

All rights reserved.
No part of this book may be reproduced or transmitted in any form or by any means, electronic or mechanical, including photocopying and recording, or by any information storage or retrieval system, except as may be expressly permitted by the 1976 Copyright Act or in writing from the publisher. Requests for permission should be addressed in writing to Abingdon Press, 201 8th Avenue South, Nashville, Tennessee.

This book is printed on acid-free paper.

Library of Congress Cataloging-in-Publication Data
Minister's annual.
   1. Sermons, American. 2. Prayers. 3. Bible—Liturgical lessons, English. I. Morentz, Jim. II. Morentz, Doris, 1929–
BV4241.M56   1986   252'.6   85-30609
        ISBN 0-687-26990-3 (alk. paper)

Scripture quotations in this publication are from the Revised Standard Version of the Bible, copyrighted 1946, 1952, © 1971, 1973 by the Division of Christian Education of the National Council of the Churches of Christ in the U.S.A., and are used by permission.

"This Week in History" sections are based on *Chase's Annual Events 1986*. Copyright © 1985 by William and Helen Chase, used with permission of Contemporary Books, Inc., Chicago.

"Story of the Week" sections are taken from *505 Jokes You Can Tell* and *2121 Funny Stories and How To Tell Them*, by William K. Pendleton. Copyright ©1978 and ©1964 by The Bethany Press, St. Louis. Used by permission.

To Bert and Peg Hovey, who taught the Christian way of life by their example

Our appreciation to the many pastors who have so generously contributed their sermons to make this book possible

To the Reverend Thomas Richards for his friendship and his assistance in the preparation of this book

To Beverly Stout, who typed every single word of this book

PREFACE

This book is divided into three sections:

SECTION I

There are fifty-two Sunday sermons with suggested scripture lessons, calls to worship, offertory scriptures, invocations, offertory prayers, and prayers for the day. All the prayers in this book are written by the editors. Also included are two hymn suggestions. You will find, in addition to the service material, a theme, This Week in History, the bulletin announcement for next Sunday's sermon, and the joke of the week.

SECTION II

This section is in turn divided into three parts:
- Special Seasons: Ash Wednesday, Good Friday, Christmas
- Special Occasions: Weddings, Funerals, Stewardship, Confirmation, John Calvin
- Special Series: This is an Old Testament Series of four sermons based on the book of Job. It may be used as a four-week series on Sunday mornings or mid-week services during Lent or Advent.

SECTION III

There is much information that may be useful during the course of the year. We have selected some information that we thought might be helpful without being overwhelming. Check it out. Maybe portions of it will be of assistance in your general preparation.

HOW TO USE THIS BOOK

First, we want you to know that we are not going to presume to tell you how to preach a sermon. You already know how to do that, and very well.

BUT

we are going to tell you how to use this book to create fifty-two successful sermons. It will be easy, but you have to at least be willing to try it our way. If you are willing to invest fifteen minutes a day, we can do it together. Here's our way:

Sunday: 15 minutes	— Read next Sunday's sermon.
Monday: 15 minutes	— Read it again.
Tuesday: 15 minutes	— Read it again. It will start to sound very familiar.
Wednesday: 15 minutes	— Read it again. Now you will start to see yourself in the sermon.
Thursday: 15 minutes	— Read it again. If you add some of your own experiences, the sermon will be a lot better.
Friday: 15 minutes	— Read it again. The author had some good ideas, but without your input this sermon would not fit your people.
Saturday: 15 minutes	— Read your sermon again. "Finally, this feels like my sermon. I'm involved, it is my sermon. I am ready to preach; let's go!"

Sounds too simple? Try it.

Suppose you really don't like one of the sermons, or it goes against what you believe. Don't use it! There are alternatives. You will have special services throughout the year, and you will have vacation Sundays—use these as substitute sermons. Move the sermons around to suit yourself. There are special sermons to fall back on.

It's all there, not cluttered with a lot of useless material—fifty-two Sunday sermons ready to go; specials for many occasions; and the usual data and information in the back that we feel will be useful. There is no perpetual Easter calendar. When did you last need to know on what date Easter would be in the year 1991? Check out the material in the back. You may find some of it very helpful.

How to use additional Sunday service material:

The major offering of this book is the fifty-two Sunday sermons. In response to the requests of many pastors, we have included material to assist in the preparation of the service according to the theme of the sermon.

Goals for Today: Here we simply attempt, in a few sentences, to show you the theme of the integrated sermon-services program.

This Week in History: We feature two past or current historical events. These may be helpful in your sermon, in other talks during the week, and as bulletin fillers. These events are often non church-related, but could be of interest, nevertheless.

Announcement for Next Week's Sermon: This is an effort to simplify your life by giving you an announcement that can be used in the Sunday bulletin, newspapers, parish paper, and so forth.

Story of the Week: We happen to believe strongly that there is not only room for humor in the church, but also that there is a great need for humor in the church. Every pastor needs at least one new good story that can be used in the sermon, in a presentation during the week, or just in conversation. We give you a new one every week.

We have done our part in the preparation of this book. If you take our suggestions and do your part, we are all going to have a good year.

CONTENTS

SECTION I:
FIFTY-TWO SUNDAY SERMONS

January 4 Dreamers and Producers—*Edward A. Beckstrom*........... 15
January 11 A More Excellent Way—*Carl Viehe*......................... 21
January 18 The Power of Forgiveness—*Roger O. Colvin*.............. 29
January 25 The Natural—*James L. Kidd*................................ 36
February 1 You Can Have Peace Within—*John Strom*................. 44
February 8 Live Religion—*Bruce V. Malchow*.......................... 49
February 15 It's the Real Thing—*D. Timothy Robinson*................. 55
February 22 The Sin That Couches at the Door—
 Richard A. Chrisman... 62
March 1 How Much Energy Do You Have?—*Glen L. Borreson*..... 68
March 8 The Near Kingdom—*Jerry L. Schmalenberger*.................74
March 15 Jesus, Lord of All—*Jon Lindekugel*............................. 81
March 22 He Loves Me . . . He Loves Me Not . . . He
 Loves Me!—*Virgil R. Anderson*..87
March 29 You Can Too!—*Raymond W. Gibson, Jr*...................... 93
April 5 Who Holds the Title?—*James M. Logan*...................... 101
April 12 To Be a Spectator—*Thomas E. Richards*.......................107
April 19 A Pharisee Speaks—*Marie Hubbel*............................114
April 26 Don't Leave Now, the Party's Just Starting—
 D. Z. Ring.. 121
May 3 Bolted Doors—*Edward A. Beckstrom*............................. 127
May 10 Biblical Images of Women—*D. Z. Ring*.........................133
May 17 Jesus, the Good Shepherd—*Peter D. Hardt*...................140
May 24 The Head of the Church—*Thomas W. McCurdy*..............147
May 31 My Peace I Give to You—*Karl M. Kindt III*................... 155
June 7 Hearing God in One Another—*James S. Vuocolo*.............163
June 14 Forth in Thy Name—*David C. Nelson*.......................... 171
June 21 How Big Is Your God, Daddy?—
 Raymond W. Gibson, Jr... 176
June 28 Has Christianity Failed?—*Charles W. Kern*...................183
July 5 Let Freedom Ring—*Thomas E. Richards, Jr*..................... 190
July 12 Clay Feet—*David C. Nelson*.. 196
July 19 Harried into Hope—*Harold G. Deal*.............................202
July 26 Teach Me to Pray—*Linda C. Beattie*..............................209
August 2 Believe in Yourself!—*Douglas K. Showalter*................. 215
August 9 Meeting God's Demands—*Richard A. Chrisman*.......... 223
August 16 On Knowing What to Do—*Carl Viehe*......................229
August 23 God's Gambling Grace—*Virgil R. Anderson*............... 236
August 30 Religion and Justice—*Charles W. Kern*......................242

September 6 What Is the Meaning of Life?—*James L. Kidd*.........249
September 13 You Want to Take It with You?—
  Glenn L. Borreson..255
September 20 To Your Advantage—*Warren A. Nyberg*...............261
September 27 On Being Different—*D. Timothy Robinson*...........267
October 4 God Promises No Rose Gardens—
  Dan Phipps..274
October 11 Grace—*Peter D. Hardt*............................... 281
October 18 The Leap in the Dark—*Bruce V. Malchow*..............287
October 25 Raising a Tudor Rose—*Jerry L. Schmalenberger*.......293
November 1 The Politics of Faith—*James S. Vuocolo*.............300
November 8 Making Yourself Miserable—*Dan Phipps*...............307
November 15 Faith Without Love—*Douglas K. Showalter*........... 313
November 22 On Dealing with Our Anger—
  Warren Nyberg...321
November 29 In Praise of Unlikely Apostles—
  Harold G. Deal.. 327

December 6 The Good Thief—*Warren Nyberg*.......................334
December 13 The Presence of Jesus: Symbol or Reality?—
  Rolf Ahlers...341
December 20 Surprise—*Terrence M. O'Neill*......................349
December 27 A Boy, a Baby, and Bethlehem—*James M. Logan*... 356

SECTION II:
SPECIAL SEASONS, SPECIAL SERMONS, SPECIAL SERIES

Special Seasons
Ash Wednesday: Death Is the Beginning—
  Thomas E. Richards, Jr.. 366
Good Friday: Complicity—*James S. Vuocolo*......................369
Christmas: Let It Be—*James L. Kidd*............................ 372
Christmas (Short Message): The Christmas Star—
  Karl M. Kindt III... 376

Special Sermons
Wedding: A Mixed or Ecumenical Marriage—
  Charles M. Chakour.. 380
  The Lord Bless You and Keep You—
    Charles M. Chakour.. 382
Funeral: A Funeral Sermon—*Thomas E. Richards*..................384

Contents

Stewardship: Give Thanks—The Tithe—*Terrence M. O'Neill*....... 386
Confirmation: The City of God—*Robert M. Belles*...................... 390
John Calvin—Servant of the Word—*Alton H. McEachern*........... 393
Electronic Preachers: Monetary Messiahs—*Dan Phipps*.............. 397
Patriotic: Christians and Government—
   Alton H. McEachern.. 400

Special Series
Old Testament—Job: The Almighty Troubleth Me.................... 406
            The Tenderizer of Our Hearts....................... 411
            Divine Target Practice................................... 416
            Overwhelming the Fatherless—
              Fred C. Lofton.. 420

SECTION III: APPENDIXES

A. Highlight Dates of the Church Year................................. 428
B. Calendars... 428
C. Colors of the Church Seasons.. 430
D. Lectionary Series for 1987.. 431
E. Blessings and Benedictions.. 435

Sermon Contributors... 439

Sunday
January Fourth

Theme: Starting the New Year Right

Call to Worship: Commit your work to the Lord, and your plans will be established. *Proverbs 16:3*

Invocation: The world needs dreamers, but it also needs doers. Let us be part of that group that dreams and then does. Your kingdom will not come on earth unless we become producers for the spreading of the gospel. Let it be so with me, Lord. Amen.

Hymn: "O God, Our Help in Ages Past"

Sermon Presentation: "Dreamers and Producers"

Goals for Today: We are your hands and your feet. We must produce or your will does not get done. Show us how we can all be producers.

This Week in History

Jan. 4—Louis Braille's Birthday—This man invented the Braille system whereby the blind were enabled to read. He gave sight to the blind and the joy of reading to millions.

Jan. 5—Twelfth Night— The end of the Christmas season and the beginning of the Epiphany season.

Announcement for Next Week's Sermon: In school when we wrote a perfect paper we got an "E" for excellence. If God graded our lives the same way, Jesus would have gotten the only "E" ever given. God expects excellence from you. Next Sunday find out how to give it your best shot.

Hymn: "He Leadeth Me: O Blessed Thought"

Offertory Scripture: When God saw what they did, how they turned from their evil way, God repented of the evil which he had said he would do to them; and he did not do it.
Jonah 3:10

Offertory Prayer: Lord, help us to start this new year as one of giving. Let us return gifts to you worthy of the blessings that you have bestowed upon us. *Amen.*

Prayer: O Lord, here we begin another year. We echo Paul when we say, "The good that I would do, I do not. The evil that I would not do, that I do." Why didn't you make it easier for us? I get so tired trying to carry the sins of all the generations that have gone before me. It just does not seem fair. We try so hard, but we fail so often.

I know all the testing builds Christian character, but I wonder if you will ever finish working on me. I want to be yours; isn't that enough? What else do I have to do to prove my love for you? This is not a perfect world, and this is not an easy place to try to live a Godly life.

Why am I going on like this? You were here in your son, you walked the same road I have to walk. You had the same problems I have to endure. You know how tough it really is. You were perfect and they hung you on a cross. Lord, forgive me for my complaining. My problem is not that my life is so hard; it is that I am trying to carry the burden on my own. Take me; be with me every step of the way. Let me take up my cross and follow you through this whole new year. Let me truly make this the year of my Lord. *Amen.*

Story of the Week: A little girl asked her Sunday school teacher, "Why do they always say 'amen' after they pray in church? Why don't they ever say 'awomen?'" Before the teacher could think of an answer to that one, a little boy in the class spoke up and said, "They do that for the same reason that all the songs they sing are 'hymns'."

DREAMERS AND PRODUCERS

Several years ago I took a graduate course entitled "Writing the Non-Fiction Book." In that course guest lecturers—some of whom were best-selling authors—spoke to us. One guest lecturer said that there are two types of people: those who are going to write a book, and those who write books. Everyone, it seems, has experiences that he or she someday intends to write a book about, but there's only a small percentage of those

January Fourth

persons who actually sit down and write books. That's the difference between dreamers and producers. *Dreamers* think about books—*producers* are the authors. But dreamers and producers are not confined to the world of literature. They are in every walk of life.

The world has many dreamers, but not an overabundance of producers. We know this to be especially true in the Christian church. A well-used statistic is that 80 percent of all the work done in the church of Jesus Christ is done by 20 percent of its people. Likewise, 80 percent of all the money given to the work of Christ is given by 20 percent of the people. Those 20 percent of persons who do most of the work and give most of the money are the producers. The rest? They are the dreamers. They're the ones who often complain that the church should be doing this, or shouldn't be doing that.

We Protestants take a great deal of pride in quoting the Apostle Paul, especially verses such as Romans 3:28 where he says, "For we hold that a man is justified by faith apart from works of law." This, of course, means that our faith alone puts us right with God, not the following of any religious, legal demands. Now, many people seem to think that this means that God rewards the dreamers—that it's more important what you think about Jesus Christ than what you do for him. It's true that you can't work your way into heaven, but it's also true that Jesus says: "I am the true vine, and my Father is the vinedresser. Every branch of mine that bears no fruit, he takes away, and every branch that does bear fruit he prunes, that it may bear more fruit" (John 15:1-2).

Apparently, Jesus was saying that he wants more than dreamers. He wants producers. The church of Jesus Christ was not built on dreamers; it was built on the blood, and the sweat, and the tears of producers.

When Jesus made the analogy of himself to the vine and the branches, he stated that if the branches receive nourishment from the vine, they'll bear fruit. If they do not bear, they are dead and should be cut off. Jesus was not contradicting Paul's idea that we are made right with God through faith alone; rather, real faith is made manifest in the way we respond to working for the kingdom of God.

Now listen again to those statistics I mentioned: 80 percent of the work of the church is done by 20 percent of the people!

In other words, only 20 percent are producers—those who bear fruit—while the others (80 percent), in Jesus' analogy, are dead branches—worth nothing in the kingdom.

Nevertheless, the church is full of dreamers.

One kind of dreamer is the person who comes to church regularly, but never gets involved with anything the church is doing. Now, I'm not talking here about the "C & E" Christians (the Christmas and Easter Christians). You know, they're the ones who come at Christmas with the question of the magi on their lips, "Where is he who has been born King of the Jews, for we saw his star in the East and have come to worship him?" But then you don't see them again until Easter, when the message is this: "He is not here, he has risen!" You see, they missed him!

No, I'm not talking about the C & E Christians, I'm talking about those who come to church regularly, but they are just never really involved. They're in church to be "inspired," to come away week-in and week-out with a good feeling, with a new insight, to sing a favorite hymn or two and have their batteries recharged for another week.

Now, there's nothing wrong with those people. God knows the church could hardly exist without them. The seats on Sunday morning would only be a fifth as full as they are now! But by the same token, the church could not exist with only those dreamers. There would be no preaching, no great hymns to sing, no corporate prayer, no anthems, no Sunday school, no church organizations, and no church building. Everyone would be sitting, just waiting for some direct inspiration, I suppose. Jesus Christ needs producers, not just these folks' dreams.

Another dreamer you might recognize is the person who thinks great thoughts about Jesus, about the church, about the Holy Spirit, but never really produces. These people mean well, and they use a lot of "Jesus talk." Usually they are vigilant at studying the Bible, praying, and dreaming great dreams about what the church ought to be doing, how the unsaved ought to be saved, how sin ought to be dealt with, how the Holy Spirit ought to be more visible in the ministry of the church, how the pastor ought to be doing more calling, and so on. But it is left to others to roll up their sleeves and get the work done.

Here's a brief illustration. See where you fit into this picture. In my years in the ministry, I have entered many homes that

January Fourth

had recently experienced the loss of a loved one. Time and time again I have seen loving, warm, concerned neighbors, friends, and relatives come to the mourning household to offer their condolences. Almost invariably they will say something like this: "If there's anything we can do, please call on us."

I think I've witnessed that scene a hundred times; yet I have never once seen the grieving one respond with a request for help. But on rare occasions the scene will be different. A neighbor or friend will come by, say just a few words to the mourning family, then go into the kitchen and start to make dinner or bake bread. Or they'll go over to the family's small children, scoop them up in their arms, and say something like: "Come on, you come over to my house for a few days and visit with me." The dreamers—"call us if you think of anything"—and the producers—"we're going to help on the spot." As I said, I have never seen a grieving person ask for help from someone who offered it; likewise, I have never seen a grieving person refuse help from someone who came in, rolled up his or her sleeves, and got to work.

The church is like that grieving person. It needs people who will come in, roll up their sleeves, and get to work.

Christ never scolded the producers, but he had quite a bit to say about the dreamers. "My Father breaks off every branch that does not bear fruit," he said.

He also said: "Not every one who says to me 'Lord, Lord,' shall enter the kingdom of heaven, but he who does the will of my Father who is in heaven" (Matthew 7:21).

About some dreamers he said:

> Beware of false prophets, who come to you in sheep's clothing, but inwardly are ravenous wolves. You will know them by their fruits. Are grapes gathered from thorns, or figs from thistles? So every sound tree bears good fruit. Every tree that does not bear good fruit is cut down and thrown into the fire. Thus you will *know* them by their fruits. (Matthew 7:15-19)

In an interesting story in Matthew's Gospel, Jesus tells of God's dividing people into two groups at the Final Judgment. He tells the people on the right-hand side that they are welcome into his kingdom because: "I was hungry and you gave me food, I was thirsty and you gave me drink, I was a stranger and you welcomed me, I was naked and you clothed me, I was sick and you visited me, I was in prison and you came to me (25:35-36).

And the people on his right side ask God when it was that they saw him like that and did those things for him. God responds by saying, "As you did it to one of the least of these my brethren, you did it to me" (25:40).

He was saying that this world is where ministry ultimately takes place, and it is done by the producers, not the dreamers. Sometimes the producers don't talk in great spiritual language, or articulate their faith in eloquent terms, but you'll know them because they have their sleeves rolled up, and they're doing what has to be done for God's kingdom.

At an Air Force base in Bitburg, West Germany, the Protestant chapel members and the Catholic parish cooperated in a number of functions together. One annual event that everyone looked forward to was the Mother's Day breakfast prepared by the Protestant and Catholic men. It was always quite an affair, with pancakes, eggs, ham, bacon, juices, and all the trimmings. It took quite a bit of planning and preparation. A Catholic man, by the name of Kelly, always coordinated the whole affair. He was just one of those delightful persons who was always there for anything that needed to be done.

But tragedy struck Kelly's life one Friday before the Mother's Day breakfast. His wife of many years suffered a massive heart attack without warning and died. Yet two days later Kelly was in the kitchen on Mother's Day, flipping flap-jacks and eggs so the Protestant and Catholic parishes could enjoy Mother's Day. Kelly was a producer who often went far beyond anyone's expectation. Jesus had a name for people like Kelly. It was "good and faithful servant." *Amen.*

Edward A. Beckstrom
Equality, Alabama

Sunday
January Eleventh

Theme: Try for Excellence

Call to Worship: Do not be conformed to this world but be transformed by the renewal of your mind, that you may prove what is the will of God, what is good and acceptable and perfect. *Romans 12:2*

Invocation: Lord, make us perfect. Don't give us A's on our report cards of life, but fill us with love; love that will not let us go; that drives us on to perfection in your sight. We don't care what the world might think. Make us God's children seeking to win his approval so that we might hear our Lord say, "You have chosen my way, not the way of the world. Yours is a life of excellence; come unto me." *Amen.*

Hymn: "I Would Be True"

Sermon Presentation: "A More Excellent Way"

Goals for Today: We all strive for excellence and perfection. To strive is not enough. Today in our service and in our sermon, we seek to find the more excellent way.

This Week in History

Jan. 14—Albert Schweitzer's Birthday—Philosopher, physician, musician, and 1952 winner of the Nobel Peace Prize. A gentle man who is a classic example of giving one's self where there is need, not comfort or acclaim.

Jan. 15—Martin Luther King, Jr.'s Birthday—Civil rights leader, minister, and winner of the 1964 Nobel Peace Prize. A man who preached non-violence all his life only to die a violent death, murdered April 4, 1968. A man who sought excellence for all men.

Announcement for Next Week's Sermon: "I hate you" is a statement we hear all too often and find so easy to say. "I forgive you" is so tough to say. To forgive is to humble yourself. Next Sunday we discover there is also power in forgiveness.

Hymn: "This Is My Father's World"

Offertory Scripture: For by a single offering he has perfected for all time those who are sanctified. *Hebrews 10:14*

Offertory Prayer: Thank you, Lord, for accepting me now in my imperfect state. Thank you, too, for offering me the chance to grow in the faith, so that I can move closer to you and to the perfection you want for me. Sin keeps me from excellence; take away my sin and make me yours alone. *Amen.*

Prayer: Don't give up on me, world. God is not yet done with me. I will get better before long. Don't give up on me, Lord. I really am trying to come closer to your expectation of me. Oh, please don't let me give up on myself. If I do, then all is lost. I certainly cannot achieve excellence without you. You cannot make me perfect without my wanting you to. I have to submit myself to you totally, completely, so that I no longer have a life of my own. It is you and me, Lord; we make it together or I will fail for sure. When I stray, bring me back. When, by my actions, I deny you, teach me to confess you to the whole world. When I am too proud, humble me. I can even stand a little pain; try me. Do whatever you will with me, but don't give up on me. Perfect me; teach me to love; save me by your grace. Your grace, Lord, is the more excellent way. *Amen.*

Story of the Week: The only part about going to church that the little fellow didn't like was the long pastoral prayer. There were times when he thought it would never end.

Then one Sunday the minister was a guest for dinner. He was asked to offer thanks. He prayer was brief and to the point, after which the little fellow said, "You don't waste much time praying when you're hungry, do you?"

A MORE EXCELLENT WAY

"Now you are the body of Christ and individually members of it . . . Are all apostles? Are all prophets? Are all teachers . . . ?

January Eleventh

Earnestly desire the higher gifts. And I will show you a still more excellent way" (I Corinthians 12:27-31).

The Apostle Paul, in his first letter to the Corinthian church, says that the church is like the human body—all parts have to work together. For healing, some are physicians; for instruction, some are teachers. Then he talks about a higher gift of the spirit. It is the gift of Christian Love, which he describes in I Corinthians 13. He introduces this chapter by saying: "I will show you a still more excellent way."

When we think of excellence in the history of our own country, we are reminded of Benjamin Franklin—but there was a schoolboy who wasn't so sure about Ben Franklin. He was asked to write an essay on Franklin's life. He squirmed in his chair, chewed his pencil, took out a piece of paper, wrote at the top of it *Benjamin Franklin*, and produced the following masterpiece:

> Benjamin Franklin was born in Boston, but her son got tired of that and moved to Philadelphia. When he got to Philadelphia he was hungry, so he bought a loaf of bread. He put the bread under his arm. He walked up the street. He passed a woman. The woman smiled at him. He married the woman, and discovered electricity.

The best-selling non-fiction book of 1983 was entitled *In Search of Excellence*. There seems to be a new concern for excellence in our land—in education, in industry, and in the growing emphasis on exercise. We are not content to sit back and watch the world go by anymore.

A former football coach for a western university was once asked by a television reporter what contribution modern football had made to physical fitness. His reply was, "Absolutely nothing." He defined football as *twenty-two men on the field who desperately need rest, and fifty thousand people in the grandstand who desperately need exercise.* To sit back is no longer enough. We strive to excel in all things.

For one thing, we have seen the tragic consequences of indifference and neglect. Senator Adlai Stevenson, former United States Ambassador to the United Nations, once remarked, "This is a rich and resourceful country. But its spirit of adventure and invention may be drying up. Nations fail when that happens."

There is a sense in our land today that that is exactly what is happening to us. Other nations are beginning to challenge our moral leadership.

A manufacturing firm once used an advertisement which stated that it wasn't the Goths that defeated Rome; it was the free circuses. Luxuries, power, indulgence had made the Roman people soft. The ad went on to say that to stay popular, the emperors gave the people more and more of the ease they craved—free bread, free circuses, and easy living. So the Romans were too soft when the ambitious, hard-working barbarians invaded, and in A.D. 410 the greatest nation the world had ever seen fell.

We are beginning to understand the danger of complacency and neglect. As someone once said: "When the grass looks greener on the other side of the fence, it may be that they take better care of it over there."

In the sixties and seventies it was out of vogue to talk about hard work. The so-called "Protestant ethic" was considered obsolete in a post-industrial society. Creative use of leisure was the concern of the day. What we forgot was that the human creature is designed in such a way that complacency and neglect are destructive to the human spirit. The time-honored principle—use it or lose it—is true. We may not like work. I personally agree with the man who said that he loved work—he could sit and look at it all day. Nevertheless, it is true that hard, enthusiastic work, with a high and lofty motive behind it, is essential to society and to the human spirit.

The search for excellence is a great Christian principle. We are stewards of our minds, our bodies, and our souls. We must seek the best. Neglect and complacency are among our deadliest enemies. As Henry Wadsworth Longfellow put it:

> The heights by great men reached and kept
> Were not attained by sudden flight,
> But they, while their companions slept,
> Were toiling upward in the night.
>
> *The Ladder of St. Augustine*

Excellence requires not only hard work, but it also requires a spirit of adventure. Bruce Larson, in *There's a Lot More to Health Than Not Being Sick*, shares a story that makes this point. He and some others were invited to try out a friend's new sailboat. A

January Eleventh

brisk breeze was blowing, and the proud new owner was at the tiller. "You know," the owner said, "I've been sailing for seventy years, and would you believe that in all those years I've never yet tipped over a sailboat?" The other men looked at him aghast. They were veteran sailors.

"Are you serious?" one of them asked candidly. "You've sailed for seventy years and never tipped over? . . . I don't think you've ever really sailed."

The veteran sailors knew that part of sailing was the possibility of capsizing. Excellence always involves risk. Paul was a man who was never afraid to risk his life for Christ. Whether he was speaking to a hostile crowd in a marketplace or shipwrecked on some island in the Mediterranean, he was a man who lived life to the fullest. The search for a more excellent way is a call to adventure.

The search for excellence also involves an upbeat, expectant attitude. There is a story about a farmer who was continually optimistic, seldom discouraged. He had a neighbor who was just the opposite. Grim and gloomy, he faced each new morning with a heavy sigh. The happy, optimistic farmer would see the sun coming up and shout over the roar of his tractor, "Look at that beautiful sun and the clear sky!" And with a frown, the negative neighbor would reply, "Yeah—it'll probably scorch the crops!" When clouds would gather and the much-needed rain would start to fall, our positive friend would smile across the fence, "Ain't this great—God is giving our corn a drink today!" Again, the same negative response, "Uh huh . . . but if it doesn't stop before long, it'll flood and wash everything away."

One day the optimist decided to put his pessimistic neighbor to the test. He bought the smartest, most expensive bird dog he could find. He trained him to do things no other dog could do. He then invited the pessimist to go duck hunting with him. They sat in the boat, hidden in the duck blind. In came the ducks. Both men fired and several ducks fell into the water. "Go get 'em!" ordered the owner. The dog leaped out of the boat, walked on the water, and picked up the birds one by one. "Well, what do ya think of that?" The pessimist answered. "He can't swim, can he?"

Some people are defeated by their attitudes before the race is ever started. Others will never be defeated for the same reason.

The man who built the Brooklyn Bridge was a dreamer. He was dreaming about spanning the East River in New York City with a suspension bridge. "Can't do it!" he was told. But he continued to dream, found some backers and started building.

Then one day a tragic accident crippled him for life. He became confined to his apartment. Only the foundations of the bridge were completed. The man then turned over the on-site supervision of the bridge to his son. But from his apartment window he could see the bridge in the distance. So every day he supervised his son's work by watching through a telescope. And the Brooklyn Bridge was built exactly as he had specified! He was able to dream, and he finished the job.

Some people will never get started—others will never quit. It is these who will find the excellent way. A man named Zig Ziglar has motivated many people to dream big dreams. I like what he says about David and Goliath in *Confessions of a Happy Christian*. He says that one night, as he was reading the story of David and Goliath, he began to add some extra embellishments to clarify the story. He realized that David's brothers were negative and afraid, that they figured Goliath was "too big to hit." David was positive and knew that Goliath was "too big to miss." The brothers compared Goliath's size to their own, which made Goliath awfully big. David compared Goliath to God, which made Goliath awfully small. Quite a difference!

A willingness to work, to risk it all, to dream great dreams—all these make up the search for excellence. But there is more—the belief that in the long run Christian love is what ultimately matters. There are many persons today who are looking for a more excellent way for the wrong reason. "I'm doing this," they say, "for me." Those are the catch words of our time—"for me." If I am at the center of my universe, what ultimate reason do I have for doing my best at anything? One day I will be gone, forgotten. No one will even remember my name. What difference will it all make then?

It made a difference to Paul. For him, to live was Christ. He did not live for himself. He knew the presence of the living Lord in his life. How could he help giving himself to God completely in everything?

In our search for excellence, let us make sure that we have our priorities in order. We are told first to seek God's kingdom and his glory. But sometimes we can't find the more excellent way

January Eleventh

because we are afraid of getting involved. Maybe your faith lately has been as tired as that of the man who spoke to the minister after church about becoming a member. But the man said that he was rather busy. "I don't want to be called on for any committee work or teaching in the Sunday school or singing in the choir. I would like to be spared from anything that would take my time." Then he added, "But also, don't expect me for worship too often." The minister thought for a moment and then replied, "I believe you are in the wrong church. The church you are looking for is down the street."

The man followed the minister's directions and soon came to another church. It was abandoned and had been boarded up. That man did not want to get involved. His faith was not excited because he was afraid to let God move him. Yet, some people never find the right way because they refuse to take even the first step.

There was a *Peanuts* cartoon once in which Charlie Brown complained to Linus about his publisher. "The publisher sent me a rejection slip," lamented Charlie. "So what?" said Linus. "Lots of writers get rejection slips." "But I didn't even submit a manuscript," cried Charlie.

In the church at Corinth, the most amazing things were happening through the action of the Holy Spirit. They were happening because the Christians there had learned to say "Jesus is Lord," in spite of the fact that the Roman government wanted everybody to say "Caesar is Lord." When a man or woman could say "Jesus is Lord," it meant that that person, man or woman, gave to Jesus the supreme loyalty of his or her life, and the supreme worship of his or her heart.

I have never known a person who had genuinely committed his or her life to God and was on the road to a more excellent way, who was ever regretful. Chuck Swindoll has a humorous story in his book, *Growing Stronger in the Seasons of Life*, that illustrates this.

A missionary was sitting at her second-story window when she was handed a letter from home. As she opened the letter, a crisp, new ten-dollar bill fell out. She was pleasantly surprised, but as she started to read the letter, she was distracted by a shabbily dressed man down below, leaning against a post in front of the building. She couldn't get him off her mind. Sure that he was in greater need than she was, she slipped the bill into an envelope, on which she hastily wrote the words, "Don't despair." She threw it out the window. The man picked it up, read it, looked up, and smiled as he tipped his hat and went his way.

The next day as she was about to leave the house, there was a knock at the door. Here was the same shabbily dressed man, smiling as he handed her a roll of bills. When she asked what they were for, he replied: "That's the sixty bucks you won, lady. Don't Despair paid five to one."

I like that. But obviously such an act of love, an act of service, doesn't always have a five-to-one payoff. Sometimes it is much more!

In our search for the more excellent way, let us be certain that we have our priorities straight. Let's work enthusiastically, adventurously, positively with commitment and service. But first of all, let us seek Christ's kingdom and his glory.

Let us pray: O God, by whose grace we are made new, may Christ and his excellence become real to us; may we go out into life, wiser to solve our problems, stronger to do our tasks, and more devoted to thy will. In Christ . . . *Amen.*

Carl Armin Viehe
United Church of Christ
Buffalo, New York

Sunday
January Eighteenth

Theme: You Can Be Forgiven

Call to Worship: To him all the prophets bear witness that every one who believes in him receives forgiveness of sins through his name.
Acts 10:43

Invocation: Lord, judge us by your mercies, not by our actions. Forgive us as we forgive. Oh Lord, we fall so far short of this goal. We cannot enter the kingdom by our deeds. We cannot make ourselves worthy. Only your great grace and forgiveness can save us. Show us your way, your truth, and your life as a great example. Forgive us our sins; save us by your mercy. Amen.

Hymn: "My Faith Looks Up to Thee"

Sermon Presentation: "The Power of Forgiveness"

Goals for Today: The sermon for today sets the whole mood of this day. It is a powerful first-person statement. It shows that God moves in strange ways to deliver his message to all of us. Ponder and preach; it will be a very special day.

This Week in History

Jan. 19—Robert E. Lee's Birthday—Military leader of the Confederacy. A great general, but also a great gentleman. Truly a man who was forgiven by all the people of the United States.

Jan. 21—Roger N. Baldwin's Birthday—Born 1884. Founder of the American Civil Liberties Union (ACLU), known as "unofficial agitator for, and defender of, civil liberties."

Announcement for Next Week's Sermon: Sometimes a movie can preach a better sermon than a preacher. Next Sunday the sermon is about that kind of movie.

Hymn: "I Would Be True"

Offertory Scripture: If thou, O Lord, shouldst mark iniquities, Lord, who could stand? But there is forgiveness with thee, that thou mayest be feared. *Psalm 130:3-4*

Offertory Prayer: Lord, we offer these gifts to you in response to your great love. We know we cannot buy your forgiveness; we cannot buy your love. We commit our lives to you so that we may receive that great gift of forgiveness. *Amen.*

Prayer: Give us courage, Lord, to forgive. It takes a lot for me to be a forgiving person. It seems that every time I have to forgive, I have to admit that I am wrong. I don't like to have to humble myself in front of other people. It just does not seem right. Lord, I know what my problem is. It is not that I don't want to forgive, it's that I am proud. Why can't I be proud of my humility? Why can't I be proud that I give a generous gift to my church? Why can't I be proud of the work I do for your kingdom here on earth? Why can't I be proud that I show your love to the poor and the lonely? All of a sudden I feel strange. I hear you saying, "Are you proud that because of your sin my Son had to die on the cross? No, child, anything you do, any love you show, any cross you bear, all of it is in response to my love for you and my sacrifice for you. You want to be proud? Be crucified with me, then you can be proud." Here I go again, Lord; forgive me for my pride. Keep me humble and never let me lose sight of your sacrifice and love for me. Forgive me, forgive me. *Amen.*

Story of the Week: The minister had given up golf during Lent. But his golf clubs were still in the trunk of his car.

One day as he passed the golf course, he decided he'd just drive a few. "That's not the same as playing," he said to himself. But, after driving a few, the minister found himself playing down the fairway in absolute disregard to his Lenten pledge.

Looking down on this was a little angel, who ran to his boss and said, "Lord, look what is happening. The minister broke his pledge. What should we do about it? What sort of punishment should we give him? How about letting me hit him with a bolt of lightning?"

"How terrible!" said the Lord. "We've got to punish him

January Eighteenth

properly. Lightning isn't bad enough. But first, let's see how he does on this next hole."

As the Lord and the angel watched, the minister teed up his ball and made a mighty swing. It soared for three hundred yards, hit a rock and bounced another hundred yards to the green, where it rolled gently into the cup.

"Did you see that?" cried the angel. "A hole in one on a four-hundred-and-twenty-yard dogleg. Why, Lord that's the greatest golf shot in the history of the game. What sort of punishment is that?"

"That is his punishment," the Lord said. "The greatest golf shot in history—and whom can he tell?"

THE POWER OF FORGIVENESS

This sermon may be a little short this morning. I hope by the time I say "Amen," you will understand why.

"If you forgive people's sin, they are forgiven; if you do not forgive them, they are not forgiven." That is what Jesus said to the disciples after he appeared to them and breathed the Holy Spirit on them.

I had set aside a couple of hours to work on this sermon text. I thought there were some very deep spiritual implications involved; I needed the time to pull them out. Forgiveness is important. *Forgive us our debts as we forgive our debtors. Do for us, Lord, as we are willing to do for others.*

I was just beginning to write when someone called to say that three women with suitcases were trying to get into the church. I expected no one, but I went to the door to see what I could do. I admit I resented the interruption because I needed the time; ideas were just beginning to come.

At the door I met a woman of around thirty years old, a middle-aged woman, and an older woman who must have been in her seventies, if not one hundred. The old woman was bent over from age. She stood with a cane, and, were it not sad it would have been funny, wore a pair of sneakers.

The youngest woman asked if she could speak to me. They had been out in the rain. I said Yes, but inside I was thinking, "Don't you know I am working on a sermon? *If you forgive people's sins, they are forgiven; if you do not forgive them, they are not forgiven.* I have a congregation that listens eagerly to what I have to say. I need my time."

She said, "Can you help us?" I looked at the old woman, whose face could not be seen because she was bent over so much. She was guided around by the young woman, and was always asking her where they were going, or what they were doing. I looked at the middle-aged woman; she was smiling. The younger woman did the talking. "Can I help you? What you need is a home, a place for this elderly woman to be comfortable and warm," I said.

"Yes, we want to get to ———" (she named a town down state) "and we need bus fare."

I knew from their accents they were not from around here. "But you cannot get there by bus."

The younger woman said, "We know."

I said, "You will have to take the train."

"Yes, that's OK." And they kept on smiling as if I had the answer to all of their problems.

I hedged because I needed to get back to this sermon. *If you forgive people's sins, they are forgiven; if you do not forgive them, they are not forgiven.* And I was beginning to feel rather unforgiving of this intrusion upon my time. But she just kept on smiling.

I pictured in my mind their getting a bus, then transferring to another to get to the train, then catching a train. "Where are you from?" I asked. The younger named the town down state. "What are you doing here?" I said.

"We were given a ride this far."

How I probed and how evasive were the answers. At every moment, I was ready to shout, "Tell me the truth! I don't need another fairytale. Just tell me the truth."

"Yes," I thought. "I can give you bus fare to get you off my back so that I can get back to working on forgiving people's sins. I'll get you out of my life with a few bucks and deal with some real truths that Jesus taught.

"Reverend," the younger asked, "would you have any food?"

"Yes, I can give you some food, but how are you going to carry it? You have two suitcases and some bags." *What a rag-tag outfit you are.* She followed me to the pantry, asked if she could have certain cans. I gave them to her, but said, "The bag will get too heavy with all the rest you have to take."

January Eighteenth

She smiled, "Yes, you are right." Everything I said was right, and she kept on smiling.

We went back to where the other women were sitting. The middle-aged woman was smiling. Why didn't these people look mean so I could get mad at them?

"Reverend, would you have any clothes?" We have sent people to the Re-uzit Shop in the past, so I pointed them down the street and said I would call and arrange to pay the bill.

I made the call then went back to work. *If you forgive people's sins, they will be forgiven; if you do not forgive them, they will not be forgiven.* There must be some great, significant truth in those verses. I did not need people taking up my time. I looked up some teachings about sin: Pride, *hubris*, making ourselves ends in themselves. I wondered how long they would be away.

After a time I heard clacking in the hallway. I could hear it from a long way off. They had returned with two plastic bags filled with clothing. I could tell that the younger had found a pair of shoes. They were satisfied with their purchases.

My mind floated back and forth between, *If you forgive people's sins* . . . and how these people were ever going to get home tonight. On Wednesday evening we had studied Jesus' teaching about the blessedness of being spiritually poor. There are two words used for poor in the Greek language. One means "not well off, having enough to live on but being far from wealthy." The other, and the one used here, means, "destitute, abject poverty, not knowing where you are going to spend the night, where your next meal is coming from."

What do you do when people throw themselves upon your mercy? I struggled to see Christ in these people. A devotional I read this past week told of a bishop who had helped a young man to get a bus ticket to where he needed to go. On his way home the bishop felt quite smug about his righteousness; then he remembered that this young man had enabled him to serve Christ.

Some people say they see Jesus in visions, that he appears as we would expect him to, in a flowing garment. I don't deny it. If only Jesus would come in that seamless robe, walking about ten inches above the street. But if he has to come to me, why does he do it in the form of someone who always smiles and takes every word I say as the truth?

My time was flying by and I had not gotten much further than, *If you forgive people's sins, they are forgiven*, and was beginning to feel anxious. How could I get these people out of my life? But what if it were Christ? Would I not be bowing and scraping before him: "Yes, Lord, what do you want me to do now?" Oh, what a sermon I could preach this morning if Jesus had appeared to me this week and I could relate our conversation.

But all I got were three women, two forever smiling and the other bent over so I could not even see her face. "Tell me the truth," I said. "I will get you tickets home, but if you are not going home, this won't do you any good."

"No, we want to go home."

I knew the trouble they would have trying to get to the train station on the bus. Sure, they could board a train here, but how long would they have to wait in the damp, cold air? I had lost so much time now, I figured I would never get back to forgiving people's sins.

It came to me that if I did not forgive these people for their intrusion into my life, would God forgive me? I could have discovered their story, sent them away empty, and been satisfied I had penetrated another charade—but would God forgive me? What a shame people have to live a lie to just stay alive.

A meditation I read this week says, "You are the salt for all mankind. But if the salt has lost its saltiness, what is it good for?"

I argued in my mind, "I am not a social worker. I am a preacher, and my sermon this week is going to be on forgiving people's sins."

I looked at the three of them. How do people get into this position? I said I would take them to the train station; I had called for information as to the fare.

The younger woman said to the oldest, "He is going to take us to the station," as if it were a few blocks away. The bent over head just moved up and down a bit, acknowledging that she understood, and maybe thankful for a chance to sit down for awhile. We loaded everything into the car. As the old woman was getting into the car, I saw her face for the first time. She was aged, weary, and, I am sure, wondering, "Where are they

January Eighteenth

taking me?" She could have been anybody's mother. It was the face of age you see so often in magazines.

I found a kind of release because I had, within myself, forgiven them of their intrusion, of taking me away from time I needed to prepare this sermon for those who eagerly, intently await my every word on a Sunday morning.

We had some conversation, but I could never find out much more about them. We got to the train station and pulled in alongside a late-model sports car. Two young fellows were getting in as we were getting out. I read what was on their minds, "There is a saint doing the Lord's business." No, I suppose it was more like, "What is that middle-class man doing with three poor people?"

I watched as the middle-aged woman helped the older one up the steps of the station, a step at a time, and they vanished from my life. Maybe they were from another world. They were. I have never had to do what they did—depend totally on someone else. I have never had to ask for food or clothing.

I depend on the word from Hebrew 13:2, "Do not neglect to show hospitality to strangers, for thereby some have entertained angels unawares." As I drove home, I prayed. I never did get to work on forgiving people of their sins. "Lord," I said, "you will have to give me the sermon for Sunday," and the words came back almost like a bell, "I already have." *Amen.*

Roger O. Colvin
St. Mark's United Methodist Church
Mount Joy, Pennsylvania

Sunday
January Twenty-fifth

Theme: The Rules of Life

Call to Worship: Or do you presume upon the riches of his kindness and forbearance and patience? Do you not know that God's kindness is meant to lead you to repentance?
Romans 2:4

Invocation: To each of us are given gifts. To some, great gifts—to others, small gifts, but to all gifts according to our abilities. Today, Lord, we look at a great gift that was almost lost. Grant that we may use what you give us to your honor and glory. *Amen.*

Hymn: "O Master, Let Me Walk with Thee"

Sermon Presentation: "The Natural"

Goals for Today: Challenge your people to take a long, hard look at themselves and to take stock of all the natural and learned skills they have. Raise the question, "Are you using everything you have to God's glory, or are you letting life rob you of all our virtue?"

This Week in History

Jan. 27—Vietnam War Cease-fire—End of the longest war in U.S. history. Treaty signed in Paris, thus ending U.S. combat role in a war which had more than one million deaths. Never again—never again.

Jan. 29—Thomas Paine's Birthday—American Revolutionary leader and author of "Common Sense" and "Age of Reason." These two pamphlets stirred the fires of the war. "These are the times that try men's souls" are the opening words of his inspirational tract, "The Crisis."

Announcement for Next Week's Sermon: If you find any peace in this crazy world, please let me know where it is or how you found it. Next Sunday let's look for it together.

January Twenty-fifth

Hymn: "Jesus Shall Reign"

Offertory Scripture: Likewise you that are younger be subject to the elders. Clothe yourselves, all of you, with humility toward one another, for "God opposes the proud, but gives grace to the humble." Humble yourselves therefore under the mighty hand of God, that in due time he may exalt you.

I Peter 5:5-6

Offertory Prayer: Lord, help us to learn that you are King of kings and Lord of all. When temptation comes, help us to resist. When our turn comes to step up to the plate to bat for you, grant that we might be ready to give our all. Give us a chance and stay with us. We will not fail with you at our sides. *Amen.*

Prayer: Father, we come before you with thankful hearts. You have touched us today and left us with your promise. Life is filled with meaning; life offers us a second chance to be born again. Life gives us a chance to do good things in your name. Life assures us that justice and righteousness will always triumph. Lord, with all the natural gifts you've given us, what more can we ask? You have loved us from the beginning and will love us till the end. You have won for us the victory. All we have to do is say, "Yes, Lord, I believe." That we should respond to so great a gift is only natural. Take me today. *Amen.*

Story of the Week: One of the local businessmen had been invited to speak to the children in the third grade. He decided to talk about the progress of the world during the past fifty years. He spent half an hour talking about the great inventions that had been developed during his lifetime.

"And now, before I go, I'd like to ask this question," he said. "What is the most important thing in the world today that wasn't here just twenty years ago?"

"Me," said a little boy in the front row.

THE NATURAL

"And they were astonished beyond measure, saying, 'He has done all things well'" (Mark 7:37).

Russell Baker, columnist for *The New York Times,* has written a book entitled *Growing Up*. In that book he has a delightful chapter in which he talks about the conversations that used to take place on the front porch back in his hometown, and how, night after night, the same wisdom was repeated over and over again. The men would all come in from the fields. Exhausted, they would sit down in their rocking chairs. But the women-folk, who'd been working all day long, continued to work and to prepare the men something to drink and to eat, some refreshment. One of the men would say, every night, "A man works from sunup to sundown, but a woman's work is never done." Everyone would nod, "Mm-hmm." They all agreed. There was no arguing with such wisdom. And when one of the children would act up, one of the adults would make the insightful observation, "Satan finds work for idle hands to do." And all across the front porch—"Mm-hmm, uh-huh."

My father used to have words of wisdom like that. One of the phrases that he frequently shared with all those who would listen was, "That which gets our attention gets us." My mother would always say, "Uh-huh." And now that I'm a little older, I also say, "Uh-huh." That which gets our attention, gets us. And that which gets our attention is stories.

Stories tell us the meaning and the purpose of our lives. They tell us how we're to put our lives together and how to relate to one another, how to understand the nature of people and the nature of life itself. The Bible is full of wonderful stories. Down through the centuries, people of faith have repeated those stories over and over again because they carry the meaning of life. They make sense. They describe and define the nature of the "really real," the way things are. Whenever we run across such a story, we know we have received a great blessing. From time to time there occurs a song, a play, or a movie in which the meaning and the purpose of life are made clear again.

The Natural, starring Robert Redford, is such a movie. It's a wonderful story. It begins with a young man playing catch with his father in very deep wheat fields. Anyone who's ever played catch knows that the ball is frequently missed, so if they dropped the ball in that deep wheat it would take them a long time to find it. I imagine all the men who watched that scene hoped that the ball wouldn't drop.

This movie portrays a marvelous relationship between father and son. This father tells his son that he's a natural. He has a

January Twenty-fifth

gift. But it's not enough to have the gift. He has to work at it and develop it. While they are playing, suddenly, out of the skies come thunder and lightning. A huge old hickory tree is split down the middle, and the boy's father dies. The boy goes to that old hickory tree, and from it he carves the wonder bat—a marvelous, miraculous instrument for playing baseball.

In time, the coach who has helped to guide and direct him to become an extraordinary athlete accompanies him to try out for a major baseball team. On the train, whom should they run into but "The Whammer"—the greatest baseball hitter of all time—who looks remarkably like Babe Ruth. The coach challenges the sportswriter friend of The Whammer. The coach says that his young athlete is the best there ever was, and that if he threw three balls at The Whammer, that would be all he would need to strike him out. The train stops; there's the opportunity to put the challenge to the test. Ten dollars rides on the outcome. In 1923 that was a lot of money for the young man's coach to bet. Three balls are thrown and The Whammer is struck out.

They make it to Chicago. There a strange and wicked woman invites young Roy Hobbs, "The Natural," to her hotel room. He walks into the room, and she asks him if he will be the best there ever was. He says that he will be. She takes out a gun and shoots him with a silver bullet, no less. You know at this point that this movie is going to be different. The screen goes dark.

The next scene is sixteen years later—1939. Roy Hobbs returns, as a middle-aged rookie, from out of nowhere to play left field for a last-place New York based baseball team. He is no longer a pitcher, but a power hitter. Now he is given a second chance to play in the major leagues. The manager doesn't want to play a middle-aged man in the major leagues, but he seems to have no alternative. So, finally, after all these years, Roy Hobbs and "the wonder bat" come to the plate. Lightning streaks across the sky. The pitch is thrown. In slow motion he swings and connects. The ball goes out of the park. Not only does he knock the ball out of the park, but he also literally knocks the cover off the ball. This knight-in-shining-pinstripes inspires his team to rise from last place to a tie for first place in the league.

Evil forces try to destroy him, but righteousness prevails. Just prior to the deciding game, the evil seductress tries to poison him. He becomes very sick. But in spite of his pain and suffering, he goes to the big game determined to play his role.

The pitcher has been paid off to throw the game, so he allows the opposing team two runs. Two times Roy Hobbs goes to the plate, and two times he strikes out. He receives a note from his childhood sweetheart, who has come to the game. Suddenly he is filled with new life, and he comes to the plate once again in the bottom of the ninth inning. The score is two to nothing. There are two men on base, two outs. Roy Hobbs swings at the ball. It's a foul knocked into the sportswriter's typewriter, destroying it. Once again he swings and hits the ball. It's a mighty blow—it would have been a home run—but it's off the side. And with this hit he breaks the bat. Then, he turns to the bat boy and says to him, "Go pick me out a winner."

Now from time to time there comes a movie that contains within it a phrase that will live in eternity. In the movie *Gone with the Wind*, there were two gems like that: "Tomorrow is another day." Remember that? And "As God is my witness, I'll never go hungry again!" In the movie *The Godfather*, people are given "offers they can't refuse." Now, in *The Natural*, Roy Hobbs says to the bat boy, "Go pick me out a winner." Previously, Hobbs had carved another miracle bat and had given it to the bat boy. Well, one hardly needs much imagination to know which bat is brought to Hobbs in this moment of crisis.

He returns to the plate. Lightning streaks across the sky! The pitch is thrown. In slow motion, he swings and hits the ball over the outfield wall and up into the stadium lights. Three runs are scored. Hobb's team wins the game and the pennant. And that's what the movie is all about.

Now, you ask, "What was *that* all about?" and, "How can that be an appropriate subject for a sermon in a Christian church?"

It seems to me there are four current secular assumptions about the way things are in the "real world." The first assumption is that life is a meaningless cosmic accident and we are on our own. The second assumption is that life is tragic and Murphy's Law is the way things are, that all things work together for bad. Third, you can't tell the good guys from the bad guys. As the poet said, "There's an awful lot of good in the worst of us and an awful lot of bad in the best of us." And in the fourth place, in the real world the bad guys usually win—they get rich, are elected to office—and the good guys lose, if they don't die young.

But this movie, *The Natural*, rejects all four of those assumptions.

First of all, this movie tells us that life is not a meaningless cosmic accident; we are not alone. Strange and mysterious things are afoot. There is more going on than meets the eye. It suggests that there is a mysterious force involved which sends lightning bolts to destroy old hickory trees from which magic bats can be carved; a force which causes a father to die leaving a young son; which causes a young man to have a miraculous gift; so we know that talent was no accident, but a gift. It was not simply natural, but supernatural. He was the best that ever was.

No, this is not a world of cosmic accident. This is a world of purpose, and grace, and mystery. When Roy Hobbs loses touch with his moral values, he is tempted and corrupted by the beautiful, but evil, seductress. He mysteriously loses his gift, his power, and he has a prolonged batting slump. But when the virtuous Iris, who is a symbol of grace, returns to stand up for him, once again the lightning streaks across the sky. The power returns, and in one game he hits four home runs. This is a world in which there is a transcendent connection between righteousness and power! And how much we need today to be reminded of that truth.

Second, this movie supports the view that there is much in life that is tragic, that bad things happen; we even get shot with silver bullets. But that is not the last word. It is possible to be born again. Iris, the good woman in this movie, tells Roy that she believes we have two lives—the life we learn and the life we live after that. Roy begins to feel sorry for himself for the bad things that have happened to him. He says that for sixteen years he could have been the best. But Iris says that we are not permitted to live in our druthers. Life is good *NOW!* She says that he is good now, and he has a good influence on children. She insists that life is filled with possibilities! When he is poisoned, Roy Hobbs ends up in a maternity hospital. One can be born again.

Scripture says that all things work together for good to those who love the Lord. Christians believe in second chances and in the act of being born again; there are crucifixions, but they are not the last word. There are resurrections, life beyond the grave and life beyond every tragic moment. There is a second act. And more than that, anything is possible for those who have faith; anything can happen. Water can be turned into wine and a good guy can literally knock the cover off the baseball. We need so much to hear that message in a world filled with cynicism.

In the third place, this movie says it's easy to distinguish the good guys from the bad guys because the good guys do good things and the bad guys do bad things. The bad guys lie, steal, cheat, and kill. Good guys don't do that. Jesus said, "You will know them by their fruits . . . every [good] tree bears good fruit, but the bad tree bears evil fruit." The bad guys love the darkness. Remember Matthew 7:16-17, the Scripture I just read to you. To be in Christ, to be in God, is to be in the light. To be in sin is to be in darkness. The bad guys love the darkness because no one can see what they're doing. In this movie the evil judge literally lives in darkness. Even when he goes to the ball game, he sits up in a booth and hides behind drawn shades. The good guys live in the light; they're bathed in the light, and they love the truth. They are not afraid to be seen.

There is a wonderful scene in which Roy Hobbs talks to the beautiful blonde seductress on the telephone. She tells him that she's alone, and she is standing there in her white slip. We can see her. She is not alone. She is with the evil gambler, Gus, and she is dressed in all black. The Bible says that Satan is a liar; when people lie, steal, cheat, and kill, they're evil—you can tell just by looking at what they do.

Last of all, this movie shows that the good guys win and the bad guys lose. It says that ultimately there are consequences to being evil, and we live in a morally just and righteous universe. God is the Lord of Life. No matter how it sometimes looks, that means that righteousness will prevail. In the words of an old hymn, "God is working his purpose out as year succeeds to year." In John 16:33, Jesus said to the disciples, "In the world you have tribulation; but be of good cheer, I have overcome the world." When Roy Hobbs hits the last home run, it's not just the baseball game that is won, not even a pennant. Rather it's the triumph of righteousness over the evil empire; it's the victory of the forces of light over the forces of dark. And as Roy runs the bases after that winning home run, he literally goes *home*. He returns to his father's house, from whence he has come. In the last scene of that movie, there he is, back in the tall wheat, back on the farm, playing catch with his own son, while the beautiful and virtuous Iris smiles upon her husband and son.

My friends, anyone who doesn't have a tear in his eye and a smile on his lips at that point will never enter the kingdom of heaven!

Someone always asks me after one of these movie sermons if I think the director really meant to put all that in a movie. And my answer is it doesn't matter what he intended because it's there. Sometimes the Lord uses people when they don't even know what they're doing, and I think the Lord used the director of this movie to proclaim a gospel which is eternal and true.

Four points—first, life is not a meaningless cosmic accident but it is filled with meaning and purpose. When we have a gift, it comes from above. When we have a talent, it's no accident. Second, life is not finally tragic, and Murphy's Law has been repealed; all thinks work together for good. We can be born again. There is a resurrection. Third, you can tell the good guys from the bad buys just by looking at what they do. And fourth, evil never wins. The good guys, justice and righteousness, have the last word. The good guy will hit the home run and be the hero. This means it's worth every sacrifice and every effort.

Christians know all of this, don't we? We know all of that because it's been revealed to us through Scripture and the revelation of God in Jesus Christ. *Amen.*

James L. Kidd
Asylum Hill Congregational Church
Hartford, Connecticut

Sunday
February First

Theme: Peace Immediately

Call to Worship: I have said this to you, that in me you may have peace. In the world you have tribulation; but be of good cheer, I have overcome the world.   *John 16:33*

Invocation: In this time of rush-rush, hurry-hurry, and the whole impersonal world in which we live, O Lord, we need a little peace, quiet time to be alone and listen to the still, small voice of God that says to us, "Here is my peace. Be still and know that I am God. All is well for those who love me, peace." *Amen.*

Hymn: "O Love That Wilt Not Let Me Go"

Sermon Presentation: "You Can Have Peace Within"

Goals for Today: As a person who preaches peace, I know how desperately we all need to find peace—that peace that puts our hearts, our souls, and our bodies at peace, at ease, and at rest. Today that message is our goal.

This Week in History

Feb. 1—Freedom Day—President Abraham Lincoln approved the Thirteenth Amendment in 1865 (Abolition of slavery). Everyone is free or no one is free. This should be a great church holiday too.

Feb. 1-7—International Clergy Appreciation Week—This week honors the four chaplains who died February 3, 1943, when they gave up their life belts during the sinking of the *S.S. Dorchester*. This week now honors all clergy.

Announcement for Next Week's Sermon: Is your religion alive? Do you feel that God talks to you each day? Do you hear voices? You may have a problem if you do or a worse problem if you don't. Bring your problem next Sunday.

Hymn: "Let Us with a Gladsome Mind"

February First

Offertory Scripture: Each one must do as he has made up his mind, not reluctantly or under compulsion, for God loves a cheerful giver. *II Corinthians 9:7*

Offertory Prayer: How do we repay you for your peace so freely given? We respond to you in kind. We give cheerfully of what we have, not because we hope to gain something, but because you gave to us first. As you gave the first fruits—your Son—so to you we give our first fruits—our tithes—to show our love and thanks. *Amen.*

Prayer: Lord, today we have talked of peace. We have this conflict in ourselves: What is peace? Is it being right with our neighbor? Is it being right with our family? Is it being right with our God? Is it all these things, all of which go to make us at peace? God, peace is such an elusive thing. To a healthy young person, continued good health brings peace. To a person who is ill, the return to good health will bring peace. To the person who is terminally ill, the release from pain and suffering that is offered only by death is the goal that brings peace. Lord, we know that fear is the great conflict in our lives. We have to fight against fear in our jobs, in our homes, and in our families. Our whole lives seem to be filled with threats and fear. Root out this uncertainty in our lives. Replace it with your peace so that we are so firmly anchored in you that nothing can shake us. Your peace can overcome the world. Your peace can overcome our fear. Your peace can overcome death. With that victory, we are at peace. Peace at last, peace at last, God Almighty, peace at last. *Amen.*

Story of the Week: The Sunday school teacher was telling her class the story of the prodigal son. "But even with all this joy and celebration," she said, "there was one who was not happy with the preparation of the feast for the return of the son, who felt only bitterness and did not wish to attend the feast. Who was it?"

After a moment's silence, a small voice said, "It must have been the fatted calf."

YOU CAN HAVE PEACE WITHIN

The word *immediately* occurs two times in our morning's lesson. We read this morning in Mark 1:21-28, that on the Sabbath Jesus appears immediately in the synagogue teaching. And then immediately Jesus confronted a man with an unclean spirit.

This man possessed of an unclean spirit cried out in the hearing of all, "What have you to do with us, Jesus of Nazareth? Have you come to destroy us? I know who you are, the Holy One of God." Then we read that Jesus rebuked him, saying, "Be silent, and come out of him!" Then the unclean spirit, convulsing the man and crying with a loud voice, came out.

That event is described plainly. Jesus commanded the unclean spirit to come out of the man. The unclean spirit obeyed the voice of Jesus, the voice of authority and power. Its coming out of the man was accompanied by a convulsion and the sound of a loud voice. The story is vivid, and the chief actor is Jesus Christ, the Exorcist!

But what are we to make of this story?

That story comes to us from the first century A.D., and we live two thousand years later. The category of demon-possession is from a pre-scientific age. In our day we do not explain abnormal behavior in terms of demons. The scientific method, that method by which we all live, merely asks what is the cause behind a certain effect. Looking at our story, we would ask: What was the cause of the man's strange behavior? What caused the convulsion? What caused the loud cry described in the story? Why was this person so highly disturbed? Is this to be explained by saying he was possessed by demons? Or is there some other factor or factors underlying his abnormal mental condition?

Believe me, I am not trying to cast doubts on the power of Jesus to calm a disturbed personality. I am not casting doubts on Jesus' ability to bring peace and tranquility to this person's innermost being, to his very soul. Indeed, I think that the central point of the story is that Jesus Christ did and does bring peace to the troubled soul.

However, we must not lightly pass over a problem in this miracle story. Inherent in the account is a first-century belief in demons and demon-possession. Jesus seems to share that belief. Jesus was a child of his generation. In the above account, Jesus either personally believed in demon-possession, or he was merely pretending to believe in the powers of demons. It seems that if we were to say that Jesus merely pretended to believe in these powers in order to accommodate his listeners, then Jesus would appear to be lacking in integrity. No, we must say that Jesus believed in the reality of demons, and that he believed this troubled man to be possessed by an unclean spirit.

A critical question then follows. If Jesus did affirm such a reality as demons, must we? Can we understand this gospel story in the light of what we call mental illness?

That the man in the story can be described as being emotionally unbalanced is beyond question. Was he suffering from what is called a *multiple personality* or a *split personality*? I think that we must take this view quite seriously. The scripture text reads, "What have you to do with *us*? Have you come to destroy *us*?" Did the disturbed man have more than one side to his personality? In other words, were there many aspects to his personality?

Modern medicine is aware of the impact of a disturbed mind upon the body. A disturbed mind causes various functional troubles. And what of the loud voice accompanying the release of the unclean spirit? When a deeply troubled mind is allowed to come clean, when a deeply troubled spirit is allowed to express itself unashamedly without fear of punishment, there is often a loud cry or scream which accompanies this feeling of relief. Counseling therapists know this well from their experiences in group work. This cry is often referred to as the *primal scream*.

Let's put the story in the category of medical science. Perhaps the man was suffering from epilepsy. When Jesus cast out the unclean spirit, there was a convulsion. I believe I am accurate when I say that epilepsy is not yet clearly diagnosed or understood. Is this disease a matter of chemical imbalance, a neurological, physiological problem, or is it a psychological condition, too? Even if this disease can be controlled by drugs, does this control mean that a clear cause of the disease has been established?

I have raised these questions because I think it is crucial that each of you ponders them. These questions are not irreverent. We do not settle for first-century modes of transportation. We do not consult witch-doctors today. When we need our teeth fixed, we do not ask our barber to do it. If in need of counseling, we do not seek it over the backyard fence. In all areas of human life we seek expertise and the best informed sources. Yet many persons are content with explanations out of the ancient world, particularly in matters of religion!

I am merely suggesting that you ask yourselves to what degree you believe in demons and demon-possession, because they are clearly biblical categories of thought. If you do not believe in such a reality, you are a modern and you have parted company with one category of biblical religion. You must be honest enough to admit this in order to maintain a healthy spiritual life.

My personal statement is that, while I do not look for demons everywhere, I think that not all human behavior can be adequately explained by mere psychological mechanisms. I think there are some cases of abnormal behavior in which evil is so deeply entrenched that an exorcist is needed—and that only the power of the Living God can effect any change for the better.

Further, I believe that there are some souls so self-centered that those persons assume demonic dimensions in their lives. Satan, as you know, is the personification of selfishness!

And I firmly believe that Jesus Christ can bring peace within. I know that Jesus Christ has brought a degree of balance, of tranquility, and of peace in my life, and that this peace within is more than the world can give. He has managed to control the demons in my existence. And as I mature, I think that there is nothing so important as this peace of God which passes all understanding. Do you have this peace within? Jesus Christ wants you to have this peace. He can give it to you. In the silence of the moment, claim it; affirm it; and live in it. *Amen.*

John Strom
St. Mark's Lutheran
Indianapolis, Indiana

Sunday
February Eighth

Theme: Religion That Works

Call to Worship: Whoever would be great among you must be your servant, and whoever would be first among you must be slave of all. For the Son of man also came not to be served but to serve, and to give his life as a ransom for many.

Mark 10:43-45

Invocation: Lord, we are called to serve, to bring a vitality and life to our faith and to our religion. Never let the excitement and joy of our first discovery of your gift, your Son, become commonplace. Keep us high on a live religion. *Amen.*

Hymn: "O For a Thousand Tongues to Sing"

Sermon Presentation: "Live Religion"

Goals for Today: Let's come to life. Let this be a happy service. The sermon is not some light, happy thing, but it does offer the challenge to come face to face with God. We should be happy to meet an old friend face to face.

This Week in History

Feb. 11—Thomas A. Edison's Birthday—American inventive genius. Over twelve hundred patents. "Genius is one percent inspiration and ninety-nine percent perspiration," he once said.

Feb. 13—First Public School in America—The Boston Latin School opened on February 13, 1635. Education of all people is the cornerstone of all democracy.

Announcement for Next Week's Sermon: What can I say to convince you that God's word is real? If you don't believe it by now, I guess we should give up on you. Never! Next week, one more time! "It's the real thing."

Hymn: "Have Thine Own Way, Lord"

Offertory Scripture: That you may know what is the hope to which he has called you, what are the riches of his glorious inheritance in the saints. (Paul's prayer) *Ephesians 1:18*

Offertory Prayer: You told us, Lord, to be doers of the word, not just talkers. That is hard. We have to love the unlovely; we have to feed the poor; and we have to give to make your kingdom come here on earth. Accept these gifts as a down payment on our debt to you. *Amen.*

Prayer: You must get pretty tired of hearing us play the humble role here for one hour a week, and then see us go out into the world as if we never knew you. If we are ever to have a live religion, it is going to have to change us. It will have to make us full-time Christians. We must change so that you and all the world can see and say, "See how they love one another." That is a live religion—that we love one another and are ready to bear one another's burdens. No one need suffer alone so long as we live our faith and are alive to all the needs that daily surround us. Where there is suffering, loneliness, hunger, fear, or a loss of faith, Lord, "Here am I, send me." Help us to return concern for our fellow man as you first reached out to save and help us. As you are always more ready to give than we are to receive, so let us be ready to give. May our giving be a reminder to all who see that we are serving because we are called to be servants. Make our religion live forever. *Amen.*

Story of the Week: The minister's little six-year-old girl had been so naughty during the week that her mother decided to give her the worst kind of punishment. She told her she couldn't go to the Sunday school picnic on Saturday.

Then, when the day came, her mother felt she had been too harsh and changed her mind. When she told the little girl she could go to the picnic, the child's reaction was one of gloom and unhappiness.

"What's the matter? I thought you'd be glad to go to the picnic," her mother said.

"It's too late," the little girl said. "I've already prayed for rain."

February Eighth

LIVE RELIGION

What does being Christian mean? The word has been used loosely to cover so much. Some people consider themselves Christian because they were baptized twenty, thirty, or forty years ago, even if they have done little with Christianity since. Some consider themselves Christian because they have had their names on a church roll for years, even if they have seldom darkened a church's door. Some consider themselves Christian because they come to church on Sunday, even though they do not let Christianity influence their lives during the week. These are all ways of dabbling with Christianity without really getting into it. We still ask, "What does being Christian really mean?"

Today's Gospel reading answers that question. In this story Peter has a moving encounter with the power of God. Peter comes to a new awareness of who God is and who he is in relation to God, and that changes his life. He commits himself fully to living for the God he has come to know in a new way. That is being Christian—responding to God's action for us by committing ourselves to living for him.

Our Old Testament lessons for each Sunday are usually chosen to match our Gospel readings. That is certainly true today. The Old Testament lesson about Isaiah's call describes an experience with the same message we find in the Gospel reading. Isaiah is in the temple one day for routine worship. He probably expects this to be like any other temple visit. But God has other plans. Isaiah has a vision of God as an exalted king, sitting on a throne in the temple. The vision is full of supernatural elements. Strange creatures, which probably look as if they are half snake and half human, fly around praising God. The temple shakes and fills with smoke. But the supernatural features are secondary. The main point is that Isaiah has encountered God.

This has enormous impact on him. For one thing, he is terribly aware of his unworthiness before God. But God deals with this feeling. He assures Isaiah of his forgiveness when one of the creatures touches his lips with a hot coal. Then God puts forth a call for a prophet. Isaiah immediately responds: "Here I am! Send me." And his life is never the same again.

Isaiah had been a believer in God. That is why he was in the temple in the first place. But now he is a follower of God in a new sense. He has personally experienced God and has devoted his life to serving God in a new way.

The Gospel story matches Isaiah's experience at every important point. Like Isaiah, Peter experiences the presence of God. It happens when Jesus guides him to a large catch of fish. One thing that makes Jesus so significant is that through him people experience the presence of God, as forcefully as Isaiah experienced it in his exalted vision.

When Peter experiences that presence, he reacts as Isaiah did. The text says: "When Simon Peter saw it, he fell down at Jesus' knees saying, 'Depart from me, for I am a sinful man, O Lord! For he was astonished, and all that were with him, at the catch of fish which they had taken" (Luke 5:8-9). The presence of God again evokes amazement and a sense of unworthiness. Again God deals with that sense. Jesus tells Peter: "Do not be afraid" (Luke 5:10). Then, like Isaiah, Peter receives a call. Jesus tells him to fish for people for the kingdom of God. Peter responds in a way that changes his whole life: "When they had brought their boats to land, they left everything and followed him" (Luke 5:11). Peter and his companions left everything—the comfort of their homes, their jobs—to be Jesus' disciples. They had been believers in God before then. But, obviously, their new experience of God has raised them to a new level of commitment.

These two biblical stories are similar because they are typical accounts of people encountering the mystery of God. That continues to happen today. People continue to have experiences in which they reach a new awareness of God. These experiences move beyond our normal ways of learning about God. Usually we learn about him through the words of other people. Our parents tell us the first things we learn about God. Sunday school teachers and pastors add to our information. Other Christians sometimes talk about their religious beliefs. So we begin to believe in God's presence.

But most people have their own experiences which make their belief in God a very personal thing. These experiences vary as much as people do. There is no way to predict when they will happen to different people. Some people experience the presence of God as a result of dealing with life's problems. When they lose confidence in their abilities to cope, they find God present and able to help them. Some people experience the

February Eighth

presence of God in certain worship occasions. Sunday after Sunday may be the same, but one Sunday we feel the presence of God. Many people especially sense his presence in the Lord's Supper. Regardless of how it happens, the main point is that we come to a personal awareness of God. The book of Job described the experience long ago. Job said to God, "I had heard of thee by the hearing of the ear, but now my eye sees thee" (Job 42:5).

When Isaiah and Peter experience God in this way, their lives are changed. They totally commit themselves to serving God. They can do that because they now know God personally and know that he is worth it. Have our experiences of God led to such commitment? If we have experienced God, we do not have to be convinced that this is the route to go. We know that it is.

What does commitment to God involve? It involves many areas of our life. I will describe just one now. Jesus made clear that commitment to God is reflected in the way we deal with the poor. We are to sacrifice ourselves for those weaker than us, as Jesus has done for us. That is an important call to us in our society. We have so much, and we have so many ways to use it on ourselves. Advertising parades an endless string of products before us. We will never reach a level of income where there will not be more than we can buy.

But that approach leads us in the wrong direction. The question is not What can we still buy? but What do we need in order to live? We need much less than advertising leads us to think. Americans can live simpler lives than we do. We need less food, energy, and clothing than we use. Even less do we need the many luxuries on which we spend our incomes.

If we were to live simpler life-styles, there might be more money available for the poor because we will have more to give to the world's needy instead of spending it on ourselves. Also, resources that we do not waste will be available for people in other places. So this is one way we can respond to Jesus' call to care for the poor.

Another way to help the poor is the manner in which we interact with them. How do we act when we meet someone down and out? I recently saw a movie in which a church leader visited a downtown rescue mission. He sat next to a man who looked like a bum and tried to talk to him. The first moments were embarrassing. But it did not take long before the two were talking. By the end, the poor man was showing the leader pictures from a dilapidated wallet. The leader had been wise enough to know that he was the same kind of human being as was the poor man. They shared with each other on the basis of their common humanity. They started sharing because the leader showed concern for this other person. That, then, is another way to care for the poor.

Care for the poor is one way that we show our commitment to God. In many such ways we show that we have personally met God. Such meetings are deeply disturbing; they make great changes in people's lives. But through them we grow toward lives that have more meaning. *Amen.*

Bruce V. Malchow
Sacred Heart School of Theology
Hales Corners, Wisconsin

Sunday
February Fifteenth

Theme: What Is Real?

Call to Worship: You will know the truth, and the truth will make you free. *John 8:32*

Invocation: Oh, Lord, you are the truth. You are all that is real in our lives. When we lose our way it is only the light of your love that leads us home to your safe refuge. Grant, Lord, that we may never stray so far from your truth that we lose our way and sight of you and your purpose for our lives. Make your truth so real in our lives that we are never afraid, that we will never doubt and never deny thee. Come into our lives; guide and control us forever. *Amen.*

Hymn: "Take My Life, and Let It Be Consecrated"

Sermon Presentation: "It's the Real Thing"

Goals for Today: We are faced with a generation that has been reared on catchy slogans and promises of the quick fix for every problem. The answer the church offers to this superficial thinking is a simple truth: A real relationship with a living God. This is not one of the choices we can make; it is the only choice we must make. Every part of the service leads to this choice.

This Week in History

Feb. 19—Nicolaus Copernicus' Birthday—This Polish astronomer and scientist revolutionized scientific thought with the Copernican Theory. He said the sun is at the center of our planetary system. *That* is how God created it, but it took almost 1500 years to discover this fact and even more years to accept it.

Feb. 20—First American in Space Anniversary—John Glenn became the first American in space to orbit the Earth. God created the heavens and the earth. Now he has made it possible to explore more of his wonders.

Announcement for Next Week's Sermon: "I got so mad at him I could have killed him." Sound familiar? Next Sunday's sermon can help you deal with anger. It could save a life—yours.

Hymn: "There's a Wideness in God's Mercy"

Offertory Scripture: Again Jesus spoke to them, saying, "I am the light of the world; he who follows me will not walk in darkness, but will have the light of life." *John 8:12*

Offertory Prayer: Lord, this is the real world. You gave it to us perfect, and we have been poor stewards of this treasure. You won't give us another world or another chance at this one. Help us to see the folly of our ways before we destroy this, your gift, and ourselves, also. Give us the wisdom to know the difference between what is real and necessary and what is unreal and destructive to your universe. You have shown us the way; now give us the courage to do what we must to follow that way and to be ready to pay the cost to be "little Christs" to our brothers and sisters here on earth. *Amen.*

Prayer: O God, we allow the world to dictate to us what we eat, what we wear, what we drink, and where we go on vacation and how we get there. That is the power of the world, to sell us what it has to offer. We are the great consumer nation. Lord, we are still in control of our own lives. No matter how hard they sell, if we don't buy it, if we don't try it, we will never know if it is the real thing. Help us to keep control over our own lives. Make us picky buyers. Do not let us fall prey to every huckster that comes along. Let me continue to be me, your chosen child, your one-of-a-kind creation. Lord, remind us that some of the best things in life are free: a perfect spring day, the smile of a baby, the cool breezes of evening after a hot day, the perfection of a rose, the kiss of a loved one, the handshake of a friend—all free, all free. But now the greatest gift of all is free for the asking. Lord, take my life and let it be consecrated, Lord, to thee. The price was paid on the cross; the gift is now free for you and me. All we have to do is ask. Take me now; make me yours; never let me go—that is God's real promise to all of us. You are mine; you are saved; you will be with me forever. Thank you, Lord, for your great gift. *Amen.*

February Fifteenth

Story of the Week: An absentminded professor went to the drugstore and said to the druggist, "I would like a box of prepared tablets of the monacetic-acidester of salicyclic acid.

"Do you mean aspirin?" asked the druggist.

"That's it," said the professor, "I never can remember that name."

IT'S THE REAL THING

We hear so much about our youth today. What we hear and what we read is not always a true picture of today's young people. As a matter of fact, we are only hearing about the radical minority. I believe that it is about time we begin to give the majority their due credit. They are a vital part of this country, and they are a vital part of this congregation. They are vibrant, alive, and sincere. The kids I know are deadly serious behind those facades of pranks and giggles. They are not second-class citizens, whose contributions to life must wait until they come of age.

There was a time when there was not too much being said about the difference between the generations of youths and adults. Then something began to happen. From World War I came the terminology of the "lost generation," and from their children came the group called the "silent generation." Then we had with us the group that has been identified as the "beat generation," supposedly the group of young intellectuals who seemed to be constantly rebelling against the world, and who sought to hide in their mystical worlds of make-believe, through the use of many and varied means. But now another term is developing . . . "Coke is it" . . . you know the slogan . . . "it's the real thing. . . . " One simply needs to turn on the T.V. to see for oneself how a clever merchandizer is appealing to the major consumer—the youth of today. In their search for "the real thing," which is to be meaningful for their existence, they have capitalized upon this false impression. Frankly, the phrase, "the real thing," does not impress me so much as does the use behind the slogan. I would assume that the board of directors discovered that they could not conquer a public whose drinking habits had been pretty well established, so they turned their attention to another generation, and look how they did it; from that old familiar expression, "give me a Coke," we now have our kids asking for "the real thing." So now we must be in "the real thing generation." It might do us within the church well to listen to what the Coke people have to say and to learn from their experiences.

It is no secret that predominant within the thinking of many clergy and lay people alike is the belief that religion is in danger of losing its appeal. Somehow the flavor of it no longer seems to be compelling and satisfying; we simply remain content to place before our youth the same old merchandise in the same old packages, and they cannot accept it! Now the startling fact about all of this is that the ingredients are basically the same, but the approaches are different. What I am about to suggest is not new; it is not revolutionary. Listen to the words of our Lord: "You have heard that it was to the men of old . . . but I say to you . . ." Now there was something new coming; it was fresh; it was vital. He came with a whole new approach to life, and it captured the hearts and minds of that generation. The early Christian church and its development were literally what we might call a youth movement. It was led by a man of only thirty years of age—this is what you and I would call the Pepsi Generation of that day. It was the real thing they were looking for, and it caught the imagination, the faith, and the hearts of the people. Their leader was not satisfied to place new wine in old wineskins. No, he said, "you must put new wine into new skins," and both are safe. So, in conclusion to these introductory remarks, I would say that we have not yet lost the real thing. I do not believe the youth have lost their faith, but I do believe that they are growing weary of all the old cliches—"Now when I was your age . . ."—maybe it is a good thing our kids don't know what we did when we were their age. Dad complains of how hard he has to work, and he probably does work hard. So he comes home at night, eats supper, then goes into the family room, grabs a six-pack, and watches T.V. for the rest of the night. Mom pops a few more tranquilizers to keep going and finally plops down in a chair beside Dad. The kids? Well, they only had three big exams in school that day. They are pooped too, but after supper they clear the table, do the dishes, and then go upstairs to study for the rest of the evening for two more big examinations the next day. I believe that when they speak of the real thing they are speaking about

February Fifteenth

something that is alive, vibrant, and vital. They want something that will speak to their needs and to the needs of the world.

Now I will attempt to suggest three areas of life which could be made more meaningful to our youth. First: They feel that religion should be intellectually honest. This point reminds me of the story of one pastor. After church an old lady was shaking his hand, commenting on the sermon. "You do not know how much help your sermons have been to my husband since he lost his mind." Isn't this often our situation? Our religious experiences never seem to involve any real mental exercise. Nothing could be further removed from the truth when we consider our adult educational opportunities and the response we seem to be getting to them. In our catechetical classes we teach about the Ten Commandments. We look at the interpretation which Christ placed upon them and compare them to the original in the sixth chapter of Deuteronomy: "You shall love the Lord your God with all your heart, and with all your soul, and with all your might." Christ reinterprets this statement by saying, "You shall love the Lord your God with all your heart, and with all your soul, and with all your mind" (Matthew 22:37). Do you see the difference? The writer of Deuteronomy leaves the mind out; Jesus puts the mind in. Your faith and mine can be relatively lifeless affairs with God if we do not work with it and seek to grow in grace. There are those who now are saying that we do not have enough emotion in our religion. To a point I must agree, but for every one person who has left his heart out of religion, I can cite dozens who have left their heads out. A man once said, "I could not be a Christian if I did not find it to be the most satisfying interpretation of life for me as far as my intellectual approach to life is concerned." I do not feel that our youth are going to be satisfied simply with a faith that is not intellectually reasonable. There is one thing for certain. We know that the youth of today will not believe all the stories simply because their elders have said that they are so. To love God, in the final analysis, means that we must also learn to love him with our minds.

My second point is that religion today must now become *morally demanding*. You have heard the complaint that this generation is the most undisciplined and morally irresponsible the world has ever known. I won't take time now to argue for or against this point, but by listening to what our youth are saying, I have been left with the impression that they want some real guidelines which will measure their conduct. They say that we of the church have given them nothing to really go by; we are one thing on Sunday, and something else the rest of the week. So, if these kids are what we say they are (and I have some reservations about this), who is really to blame? I am not going to advocate a return to the "thou shalts" and the "thou shalt nots," but I am suggesting that we make an honest attempt to work out with them some solutions to their questions about adult behaviors, about saying one thing and doing another.

There is no doubt about it, they are looking for the real thing, sure signs in a positive direction. And all too often when these signs appear, young persons are not certain if the signs are real. I am convinced that this generation is looking for a faith and a religion which have some real teeth in them, a faith that will make a decided difference in the kind of real person you are, a faith which builds sound and secure lives.

My third, and last point is that we must come up with a religion which is spiritually challenging. Here is where I hear the major portion of their doubts and misgivings. As they view the church of which you and I are a vital part, they see little which is really challenging to them.

In an issue of the comic strip "Peanuts," Charlie Brown is pretty clever. When three big boys chase him, he runs and runs. They get closer and closer, so he stops them and organizes a discussion group. This may well be an answer, but simply having a discussion group will not challenge a generation of youth today to give their lives to Christ without some positive action within that group.

When the Lord of life said, "Follow me," he set his steps toward Jerusalem. And when he arrived, the people had a cross waiting for him. There are a lot of crosses out there for each one of us who is willing to take Christ seriously and honestly, and these crosses have your names and mine written on them. Whether you wish to assume a position on that cross in sacrifice and dedication determines the degree of your faith—young and old alike! This is what our young people need today, to see more people willingly and sacrificially step up into the arena of life and assume the role of servant to man. For it to be meaningful to you and to them, it must cost us all something. God cared

February Fifteenth

enough to send the very best. These kids today can become either the best generation, morally and spiritually speaking, this world has ever seen, or they can be the last.

This then appears to be our responsibility as Christians. Our challenge, as mature adults, is to lift up to this generation, and the generations to follow, a faith in our God and our Lord which is intellectually honest, morally demanding and above all, spiritually challenging. It is no secret. The hour is now upon us. Will this generation go down in history as only the "real thing" generation, or from them, will we, by the help of God, develop within them The Real Thing—the Christ generation? "If any man would come after me, let him deny himself and take up his cross and follow me" (Matthew 16:22). This, to me, is the Real Thing. *Amen.*

D. Timothy Robinson
St. Mark's Lutheran Church
Isle of Palms, South Carolina

Sunday
February Twenty-second

Theme: A Case of Murder

Call to Worship: Know this, my beloved brethren. Let every man be quick to hear, slow to speak, slow to anger, for the anger of man does not work the righteousness of God. *James 1:19-20*

Invocation: Lord, guard our minds, our hearts, and our tongues from thinking or speaking in anger. We know that the only way to overcome anger is to replace it with love. Fill us so full of thy love that there is just no room for anger. *Amen.*

Hymn: "Dear Lord and Father of Mankind"

Sermon Presentation: "The Sin That Couches at the Door"

Goals for Today: To face the fact that most anger is a display of the sin that is in us. To try to understand the strange paradox that the only anger acceptable is God's righteous anger. Our anger is always unacceptable to God.

This Week in History

Feb. 22—Lord Robert Baden-Powell's Birthday—British army officer who founded the Boy Scouts and Girl Guides. These two organizations have made such a great contribution to the growth of so many American young people.

Feb. 23—George Frederick Handel's Birthday—Born in 1685. Handel's most frequently performed work is the Oratorio, Messiah, first heard in 1742. It was truly inspired by God as Handel claimed.

Announcement for Next Week's Sermon: "I am just plain tired." That seems to be the new theme of most people today. What must you do to have energy? Next week we find the answer.

Hymn: "How Firm a Foundation"

February Twenty-second

Offertory Scripture: Beware lest you say in your heart, "My power and the might of my hand have gotten me this wealth." *Deuteronomy 8:17*

Offertory Prayer: If you have anger in your heart when you bring your gift to the altar, leave the altar; go make peace with your brother. Then come and present your gift. Lord, help us to practice forgiveness and remove all anger from our hearts so that these gifts are acceptable to you. Amen.

Prayer: Lord, you must get so tired of seeing people with short fuses. You made us in your image—tolerant, loving, and forgiving. Sin came into our lives and made us angry, unable to love, and unable to forgive even the smallest thing. You have every right to give up on us. We have no explanation for our anger and no defense for our sin. All we can do, Lord, is to fall back on your promise at our baptism: to never desert us, never give up on us, to always be ready to forgive if we are ready to come and say, "Forgive me, Lord."

Now, Lord, in the quiet of this moment, in this your holy house, cleanse us of all anger, all hatred, and make us new people of God. Renew us, forgive us, help us as we go out into the world this week. We need nothing spectacular, just a few little changes—a kind word, a forgiving gesture, a loving deed. Every day, in every way make us more like you. Amen.

Story of the Week: A young man had been arrested for fighting and the judge told him to tell his side of the story.

"Well, your Honor," the young man said. "I was in a telephone booth talking to my girl friend, when this man suddenly opened the door, grabbed me by the neck and threw me out in the street."

"And that is when you struck him?" asked the Judge.

"No, sir, I didn't hit him," the fellow said, "until he grabbed my girl friend and threw her out, too."

THE SIN THAT COUCHES AT THE DOOR

> The Lord had regard for Abel and his offering, but for Cain and his offering he had no regard. So Cain was very angry,

and his countenance fell. The Lord said to Cain, "Why are you angry, and why has your countenance fallen? If you do well, will you not be accepted? And if you do not do well, sin is couching at the door; its desire is for you, but you must master it." Cain said to Abel his brother, "Let us go out to the field." And when they were in the field, Cain rose up against his brother Abel, and killed him. Then the Lord said to Cain, "Where is Abel your brother?" He said, "I do not know; am I my brother's keeper?' (Genesis 4:4b-9)

The problem of anger appears early in the Bible, just as it does in life. Even very young children, as we all know, can become terribly angry.

Anger can be defined as *a feeling of displeasure resulting from injury, mistreatment, opposition, and the like, and usually showing itself in a desire to fight back at the supposed cause of this feeling.* Cain blamed Abel for his problem and killed him.

The typical anger reaction is to strike out against someone or something. It does not always lead to murder, but often enough it does. How many domestic murders are the result of anger, not premeditation, but spontaneous, uncontrolled anger? The desire to hurt is there, whether it leads to murder or not: "I'll get you for that!"

The Old Testament is realistic about people and human nature. While looking through a concordance, one sees many references to people being angry. Even the heroes of the faith—Jacob, Moses, Samuel, Saul, Abner, David, and many others—were all said to be angry at some time or another.

The same tendency continues into the New Testament as well. Even Jesus and Paul are depicted as being angry at times. Jesus, however, addresses the problem of anger, and was aware of the relationship between anger and murder. He takes the commandment not to kill back a step, saying that the desire to kill breaks the commandment against killing. Don't be angry; avoid the feelings that can lead to murder.

But how can this be? Anger is a physical reaction. Ordering us not to be angry is like telling the wind not to blow or the sun not to shine. Furthermore, psychologists tell us that repressing anger is a major cause of depression and other ills. Frequently, Jesus' command is taken to mean that we must repress our anger. Christians can't fight; parents can't become angry with their children, or children with their parents. This is especially

February Twenty-second

true of those of us who are preachers. Preachers are expected to be models, to be beyond the normal weaknesses of human nature. An expression frequently used to express frustration at a particularly trying situation is "that's enough to make a preacher cuss."

Yet, despite all this, twice the Bible says: "Be angry, but do not sin" (Ephesians 4:26) and "Be angry, but sin not" (Psalm 4:4).

Anger is not totally repressed in the Bible. God is frequently pictured as being angry. *The wrath of God* is an expression used throughout the Bible. Jesus is pictured as being angry, as, for example, when he heals a man on the Sabbath and is criticized for it: "And he looked around at them with anger, grieved at their hardness of heart" (Mark 3:5). Likewise, when parents were bringing children to Jesus to be blessed, the disciples rebuked them: "But when Jesus saw it he was indignant" (Mark 10:14). Near the end of this ministry, when he drives the money changers from the Temple, we can imagine there was a touch of anger as he rebukes those who were turning a house of prayer for all the nations into a den of thieves. We just cannot imagine Jesus as being emotionally flat, unable to feel the emotions which well up within us as we confront the experiences of life.

What, then, can we make of this? We must admit that anger is real, and that there is danger in denying and repressing it. But this gives us no license to express anger without thought of its effects upon others or upon ourselves. Anger should not be completely repressed, nor should it be thoughtlessly expressed.

How, then, can we handle anger?

First of all, let's not make a virtue of expressing anger. Some time ago, a magazine ran a picture of a man in an obvious state of anger. The caption read: *I don't get ulcers, I give them.* Likewise, let us not be fooled by the church person who says, "I'm not mad, I'm just filled with righteous indignation." As James advises us: "Let every man be quick to hear, slow to speak, slow to anger, for the anger of man does not work the righteousness of God" (James 1:19-20). Proverbs advises us: "He who is slow to anger is better than the mighty, and he who rules his spirit than he who takes a city" (Proverbs 16:32). We do need to exercise control, even of our anger. A lack of control damages ourselves, others, and the work of God.

But, then, we have to find ways of dealing with anger. One way is to drain off the harmful effects, as lightning rods drain off the electrical charges which could destroy a building. One way to do so is by participating in physical activity. In years past we could do that by chopping wood or beating the rugs during spring housecleaning. Today many persons accomplish this by tennis and other vigorous activities—jogging, running, swimming.

Another way is through prayer. The psalmist, who feels that others are angry with him, suggests that they "be angry, but sin not; commune with your own hearts on your beds, and be silent" (4:4). Paul also says to put the situation before God: "Be angry but do not sin; do not let the sun go down on your anger, and give no opportunity to the devil" (Ephesians 4:26-27). The writer Thomas De Quincey wrote: "Call for the grandest of all earthly spectacles, what is that? It is the sun going to his rest. Call for the grandest of all human sentiments, what is that? It is that man should forget his anger before he lies down to sleep" *(Confessions of an English Opium-Eater)*.

Above all, we must never forget our ties to one another. This was Cain's problem. "Am I my brother's keeper?" (Genesis 4:9). Jesus said:

> You have heard it was said to the men of old, "You shall not kill; and whoever kills shall be liable to judgment." But I say to you that every one who is angry with his brother shall be liable to judgment; whoever insults his brother shall be liable to the council, and whoever says, "You fool!" shall be liable to the hell of fire. (Matthew 5:21-22)

Then Jesus immediately adds: "So if you are offering your gift at the altar, and there remember that your brother has something against you, leave your gift there before the altar and go; first be reconciled to your brother, and then come and offer your gift" (Matthew 5:23-24). It is our responsibility to try to overcome the strained relationship, to do all in our power to deal with one another in ways which maintain the unity we have. Also, Paul says: "Therefore, putting away falsehood, let every one speak the truth with his neighbor, for we are members one of another. Be angry but do not sin; do not let the sun go down on your anger" (Ephesians 4:25-26). Thus Paul is saying the same thing Jesus says, that we should try to maintain

February Twenty-second

brotherhood; we are *members one of another*. Remembering that should help us deal with the anger we may feel toward one another.

In conclusion, we remember that Jesus is reminding us of the close ties between thought and action; that anger is incipient murder. It is the first step which may take us into disastrous action. We remember that we are creatures of emotion as well as of reason; that anger is a normal, natural reaction to certain situations, and cannot be repressed without damage to us. Furthermore, being a Christian does not destroy our emotions, or at least it should not. Having the human capacity to love also means we have the capacity to be angry. But we are not simply the prisoners of our emotions. Our faith assists us in channeling and directing our emotions.

God said to Cain: "Sin is couching at the door; its desire is for you, but you must master it" (Genesis 4:7). Anger threatens to cause us to sin, but we can master it, not by repression and denial, but by acknowledging it. Be angry, but do not sin. Work it off; pray it off. And let us never forget that the one we are angry with is our brother, and we are responsible for our brothers. As we assume responsibility for each other, we overcome the sin that couches at the door. *Amen.*

Richard A. Chrisman
First United Methodist Church
Mason City, Illinois

Sunday
March First

Theme: Give Me Strength

Call to Worship: "Come to me, all who labour and are heavy laden, and I will give you rest." *Matthew 11:28*

Invocation: Life is full of choices, good ones, bad ones, holy ones, unholy ones. When we make them alone they all seem to turn out to be bad. When we make them with you they are good. Lord, let us learn to include you in all the choices in our lives. Then our lives and choices will be acceptable in your sight. *Amen.*

Hymn: "Lord, Speak to Me"

Sermon Presentation: "How Much Energy Do You Have?"

Goals for Today: We have just so much time and so much energy. How will we use these valuable commodities? It is the proper balance in our lives that brings happiness. Choose wisely.

This Week in History

March 1—World Day of Prayer—This day celebrates the worldwide expression of prayer and Christian unity.

March 1-7—(This week must be noted in your bulletin or parish paper.) Return the Borrowed Book Week—Purpose: To remind you to make room for all those precious old volumes that will be returned to you, by cleaning out all the worthless trash your friends are waiting for. A little reminder and a little humor never hurt.

Announcement for Next Week's Sermon: The kingdom of God is at hand. Paul and Peter believed Jesus would return in their lifetimes. If he comes back in your lifetime, you'd better be ready. I don't think this will happen, do you? Just in case, are you ready? Don't miss next Sunday.

Hymn: "Christ for the World We Sing"

March First

Offertory Scripture: For Christ also died for sins once for all, the righteous for the unrighteous, that he might bring us to God, being put to death in the flesh but made alive in the spirit.

I Peter 3:18

Offertory Prayer: The goods of this world are our energy converted into money and worldly goods. We willingly give of this energy because we want the comforts of this world for ourselves and our loved ones. That is good. Leave enough energy to do God's will; that is your eternal need and the will of God. Accept our converted energy. *Amen.*

Prayer: Renew us every day, Lord, or we will run out of gas. We need to learn to relax. We need a good night's sleep. We need good food. We need to be surrounded by love just to survive. You have taught us by your life's example that just surviving is not enough. We must give and give and give. We must never become weary of doing good deeds for our fellow human beings, wherever they may be and whatever their needs. The deeds we do are not an "if you feel like it" thing. They are a command from God. Do it! Lord, we know all too well our energy will give out before the job is done. Remind us of your secret source of power in our time of trial. Let's get down on our knees and pray; rise up and finish the job. It never failed you and it will never fail us. *Amen.*

Story of the Week: One hot day down in Georgia a fellow named John Henry Simpson took a job with a road contractor. The crew was building a new road through the red clay hills of the state. The temperature was more than 100° in the shade and the foreman was working his men relentlessly. After several hours of this sort of grueling labor, John Henry went over to the timekeeper and asked him: "Boss, ha[ve] you got a fellow on your list named Simpson?"

The timekeeper looked at his time sheet and then said, "Yes, I've got a man on my sheet named Simpson. What did you want to know about him?"

"Oh, nothing, boss. But, from the way they'[ve] been working me, I thought maybe they had it down as Sampson."

HOW MUCH ENERGY DO YOU HAVE?

Jesus said, "No one can serve two masters; for either he will hate the one and love the other, or he will be devoted to the one and despise the other. You cannot serve God and mammon" (Matthew 6:24).

Was Jesus right? Is it true that a human being can serve only one master? Or, to ask it another way, can you and I have only one center for our lives? Let me put before you an illustration.

A man works forty hours a week at his job. He does it well, but the pay he receives does not give him the nice things he would like to have. So he takes on an evening job, makes more money, and buys more things—things he likes so well and his neighbors admire so much, that he adds a third job he can fit into his spare time! Trouble is, his family doesn't seem to appreciate all that he's doing for them. All they do is complain that they never see him. And then he finds himself falling asleep when he does go places—not only at church listening to sermons (which, of course, everybody understands), but even in the school gymnasium when the basketball game goes into overtime! Then his daytime boss hints that his work isn't so good as it used to be, the sales on his third job go down, and he finds himself irritated and angered when anyone makes a request of him. If I were to ask you how many masters he has, what would you say? Three? One for each job? Would you say many, because of all the demands on him? Or would the answer be "money" or "having nice things"?

However you'd answer that question, if we were to ask him, as he slid into the church pew on a Sunday morning, "How much energy do you have?" he'd probably say what you and I know that we sometimes must answer, "Not enough!" And to that wearied reply would come the words of Jesus, "Yes, I know. No one can serve two masters. There is another way to live!" What Jesus does in the words of today's lesson is hold a mirror up to us to show us that what we are trying to do is self-destructive if our lives have any other centers than serving the purposes of God! A literal translation of Jesus' words is, "No one is able to serve two masters." But I'd propose that what that means is this: *No one of us has enough energy to serve two masters!*

We have limits. Sometimes we are exhausted because we have pursued the will of God in service to our neighbor. But

March First

maybe more often we become worn out because we have lost a sense of that divine center to our lives. Whether then—like the man in my opening story—we frazzle ourselves under a myriad of demands or spend all our efforts in a dizzying pursuit of ever "more and nicer things," we are driving ourselves to destruction. We are ruining that beautiful creation which is intended to serve God alone!

What Jesus, in his great love, shows us is that we really cannot live with a divided heart. I know people who say, "A little religion can't hurt you," so they come to church . . . but they keep this "God-business" pretty casual. It seems that Jesus would say to them, "A little religion won't help you either!" Why? Because a relationship with God is not one thing among many! It is the only thing! It is the center from which all of life flows! When Jesus said, "Seek first his kingdom . . . " he did not mean, "Do your religious duties first and then you can do the things you want to do!" Oh, no, when he said, "Seek first his kingdom," he meant, *Seek only his kingdom!* That is, seek God's will in everything you do. You don't have the energy to do more than that! Why? Because God wants all of you, not just some part left over after you've got what you want! Until God has all, our exhausting dividedness will continue.

Augustine put his discovery of that in these words, "The heart of man is restless until it finds its rest in thee" *(Confessions).* We have enough energy to serve God, no more, no less—and that is learned only in and through Christ! Where can you and I find someone of truly undivided heart? Only in Jesus Christ. Where can we find a mind without the double-mindedness of our own? Only in Jesus Christ. So then, if we really want to find a different way of living, we go to him. We see him as the One who really *sought first the kingdom.* We see him, now at the beginning of Lent, setting his face toward Jerusalem even knowing that it means death. We see him later in a garden praying, "Father . . . not as I will, but as thou wilt." Now tell me, why in the world did Jesus do that? Was it simply to be admired by the pious and scoffed at by others? Oh, no, it was much more—including a living example of how we are to live: totally for God! Life is not about getting our way; it is about going God's way!

It sounds so simple when the preacher says it, but on the other side of these sanctuary walls it's not so simple. But that's no reason at all to adopt a "poor me" attitude—or a "forget-it-it's-too-difficult" mentality. If our very lives are involved, it must be worth our attention. So let me offer a little gauge by which you can test what's happening in your life. Paul wrote to the Colossians, "Whatever you do, in word or deed, do everything in the name of the Lord Jesus, giving thanks to God the Father through him" (Colossians 3:17). Hear it again: do everything in the name of Jesus. Let that be the test! Can I do what I do in the name of Jesus? Is the mind of Christ working in me, or is some other power? Am I seeking the glory of God, or my own interests?

That's not so complicated—sometimes difficult or even impossible without God's help—but not so complicated. Let me offer some possible examples. In the name of Jesus, can I:

—worry about not having enough food to eat or fashionable clothes to wear?

—spend hundreds of thousands of dollars on me, like the T.V. ad says, "because I'm worth it," while giving only a fraction of that to help someone who has virtually nothing?

—fill hours with leisure—tennis, golf, card playing, weekend outings, and so on—and at the same time dare to complain that I was asked to teach Sunday school again?

—daydream and worry about how I am going to get my way about something I want, while never once praying to God about what he wants? Can I do that in the name of Jesus?

Ridiculous! Yet we do these things, forgetting that the mind of Christ needs to be formed in us. We need a mind that trusts God, that trusts that we will be cared for even when we haven't put ourselves first and foremost. For trust is at the heart of the matter. Let me ask: have you ever awakened some morning, gone about getting dressed, brushed your teeth, and gone to work—only to panic, absolutely panic, a couple of hours later—"Oh, no, I forgot to pray this morning! I'll starve, I'll freeze to death, I'll go bankrupt!" I doubt that that has happened to any of us because we know that the amazing mercy and love of God comes to us without our prayer; it comes to us when we've loved God and when we've treated him like an unwelcome relative. That lesson of his care must come to affect every corner of our lives; it must.

Jesus is right, of course; we don't have energy for everything—especially for seeking both God's will and our own

March First

at the same time. How much energy do you have? Enough to serve God, to seek his kingdom, not as one thing among many, but as the only thing. *Amen.*

Glenn L. Borreson
First Lutheran Church
Decorah, Iowa

Sunday
March Eighth

Theme: So Near and Yet So Far

Call to Worship: For you were called to freedom, brethren; only do not use your freedom as an opportunity for the flesh, but through love be servants of one another. For the whole law is fulfilled in one word, "You shall love your neighbor as yourself." *Galatians 5:13-14*

Invocation: Lord, your kingdom is here right at hand, here, where we live. It is our neighbors, our friends, and, yes, even our enemies. Help us to see the needs that are all around us, to see them and to respond to them with courage and in love. If we harden our hearts to your call at home, we are lost. Teach us to love and to serve in your name. *Amen.*

Hymn: "Stand Up, Stand Up for Jesus"

Sermon Presentation: "The Near Kingdom"

Goals for Today: To learn the truth of the old Russell Conwell sermon, "Acres of Diamonds." We don't have to look around the world for a place to serve. All we need to do is to look in our own backyards. Start serving right where you are.

This Week in History

March 8-14—Girl Scout Week—To mark the founding of the Girl Scouts USA, the largest voluntary organization of girls and women in the world, which began March 12, 1912.

March 13—Good Samaritan Involvement Day—To emphasize unselfish aid to those who need it. The anniversary of the death of Kitty Genovese, whose killing was witnessed by thirty-eight people who did not want to get involved.

Announcement for Next Week's Sermon: We are surrounded by choices. That is a great thing about America—we do have freedom to choose. You may lose some of these choices if you

March Eighth

choose Christ. That may turn out to be your toughest choice of all. Will you choose him?

Hymn: "All Hail the Power of Jesus' Name"

Offertory Scripture: Which of these three, do you think, proved neighbour to the man who fell among the robbers? He said, "The one who showed mercy on him." And Jesus said to him, "Go and do likewise." *Luke 10:36-37*

Offertory Prayer: Let us serve our neighbors. They are the near kingdom. Let us serve the world, for through an almighty God all the world is our neighbor. Let us serve the Lord with our lives and our worldly goods because it is due him for his great gifts to us. *Amen.*

Prayer: As cars have changed, so has our concept of who is our neighbor, in a geographical sense. As jets have changed the world and shrunk it to a very small planet; as space travel has put a great part of the universe within our reach, so, too, a God who is omnipotent and omnipresent makes everything small and keeps us humble as we see this majesty. Whatever happens anywhere in the world today happens to and involves us as residents of this planet. This earth and all who live on it are a part of God's kingdom. We can close our eyes to the plight of our neighbors, but those problems will not go away. We must bear our brothers' and sisters' burdens. We must fight for all our neighbors, or we will lose all of them. And in this process we will surely lose ourselves. Yes, Lord, we are our brothers' keepers. We must bear their burdens; we must share our bounty; we must share the good news that we worship a living, caring, and loving God. Grant us thy grace to be worthy. *Amen.*

Story of the Week: The old man was celebrating his hundredth birthday and the reporter was interviewing him.

"To what do you attribute your longevity?" the reporter asked.

The old man thought a moment and then said, "I never smoked, drank whiskey, or stayed out late. And I always walked two miles a day."

"But," said the reporter, "I had an uncle who lived that way, yet he only lived to be eighty. How do you account for that?"

"He just didn't keep it up long enough," the man said.

Minister's Annual

THE NEAR KINGDOM

According to Mark, the earliest gospel writer, the story went like this: John the Baptist was preaching outside Jerusalem, down toward Jericho. Jesus, his cousin, came out to hear him and was baptized in the Jordan River. During the experience, Jesus became convinced that he was the long-awaited Messiah and God's Son.

So Jesus started his ministry. First came time alone in the wilderness caves of Qumran by the Dead Sea. It was a time when Jesus had to consider the temptations of all sorts of models of ministry he could pursue—

A miracle worker
The temptation to appeal to the crowds with the spectacular
Using his newly discovered powers to make life rich and easy for himself
A political leader manipulating crowds, armies, and peoples.

Soon cousin John got into serious trouble. He was put in prison and would be beheaded for speaking out against Herod, the king.

We take up the story today as Mark tells of Jesus' beginning his public ministry back home in Galilee.

". . . Jesus came into Galilee, preaching the gospel of God" (Mark 1:14). Notice that Jesus was a preacher.

There are days when I wonder if anyone hears or cares what is said in this pulpit. If the sermon is bland, general, and ineffective, no one seems to mind, except the youth who rightfully claim it is boring and of no consequence. If it hits people right between the eyes, those hit resent it and get mad at the preacher instead of considering how we ought to change our lives and behaviors.

A pastor once likened being a preacher in his congregation to standing in the middle of the race track at the State Fairgrounds and dodging the cars as they came by.

Sometimes it seems that many come to church only to have their prejudices made even more hard-set rather than to consider a new idea from God. Sometimes it seems as though the liberals, who want statements of social action from this pulpit, are never here when that happens. Those who dislike

March Eighth

me think that nothing I ever say from the pulpit could be godly or correct or important.

Rarely, but once in a great while, I despair of preaching altogether and almost say, "What's the use?" That is especially true when the Republicans say I am a Democrat, when the Democrats claim I am a Republican, the John Birch Society says I am a Communist, and the Fundamentalists claim I am not even Christian—all from the same sermon on the same day!

In 1532 Martin Luther wrote:

> Let us preach to the glory of God and pay no attention to the judgment of people. If someone can preach better, let him or her preach better. Let us preach only Christ and the Catechism. This is the wisdom that exalts us, because it is the Word of God. Praise and censure mean nothing to us.

Jesus was a preacher! The *Interpreter's Bible* mentions that he didn't write books; he trusted his most precious sayings to the blemished reputations and precarious memories of his friends.

Mark begins to tell of Jesus' ministry by saying that Jesus went to Galilee and preached the Good News from God. We are to be encouraged.

"The time is fulfilled, and the kingdom of God is at hand" (Mark 1:15).

This verse is the center and key to the whole Gospel of Mark. *The kingdom of God is near*. It is the main subject of Jesus' preaching and teaching throughout the rest of his three years of ministry.

What in the world is this kingdom that is so near? Ernest F. Scott states that the kingdom, as Jesus conceived it, was at once the higher, spiritual order, the better righteousness, the larger human brother and sisterhood, the life of inward fellowship with God. None of these excludes the other.

So, is that really very near? Sometimes—and certainly it was wherever Jesus went.

The kingdom is the reign of God, his sovereignty over mind, heart, will, and the world. It is Christ's kinship to God. When we see ourselves as brothers and sisters with other people, the kingdom is near.

It is in the future. Whenever a human life is brought into harmony with the Father's purpose, it is even present with us.

The main theme of Jesus must be the main theme of his disciples and messengers if we really are going to proclaim the news he wants proclaimed. It has always been a disaster in church history when Christians have gotten away from this proclamation of the near kingdom and made it secondary or forgotten it altogether. When Christian teaching and preaching has been a dividing force in the body of Christ—whenever it has pitted brother against sister—whenever it has failed to catch the imagination of folks, it has been a long way from the teaching and preaching of Jesus, who went to Galilee and preached the good news from God. "The time is fulfilled," he said, "and the kingdom of God is at hand."

You and I must preach it and teach it and live it so that those around us will say, "Look, there is the kingdom!"

We often see that kingdom at the baptism of a child, at the communion rail, during a beautiful anthem, when giving to children at missions, in the embrace of a refugee family at the airport, in the tears of a grieving and comforted widow, during the visit to a prisoner in jail, in the handclasp beside the hospital bed, in the check placed in the offering, in the reconciliation with a spouse, and in a thank you note from a daughter or son.

The kingdom is very near in the hug of a lonely person, or when folk of different colors come together in a church and worship God as one family. It is there when leaders of nations sit down to talk about arms reduction and peace. Certainly, the kingdom is near when the leaders of our church gather hurting people together for help and encouragement. It is certainly present in the wafer and wine in the homes of shut-ins as a pastor takes the sacrament to them.

A woman told me of a relative of hers whose wife was expecting a baby during the colder portion of winter. To make sure that he would be able to start his car to take his wife to the hospital, in the middle of the night, he took the battery out of the car each evening and kept it in his kitchen to keep the battery warm. At any moment he was prepared and ready.

That's the kind of expectancy Jesus taught—to be ready—to expect the kingdom to come at any moment in our own lives.

Jesus pointed out the kingdom to his disciples in the way that a widow gave all she had in the temple offering one Sabbath. He used the example of the mustard seed to instruct the disciples in the possibilities of the kingdom in the smallest of things. He told

March Eighth

stories about lost coins, lost sheep, and lost sons to illustrate the kingdom's concern for all creatures. He told about a farmer's sowing seed in the most unpromising ground to illustrate how the kingdom needed to be shared everywhere.

Jesus went to Galilee and preached the good news from God. I am encouraged and affirmed by that. *The right time has come,* he said, *and the kingdom of God is near.* Watch for it! Work for it! Expect it to pop up and out, wherever God's people are doing the ministry and living out the faith as God would have them do.

Notice that it's a *near* kingdom. You and I must not only preach and teach it, *but we must also live our lives and ministry in the world that it comes where we are.* For a brief, delightful moment it is here and we are in it.

A pastor once told me about an experience he had had. A call came at 1 A.M. He put on his clothes and drove to the phone booth where a nineteen year old girl had said she and her new baby would be waiting. It was a sight he would never wipe from his memory. The girl was sitting on the floor, the baby in her lap. Her feet were against the door so that her drunken husband could not get to her. She had been badly beaten. The baby was screaming. The pastor recognized them because he had baptized the child a few weeks before.

He hid them in a motel room the rest of the night. As he wiped off some of the blood from the baby's face, he thought he got a glimpse of the kingdom in a tiny smile from that infant child.

Notice what Jesus says we are to do about the nearness of the kingdom: "Repent, and believe in the gospel" (Mark 1:15).

So we hear our theme of "repent and believe." We hear from Jesus that the nearness of his kingdom ought to move us to turn from our sins. But often we do just the opposite. We try to find ways to justify those sins:

We point to what everyone else does.
We show how it's been done that way for years.
We try to show how it's not really that bad.
We exclaim that we want to be an all right man or woman.
We point to the money we make.
Or, we simply say it feels so good.

Yet, Jesus said that when we become aware of how close the kingdom is, we'll face the truth about ourselves. It is true that we are bigoted and self-centered. We are greedy and often lazy when it comes to kingdom work. We do have large egos and narrow minds. In fact, our minds are often like concrete, all mixed up and hard set. Pride and selfishness rule us, and we often judge our church not by what we can do to enable the kingdom to come, but rather what we can get out of it.

To all this, the message from this pulpit is the same today as it was from the first Christian preacher during his ministry in his home of Galilee: *Turn away from your sins and believe the good news.*

There was a movie a few years ago entitled *Witness*. It tells of the Amish of Lancaster County, Pennsylvania. A little Amish boy witnesses a horrible murder. Because of that, a hard, streetwise cop ends up in the simple Amish home of the young lad's grandfather. The little boy, named Samuel, finds the cop's gun and is examining it when he is discovered. His grandfather tells him that what he takes into his hand, he soon takes into his heart. We have taken all sort of things into our hands—we need to rid ourselves of them and clean out our hearts as well.

When we do turn from our sins, when we repent, oh, how God loves to forgive and take us back home again! That's what the preacher Jesus meant about the good news. It's the good news about his near kingdom; there is forgiveness and new life.

What a preacher! What a kingdom! What good news!

After John was arrested, Jesus came into Galilee, preaching the gospel of God, and saying, "The time is fulfilled, and the kingdom of God is at hand; repent, and believe in the gospel" (Mark 1:14-15). *Amen.*

Jerry L. Schmalenberger
St. John's Lutheran Church
Des Moines, Iowa

Sunday
March Fifteenth

Theme: The King of Kings

Call to Worship: Keep yourselves in the love of God, wait for the mercy of our Lord Jesus Christ unto eternal life. . . . Now to him who is able to keep you from falling and to present you without blemish before the presence of his glory with rejoicing . . . .
Jude 21, 24

Invocation: Lord, let us be your children and let us allow you to be our God. It is not always easy. We are constantly tempted to make our own rules, to rebel against your power in our lives. Help us to relax and know that peace comes from our obedience to you and your law. *Amen.*

Hymn: "O Master, Let Me Walk with Thee"

Sermon Presentation: "Jesus, Lord of All"

Goals for Today: Life is filled with choices. Some we are free to make without consequences. Some choices cost us dearly. Today we try to sort out where our freedom of choice under God starts and stops.

This Week in History

March 17-23—National Wildlife Week—To call attention to the importance of wildlife to the balance of nature and man's need to maintain the creatures of the world.

March 21—National Agriculture Day—A day set aside to honor the farmer and the soil. In recognition of the nation's "most basic industry, thanksgiving day for the growers, not the food."

Announcement for Next Week's Sermon: "He loves me . . . he loves me not . . . he loves me." That isn't just a child's game with daisy petals; it is also a matter of life or death.

Hymn: "Are Ye Able"

Offertory Scripture: Therefore, brethren, be the more zealous to confirm your call and election, for if you do this you will never fall. *II Peter 1:10*

Offertory Prayer: Lord, we did not choose you. You chose us first, while we were yet sinners. You have given us freedom to chose how we spend our lives and how we spend the gifts you have given us. Accept these gifts as a token of our recognition of our total dependence on you. *Amen.*

Prayer: Why do you have to complicate our lives? Why did you give us all this freedom? I feel as Paul did—all the good choices I would like to make I don't seem to make. All the bad choices I do not want to make, these I seem to make. It is all your fault. You should have known better than to trust anyone as weak as I. I am just messing up my life until it will be almost beyond redemption.

Lord, we thank you for that word *almost*. Oh, I have messed up, but you have not given up. *Almost* means there is still time to come back and say, "Help me to start choosing wisely. Help me to throw myself on your mercy." That is the only chance I have. I tried and tried to do it on my own—it just doesn't work. The only chance I have is to say, "Take me; remake me; don't forsake me. I am yours." Only then, with that one great and right choice, can I live with you. Choose me again to be one of your children. *Amen.*

Story of the Week: "Wonder drugs won't help you," the doctor told his elderly patient. "What you need is complete rest and a change of living. Go to a quiet country place for a month. Go to bed early, eat lots of vegetables, drink plenty of good rich milk, and smoke just one cigar a day."

A month later the man returned to the doctor's office. He looked like a new man.

"Yes, doctor," the man said, "your advice certainly did me a world of good. I went to bed early and did all the other things you told me. But that one cigar a day almost killed me at first. It's not easy to start smoking at my age."

March Fifteenth

JESUS, LORD OF ALL

One of the great luxuries we enjoy in our free society is the luxury of choice. We can choose our own means of living, the cars we drive and the direction we want to drive them. We can choose our clothing, our food, the communities in which we want to live, and even the way we want to live in them, so long as we do not infringe someone else's freedom of choice. We often choose our own friends, and sometimes our enemies. The free choices we have are numerous and plentiful.

It's hard not to believe that this is the kind of society that God has in mind for all people. We are able to exercise the free will that God has blessed us with in the first place. We need to walk cautiously here, of course, and be careful not to say that American democracy is the model for the kingdom of God, or that the free will we have from God is the same as the will we are free to express as American citizens.

There is no question that we have a free will of some kind. It is supported by scripture, but it is especially evident in our own daily experiences of decision-making. Scripture also makes it clear that human free will, though very real, is very imperfect. That is to say, we have the will to make choices; we just don't have the will to make every choice the right one. We lost that ability long ago when we decided to be gods, ourselves, rather than to be God's own. Instead of wanting to be ruled by God, we chose to be free of his rule. Thus we lost our innocence, our trustworthiness, and our freedom. So the real status of our lives is not the exercise of a perfect, unbridled will that is perfectly able to choose right from wrong, but rather the exercise of a will that is absolutely limited by sin. In short, we have a will that is free, but which is not able to choose to be free.

Christian psychiatrist M. Scott Peck *(People of the Lie)* says that there are really only two states of being: submission to God and his will and goodness, or refusal to submit to anything beyond one's own will, which automatically enslaves one to the forces of sin and evil. It is a view shared also by C. S. Lewis, who said, "In the universe there is no neutral ground: every square inch, every split second is claimed by God and counterclaimed by Satan" *(Christian Reflections).*

We have the freedom to choose, to choose our friends, to choose our church. But when it comes to choosing who is to be our Lord, our God, it is not a matter of asserting our free will, but a matter of submission—of yielding, of giving up our lives. A Lord is one in whom we trust and whom we rely upon, one to whom we give our prime allegiance and submit ourselves to in complete obedience. Who is that person for you? Who or what is your Lord?

There is an assumption behind that question: All people who wish to be called *Christian* are those who follow Christ and believe in the power of the cross to save. But I am also aware that in this world we are surrounded by a host of so-called Lords that vie for our allegiance and loyalty. A question we need to wrestle with is: Do we see Christ merely as one of the many options available? Do we choose him as Lord much like we select a new suit or car? If he fits and feels good, we'll wear him. Or does he stand quite apart and alone? Is he just a good bet or is he the only game in town? Does he offer you one way to live or the only way to live? Is he the one Lord or one among many?

Think carefully and speak your answer carefully. Don't speak too quickly, for your choice is truly a matter of life or death. If you choose to say that Christ is a good option, you choose initially the safest route to go. There's very little to risk, or so it would seem.

To regard Jesus as an option among others means you can have a very casual relationship with him. You can attend worship whenever the spirit moves you, but if you feel that you have earned a little rest, skipping a few occasions isn't such a big deal. As long as you get to Holy Communion now and then, that's really all that matters, right? Make Jesus just an option among others and you can enjoy all the benefits of being a member of the Body, without any of the responsibilities. It's a free country, isn't it? If you want to become more seriously involved, it's still your choice, isn't it? And if you don't want to, it's your choice as well.

It's such a safe, easy life when we make Christ one of many optional Lords to follow. It seems to give us the freedom to shuffle our allegiances around. Christ is definitely more important to us at specific times in our lives—baptisms, weddings, funerals, Christmas, and Easter. But *church* isn't the only obligation we have, is it? We have careers to work on, bills to pay, places to go, things to see, people to meet. We have lots

March Fifteenth

of choices, lots of options. A person just has to set some priorities now and then.

We need to think again how safe and easy a life it really is. Remember Dr. Peck's formula: "One either submits to the will of God, totally and completely, or refuses to submit to anything beyond one's own will." Making Christ and church membership a casual choice is submitting yourself to nothing more than your own will, and that is regarding yourself as Lord. That is also idolatry, and that makes living not so safe at all. It leads us down a road to death.

But now, if we choose to be more serious and less casual about following Christ, then we need to be warned. To submit to Christ as our only Lord of Life means we will lose something; we will lose our freedom of choice.

When Christ becomes our Lord, we will no longer have the luxury of deciding who is our neighbor and who isn't. We will no longer have the option to love only those who do nice things for us. We will no longer simply enjoy the benefits of being *Christian*, but must now take on the responsibilities of that name. Christ will own us, possess us. Our life will no longer be ours, but his.

It's not a safe choice. There are others that are definitely more safe. On the other hand, there are no others that make the kind of promise that Christ makes: "He who believes has eternal life," (John 6:47).

The casual believer may think it all too risky, and would rather have greater choices. He or she would rather have that luxury of borrowing from both worlds as he or she sees fit. Jesus said, "Not every one who says to me 'Lord, Lord,' shall enter the kingdom," (Matthew 7:21), which is to say to those whose casual attitude goes no further than that: There is no such thing as standing on neutral ground with faith. One cannot stand in the middle between submission to the Lordship of Christ or the following of one's own will. To do so is to be ultimately torn apart!

Jesus did not come to earth to be one of the many candidates running for King of kings. God didn't send him our way that we might merely ponder his words, or think about his parables, and take them simply as good advice. God didn't ask our permission; he didn't call for a vote; he didn't wait for us to say yes—or no.

In absolutely perfect freedom, God chose us! He sent us Jesus, hoping we would follow. Whether we do does not change the fact that he has been established by God as Lord of all! We can reject him but not make him go away. The cross is history, never to be repeated, thus never to be forgotten or ignored.

We really don't have a choice. Choosing not to believe at all, or deciding to live a casual relationship with Christ, holds very little risk and very little promise. But choosing to submit to Christ's lordship is to relinquish all rights and claims on our lives by other lords.

By no other lord are we genuinely safe. Christ's lordship is one of shepherding, of providing, of making us whole people. Jesus, our friend—Jesus, our comforter and life-giver—Jesus, Lord of all! What will it be? A matter of choice or a matter of submission? A lord of your choice, or the Lord that has chosen you? It's the only choice in life that matters. *Amen.*

Jon Lindekugel
Christ the King Lutheran Church
Hutchinson, Minnesota

Sunday
March Twenty-second

Theme: Love Is Forever

Call to Worship: We know that in everything God works for good with those who love him, who are called according to his purpose.

Romans 8:28

Invocation: We are compelled by your life of love to love one another. As we look at our own lives filled with failed attempts to love as you love, we are forced to turn to you and admit that without your leadership, our lives just drift. Show us how to love and give. Teach us that as we are able to give of ourselves we are able to love. Take our feeble efforts and turn them into loving triumphs for you. Amen.

Hymn: "Blest Be the Tie That Binds"

Sermon Presentation: "He Loves Me . . . He Loves Me Not . . ."

Goals for Today: To discover that life is never perfect but you are loved. When we suffer it should bring us closer to God's love. If we understand him, we understand love.

This Week in History

March 23—Liberty Day—Anniversary of Patrick Henry's speech at St. John's Church, Richmond, VA, in 1775. "I know not what course others may take, but as for me, give me liberty or give me death." A creed we can still subscribe to today.

March 24—World Humanist Week—To celebrate the Humanist ideals of universal brotherhood, humane concern, and a life guided by reason.

Announcement for Next Week's Sermon: Don't be chicken, try it! God does not expect us to try to do stupid things. He does expect us to show real Christian courage. Try; you can do it.

Hymn: "Love Divine, All Loves Excelling"

Offertory Scripture: And now, Israel, what does the Lord your God require of you, but to fear the Lord your God, to walk in all his ways, to love him, to serve the Lord your God with all your heart and with all your soul.

Deuteronomy 10:12

Offertory Prayer: Lord, how can I say to those whom I love that I care and then not support them as I am able? Lord, I love you. Accept these gifts as a true demonstration of my love for you.

Prayer: Love, Love, Love. You must get pretty weary of hearing that word drift up to you in prayers. I am sure it must make you weep as we toss that word around so casually. We talk of love, but we kill with guns; we kill with words; we kill with deep-seated prejudice and hatred. How long, O Lord; how long will it take us to learn that love is not a word but an action? If I say I love you and do not show it, I am a clanging cymbal. If I say I love but do not help my fellow man, I am a hypocrite. If I say I love you and do not bring my gifts to the altar, I am robbing God—a strange kind of love. Help us to learn how simple it is to love. All we have to do is dump all our sins on you. We confess and you forgive. We say take my sins; I can't handle them; wash me and I will be whiter than snow. Now that I am back in a right relationship with you, I can love. Help me to love. *Amen.*

Story of the Week: The editor of a small-town newspaper in New England was trying to sell advertising.

"Don't need to advertise," said the owner of the store. "Been in business nigh on forty years and never advertised."

"Could you tell me what that building is on the hill?" asked the editor.

"That's the village church," the man said.

"Been there long?" the editor asked.

"Oh, about one hundred fifty years," said the storekeeper.

"Well," said the editor, "they still ring the bell every Sunday, don't they?"

March Twenty-second

HE LOVES ME . . . HE LOVES ME NOT . . . HE LOVES ME!

or
IS GOD GOOD?

Today's odd sermon title is telling a story. Maybe you have never done it, but just imagine a lover—a girl or a boy, it makes no difference—alone, deep in thought, thinking of the other and wondering: Does he love me? Does she love me? The lover reaches out, pulls off a daisy bloom, and meditatively and deliberately pulls each petal, saying, "He loves me, he loves me not, he loves me," and so on. Have you ever done that? Well, it matters not whether you did. Everyone at some time and in some way has played a game like that with God. Many still are; yes, many are still playing that game!

Instead of a flower blossom, they and we have used events and experiences for "petals," and say, if treated well and given a good experience, "He loves me!" But if hurt or given a bad experience, "He loves me not." Maybe we let our feelings be the petals. If we are filled with excitement, "He loves me!" If we are down low, almost to the ground, "He loves me NOT!" Then we are in the pits.

Is that the way we live? Is that a description of our relationship to God and Christ? If good, well, and rosy—he loves me! If rotten, sour, thorny—he loves me not? I am afraid many do live this way.

Look at Abraham. What was his faith like? A yo-yo, up and down? Or a railroad track, level and straight? Did Abraham play that game, too? When he counted the stars and God said, "So shall your descendants be" (Genesis 15:5), Abraham felt good. His faith was reassured. *God loves me.* But when Sarah couldn't seem to bear him a child, for forty, fifty, seventy years, still no child, then, *God must not love me!* Is God good? Yes, just by knowing human nature we know that Abraham's faith was like that, too. Sometimes I'm up, sometimes I'm down, Lord. And sometimes I'm almost to the ground!

Isn't that our experience sometimes? Aren't those our feelings, sometimes? Well . . . yes! They were for Abraham, too, sometimes. Genesis 22 is one of those times. Isaac was finally born. (Abraham was one hundred years old, Sarah was past ninety.) Isaac must have been about thirteen at this time, big enough to carry a bundle of kindling, a handsome young boy just coming into his manhood. He was the apple of his dad's eye. He loved his dad, too. He obeyed his every word. Isaac was Abraham and Sarah's only son. Their son of promise! Their thoughts must have been, "Yes, God is good. Surely God loves us!" Now see the yo-yo in their faith? Why did they feel good? On what was based their conviction that God loved them? It was the physical, human, earthly reality of Isaac! Therefore, we have Isaac; he's our son of promise, all is well. God is good! Yes, he loves us! But what if this very physical, earthly, very, very human evidence of God's love and goodness were to be removed? What if it were to be taken away?

God knew that Abraham and Sarah were strong in their faith. He knew how much of the yo-yo was in it, and how much railroad track it had. Infinitely so, divinely so. So, God administered his test to Abraham. He coached his faith. *Abe! Give me your son! Yes, that one you love.* Hadn't God put himself under trial, even more than had Abraham?

Right away, God knew the tornado his command would release within the person of Abraham. Why? "He is my only son. He's the son of promise. Isaac, my Isaac. I love him!"

Hot tears, clenched teeth, anger, wonderings, were all his. But especially that question again, "Is God good? Does he love me?"

He packed for the long trip to Mt. Moriah. He laid the wood on Isaac. He took the fire and the knife himself and . . . they left. The two of them together. A three-day journey. Three days for Abe to think and wonder . . . he loves me, he loves me not, he loves me . . . and hope and think some more. Until finally they arrived at the mountain. Isaac laid down his wood. Abraham prepared the sacrifice, both of them unaware that nearby a ram was caught by its horns and that it (not Isaac) was to be the sacrifice that day. Neither Abraham nor Isaac knew that, but God did. God did provide, didn't he? Just as faithfully, lovingly, graciously as when, two thousand years later, on that same mountain at that same scene, God "gave his only Son, that whoever believes in him should not perish but have eternal life!" (John 3:16).

Once again, Abraham's faith ascended! It yo-yo'd up, up, up! Once again Abraham's faith was independent of earthly, physical, human criteria (like the physical presence of Isaac). Now it was on the power, the word, and the promise of God himself. It was a railroad faith. Once again, Abraham knew (believed). "Yes, God is good! Yes, God loves me! This I know because his word has told me so." It was that faith response that saved Abraham.

Beloved hearers of God's word, that is the way God works with us too. We, also, being human, have a yo-yo faith. In the 1970s prices were up, crops were good, loans came easily, it was safe to invest. Many did. We considered our physical well-being, our material prosperity; and our faith yo-yo'd up. We smiled, "God is good. God loves me!" But now prices are down, crops are thinner, loans are hard to get, and debts even harder to repay. Some of us, like Abraham, are wondering. There is a tornado inside us. Is God good? Does he love me?

Tell me, why did God do that to Abraham? Why? Because he liked to see him sweat, squirm, and struggle with his faith? No! God hates to see his children suffer. Our hot tears hurt him just as much as our children's tears hurt us. If you do not believe so, just look at what happened at Gethsemane and on the cross. Why, then, did God do that to Abraham, threatening for three days to remove the one he loved, to take away the apple of his eye, the son of promise, the very one upon whom his confidence, his yo-yo faith in God rested! There is our key. God was coaching Abraham from a faith less and less based on the physical and the material to a faith more and more based instead on the plain word, power, and promises of God.

In Genesis 15:5-6, we are given a very short story about Father Abraham: "and [God] brought [Abraham] outside and said, 'Look toward heaven, and number the stars, if you are able to number them. Then he said to him, So shall your descendants be!' " God's word and promise. "And [Abraham] believed the Lord; and he reckoned it to him as righteousness." That was the faith God was restoring to Abraham later on in Genesis 22, a faith that knows that God is good, that God loves him whether the yo-yo is up or down.

Have you ever wondered if that might be why some of these physical, material things that have been only crutches for a yo-yo faith are being removed? Might it not well be that God is coaching us, also, upwards onto a railroad track faith? Lord, I believe. Help my unbelief. Are we still plucking daisy petals,

"He loves me, he loves me not, he loves me?" You probably are, so am I; we probably will continue through this crisis and the next, over this mountaintop and the next because we are all human and that's the way our faith grows. But through all these ups and downs, highs and lows, let us always remember and never lose sight of the fact that God is good. He does care. Yes, he loves us! He loves us every one. *Amen.*

Virgil R. Anderson
Wallingford Lutheran Church
Wallingford, Iowa

Sunday
March Twenty-ninth

Theme: I Can Do All Things

Call to Worship: I therefore, a prisoner for the Lord, beg you to lead a life worthy of the calling to which you have been called. *Ephesians 4:1*

Invocation: God, give us the courage to dare. We would also like to succeed, but that is not so important as our show of faith that we are willing to try. You want us to be daring for you. You showed us the way. You put your life on the line for us and you lost. You lost your life so that we could be winners forever. Give us grace and faith to be fools for Christ. *Amen.*

Hymn: "How Firm a Foundation"

Sermon Presentation: "You Can Too!"

Goals for Today: Courage is a very scarce commodity for today's world. It is even true in the church. Try to get your people to stand up and be counted out in the world. God gives us the courage to be one of his witnesses: "I can do all things through Christ who strengthens me."

This Week in History

April 1-30—Cancer Control Month—To make America aware of this dread killer and the progress that has been made in treating it, but that there is still a long way to go. Christians surely will want to support this great effort to wipe out this killer.

April 2—Frederic Bertholdi's Birthday—French sculptor born in 1834 who designed what is now known as the Statue of Liberty, a symbol of freedom for all humankind.

Announcement for Next Week's Sermon: If you go in business with someone, get everything in writing. That's always good advice. God is in the business of life with us and it is all in writing. Come renew your contract next Sunday.

Hymn: "Praise to the Lord, the Almighty"

Offertory Scripture: God, who saved us and called us with a holy calling, not in virtue of our works but in virtue of his own purpose and the grace which he gave us in Christ Jesus ages ago. *II Timothy 1:8-9*

Offertory Prayer: Lord, against all odds you and I are a majority. As long as I put my trust in you, I cannot fail. Bless us now as we show our gratitude for your great blessings. Accept these, our gifts of thanksgiving. *Amen.*

Prayer: O God, make us positive people. Make us the kind of people who see all challenges as opportunities to do your will and to spread the Good News. When we look beaten we scare people away from your house and your free salvation. Make us happy and exciting people to be near so that we glow with the assurance that you have won the victory and that all we need to do is to say, "I am yours," and we share in that victory and success. The future of the church is in our hands. If we don't do it, it will not be done. Make us can-do people. Let us see the hungry and the poor, the lonely, and those who mourn. Give us the energy and the spirit to step in and say "May I, on behalf of my Savior, be of service?" Make me a blessing in this, your world, and take me to the world to come. *Amen.*

Story of the Week: A young lady from a small town was visiting the city for the first time. At a street crossing she completely ignored the light which read, "Don't Walk."

She was halfway across the street, when a policeman stopped her and said, "What's the matter lady, can't you read?"

"Why, yes," she said.

"Well, then, why did you walk across the street when the light up there said 'Don't Walk'?"

"Oh," she said, "I thought that was an advertisement for the bus company."

YOU CAN TOO!

"I can do all things in him who strengthens me" (Philippians 4:13).

Those who remember World War II may also remember a remarkable group of men called the *Seabees*. Seabees was their nickname, but their official designation was the U.S. Naval

March Twenty-ninth

Construction Battalions. They were the men who went ashore behind the Marines during the Pacific Island battles and constructed the facilities necessary for the support of the initial assault forces. They referred to themselves as "can-do" people, and were often quoted as saying, "The difficult we do immediately; the impossible takes a little longer!"

All of us can be can-do people—if we want to be. Throughout history there have been individual Christians and churches who were can-doers. Paul was such a Christian, and the little congregation at Philippi was such a church. Paul began his letter to the Philippians by thanking them for their can-do brand of Christianity, which had made them his full partners in the gospel of Jesus Christ, even while he was in a Roman prison. He was aware that it was their can-do prayers which sustained him and gave him hope. He knew that it was the Philippians' can-do spirit which enabled them to support him with their gifts, even when he was absent from them. Paul was so inspired by their willingness to attempt anything for Christ that he concluded his letter to them with an affirmation that literally sings as an anthem of confidence: "I know how to be abased, and I know how to abound; in any and all circumstances I have learned the secret of facing plenty and hunger, abundance and want. I can do all things in him who strengthens me" (Philippians 4:12-13).

I can do all things through Christ who strengthens me. No matter how you say it, that is quite a statement! In the New King James Version of the Bible, verse 13 says, "I can do all things through Christ who strengthens me." J. B. Phillips translates Paul as saying, "I am ready for anything through the strength of the One who lives within me." The New English Bible translates Paul's statement as, "I have strength for anything through him who gives me power." Good News for Modern Man makes Paul's words as contemporary as the morning newspaper: "I have the strength to face all conditions by power that Christ gives me." No matter which translation is used, Paul makes it clear that Christians can do anything if they remember first of all *what* they have to do.

What is it that Christians have power to do in living the Christian life? Paul wraps that answer up in two words: all things. Everything. Anything. Literally, there is nothing that a Christian cannot do. To be a can-do Christian means that we can apply our Christianity in the place we earn our living in how we relate to our fellow workers and our bosses; in the way we vote; in the use of our money and time; even in what we eat and drink and wear. "The earth is the Lord's and the fullness thereof" (Psalm 24:1). All things are his: the cattle on a thousand hills, the hills themselves, and everything under, above, and around the hills. A Christian is one who accepts this as a joyous fact; he is a faithful steward. Therefore, he knows he can do all things that his Lord wants him to do, and does those things in a redemptive, loving manner which will reveal the presence of God in him.

Glenn Cunningham was twelve years old when a kerosene stove blew up, killing his brother and burning Glenn so horribly that he almost died as well. Glenn recovered, although the burns left his leg muscles paralyzed by atrophy. It seemed certain that Glenn Cunningham would be crippled for life. But Glenn Cunningham's mother was a can-do Christian, and Paul's motto was engraved upon her very soul. She told her son, "The Lord made you whole and he wants you whole now. You'll not only walk, Glenn, you'll run and play. I believe it and if you believe it, it will happen." So day after day, week after week, month after month, she massaged his useless legs for hours at a time. When she could not do it, she made Glenn do the massaging himself. It took a long time and progress was agonizingly slow, but there came a day when Glenn Cunningham began to walk and then to run. He kept at it until, in 1934, he broke the world's record for the mile run. In 1938 he did it again, breaking his own record. Glenn Cunningham's mother believed he could do anything with Christ's help, and she taught Glenn to believe it, too—and he did!

An isolated success story? Absolutely not! You can do it, too! Glenn Cunningham's name might as well have been Legion, for there are countless Christians like him. Think of Helen Keller, deaf, dumb and blind, who believed she could do all things—and think of what she accomplished. Think of stone-deaf Ludwig von Beethoven. Listen to his Ninth Symphony and consider what he did. Consider Susanna Wesley—or Theodore Roosevelt—or David Livingstone—or Clara Barton—or any of a host of well-known winners of stringent adversities; invariably you will find Paul's can-do affirmation was the watchword of their lives. Look around at

March Twenty-ninth

the real, honest-to-God Christians in our own community who have overcome sickness or adversity. Ask them how they did it. The chances are overwhelming that they will answer in some fashion, "I can do all things through Christ . . ."

"Through Christ . . ." Don't dismiss those two words! "Through Christ . . ." They tell us *who* enables us to do *what* we have to do. "I can do all things through Christ . . ." Paul was calling attention not to what he—Paul—could do; rather what he could do because he was enabled through Christ. Whenever we read Paul's letters, we should always remember that we really are reading not what Paul wrote, but what Christ told Paul to write. Paul was a Christ-possessed man. Christ was in Paul's heart, mind, and deeds. This is clearly evident because one of Paul's favorite expressions was *in Christ;* it occurs dozens of times in his letters. More than anything else, Paul wanted to be a man in Christ. He told the Philippians that it was his "eager expectation and hope that . . . always Christ will be honored in my body, whether by life or by death" (Philippians 1:20). Again he told them that for Christ's sake, "I have suffered the loss of all things . . . in order that I may gain Christ and be found in him" (Philippians 3:8-9). He said that the whole goal of his ministry was to be as nearly like Christ as possible (Philippians 3:12-14). He triumphantly affirmed to the Galatians, "It is no longer I who live, but Christ who lives in me; and the life I now live in the flesh I live by faith in the Son of God, who loved me and gave himself for me" (Galatians 2:20). If it had not been for Christ in him, Paul would not have been effective as either a preacher or a church builder. In fact, if it had not been for Christ in him, Paul would not have been Paul, the greatest Christian missionary of all time. He would have been only Saul, the hate-filled Pharisee who served as an accomplice in the murder of Stephen, the first Christian martyr.

A pastor once counseled a lady who was a new Christian. She was attempting to deal with a personal problem which seemed overwhelming. Her husband was not a Christian and was giving her a hard time. He mocked her faithfulness in worship and prayer, and try as she would, she could not persuade him to join her.

"I just can't witness to my husband," she said. "It is impossible for me to win him."

"I agree with you!" the pastor replied. "It is impossible for you to win him for Christ, but it is not impossible for Christ to win him through you."

"But how, preacher? How can Christ win him through me?"

I encouraged her not to nag her husband, but to love him; not to push him, but to lead him by example and patience. She agreed to try, and for months thereafter she did. Eventually, he began to attend church with her and finally accepted Christ as his Savior and Lord.

When he told me of his decision, his exact words were, "It wasn't your preaching that led me to this moment; nor was it because I was convinced by the Bible or anything like that. I took Jesus as my Savior because I have seen what he did in my wife. She is the most genuinely loving person I know, and I wanted to be like her. If Jesus Christ can do that sort of miracle in her, I know he can do it in me, too!"

In Marc Connely's magnificent play, *Green Pastures*, there is a powerful scene in which Moses turns over the leadership of the children of Israel to Joshua. The people don't understand the reason for the change in leadership. When they ask why God is treating Moses this way, he tells them that God has plans for him. He then watches the people of Israel march away, leaving him alone. Moses feels desperately lonely when suddenly he feels a hand on his shoulder. He knows it is the hand of God because he has felt that hand before. Moses says, "You're with me, aren't you, Lord?" and God replies, "Of course I am, Moses."

That same sort of assurance is given to every Christian. God is with us always and forever in Jesus Christ. We have his word on it. Therefore, we can say with Paul, "I can do all things through him who strengthens me."

Don't forget those last three words in Paul's lovely affirmation! Genuine Christians can do all things; that is the *what* of their lives of discipleship. They can do them through Christ; that is *who* enables them to do all things. "Who strengthens me" tells us *how*. We discover how to do whatever we have to do through the power which Christ alone supplies. Through Jesus Christ, we are supplied with the power which Christ alone supplies. Through Jesus Christ, we are supplied with the power we need to love the unlovely, to forgive the hateful, to reach out to the lonely and the outcast, to care about those who do not even care about themselves.

March Twenty-ninth

But how does the power of Christ work to strengthen us for daily living in good times and bad? There are three primary ways: through prayer, the Bible, and worship. Two of our most familiar religious cliches affirm this statement, "All things are possible through prayer" and "The greatest power in the world is prayer-power." They may sound trite, but the fact is that they are true. They are true because they recognize that, as human beings, we are not able to do everything on our own. Quite frankly, prayer is an admission of our weaknesses. This is not easy for many of us to admit because we like to boast, "I am a self-made man. Everything I have, I got on my own." The truth is, however, that none of us are *self-made* persons, sufficient unto ourselves. We all have weaknesses, and when we admit those weaknesses we are brought closer to God. Once we admit them, God can replace them with his strength. Paul had to learn this lesson himself. He told the Corinthians,

> A thorn was given me in the flesh, a messenger of Satan, to harass me, to keep me from being too elated. Three times I besought the Lord about this, that it should leave me; but he said to me, "My grace is sufficient for you, for my power is made perfect in weakness." (II Corinthians 12:7b-9a)

As a result of his confession of weakness through prayer, Paul was able to say, "I will all the more gladly boast of my weaknesses, that the power of Christ may rest upon me" (II Corinthians 12:9b). If this was true for Paul, it is much more true for us! When we surrender our weaknesses to God in prayer he makes his power available to us, power to do all things.

The power of Christ is also available from the Bible. The Bible is the most widely owned book in the world, but the Bible also is one of the least-used books. Owning a Bible and not using it for power for daily living is like living next to a nuclear power plant and lighting your home with candles. If Christians really knew the power of the Bible, they could change the world for Christ's sake. The Bible, as the Word of God, has the power to cleanse society of sin. When Jesus was tempted by Satan in the wilderness, he drove the devil away with the power of God's Word. Martin Luther spoke of the power of God's Word to overcome evil when he wrote in his great hymn, "A Mighty Fortress Is Our God": "One little word shall fell him." God's Word is truth; falsehood cannot withstand truth. Neither can darkness withstand light, and the Bible truly is "a lamp to [our] feet and a light to [our] path" (Psalm 119:105).

Finally, Christians find power for daily living through worship. There is so much power available through worship that it is incredible. This is true because the church as a worshiping community is a divine institution, even though it is made up of sinful human beings. When we Christians join together in worship, the Holy Spirit is present in our hymns, prayers, sacraments, and sermons. His power is available even to the weakest. Once, after being served Holy Communion in her home, an elderly lady crippled with arthritis said to her pastor, "Oh thank you, Pastor. Now, I have the power to go on living again. Sometimes I feel so helpless and forgotten, but when I receive the Lord's Supper, I know I can do anything God wants me to do!" Exactly! That eighty-five-year-old lady received the power of the Holy Spirit through worship, and that same power is available to all Christians who regularly and faithfully worship in their churches.

A man once purchased a power chain saw. The clerk who sold it to him said that it could cut twenty cords of wood in a single day. Some time later, the customer went back to the store, quite angry and upset. He wanted his money back because he said that, try as he would, he could not even cut one cord of wood in a day. The salesman took the saw, turned on the switch and cranked it up. The saw came to life with a roar, as the cutter chain went 'round and 'round. The customer was dumbfounded. He had been trying to cut wood without turning on the power. There are many Christians like that man, who have never discovered the tremendous power available to them through Jesus Christ. They have never turned on the switch of faith.

Paul, however, was one who did turn on the switch of faith. Because he did, he was able to do all things through Christ who strengthened him.

You can, too—if you believe in Jesus Christ, as Paul did. Do you? *Amen.*

Raymond W. Gibson, Jr.
Kentucky Conference
of The United Methodist Church
Lexington, Kentucky

Sunday
April Fifth

Theme: "This Is My Father's World"

Call to Worship: Do not lay up for yourselves treasures on earth, where moth and rust consume and where thieves break in and steal. *Matthew 6:19*

Invocation: All that we are and all that we own comes from you. Make us grateful for these gifts which you so freely give. Never let us forget the sacrifice you made by the death of your Son so that we might have life and live more abundantly. *Amen.*

Hymn: "All People That on Earth Do Dwell"

Sermon Presentation: "Who Holds the Title?"

Goals for Today: "Remember, the land is mine." This Old Testament admonition is our theme today. All we are, all we own is just a trust from God. You'd better believe it.

This Week in History

April 7—World Health Day—Celebrates the founding of the World Health Organization in 1948. This is a United Nations sponsored effort to improve health around the world.

April 11—Civil Rights Act of 1968—Anniversary of the signing of the act protecting civil rights workers and providing anti-discrimination measures in employment and housing. Signed into law by President Lyndon B. Johnson.

Announcement for Next Week's Sermon: Wave your flags, tap your foot to the music of the bands. Stand on the curb as the parade goes by. When it is over, you'd better get moving. The parade should inspire you to action. Don't settle for just being a spectator.

Hymn: "How Great Thou Art"

Offertory Scripture: No one can serve two masters; for either he will hate the one and love the other, or he will be devoted to the one and despise the other. You cannot serve God and mammon. *Matthew 6:24*

Offertory Prayer: It is all yours, Lord. The sooner we learn that lesson, the sooner you can accept us as full partners in your kingdom. I have learned my lesson. Take all of me forever and ever. *Amen.*

Prayer: How far, O Lord, will we go to try to take it with us? We know you are God; we know we cannot fight you and win. We know that your will will be done in the end no matter how much we try to impose our will upon you. Somehow, Lord, get through to us. Make us willing sharecroppers with you. You are the landlord; we are the tenants. Thank you, Lord, for not just letting us be your tenants, but for insisting that we be your children, heirs to your kingdom, children so valuable in your sight that you sent your Son to die for us and signed the deed to our part of your world in his blood so that all people might see your love and believe. Make us worthy stewards of your promise. *Amen.*

Story of the Week: The teacher was giving a talk on science. "Can anyone tell me," she asked, "why lightning never strikes the same place twice?"

"That's because the same place isn't there after lightning strikes it," a little girl said.

WHO HOLDS THE TITLE?

"The land shall not be sold in perpetuity, for the land is mine; for you are strangers and sojourners with me" (Leviticus 25:23).

In the old Jewish economy, every fiftieth year was designated as the year of jubilee. It was so named because land reverted back to the original owners at that time. It was a year of liberty and a time of justice. All who had been sold into slavery were freed. All public and private debts were wiped off the books. In the words of the writer of Leviticus, "What a happy year it will be!" Most of us would wish that a jubilee year would come around for us once in a while. What a year that would be!

Not only was the year of jubilee a time which would bring about freedom and justice, but it was also a time to remember. Many years later, David, the writer of the psalms, begins the

April Fifth

twenty-fourth psalm with these words, "The earth is the Lord's . . . the world and all who dwell therein." Whether it is the writer of Leviticus or David, the theme is the same. God is the owner; we are the managers.

Let's use this as our starting point: *The earth belongs to God.* That statement flies in the face of most economic theory. In the philosophy of private enterprise there is what we call the *right of ownership.* People, individuals, corporations own land, property, buildings, and make investments.

In the Communist philosophy of land ownership, the land belongs to the State. It is held in trust for all the people, at least that's how it should work. But that land was there long before the Communists came into power and took over ownership, or should I say trusteeship. Before them the Czars controlled the land. In other countries it belonged to kings, feudal lords, protectors, or caesars.

No matter who the owner was, the sharecropping duties had to be passed on. The truth of the statement "The land is mine," still holds true, even in our large cities! *Time* magazine recently reported that most of the property in Manhattan has changed ownership four times since the Indians sold it to those early settlers.

I like the story about a New York law firm that was engaged to clear the title to some property in New Orleans. The New York firm engaged a law firm in New Orleans to search for the title and to obtain the necessary data. The New Orleans firm traced the title back to 1803, but the New York firm wrote saying that they hadn't gone back far enough. In due time they received a reply something like this:

> Gentlemen: Please be advised that in the year 1803 the United States of America acquired the territory of Louisiana from the Republic of France by purchase. The Republic of France in turn acquired title from the Spanish crown by conquest, the Spanish crown having obtained it by virtue of the discoveries of one Christopher Columbus, a Genoese sailor, who had been authorized to embark by Isabella, Queen of Spain, who obtained sanction from the Pope, Vicar of Christ, who is the Son and heir of Almighty God, who made Louisiana.

Well, that goes back far enough, doesn't it? And behind the humor is a solid truth. "The land is mine." God holds the title. A minister once delivered a sermon on God's ownership. Later in the day his host, a man who had considerable means, showed the minister his plantation. At one point, looking over his broad acres and remembering the morning sermon, the host asked, "Do you mean to tell me, Pastor, that this land does not belong to me?" The answer came back, "Ask me that one hundred years from now."

There is a Spanish proverb which says, *There are no pockets in our shrouds.* People who believe otherwise are not wise; our Lord once called them fools. There was one who believed that the crops, barns, and possessions were all his. "Fool," was the response "tonight you die. Then who will get it all?" That's no hypothetical situation, for it is cut out of the fabric of life even in the twentieth century.

Who holds the title? Scripture, life, and experience all come to the same conclusion. The earth belongs to God, but let's move on to affirm that God has summoned us into a partnership. "The land is mine." We are merely tenants and sharecroppers, an ancient truth which has come home to us in the past decade with greater force than ever. This tending of the garden called earth isn't just a story recorded in the beginning chapter of Genesis. It is a continuing saga in man's history. God is the owner—man is the manager.

What happens when we fail to recognize this? Some of you who lived in the mid-section of the United States back in the thirties know from experience what happened. When there is the attitude, "This land is mine and I'm free to do with it whatever I like," there is nothing ahead but disaster. For years pioneers, settlers, and farmers had been abusing and misusing the partnership. The result was a dust bowl! Hundreds of miles and thousands of acres of land lost valuable top soil as the wind scattered it to the states of Indiana, Illinois, and Ohio.

We are partners. Though the writer of Leviticus didn't use the words *conservation* or *ecology*, that essentially is what was understood. Fields were to lie dormant for a period of time so that the valuable land would be conserved. There are only four to five inches of productive soil, which someone has described as "the planet's skin." To allow that skin to be scattered to the winds to erode and be washed out to sea is to commit suicide.

April Fifth

Yes, I realize that none of us here may be farmers, but the import of these words goes far beyond farming and soil conservation. It goes to the very depth of our lives. Either we see ourselves as partners with God in what we do or we view ourselves as owners and are, therefore, free to do what we please. Simply because we may give ten percent of our income away does not mean that we are free to do as we please with the other ninety percent. Either God is our partner in all of life or we are pretenders to the crown.

What happens when we take this business of partnership at full face value? R. G. LeTourneau, a man of middle age, found himself heavily in debt with only a grade school education. The concept of God's partnership got through to that man and he developed it. He eventually became head of the largest maker of earth-moving machinery. William Colgate was seized by this concept of God's ownership, he as a partner. Penniless when he left home, he founded one of the largest soap businesses in the world. The name J. L. Kraft is known because of a cheese company which bears his name. Any Baptist who has been to Green Lake or visited North Shore Baptist Church, in Chicago, is well aware of what Mr. Kraft did to benefit others, simply through this partnership with God.

There's no secret about it! The formula is simple. Take God into partnership in whatever you are presently doing. Give this partner ten percent of whatever you earn, but with the understanding that you are using the other ninety percent as a loan. Have you noticed that to any word we use to describe this arrangement there is the suffix *ship;* stewardship, ownership, and partnership all imply relationship. There is an interrelatedness about life, even in the city. If you don't believe this, then let the trash collectors go out on strike—or the police and firefighters—and we begin to catch a glimpse of how interdependent we are even in urban America.

Which leaves us with but one final reminder: *Everything we do either promotes or demotes this partnership.* When we see our lives, how we earn our livings, what we do with our time, how we use our abilities and talents all as a part of a package of humanity bound together, then this concept of partnership is promoted. Life does become more livable both for us and others. Someone once overheard a conversation between two men who were discussing a house one of them was contemplating buying.

It was a new home. The first man mentioned the name of the builder of the house and said to the other, "You need not hesitate to buy one of those houses. He builds his Christianity into them."

You see, it makes a significant difference as to how we view what we are doing. If we are God's partners then it makes a difference how we teach. We will be better managers of our households. We will be better nurses or physicians. As one doctor said, "I merely set the bones, God does the healing."

In a political year we often hear the phrase, "you can't mix religion and politics." It may be that until we do mix religion and politics, religion and our business, religion and our personal relationships, we will never prove our religion nor will we improve our business, political affairs, and our everyday lives.

Would it not make a difference if we could get a sense of God in the ordinary, daily affairs of our lives? If we could take with us a sense of "God is in this with me"?

The land is mine. . . . The earth belongs to God. But then along comes the Apostle Paul to add one final dimension to this, "You were bought with a price." For the Christian, therefore, the cross of Christ means the re-evaluation of all values and the casting of the whole of life into the form of debt. In the words of the hymn,

> Jesus paid it all;
> All to Him I owe.

We need this reminder that stewardship is not the leaving of a tip on God's tablecloth; it is the confession of an unpayable debt. *Amen.*

James M. Logan
Catalina Baptist Church
Tucson, Arizona

Sunday
April Twelfth

Theme: The Church Is Packed

Call to Worship: God is our refuge and strength, a very present help in trouble. Therefore we will not fear though the earth should change, though the mountains shake in the heart of the sea.

Psalm 46:1-2

Invocation: You are God! It is so nice and safe to be here in your temple. We worship and adore you. Enough of this comfort; now go out and become doers of the word, not just listeners. Amen.

Hymn: "God of Our Fathers"

Sermon Presentation: "To Be a Spectator"

Goals for Today: To be sure we all understand that the Christian faith is an active faith not a passive one. We show our faith as we work in response to God's first love.

This Week in History

April 13—Thomas Jefferson's Birthday—Third President of the U.S. Author of the Declaration of American Independence. The father of the demand for religious freedom in all United States documents.

April 12-20—National Library Week—To recognize the contribution of all libraries, public and private, to the education and enjoyment of all people. To honor the freedom of the press, so vital to our personal freedom.

Announcement for Next Week's Sermon: Easter is a great day for visiting friends and family. Do it and enjoy it. Don't miss next week; we have a special Easter message for you.

Hymn: "Lead On, O King Eternal"

Offertory Scripture: But when the disciples saw him walking on the sea, they were terrified, saying, "It is a ghost!" And they cried out for fear. But immediately he spoke to them, saying, "Take heart, it is I; have no fear."

Matthew 14:26-27

Offertory Prayer: We can't just be spectators; we have to jump into the world and be a vital part of it. We start here and now by offering these our gifts that are such an important part in maintaining and spreading your word of salvation. Take them as a symbol of our participation. *Amen.*

Prayer: Lord, I don't want to be a cheerleader. I want to play in the big game of life. I want you to know I am ready to go where you send me. I am ready to do whatever task you assign me. I want to be active in the battle against sin. I want to be on your side when victory is declared. Remember, Lord, after all this big talk we know we are nothing without you. If you don't give us the strength and courage to do the task, we will fail. Help us to realize that we can do anything if we start on our knees—if we acknowledge that you are the Lord of all, that all good works start with you. Let us be in the thick of the action, but never let us forget you are our armor and protection. Take us off of the curb as spectators and let us join those who march to your triumphant song till the victory is won. *Amen.*

Story of the Week: Four men were putting out on the 18th hole when a ball landed at their feet and rolled within six inches of the hole.

"Who would do a silly thing like that?" one of the men cried. "He didn't even holler at us. It might have hit somebody."

"I don't know about that," one of the others said, "but he sure made a good shot. He almost got a hole in one."

"Hey," said the third, "Let's give him a big thrill. Let's kick it in the hole and when he comes up in a few minutes, he'll think he got a hole in one and it will tickle him to death."

That's what they did. In a few minutes, a man walked up with his putter in his hand. "Did anybody see a ball come this way?" he asked.

"Yes," said one of the foursome, "there it is—in the hole."

"In the hole?" the man screamed. "Wonderful, I made a nine."

April Twelfth

TO BE A SPECTATOR

Palm Sunday

From time to time I have a dream: I'm a citizen of Troy. We Trojans have been at war with the Greeks for nine years. One morning we wake up and look outside the city gate to find that the soldiers have left. All that is there is a large wooden horse.

Those Greeks are tricky. But our leaders do something incredible—they open the gates and bring the horse inside. Don't they know that it could contain Greek soldiers? For nine years we've kept them from storming our city. Now our leaders are opening the gates and dragging in this beautiful horse, a horse full of soldiers who will capture our city, kill our soldiers, take away our wives and daughters. I watch as the first soldier comes out of the wooden horse. It's too late. I can only watch as the destruction begins. I'm a spectator to one of the greatest acts of folly in the history of mankind.

Then, from time to time, I have another dream: I'm a newly commissioned officer in the Merchant Marines, and I've been assigned to a new ship on its maiden voyage. I've been left on the bridge of this luxurious ocean liner. I'm a little worried, for in the last fifteen hours we've been receiving radio messages warning us about the danger of icebergs in our path.

The captain doesn't seem too concerned. He's down below. The passengers are enjoying a full program of fun—dancing and drinking—while our powerful engines push us full speed ahead. I'm nervous; I don't know what to do; I'm new at this. I guess the captain knows what he's doing. I'm really only a spectator. But I'm worried. At the end of my dream I catch a glimpse of the name of the ship painted on the hull. I can barely make it out, but it spells *Titanic*.

Then there is a nightmare that I have from time to time: I'm a Jew who has come to Jerusalem for the Passover. I've heard the excitement about the coming of the Messiah. People are cutting down palm branches to put in his path. Others are taking off their coats to put on the road so that the feet of the donkey on which the Savior is riding will not touch the ground. But in the days that I've been in the city I've seen some of the Scribes and Pharisees gathering together and whispering plots about having Jesus crucified. I want to warn Jesus, or at least one of his disciples. The crowd is so big, all I can do is watch. I can't warn my Lord about what the religious leaders are planning. Being a helpless Palm Sunday spectator is so hard.

There are some other dreams and nightmares that I must share with you this morning.

So often we think that things like violence in the home; spouse abuse; child abuse; tension between parents and children, husbands and wives; teenage suicide; drug and alcohol abuse, all happen somewhere else to some other people. If you think these are the kinds of things that other people do while we watch, then you need to think again.

We look at our world and see all sorts of crazy things going on. It seems that we have gone insane. We see wives who honestly believe that they deserve the beatings they receive from their husbands; children who opt for death over life because living has become such a problem; families in which communication has broken down; children who are sexually and physically abused. Sixty percent of the applicants for jobs in the post office fail a test for proof of illegal drugs in their systems; massive drug raids occur all over the nation. Sometimes we think that all we need to do is to circle our wagons and wait out the problems. Some people hope for a miracle cure, others accept the world as it is. But as your pastor, as your brother in Christ, as your partner in ministry, I need to tell you that the wooden horse is inside the gates—the wooden horse of sin that threatens to undo us.

On this Palm Sunday, I need to tell you that the icebergs—child and spouse abuse, drugs, alcohol, teenage suicide, and sexual promiscuity—are directly in our path and many of us are moving full speed ahead. The band is playing, everyone is dancing, and people are not really giving a damn. These things are happening in our church family not as occasional, isolated incidents, but with alarming frequency and severity.

On this Palm Sunday, we need to ask ourselves, "How can we dare to be spectators of all this? How can we just stand idly by as these things happen around us? Didn't Jesus say we were like a light in a world full of darkness?" The world's attention seems riveted to the starving people of Africa. The Africa situation is a tragedy and we should do our best to help these people, but we cannot ignore the cries and needs of our people

April Twelfth

who are hungering for truth and righteousness and thirsting for hope right here.

What are we to do as a family of God? First of all, if you feel that this can't be true, then I pray that you would receive the ability to listen to the cries for help and see the seriousness of the situation. Jesus spoke about those who have eyes but see not and those who have ears but hear not. Denying that a problem exists has never made that problem go away: case in point, the *Titanic*.

Second, we need to look to our Lord to find the method for dealing with actions that go against the will of God, as well as dealing with the people who perform these acts. You see, the Pharisees had one method. Theirs was one of pointing the finger of blame and casting out the sinner. It was to them that Jesus said, "Let him who is without sin among you be the first to throw a stone" (John 8:7).

With ultimate authority, Jesus taught about our sinfulness. But he was emphatic in pointing out that even the worst sinner could be saved by God's grace. Jesus rejected the actions, but not the actor. He rejected the sin, but not the sinner. No one is beyond God's mercy. Jesus often talked about the need for repentance. In fact, he claimed that there is a great deal of joy in heaven when a sinner cries to God, "God be merciful to me a sinner" (Luke 18:13).

In this Lenten season we have talked about many of the challenges of being a Christian. Sometimes the toughest thing to do is to look at our lives and say "It's time to make a change. It's time to turn from my sinfulness and ask God's forgiveness. It's time to turn my life around, to break with the past." Like the prodigal son who was so far away from home, it's time for us to sit down and look at our lives. Sitting there among the pigs—monetarily and spiritually bankrupt—he saw things from a different perspective. All the glamour had faded. All the excitement was gone. The only hope he had was that his father would forgive him. He had the confidence and trust in his father's love that he could return home. He would be forgiven.

Sometimes just looking at the situation isn't enough. Sometimes we need to be like Paul, who was knocked off his horse before he could turn his life around from being a persecutor of the faithful to being a preacher of the faith. We need to remember that we can never hope to hide anything from our Lord. He knows our every action—our every feeling, our every thought. All of us have sinned! All of us have fallen short of God's expectations! All of us need God's forgiveness. It is time for us to turn from lost lives to real living. How much is your life worth? How much is the life of one of your loved ones worth? Is it worth making changes?

Let's talk about our children first. So often people are quick to blame parents for their kids' problems. That is the easy way out. I've met often with parents and I realize that they are looking for answers. Being a parent is a tough job. It is time for us to begin offering help so that people can develop parenting skills. We must begin to work on developing a program on parenting skills. The time has come for families who are lacking in communication skills to learn them. It is time that all of us who are parents must learn to anticipate problems in the family, to find constructive alternatives to physical and sexual violence. It is time for those who are suffering from addictions to say, "I've had enough. God wants me to be sober, and I want to be sober." If a loved one has a problem in this area, the time has come to stop being a spectator and to do something about it. We, the church, can help. It is time to stop hoping for a miracle cure. It is time to stop accepting the world as it is.

This is a call to arms. We need to realize that we have members who are a threat to themselves, their families, and to us as a communion of saints. They need help. It is time for us to stand up for what we believe in or realize that we will stand for just about anything. We need to look and realize that there are things like despair, doubt, and hopelessness that can sink us. But it's time to ask God's help to keep us afloat and lift us up. If you, or someone you know, are thinking about committing suicide, then it's time to stop watching and reach out for God's helping hand.

It's time that we make sure we have our priorities in life straight. Luther said that God is whatever or whoever is the most important thing in our lives. It's time we all check our priorities. I heard about a church that changed its mid-week Lenten services because the bowling team, including the pastor, bowls on Wednesday nights. Church isn't important in many people's lives. Christ isn't important either. Where does he stand with you?

April Twelfth

There were spectators on that first Palm Sunday. There were spectators at the trial of Jesus. They watched as the crowd cried, "Crucify him!" There were spectators at the foot of the cross who watched as Jesus died for the sins of the world while people mocked him. There were spectators at the stoning of the first Christian martyr, Stephen. One held the coats of those who were doing the stoning. His name was Saul—he later changed it to Paul, but he also changed his whole style of living.

Someone once said, "Sneaking evil past the people of God should be like trying to sneak the sunrise past a rooster." Today is Palm Sunday and this is Holy Week. Next Sunday we will be celebrating Easter and the forgiveness it means to us as well as the victory over sin and death that God shares with each and every one of us. But Easter also means an opportunity for new beginnings in our lives. This week I ask each of you to seriously look at your life and your family's life; after you've looked, think about the changes you need to make. Ask God to help you. Ask your church to help you. Take up your Lord's promise "Behold, I make all things new" (Revelaton 21:5). The time for being a spectator is past. Now is the time to act. *Amen.*

Thomas E. Richards
St. Paul's Lutheran Church
Tannersville, Pennsylvania

Sunday
April Nineteenth

Theme: He Is Risen

Call to Worship: For I delivered to you as of first importance what I also received, that Christ died for our sins in accordance with the scriptures. *I Corinthians 15:3*

Invocation: On this holy day of Easter we come to you with joyful hearts. We know that our redeemer lives. What sweet comfort this thought gives. He is risen! He is risen, indeed! *Amen.*

Hymn: "I Know That My Redeemer Lives"

Sermon Presentation: "A Pharisee Speaks"

Goals for Today: To make the risen Lord a reality in the life of every member present today. He is risen. He is risen, indeed.

This Week in History

April 19—Easter, the Resurrection of Christ—The date of Easter, a movable feast, is derived from the lunar calendar (as prescribed by the council of Nicea, A.D. 325): the first Sunday following the first full moon on or after the Vernal Equinox (March 20)—always between March 22 and April 25.

Announcement for Next Week's Sermon: If you like a party, be here next Sunday. Today is Easter. It is party time. The party goes right on next week.

Hymn: "Crown Him with Many Crowns"

Offertory Scripture: I have been crucified with Christ; it is no longer I who live, but Christ who lives in me; and the life I now live in the flesh I live by faith in the Son of God, who loved me and gave himself for me. *Galatians 2:20*

Offertory Prayer: Lord, you have given your all, your Son Jesus Christ. How can we respond to so great a gift? Humbly, we

April Nineteenth

submit these our gifts of celebration to thy honor and glory. He is risen! He is risen indeed. *Amen.*

Prayer: Easter day is always such an easy day to pray. It is such a happy day. We have passed through Holy Week with all the sadness and injustice behind us; now we look with joy at the resurrected Lord in his victory over death as he brings us new hope. We now have the courage to look at God as Father, and we have the rights of Sonship, joint heirs in the kingdom. Now we are the saints of the church. As saints we must accept the cross that is laid upon us. We must proclaim the good news, we must be ready to fight and suffer to be sure that his kingdom will come on earth as it is in heaven. Why, right in the midst of the joy of this Easter day, do we have to talk about suffering? That is the message of Easter. Through joy, sorrow, suffering, and even death, we have a risen Lord who is with us always. He is in our life. He is with us now. He is with us forever even to the end of the world. He is risen. He is risen indeed! *Amen.*

Story of the Week: A minister, called suddenly away and unable to officiate at the Christmas services in his own church, entrusted his new assistant with the duty. When he returned home, he asked his wife what she thought of the young man's sermon.

"The poorest I ever heard," she said. "Nothing in it at all. It didn't even make sense."

Later that day, the minister, meeting his assistant, asked him how he had managed.

"Fine, sir, absolutely wonderful," he said. "I didn't have time to prepare anything myself, so I preached one of your old sermons."

A PHARISEE SPEAKS

My name is Josiah, son of Jonathon.

I lived in the time of Jesus of Nazareth, observed him first-hand for three years. I come to tell you my story.

I was one of the favored ones of my time for I was born a Pharisee—son of a Pharisee—and part of the most select group of Jews. We were guardians of the sacred law and traditions of our fathers.

I was educated under the best rabbis, learned the laws of the Old Testament by heart. I knew how to argue the finest legal point and interpret the writings and the prophets.

I lived in Jerusalem, the blessed city, and taught in the holy temple. Finally I was elected to the highest council. Life seemed complete with its round of teaching and dealing with court cases.

In my personal life I was faultless—outwardly. I gave tithes of all I had, fasted twice each week, watched every move on the Sabbath, kept myself apart from sinful people, like tax collectors. I was one of the pure and undefiled, but, truth to tell, one of the inwardly unsatisfied. The more I kept at keeping the letter of the law, the more burdensome it became. Regulations increased. I wrote my share, but for all my trying they were hard to remember and harder to keep.

Then Jesus of Nazareth came into the world and my whole life was turned upside down with worry, questions, and the need to silence this man forever.

Reports about Jesus were forwarded to us in Jerusalem from the country where our scouts were looking for those who broke the laws. First we heard about a wild-looking man called John the Baptizer. He was stirring up mobs of people at the Jordan, telling them the Messiah was at hand. We didn't need that—a lot of people getting us into trouble with the Romans. We sent priests and Levites to check this out, and their reports were disturbing.

This John called the temple messengers *snakes* and *sinners* and made some wild statements about God's being able to turn stones into children of Abraham. Common people went down to the river like sheep, and he baptized them and told them a Savior was close at hand. Our spies were getting ready to come home when John let out a shout, pointed to a certain young man, and cried, "There is the Lamb of God who takes away the sin of the world!"

Before long, that man, who was Jesus of Nazareth, in Galilee, had a bunch of common people following him. The situation looked so serious that some of us were assigned to go and see what this new *Messiah* was up to. It was my lot to see first-hand what he did and to hear his stories and feel the tingle of shame when he singled out scribes and Pharisees as hypocrites.

I went north to Galilee. I endured travel, rude people, shoving mobs of the common and sinful people who turned up wherever Jesus was.

April Nineteenth

Legal experts came from nearby towns. We made a very strong showing, but we had to watch in helpless amazement the crowds hanging onto this man's every word and story.

Let me tell you one strange incident. We were crushed into one house, listening to Jesus, when a man was let down through the roof tiles in front of Jesus. It was a helpless, paralyzed man. Jesus bent over him, and we were shocked to hear him say, "Man, your sins are forgiven." Instantly, we were on guard, looking at one another, thinking, "Who but God can forgive sins?"

Jesus turned to us, reading our minds, and said, "I will show you I have authority to forgive sins." Then to the man, "Get up and walk." And he did, instantly. And so he had us. If he could raise the paralyzed, it was obvious he could forgive with the same power. We should have learned that day who he really was, but we were just beginning our battle.

He took up with the most wretched, ungodly people. We couldn't believe our eyes when someone calling himself *Son of Man* chose tax collectors for friends. Matthew, for instance, had a dinner for Jesus and a lot of the riff-raff were invited. We looked on in amazement and, I must say for myself, with envy. They looked so free. Jesus was laughing and everyone was having a wonderful time—so different from our cautious meals when we were constantly on the watch lest we break the least command about food.

And that wasn't the worst of it. We caught him many times talking to children and to women we wouldn't admit even existed. I saw him touch lepers. He took up with such types as Zacchaeus the rich reprobate of Jericho. We documented case after case, but he kept going, disregarding our legalism as though he were following some other law.

We questioned his followers and he sent word that he didn't come to heal the righteous, but the sick. I had never thought about that before, but we did spend all our time on the clean and sacred and legal. But this madman had to be stopped.

The crowds around him increased; and the ignorant, the outsiders, even the *dogs* of the Gentiles followed him. A child could understand his stories, and he even turned those stories on us. Once I thought he had picked me out when he told of a Pharisee's praying in the temple, reciting his goodness in fasting, tithing, and keeping above the common herd. But then he pointed out a sinful tax collector's praying for mercy. Jesus said the sinner was justified before me (the Pharisee). That story must have been the beginning of my battle.

However, it wasn't his teaching that was the worst. We were shaken to the core by Jesus' attitude toward the law and sacred Sabbath.

We had kept on his trail from synagogue to synagogue, building our case against him. One man came in with a dried-up hand; we leaned forward to see what Jesus would do. Would he dare heal on the Sabbath? He looked at the man, told him to come forward. In the breathless silence Jesus turned to us, asking, "Does our law allow us to help or harm on the Sabbath? To save life or destroy it?"

Not a soul spoke, and across Jesus' face came such an expression of anger at us all. I trembled at such holy wrath. Then there came the swift tide of pity, for he saw us to be so blind and stubborn.

He told the man to stretch out his hand, and instantly it was normal, right, useful. There was a catching of breath, a murmur at the miracle. It was wonderful to see the man's joy and gratitude. But we remembered ourselves in time, jumped up, and marched ourselves out of the synagogue.

In our anger we gathered some of King Herod's men we wouldn't have trusted any other time. In council we all decided Jesus must be stopped before the whole Sabbath law was disgraced before God and the world. This time we said it aloud—he must be killed.

Even as we plotted and stormed, Jesus walked through grain fields rubbing out the heads, a work forbidden on the sacred Sabbath. And then he told his critics, "The Sabbath was made for man and not man for the Sabbath."

We put these words down on our scrolls and waited to spring our trap . . . and I was thinking how different life would be if the Sabbath were a day of peace and enjoyment and not of the dread lest we break an obscure rule.

Reading gives such a faint picture of what it was like to watch Jesus, with those unbelievable hands, give health to a leper, sight to the blind, and strength to the paralyzed. They came in such streams and he never turned any away. He embraced them all, and I found I was leaning toward his touch until I recalled he was a lawbreaker and a rebel.

April Nineteenth

After three years, I was worn out with the crowds, my inward doubts, and the travel back and forth to Jerusalem to report to the council. Then those last days swept over us and brought his certain doom, from which he never flinched. I thought he must have had courage from God or the devil.

He shouted into an open grave in Bethany and a dead man got up and walked out of the tomb. That did it. We said, "If we let him go on in this way, everyone will believe in him, the Romans will come and destroy the temple and our nation."

The high priest reminded us that one man must die to save the people. So we began our final plans for his destruction. First, we would get him to make statements we could use in trial against him. It looked easy, for he was in Jerusalem openly teaching, after that awful day he went on a rampage and sent the money changers flying. We lost a lot of cash that day, I can tell you.

We tested him from Scripture, but he could argue from it and open it up in ways we never dreamed. The Sadducees tried their trick story of the wife who married seven successive brothers. They asked whose wife she would be in heaven (a heaven they didn't believe in, of course). Jesus quoted Moses to them, to their utter confusion, and said that God was a God of the living and not of the dead.

That day I stepped forward with my question. It was a trick, but it mattered to me more than I would admit even to myself.

"Teacher," I asked. "What is the great commandment?"

Without hesitation he told me to love God with heart, soul, mind, and strength, and to love my neighbor as myself.

I was moved in spite of myself as he spoke with reverence and such authority.

I answered, "Well done, Teacher! It is more important to obey these two commandments than to offer animals and other sacrifices to God."

Jesus looked at me, saying, "You are not far from the kingdom of God."

I felt an almost physical tearing as I leaned toward this man, wanting his kingdom, but at the same time I was clutched by the law.

A little later we heard him blaspheming by saying that *One God* was his father and that before Father Abraham lived, he, Jesus, had lived. I felt something hard in my hand and looked down to find I had grabbed up a stone to hurl at his words. All of us were growling and ready to swing our stones when he calmly walked away. I dropped my stone with a thud, kicked it away with my foot. I hated it, or was it myself I hated for having the thought to fling it at a good man claiming to be the Messiah?

A tug on my sleeve pulled me into a room where council members stood with a shifty-looking man who turned out to be one of Jesus' disciples. He was making a deal with us.

"Pay me," he said, "and I'll get the Teacher for you."

How quickly we counted out his price and even thanked God for sending such a traitor to us.

The next hours are a blur. I was so tired of the struggle, the endless arguments, the building of the case. I had to hate Jesus, but I could not.

I saw him dragged in, beaten, insulted and bearing the scalding, irrational hate of our council and High Priest. Jesus acknowledged that God was his father and that he would be at God's right hand for us all to see.

"Blasphemer!" "Death to the heretic!"

We had to call in the Romans to do the execution. I dragged myself home when it was over, hoping for peace and the old life, but that was not to be. I saw him everywhere. I heard him and lived again and again the scenes in Galilee. I wept for him and for my poor self.

A knocking at my door—the agitated Pharisees of Council.

"They say that Jesus was stolen out of that tomb. Some even say he is alive again."

My heart leaped with hope. He said he would rise from the dead!

Yes, I saw him alive again. I gladly flung away my old life; it was like a straw in the wind. I grasped the reality of freedom, love, and eternal life. I found them all in Jesus, my Messiah and Lord. He is the Son of God. He is the Master of all and of my life.

I leave you to go back across the centuries, but I say to you who live now: *Jesus Christ is worthy of all your allegiance and your love. I beg you to follow him with all your heart. Amen.*

Marie Hubbel
Chico, California

Sunday
April Twenty-sixth

Theme: Easter Is Only the Beginning

Call to Worship: It is written, "You shall worship the Lord your God and him only shall you serve." Matthew 4:10

Invocation: We are gathered here to again celebrate the victory of Easter. Make this a day of victory for all the faithful who have come to worship the risen Lord. *Amen.*

Hymn: "The Church's One Foundation"

Sermon Presentation: "Don't Leave Now, the Party's Just Starting"

Goals for Today: To praise the faithful who are here today and to make them aware that they are like the twelve who continued to follow Jesus.

This Week in History

May 1—Law Day—To advance equality and justice under law; to encourage people to support and respect the law.

May 1-31—Older Americans Month—To encourage respect for older people. To assure a life of dignity for all people.

Announcement for Next Week's Sermon: Have you ever been afraid? I mean really afraid? You locked all the doors and that made you feel safe. Bolted doors are not the answer. See you next Sunday.

Hymn: "Faith of Our Fathers"

Offertory Scripture: But the hour is coming, and now is, when the true worshipers will worship the Father in spirit and truth, for such the Father seeks to worship him. God is spirit, and those who worship him must worship in spirit and truth.
John 4:23-24

Offertory Prayer: Lord, you bless us and all that you ask in return is that we be faithful. Let these our gifts show you our faithfulness. *Amen.*

Prayer: We must be faithful. We do not have to find the road to faith alone. Lord, you showed us the way so many times during your life here on earth. You were tempted by the devil just as we are. You remained faithful. You had to face angry crowds who cursed you and threatened you; you remained faithful. You suffered and died for us; you knew the agony of pain in your body and rejection in your heart, but you remained faithful. This is not an easy world in which we live, you know that. Your temptations, your agony, your faithfulness through all give us courage to try each day anew. By your example, by your victory over sin, temptation, and even death on the cross, we are filled with hope that we, too, will win against all odds and in the end hear you say, "Come to me, you good and faithful servant." So let it be with me. *Amen.*

Story of the Week: The kids were fighting again and mother shouted from the kitchen where she was working, "Stop that fighting. Haven't I told you to go by the Golden Rule."

"Yes," came a voice from the recreation room, "but he did it unto me first."

DON'T LEAVE NOW, THE PARTY'S JUST STARTING

I attended college at a fairly large school which had a great many students on a single campus. I recall sitting in a math class, as a first-quarter freshman, in a huge auditorium, with about five hundred other brand new students like me. On the first day of class, the professor said, "I want everyone to look at the person on your left. OK. Now, look at the person on your right. OK. Before this ten-week quarter is over, one of them won't be here anymore."

Last Sunday, which was, of course, Easter, I was tempted to try that little exercise with the congregation at this church. For I knew, as you did, that one-third to one-half of those who were with us in worship last week wouldn't be here today. Among pastors, we refer to the Easter crowds, and similarly to Christmas and Mother's Day crowds, as *celebration Christians.* You'll never see such folks when there's a lesson to be studied or a class to be taught or a wall to be painted. They'll never be around to hear a sermon on morality, or self-denial, or the

April Twenty-sixth

meaning of the cross. Celebration Christians show up only when there's something extra-special to celebrate—when it's *party time* at the church.

It's the Sunday after Easter this week—the hoopla and the hullabaloo have died down, and we're back, pretty much, to our routine, regular group of worshipers today—persons who regard faith in Jesus Christ as an ongoing commitment, and not just a once or twice a year party time. I want to salute this congregation today—you are the indispensable backbone which keeps the church of Jesus Christ alive—so it will still be around to receive the party-goers next Easter. And I want to let you in on a secret that the Easter-only crowds haven't found out about. (Whisper) Easter isn't the only time of the year when Christians are allowed to celebrate. (Repeat, louder) Easter isn't the only time of the year when Christians are allowed to celebrate. Since that first Easter morning, dedicated Christians have been celebrating, night and day, for nearly two thousand years. We're the church of the permanent party. We've got enough reason to celebrate from now until the end of time: Jesus has been raised from the dead, and we've been granted eternal life. That's not just the message of Easter morning. It's the joyous shout of every morning. Praise God! Jesus is alive!

Human nature being what it is, though, any other day besides the real one—Easter itself—doesn't feel quite the same. You're here today because, for the most part, you're faithful Christians. But even so, I'll bet this Sunday doesn't quite have the same *zing* for you that last Sunday had. It's all well and good to suggest that we try to sustain the Easter spirit—or the Christmas spirit when it's December—for the whole year around, but people, realistically, just aren't built that way. Even though God's victory over sin and death is worth celebrating each and every day, we just can't seem to keep ourselves up for such celebration all the time.

The Gospel of Luke gives more insight into the first Easter and its aftermath than do either Matthew or Mark. In Matthew and Mark, the Resurrection is covered only briefly—the tomb is found empty early in the morning; Jesus immediately appears to the disciples and encourages them; everyone gets excited and filled with joy; and there the story ends, on a supremely high note. But Luke tells it a bit more completely. The amazement, the joy, the excitement of Easter morning are presented—as in the other two Synoptic Gospels—but Luke carries the narrative a bit further. By Easter evening, the very same day, the raw emotional edge of the morning's excitement has abated. The disciples have come together for the evening meal, and each has begun to wonder about the day's events. Was it for real? Was it truly so miraculous? Or was it just mass hysteria—a grand and glorious emotional high from which they're now coming down—a "mountain-top experience" with little lasting effect?

In this context, Luke presents Jesus' coming to the disciples during their evening meal. Correlating his Gospel with the others, we know that this is Jesus' second appearance to all except Thomas. But the reception Jesus receives the second time is quite different from the first. The jubilation and the excitement are largely gone. They've had time to recover from the emotional shock of seeing a dead man come back to life. And now there are questions—doubts—even fright! *Is he a ghost come back to haunt us because we deserted him when he needed us? Maybe having Jesus come back from the dead isn't such a good thing after all.*

Jesus, ever the master analyst of human nature, is well aware of what is going on in the disciples' hearts—the turmoil, the uncertainty, the confusion. So he appeals to their minds—the rational faculties—and not to their emotions at this point.

"Why are you troubled, and why do doubts rise in your minds? Look at my hands and my feet. It is I, myself! Touch me and see; a ghost does not have flesh and bones, as you see I have."

And so they do this, and find solid evidence of the physical reality of the Resurrection. Then, lest this confirmation provoke another wave of the earlier emotional hysteria, Jesus keeps them on a very mundane, down-to-earth level.

"Do you have anything here to eat? I'm hungry—how about rustling up some of that fish, and let's have dinner." No praise, no worship, no theological discussion—not yet. Let's eat, first!

After the meal, when they have become more used to the fact of having the Master, the one they had thought to be dead, around with them again, Jesus appeals a second time to their minds.

"You know what I taught you before. You know what the scriptures said about me. You know that I promised to return—and I have. All of this is God's plan—predicted and fulfilled exactly as he promised. You are witnesses of these

April Twenty-sixth

things. And now you are going to be witnesses of them to others."

Jesus knew that their emotional reactions to his Resurrection would quickly subside, especially when he returned to his father in heaven. The evidence is clear throughout the Bible—miracles can be convincing for a moment, but they don't produce true, lasting faith. So Jesus gave his disciples a clear explanation of the facts. God had promised. Jesus had explained God's promises as he taught. God had fulfilled his promises—to the letter. And now they, the disciples, were part of God's plan for the future. The Resurrection morning wasn't the final chapter in what they were to experience. There was more, much more, yet to be accomplished in God's plan. The party was really just starting. Don't leave now—good things are just starting to happen!

I shudder to think of what might have happened to the world if a third, or even half, of the original disciples had simply packed up and gone home after that first Easter. If, for example, five of the eleven—Peter, Thaddeus, Simon, James, and Bartholomew—had decided they'd seen everything worth seeing, that Easter was now over, and had gone back to their former occupations, I doubt that the early church could have gotten off the ground with just half—or even two-thirds—of the disciples behind it. But, praise God, nobody went home after the first Easter. They all stayed. They all witnessed. They all worked. And because they all committed themselves to being more than just celebration Christians, the church got its start. Because of persons committed to Christ throughout the ages, you and I are privileged to hear the gospel of the Resurrection this morning. If Christians throughout the centuries had come just to hear about Easter—to "celebrate" Jesus once a year, I'm quite sure there would have been no celebration of Easter this year. The whole idea would have been forgotten centuries ago.

A few years back, an older and wiser pastor told me this—"Never," he said, "never criticize the persons who are present in a worship service because of those who are absent. The folks who are there deserve praise, not criticism." That's exactly what I want to say this morning. I salute you, the regular worshipers at this church today. You are the faithful disciples who will keep this church alive. I can't promise you the excitement of an Easter morning every Sunday that you come here. I can't guarantee that there won't be times, in the coming year, when it will be hard for you—or me—even to remember that there was an Easter. But I can promise you that God will remember your faithfulness and reward it. Someday, somewhere, we have his promise that there will be a permanent party—where Easter is celebrated every day of every year unto eternity. God keeps his promises. So—don't leave now, the party's just starting! *Amen.*

D. Z. Ring, III
St. Mark's United Methodist Church
El Paso, Texas

Sunday
May Third

Theme: The Other You

Call to Worship: Let us hold fast the confession of our hope without wavering, for he who promised is faithful.
Hebrews 10:23

Invocation: We play games with our friends, our family, and our God. Lord, help us to relax and just be ourselves. People will love us, our families will love us, and God will love us. Take me as I am. *Amen.*

Hymn: "All People That on Earth Do Dwell"

Sermon Presentation: "Bolted Doors"

Goals for Today: To get people to realize that God's love knocks down all doors, or any other defense we may try to put up to keep him out of our hearts. Don't fight him; you have lost already.

This Week in History

May 3-9—National Family Week—To celebrate the family and especially the influence that the Christian concept of family has had on the family unit in America.

May 8—Victory in Europe Day—Commemorates the unconditional surrender of Germany to Allied Forces in 1945, ending World War II in Europe. Peace at last.

Announcement for Next Week's Sermon: Women did not always do too well in the Bible. Let's take a look at some of the strong women who made a difference.

Hymn: "O Jesus, Thou Art Standing"

Offertory Scripture: Blessed is the man who endures trial, for when he has stood the test he will receive the crown of life which God has promised to those who love him. *James 1:12*

Offertory Prayer: Anyone who understands the Christian faith knows all about surprises. Jesus died for a worthless soul like me; that is the biggest surprise of all. Accept these gifts as our response to your great surprise. *Amen.*

Prayer: Masks, masks, masks—which mask should I wear today, O Lord? Maybe the mask of self-reliance, I like that one. It tells the world that I'm strong, that I'm tough, that I'm in charge. This is the mask that hides my feelings of insecurity. This is the mask that I need when I face challenges or adversity.

Perhaps I'll wear the mask of knowledge. I don't want people to think I don't know what's going on. What's the old saying: *sometimes wrong but never in doubt.* If I can only wear this mask of knowledge and impress people with my reason and logic, they won't ever guess that I have my moments of doubt and indecisiveness. I might even be able to fool them into thinking I never make mistakes.

Then I need to wear my mask of self-righteousness. If I admit that I'm a sinner in need of your forgiveness and your love, then people will realize I'm not perfect. Then they will wonder if I really am all that smart or strong.

It's tough, Lord, wearing the right mask for the right situation. It's tough telling the world one thing while behind the mask I wrestle with the truth. I want to be honest with others, with myself, but most of all with you.

Help me to be myself. Help me to know that you love me and care for me so much that you were willing to die for me on the cross. Help me to know that you love me in spite of the masks I wear. You love me for what I am and because you do I can love myself. Given the opportunity, my family and friends will love me, too. *Amen.*

Story of the Week: The man had just put the finishing touches on the concrete driveway, when a little boy chased a playmate right across it. The man got back on his hands and knees and worked for an hour to erase the footprints and smooth out the damage. As he worked, he kept muttering about the kids who had caused all the trouble.

A man passing by heard him and said, "It sounds as though you don't like children. You shouldn't feel that way."

"Oh, I don't dislike children," the man said. "I have children of my own. I like children in the abstract—but not in the concrete."

May Third

BOLTED DOORS

In Eugene O'Neill's play *The Great God Brown*, the characters hold masks in front of their faces when they are talking to others. They remove their masks to talk to the audience and to reveal their real feelings.

We all wear various masks in front of others. When we're young, we wear our courting masks, letting our boy or girl friends see only the side of us we want them to see.

When we're at the job, we wear our business masks, trying to assure ourselves of that next promotion or maintain job security.

When we're with friends, we wear our friendly masks, guarding our prized friendship.

Few people know us as we really are; in fact, we probably don't even know ourselves completely. That's why, in public confession, we confess sins that we don't even know we have committed. We always jealously guard those parts of our personalities that make us vulnerable to hurt. Our minds block out many of the memories that would be very painful to recall, and it's probably a good thing. It's the way God made us. Only he knows us as we really are.

Yes, we shut out the world from much of our private lives. We bolt the doors to our hearts to protect us from hurt. Intimacy can be defined as our allowing another person to enter, however little, into our personal hiding place where we are protected from hurt.

Even the disciples, after the Resurrection of Jesus, found their hiding place. It's somewhat amazing that even after being told that Jesus had been raised from death, having seen the empty tomb with their own eyes, they should still go into hiding. They had so much to be joyful about, so much to live for; yet Easter night found them behind bolted doors.

I think the reason for that is that they had experienced too much hurt in the days before, and they were afraid of being hurt again. The horrible events of Golgotha were too fresh. They were still afraid that their lives were in danger, so they hid from the world.

But the truth of the matter is that no matter how desperately we hide from the world, Christ seeks us out. He searches out our hiding places, penetrates our bolted doors, appears in our midst.

I'm sure you all remember that beautiful poem by Francis Thompson, "The Hound of Heaven." It pictures God in relentless pursuit of the one who tries to flee him and hide from him:

> I fled Him, down the nights and down the days;
> I fled Him, down the arches of the years;
> I fled Him, down the labyrinthine ways
> Of my own mind; and in the mist of tears
> I hid from Him, and under running laughter.
>   Up vistaed hopes I sped;
>   And shot, precipitated,
> Adown Titanic glooms of chasmèd fears,
> From those strong Feet that followed, followed after.
>   (ll 1-9)

Finally, when the speaker can run no more he must give in, and the pursuing God reaches out to him with these final words: "Rise, clasp My hand, and come!" (l 176).

That scene has been reenacted again and again throughout history. We cannot hide from God. We cannot bolt our doors to keep him out. He seeks out our hiding places, appears in our midst, and says to us, as he said to the disciples: "Peace be with you" (John 20:26). Then he showed them his hands, and he showed them his side—symbols of how diligently he wants to be in our midst—and the disciples were filled with joy at seeing the Lord.

In the Revelation to John, the last book of the Bible, Jesus says to us: "I stand at the door and knock; if any one hears my voice and opens the door, I will come in to him and eat with him, and he with me" (3:20).

Of course, it is true that Christ wants us to open our doors to him, but it is also true that there are times in our lives when, for one reason or another, our doors are bolted shut and we are reluctant to open to anyone—even Christ.

The story of that Easter night, however, teaches us that Christ can, and often does come, into our midst despite the bolted doors of our hearts. The doors to the disciples' hiding place were bolted; yet Jesus appeared to them—regardless of their bolted doors.

May Third

One reason we bolt the doors to our hearts is out of fear—fear of the world—just like that of the disciples. Or, perhaps, fear even of Christ. But Christ wants us to know that there is no reason to be afraid of him. *Peace be with you!* he told the disciples.

Another reason we might bolt the door to him is because of honest doubt—like Thomas'. Even though the disciples had told him that Jesus had risen and had appeared to them, Thomas needed to see with his own eyes. He was no different from the rest of the disciples—they had also hidden themselves until Jesus appeared to them. Thomas, just like them, was a practical man, a realist. He didn't want to build his faith on rumor.

"Unless I see in his hands the print of the nails, and place my finger in the mark of the nails, and place my hand in his side, I will not believe" (John 20:25).

And so again, Jesus had to make his appearance despite Thomas' bolted doors, and when Thomas saw he cried out: "My Lord and my God!" (John 20:28).

Thomas, like the others, didn't really want to lock Jesus out, but he was afraid—afraid of his own doubts—so he bolted the door to his heart; yet, Jesus came in.

Yes, we'll sometimes hide behind bolted doors because we are afraid, or because we have honest doubt, but there are times when we bolt the doors to our hearts with the express purpose of keeping Christ out! Saul of Tarsus did that as a young man. Before he became Paul the apostle, he locked his heart to Christ—to keep him out. Saul's zeal for God was so great he couldn't conceive of God working in any way other than the way Saul thought. The idea that Jesus was the Christ was not in his thinking. To him, Christ was an impostor, an impediment in God's plan.

But Christ wanted Saul. He knew that Saul had the potential of great work for him. So he broke through Saul's locked heart and literally tore down that bolted door. It happened on the way to Damascus when Saul was about to ferret out Christ's followers and have them arrested. In a blinding light Jesus burst through the barred door and called out: "Saul, Saul, why do you persecute me? It hurts you to kick against the goads!"

Goads are cattle prods—sticks with nails in the end of them to keep the cattle moving in the direction the herdsman wants them to move. Fighting the goad can be painful for the cattle.

Well, Christ was telling Saul that he was prodding him just as herdsmen prod cattle. He was telling that Pharisee, Saul: "From now on, it's going to be painful for you if you continue to fight the will of God."

In other words: "If you keep locking your doors on me, Saul, I'm going to keep knocking them down until you tear them down yourself. There's no way you can lock me out forever!"

We know the rest of the story—how Saul did open up to Christ and became the Apostle Paul. You and I are here probably because of him. After all, he was the first missionary to the non-Jewish nations.

There are many reasons that we hide behind locked doors. It may be because we are afraid to open our hearts to the world, or even to Christ. Or it may be that our doors are bolted because, like Thomas, our lives are filled with honest doubt. Or maybe it is because, like Saul of Tarsus, we are so filled with zeal for God that we have left no room for him to work in our lives as he wants to work. But whatever the reason, Christ can, and often does, come to us despite our bolted doors.

Hide from God? It is impossible. The Psalmist knew that:

> O Lord, thou hast searched me and known me!
> Whither shall I go from thy Spirit?
> Or whither shall I flee from thy presence?
> If I ascend to heaven, thou art there!
> If I make my bed in [Hell], thou art there!
> If I take the wings of the morning
> and dwell in the uttermost parts of the sea,
> even there thy hand shall lead me,
> and thy right hand shall hold me. (139:1, 7-10)

Those of us who have experienced the Risen Christ know that there is nothing that can keep Christ out of our locked doors forever. Our Lord is a searching Christ—searching us out even when we hide from him, and he comes in to us there, to meet us with these words of comfort: *Peace be with you!*

Amen.

Edward A. Beckstrom
Equality, Alabama

Sunday
May Tenth

Theme: Women, God Bless Them

Call to Worship: There were also many women there, looking on from afar, who had followed Jesus from Galilee, ministering to him.
Matthew 27:55

Invocation: Lord, you have made us male and female, but all one in the sight of God—all one family; all one cause; all one Lord—one victory over death. *Amen.*

Hymn: "Christ Is Made the Sure Foundation"

Sermon Presentation: "Biblical Images of Women"

Goals for Today: To make Christ the binding and healing power of the church so that there is no distinction between male and female. All one body!

This Week in History

May 10—Mother's Day—A day to honor all women, with a special emphasis on mothers. First observed in Philadelphia in 1907.

May 11-16—National Salvation Army Week—To bring attention to the religious and social welfare ministry of this great organization.

Announcement for Next Week's Sermon: I have not seen a sheep for at least a couple of weeks. Why would we want to talk about sheep next Sunday?

Hymn: "Onward, Christian Soldiers"

Offertory Scripture: There is neither Jew nor Greek, there is neither slave nor free, there is neither male nor female; for you are all one in Christ Jesus.
Galatians 3:28

Offertory Prayer: We thank you, Lord, for the gift of those who have guided us throughout our lives. Today especially we ask a special blessing on our mothers. Through their lives and examples we have learned so much. Bless them all. *Amen.*

Prayer: Today, Lord, we honor all women for the role they have played in the growth and progress of your church. As the hymns of praise are raised from your church here on earth to your throne on high, you hear the voices of women singing your praise. We depend on women so much here in your church, so, also, let us honor them for their service. Let us not just let this day be Mother's Day, but every day a day of honor for mothers. You set the example from the cross. You showed your concern and love for your mother. Help us to follow this example by caring and loving our mothers, so that their lives may be full and rich, happy and carefree, until they go to live with you. They cared for and loved us, now let us show our love for them, and through this action, prove our love for you. Thank you, Lord, for the blessing of all mothers. *Amen.*

Story of the Week: The little boy who had been playing in the back yard all morning came through the kitchen door and said to his mother, "Who am I?"

His mother thought she was supposed to play some kind of guessing game and said, "Oh, I think you must be Tarzan."

"I guess Mrs. Wilson was right," he said. "She said I was so dirty that my own mother wouldn't know me."

BIBLICAL IMAGES OF WOMEN

We are set free from the old law; there is neither male nor female—all are one in Christ Jesus.

I want to begin today's message by calling your attention to something obvious. Have you ever noticed how women outnumber men in church worship services? Look around you for a moment. The women here today outnumber the men by at least two to one, maybe even three to one. This isn't just an idiosyncrasy of this church, either. In every Christian church or denomination I've ever been in, or seen any statistic about, the women outnumber the men. I used to wonder a great deal about that. *Why does Christianity have such an overwhelming*

May Tenth

attraction for women? Then I did some studying of other religions. Even today, in an Orthodox Jewish synagogue when attendance is taken only the men are counted. The women might as well not be there—they simply don't count. In Moslem countries women are regarded as property—either of their fathers or of their husbands. In areas of the world where Hinduism is practiced, cattle are regarded as superior to women. Of the major religions of the world, only Christianity—even in the twentieth century—only Christianity affords women a measure of acceptance—and even equality—in the eyes of God. "There is neither Jew nor Greek . . . slave nor free . . . male nor female; for you are all one in Christ Jesus" (Galatians 3:28).

In recognition of the fact that I'm usually speaking to an audience of more women than men, plus the added fact that today is Mother's Day, I thought I would dedicate this sermon specifically to the ladies. Now, men, please don't fall instantly asleep at that cue. You just might learn something from this sermon, too. Hang in there!

Just what does the Bible have to say about women? Let's begin by being honest. The majority of biblical passages that deal specifically with women do so in a negative context. I'm aware that it's become very popular in recent years, especially in our church, to pick out the positive images of women in the Bible and to show those off, ignoring the negative ones. But the fact remains that most biblical images of women are negative, for two obvious reasons. First, three-fourths of the Bible is the Old Testament—the basis for Judaism—and we've already mentioned the traditional Jewish view of women. Women were seen primarily as property among the Israelites. We get this sense even in such prominent scriptures as the Ten Commandments. Exodus 20:17, the commandment against covetousness, reads as follows: "You shall not covet your neighbor's house, you shall not covet your neighbor's wife, or his manservant, or his maidservant, or his ox, or his ass, or anything that is your neighbor's." The use of masculine pronouns throughout makes it clear that this commandment is intended to govern relationships between two men. Its focus of concern is the property of another man. The wife of a man is simply an entry on the list of possessions—inferior in the listing to a man's dwelling, but more important than his hired servants.

The second, more important, reason why most biblical images of women are negative is that the Bible depicts all of humankind as a flawed, fallen creature in need of salvation. "All have sinned and fall short of the glory of God," to quote Romans 3:23. Both men and women are sinners in need of God's grace. Ladies, there's no *pedestal* of acclaim for you in the Bible. Men need Jesus. Women need Jesus. In that sense, the bible teaches a very radical sexual equality. All have sinned—all need Jesus.

Even in the Old Testament, however, there are some strong, positive images of women that can't be ignored. The Genesis accounts of the creation of Adam and Eve reflect God's original design and intent that prior to their fall, man and woman were to be equals. The woman, Eve, is created to be a fit, co-equal companion to the man, Adam—sharing fully in the task of ruling the earth. God addresses his blessings and commands to both of them. When they disobey God, their fall from grace becomes the occasion for the original solidarity between the sexes to be shattered, as each attempts to blame the other for their joint wrongdoing. The ages-old "battle of the sexes" is a specific part of the curse God levies upon them both for the wrongdoing in Genesis 3:16-19. Sexual equality was God's intent for men and women. Our present struggle with inequality reflects our sinful, broken natures.

In the New Testament, the image of women continues to be mixed. Of course, I suppose just about everyone is aware of the three letters of Paul—I Corinthians, Ephesians, and I Timothy—in which Paul gives discourses on specific subordinate roles of women in the Christian community. Christian churches have long used these letters as ample justification for establishing and maintaining male domination at almost every level of church decision-making, in spite of the minority numerical status of men in practically every Christian denomination—Catholic, Orthodox, or Protestant. And I'm not saying we've necessarily erred in some of this—Paul's letters are part of God's Holy Word to us, and we've got to take them seriously. I don't think God would have allowed Paul's teachings about women to come into the Bible if God didn't want us to pay heed to them. However, for men or women to pull out selected verses of Pauline writing to hold up against women—no talking

May Tenth

in church . . . cover your head . . . be submissive to your husband—is to misinterpret the Scriptures as a whole. The same Paul who wrote "it is shameful for a woman to speak in church" in his letter to the Corinthian church also wrote to the church at Galatia: "There is neither Jew nor Greek . . . slave nor free . . . male nor female; for you are all one in Christ Jesus." Which verse would you choose? Both are Paul's writing—and both are God's Word.

Ultimately, when Christians are searching for the truth about a complex, ambiguous, or controversial matter—such as the image of women in the Bible—the best criterion to which we can turn is our Lord and Savior, Jesus Christ. His life, his teachings, his actions are the centerpoints around which all else must gather. And while I do not believe that any part of God's Word ever directly contradicts any other part, I would submit that the best test of any teaching, idea, or doctrine found elsewhere in the Bible is to look at it in the light of the Gospels, where we most directly encounter Jesus. On the issue of women, it is highly important to recognize that in the Gospels—in the life and teachings of Jesus—we find almost universally positive images of women. In fact, 90 percent of all the positive statements about women in the entire bible are found in the four gospels—Matthew, Mark, Luke, and John.

Let's consider, briefly, some of Jesus' images of womanhood. In the first gospel—that of Matthew—in chapter 19, Jesus takes the side of the woman in interpreting the Mosaic law on divorce. His disciples, who have always been taught to interpret this law for the benefit of husbands, are astonished at this "even-handedness" on Jesus' part. In Mark 5, and again in Mark 7, we have two separate cases of women, one with a disease herself and the other with a sick daughter, who are commended by Jesus for their great faith in Him—and the males present come off looking awfully foolish by comparison. But it is in the Gospel of Luke that we find the most extensive positive imagery concerning women in relation to Jesus. It is in Luke that the sisters Mary and Martha, mentioned only in passing in the other Gospels, are accorded a relationship with Jesus as close or closer than that of any of the traditional twelve male disciples. In several of Jesus' parables in Luke women are the chief actors. Jesus' parable of the lost coin, in Luke 15:8-10, must have been a revolutionary bombshell of teaching to the Jews of his day. In this parable, a woman is placed in the position of seeking, finding, and saving the coin which was lost. This may not seem important or unusual to us, but to the Jews it was obvious who the one who seeks, finds, and saves must be. Jesus was allowing a woman to fill the role of Almighty God in this parable. This was unheard of—God must always be male, mustn't he? In Luke 20, Jesus states flatly that, in the kingdom of heaven, unlike the society of Israel, women will not be the possession of any husband, but the same as men, will be like the angels. I'm sure such anticipated equality made Heaven seem less desirable to many of the Jewish priests, some of whom claimed up to four wives among their earthly possessions. In the last chapter of his Gospel, Luke presents three women—Mary Magdalene, Joanna, and Mary the mother of James—as the first witnesses to the resurrection of Jesus on Easter Day. Small wonder that so many Jews rejected the resurrection since, to them, the witness of a woman was completely invalid, always inadmissable, simply on the basis of her sex, in a Jewish court of law! The last Gospel, that of John, also presents several favorable images of women, notably the story in John 8 of the woman caught in adultery in which Jesus rejects the Jewish double standard on sexual sin, which would have had the woman stoned but allowed the man to go free. Women fare well in all of the Gospels, and the Gospels are the heart of God's Word to us.

Well, that's it, a survey of the Bible's teachings about women. And how might we respond to such a message? Let me suggest two possible ways. First, specifically for the women, you've come a long way, baby. And you'd be wise to recognize and acknowledge where the roots of your progress began, with Jesus Christ, the God who came down to earth to show us all what it means to be truly human. Second, and finally, something for everyone. We're in the midst of a turbulent, confused time concerning the sexes. Roles and ideas about men and women are changing as never before. Women's lib, men's lib—we're all unsure, uneasy about what these things will mean. In the midst of all this let's hold fast, in the Christian church, to the writing of an old male chauvinist of nearly two thousand years ago—"There is neither Jew nor Greek, there is neither slave nor free, there is neither male nor female; for you

May Tenth

are all one in Christ Jesus." Whatever else may happen, that is God's eternal truth for us all! We all need Jesus Christ. We all stand in need. Male, female, old, young, white, brown, rich, poor—whatever. We all need one thing. We all need Jesus. *Amen.*

D. Z. Ring
St. Mark's United Methodist Church
El Paso, Texas

Sunday
May Seventeenth

Theme: His Sheep

Call to Worship: And when the chief Shepherd is manifested you will obtain the unfading crown of glory. *I Peter 5:4*

Invocation: O Lord, why must I always follow like a sheep? Why can't I lead for a change? Is this some sort of exercise in humility? Must I always walk in somebody else's dust? Please, God, let me be right up front next to you for a change. Forgive me my pride, Lord. All through your ministry here on earth, people wanted to be close to you, but when it came to the cross, they all left you alone. Just let me be one of your sheep. Give me the courage to stay in the flock and the humility to know that, though I am one of many, the shepherd knows me by name. That's enough for me. *Amen.*

Hymn: "A Charge to Keep I Have"

Sermon Presentation: "Jesus the Good Shepherd"

Goals for Today: Today is *Good Shepherd Sunday* in the church year. On this day we are all called to a new awareness of Jesus in the role of the Shepherd and we are his flock in the role of the sheep. We must see this illustration of Jesus as more than a pretty picture of a nice little Sunday school story. Today we drive home the absolute fact that we are willing to be his sheep and to totally submit ourselves to him or die. We must be ready to accept him as the Shepherd and to follow, without question. This sermon offers the life or death choice. Will you follow him?

This Week in History

May 20—Council of Nicaea I—The first ecumenical council of the Christian church, called by Emperor Constantine I in the year 325. It formulated the Nicene Creed and fixed the date of Easter.

May 20-21—Lindbergh Flight Anniversary—Charles Lindbergh landed in Paris in 1927. This was the first solo transAtlantic

May Seventeenth

flight. "Lucky Lindy" was lucky because he prepared well and had the courage to challenge the unknown.

Announcement for Next Week's Sermon: Some dream dreams and do nothing. Some dream dreams and do. If you are a doer, you'll love next week's sermon.

Hymn: "Jesus Calls Us O'er the Tumult"

Offertory Scripture: But it shall not be so among you; but whoever would be great among you must be your servant.

Mark 10:43

Offertory Prayer: As we are all your sheep, so we must worship you in our own way. We give to you as we are able. We give our gift as a sacrifice so that we might do honor to that great sacrifice the Good Shepherd made on the cross to save his flock from death forever and ever. *Amen.*

Prayer: Lord, on this Good Shepherd Sunday, we sit and try to picture you as the Good Shepherd. It really isn't too easy for us today. We do not live on farms. We do not raise sheep. We do not know how dependent the sheep are on the shepherd, and we don't know how independent sheep can be. How can we better understand the signifiance of that relationship?

Lord, show us through our families; that is something we can all understand. The good mother who cares for and worries about her children—she knows them so well. They are each different, but she loves them all. She gives of herself equally to them all. She would lay down her life to save any one of them and she cares for their every need. If we can understand that about our mothers, how much more so we can expect that kind of care, and more, from our Father in Heaven? He knows us. He loves us. He cares for us, and he has proved his concern by laying down his life for us so that we might have life and overcome death once and for all. Good Shepherd, continue to lead and I will follow. *Amen.*

Story of the Week: A sheepherder finally struck it rich. Among other things, he bought a Rolls Royce limousine. On his next trip to town, the car salesman asked him how he liked his new car.

"Say, fella," said the sheepherder, "that is a real nice car. I sure do like that window that rolls up in back of the front seat."

"I didn't know you had a chauffeur," said the salesman.

"I don't have no chauffeur," said the owner of the Rolls, "but I sure like that window. It keeps the sheep from licking my neck when I'm taking 'em to market."

JESUS, THE GOOD SHEPHERD

I really tried to borrow a sheep for this morning's service—it just didn't work out. But I've got the next best thing (pull out sweater) . . . 100 percent wool! John 10:14-18 is about sheep and a shepherd. It's an unforgettable portrait of the relationship between Christ and his people. Won't you follow along with me as I read? Jesus is the Good Shepherd: "I am the good shepherd" (John 10:14a). That makes nice poetry, but what does it mean? There are some areas where sheepherding still goes on, but people generally don't know much about sheep today. Sheepherding, a respectable vocation, was one of the major occupations in Palestine. Shepherds didn't use dogs or horses, helicopters or Hondas to herd sheep as is done today. A sheep's fate rested entirely with the type of man who owned it. There were poor shepherds, whose sheep would struggle, suffer, and waste away. And there were good shepherds, whose sheep would flourish and thrive contentedly.

We all like to hear that we're good at what we do: "You're a good: housewife, clerk, foreman, realtor, or whatever . . . ." It means we know what we're doing and we're dedicated to doing it well. A good shepherd was one who managed his flock with maximum skill. He had one objective: the well-being of his flock. There was no price too high to pay for their health and safety. The good shepherd was committed to his sheep. But the Greek word translated here as "good" *(kalŏs)* goes even farther than that. It points to Jesus' power to do good for his sheep. But it also directs us to the marvelous goodness of his *own* personal character. Now one of the specific characteristics of Jesus, the Good Shepherd, is that: *He knows his sheep*—"I know my own and my own know me, as the Father knows me and I know the Father," (John 10:14b-15a). But first we should ask, "Who are the sheep?" We are! We are the objects of his loving attention

May Seventeenth

and intense concern. We're familiar with the barnyard insults referring to someone as a "pig," or as acting "chicken," or being "as stubborn as a mule." But being called a sheep isn't an insult; there are many parallels in the way we behave. God's people are called sheep in at least a half dozen books of the Bible.

So, to say "The Lord is *my* shepherd," as David did in the twenty-third Psalm, isn't just religious fantasy. It depicts a profound practical working relationship between us and God!

The word "know" here means more than mere factual knowledge. You can read about someone and know all the facts, but still not know him or her. The Greek word means *knowledge gained by experience*. It describes a relationship built on trust and intimacy. David wrote about God's knowledge of us in Psalm 139:1-4:

> O Lord, thou hast searched me and known me!
> Thou knowest when I sit down and when I rise up;
> thou discernest my thoughts from afar.
> Thou searchest out my path and my lying down,
> and art acquainted with all my ways.
> Even before a word is on my tongue, lo, O Lord,
> thou knowest it altogether.

Just think of it! We are under the care of one who fully and completely understands us through and through! Even though he knows the dreadful truth of our sinfulness, he still loves us with an everlasting love. We are known!

Jesus is shown to be the Good Shepherd also in that: *He sacrifices for his sheep*—"and I lay down my life for the sheep," (John 10:15b). Jesus' central purpose was the salvation and health of his sheep. The cross of Calvary graphically demonstrated the depth of his desire to have men and women, boys and girls come under his benevolent care. About this, Peter wrote: "He himself bore our sins in his body on the tree, that we might die to sin and live to righteousness. By his wounds you have been healed. For you were straying like sheep, but have now returned to the Shepherd and Guardian of your souls" (I Peter 2:24-25).

But to "lay down" his "life" means more than death. The word for life is *psuche* in the Greek. It is more than just physical life; it includes personality, and could even be translated as "soul." Gymnast Mary Lou Retton thrilled the country with her electrifying performances in the 1984 Summer Olympics in Los Angeles. But to do so she had to make gymnastics her life: to eat, breathe, and think gymnastics. And so it is with a good shepherd. His sheep are literally the recipients of his life, his attention, his time, his care, his labor, and so forth. Jesus, the Good Shepherd, lays himself out for us continually by interceding, guiding, empowering, and working on our behalf.

Why did he come? Why did he suffer and die? Why does he continue to give us his very life? *For the sheep!*

Sheep are practically defenseless without their shepherd. They are endangered by predators, both the two-footed and four-footed kind. There were rustlers who would steal or kill sheep. These are the ones Jesus spoke of in John 10:8, "All who came before me are thieves and robbers." They were opportunists and imposters who would pillage other's lives if they could. They were people preaching false values, ideas, and standards—such as the religious leaders of Jesus' day. They were wolves in shepherds' clothing! There were no burglar alarms in sheep pens, and no judo classes for the sheep! The shepherd, if he was a good shepherd, was their protector!

Not only are sheep defenseless, but they also cannot take care of themselves. Sheep require more attention than any other class of livestock. The shepherd tended their injuries and led them to the food and water. In verses 9 and 10, Jesus says of the sheep that "he will go in and out and find pasture . . . . I came that they may have life, and have it abundantly." He's talking about more than just physical life here. He's talking about a certain quality of life: the abundant, overflowing surplus. He's talking about abundant life in every area: physical, mental, moral, emotional, spiritual. With Jesus as our shepherd, we can experience the best that life can offer!

The good shepherd, then, knows his sheep and sacrifices for them. But a good shepherd does something else as well:

He seeks and gathers his sheep—"And I have other sheep, that are not of this fold; I must bring them also, and they will heed my voice. So there shall be one flock, one shepherd" (John 10:16).

Isaiah reflected that "all we like sheep have gone astray; we have turned every one to his own way" (Isaiah 53:6). Many in his audience then, as now, refused to believe they were lost.

May Seventeenth

People look at their possessions, positions, education, religiosity, and morality and conclude that they're OK. But if they're not following the Shepherd, they're lost! That's the bad news. The good news is that Jesus cares enough to seek out, save, and restore lost men and women. He clearly said, in Luke 19:10, that he had come "to seek and to save the lost." As a parent would expend every ounce of energy looking for his lost child, so does God love and long for those who yet refuse him.

The scope of his "search" was not to be limited to Jewish Palestine. No! His mission is a world mission! God aims to bring into his flock people from every land, tongue, and race. Jesus said, "Go . . . and make disciples of all nations . . . " (Matthew 28:19). And as the angels of Bethlehem announced, the gospel was to be "good news of a great joy which will come to all the people" (Luke 2:10).

How do we come under his control? How do we come to be his sheep? By listening to his voice. This means, first of all, recognizing that it is God who calls us to himself. Then it means responding to his call; taking him seriously; trusting him to lead us and protect us; giving him what is already his—the right to control our lives. This calls for hearing which results in doing (James 1:22). The Jews heard the words, but most didn't do anything. His sheep hear his voice, and follow!

But wait! The two final verses of this passage tell us some important things about the plan of our Shepherd:

His plan is God's plan—"For this reason the Father loves me, because I lay down my life, that I may take it again. No one takes it from me, but I lay it down of my own accord. I have power to lay it down, and I have power to take it again; this charge I have received from my Father" (John 10:17-18).

His concern for his sheep required that he lay down his life in death. But note two important things here. First, his death was voluntary. Strictly speaking, no one took his life. He chose to die that way on the cross. His power was such that no human hand could have touched him without his consent. Earlier in his ministry people had tried to arrest and kill him, but had failed each time. On the cross he voluntarily laid down his life to turn aside the Father's wrath and take away the penalty for our sins.

The second thing to note is that his death was not the end. It was the first step of a plan to submit to death and then to emerge from it triumphantly alive. Early in his ministry, Jesus had predicted about himself that "the Son of Man is to be delivered into the hands of men, and they will kill him, and he will be raised on the third day" (Matthew 17:22). And this is indeed what did happen on that resurrection morn. Jesus stepped out of that tomb alive and erased forever any doubts we might have that he was indeed God the Son. Anyone could lay down his life, but only the Son of God could choose to take it back up! He was no helpless victim. He had the authority, the right/power/privilege, to become the instrument of reconciliation between God and man, and between man and man.

This was the Father's plan. Jesus said in John 6:38, "For I have come down from heaven, not to do my own will, but the will of him who sent me." And, indeed, Jesus fully completed the difficult work committed to him. Following him as our Shepherd is God's way to salvation and safety. Jesus decisively ruled out any other way when he declared, "I am the way, and the truth, and the life; no one comes to the Father, but by me" (John 14:6). Some people like to think that there are two ways, man's and God's. But man's way is no way at all; it ends in separation from God and everything good. God's way is narrow, but it is the narrowness of truth!

Because he rose again from death, Jesus continues to be the Good Shepherd to all who will follow. We've all seen jobs that were filled by one person after another. Well, there's no turnover here. Jesus Christ will be our shepherd into eternity itself (Revelation 7:17). Through my words this morning, and in many other ways, he is calling you to himself. He does not override our wills; he offers us a choice:

—to live in bondage to sin and self, or
—to begin the productive and satisfying adventure of knowing God as our Shepherd.

It is a staggering choice which each of us has had to make. Who better could care for you? He calls you to follow him, to be his sheep and let him be your shepherd. Will you? *Amen.*

Peter D. Hardt
Castro Valley, California

Sunday
May Twenty-fourth

Theme: Who Is in Charge?

Call to Worship: In the beginning was the Word, and the Word was with God, and the Word was God. He was in the beginning with God; all things were made through him, and without him was not anything made that was made. *John 1:1-3*

Invocation: We have opportunities spread out before us, another new beginning, a clean slate. What will you have us do, Lord? Feed the hungry, visit the suffering, minister to those in need, visit the sick and bereaved? If we are to understand your call to discipleship, we must do all these things. If we understand your call to stewardship we must give of our money to make your kingdom come here on earth. If we do all of these things and forget to submit our lives to your will, it is all for nothing. Take our lives, use us as you see fit. Help us to let go of our lives so they are truly in your service. Take my life and let it be totally controlled by thee. *Amen.*

Hymn: "All Creatures of Our God and King"

Sermon Presentation: "The Head of the Church"

Goals for Today: It is so easy to say, "Christ is the head of this church." We live in a real world with all sorts of people who have all sorts of needs and motives to fill in the church. We are members of denominations that impose rules and orders on the lives of our congregations. Today we take a realistic look at some of the factors that help us arrive at the final conclusion, "Christ is the head of this church."

This Week in History

May 25—Memorial Day—By Presidential proclamation, calling for Memorial tributes to the dead and prayers for peace.

May 29—Ascension Day—Forty days after Easter. Commemorates Christ's ascension into heaven. Observed since A.D. 68.

Announcement for Next Week's Sermon: Peace is the absence of war. Inner peace is the absence of fear and sin. Discover peace next Sunday.

Hymn: "Glorious Things of Thee Are Spoken"

Offertory Scripture: Whatever your hand finds to do, do it with your might; for there is no work or thought or knowledge or wisdom in Sheol, to which you are going. *Ecclesiastes 9:10*

Offertory Prayer: This church was built by producers. This church has grown thanks to the chosen producers. Accept these our gifts as the products of our love for you. *Amen.*

Prayer: Lord, I'm wondering where I stand in your kingdom. Oh, I believe that you died for me and your promise to me of eternal life in your kingdom is the foundation for my life and my faith. But to be honest, Lord, I'm wondering if I'm one of the dreamers or the producers. Am I one of the 80 percent of those who talk a good game, who always promise to get more involved tomorrow, who have good intentions but little else?

It seems so unfair that four of us call ourselves by your name but only one of us is really doing the work that needs to be done in your kingdom.

Lord, you have the power to turn water into wine, to turn sickness into health, to change us from sinners into saints, even to give life to those who are dead. Lord, change me from a dreamer into a "doer." Help me to see that you have given me the gift of faith so that I might bear fruit in your kingdom. Help us to use our God-given time, talents, and treasures to turn our dreams into realities. Help us to open our minds, our eyes, our hearts, and our hands to those around us in need.

To those who are weak, may I bring them your strength; to those who are troubled, your peace; to the suffering, comfort; to those who are indifferent, enthusiasm; and to those who are dying, your assurance of everlasting life.

Help me to roll up my sleeves and dig in today, O Lord, so that at the end of my life you will welcome me with the words, "Well done thou good and faithful servant." *Amen.*

Story of the Week: The zookeeper had a new secretary. She was faced with the problem of the plural for the word

May Twenty-fourth

"mongoose" when she was told to order a pair of them for the zoo.

She started out by ordering two "mongeese." On second thought she decided that didn't look right and rewrote the letter. This time she spelled the word "mongooses." Since that didn't seem to be right either, she finally wrote as follows: "Gentlemen: Please ship us one mongoose as soon as possible. Sincerely yours. P.S. While you are at it, please send us another one."

THE HEAD OF THE CHURCH

Consciously or unconsciously, you and I often look at the church and church leadership in ways different from the New Testament concepts. We tend to refer to the church as "my church" and a minister, deacon, or another church leader as "my minister" or "my deacon" or "my" this leader or that leader.

Don't think that ministers, deacons, and other church leaders are not to be caring and personal in their service—they are; nor do I mean to imply that church members are not to regard their leadership in personal ways. This regard for one another is the essence of Christian love.

We must re-evaluate our concepts of *what* the church is and to *whom* the church belongs. It is easy to assume a comfortable security in regard to church through familiarity. You have heard the saying, "familiarity breeds contempt." None of us here would say we have contempt for our church. Keep in mind that contempt does not always show itself in highly visible ways. Sometimes contempt is revealed by way of disregard for New Testament teaching, primary of which is the instruction that we give ourselves as "a living sacrifice, holy and acceptable to God," and that we "love one another in brotherly affection" and "outdo one another in showing honor" (Romans 12:10).

New Testament Positions of Leadership

In the New Testament there are basically two groups of leaders in the church. There is the position identified by three names—elder, bishop, and overseer. We see these as titles primarily of responsibility rather than that of position. So we have these names all under one category, that of pastor. The pastor is the spiritual "elder," the spiritual leader in that sense. He is the "bishop," he is the "overseer," overseeing the flock for the Lord Jesus Christ.

The other position is that of "deacon." This word means *servant*, and I think we could conclude that every worker in the church—every deacon, Sunday school worker—could come under the title. We do not want to say there is a "laity" or "clergy" by any means dividing our church into two different working bodies. We'll see later that as we come together there is a unity among us.

So, in these positions we think of everyone this church elects to a position of responsibility. It makes no difference what the position; if this church has elected someone to any place of responsibility that person comes into the category of deacon or servant. The question we face is: "Who is head of the church?" Is it the pastor? The church council? Is it any group of people or any one person in our congregation who should be the head of our congregation, who should be the head of our church?

Leadership can be gained in several ways. Children learn this game early, and many learn it very well. When they are opposed by another person the one having the greatest number of friends votes down the opposition.

Then we see that child who is a somewhat demanding individual. He's the "bully on the block." He's going to demand that everyone do what he says.

Sometimes this shows up when seniors run for class office. Possibly the most popular person in school is the senior class president. Many times, this one, over the years, has earned the respect of other children who will elect him or her to office.

As we look at the Bible we see that it talks about several kinds of church governments which developed through history and time. I will speak of these organizations in terms we are familiar with. By this I'm not putting down different denominations. I'm simply recognizing that there are different ways in which we function.

First there is the "papal" authority. This is an authoritative individual who sits over all of the church. Because of some churches' concepts this one person receives a word from God and in turn passes the word down, in a Christmas tree effect, until it gets down to every congregation.

May Twenty-fourth

Then there is another group of churches; somewhere along the line someone selects who will run the political process in that church. Here we have our Methodist brethren who have a bishop who tells the pastor, "You have been here long enough so you may move to another church" and "Church, like it or not, this man will be your pastor."

Then there is a body like the Baptists who fall into a congregational form of government. In other words, the congregation runs the congregation, the church runs the church. By "church" I am speaking of the local body of believers who come together to worship. Nevertheless, the local congregation determines its own direction, its own purpose.

Determining Who Is to Lead

The biggest difficulty in any church is determining who is going to lead.

In the congregational type of government there is a tendency to form a government in the exact way children learn how to control each other and how to be king-pin on the block. In our churches many times someone will make friends with as many people as possible. Then when an issue comes up in the church he or she contacts all of these friends and says, "Folks, we have to vote this down!" So they show up en masse and vote it down.

We also have a danger of developing within our church a "bully" type, a person who would push his or her influence or whatever he or she could do to soon be running the local congregation.

Then there is the congregation, and probably very few, that allows the members to lead in creating the program to run the church. There are some pastors who run the church. The system in that local church is such that whatever the pastor wants, the people say, "That's it!" In a sense people who accept what the pastor says as being a "word from God" allow a papal type of government to be established within that local congregation.

We are allowing these different forms of government to develop within the local body whether we like them or not. We struggle with this in our churches.

Consider Some Biblical Principles

There are some doctrines within the Scripture which I think

we should really consider in thinking about the government of our own local congregation.

The first of these doctrines is one we call "Priesthood of Believers." This doctrine is opposed to the Old Testament practice of the priest's representing the people before God, and in turn, representing God before the people. That priest also offered sacrifices for all of the people, but first had to offer a sacrifice for himself. Then he could enter the Holy of Holies into the presence of God. In the New Testament, after Christ lived on this earth, we see that every single person is important in the eyes of God. Every person has the right to go into the presence of God for himself. If you don't believe in the priesthood of believers, you have no way to approach God and ask forgiveness for your sin. As you ask God to forgive sin, you should become part of a local body. This is why Christians are encouraged to join a church, to get involved with other believers. We pray to God and study his word searching for that leadership. Then, as God reveals that leadership, how can the pastor say that God does not speak to any other people the same as he does to the pastor? Who is any other person of this congregation to say that God does not speak to anybody else the same as he does to the pastor? This would eliminate the "bully" type government. This would eliminate the political church government because as we priests approach God, searching for his will and leadership, we will come back into the church to do his will with less squabbling.

There is another doctrine that is very important. That is the doctrine of the autonomy of the church. By this I mean that no person or organization inside or outside the local church has any right to tell the church what it is going to do.

The church is in danger of playing childhood games in determining who is going to lead it. When people within the church are not willing to accept their responsibilities, the church soon gravitates to a non-biblical form of government. It may develop a papacy, and that might be the pastor or one person within the congregation. It might develop a political type of government, then begin to play politics, manipulating everyone in the congregation to get what "I want." That's really a personal papacy. Or it develops a presbytery when it allows the deacons, church council, or any other organization in the church to rule the church.

May Twenty-fourth

In Ephesians 5:23, Paul states that Christ is the head of the church. We are a Christ-centered church. Only as every member of this congregation prays searching for God's will and leadership can we keep Christ as the center. If we're not praying, searching for God's will, we had better be careful. We are in danger of putting ourselves, or some other self, in the center. In I Corinthians 11:3 we read a line of authority. It is not that the man is superior to the woman, but it is in the sense that "when three people sit on a horse only one can sit in front." Somewhere along the line we must have a sense of authority. If we don't have someone saying that is how God lined us up, we must recognize it, join it, and go on. God, Christ, Holy Spirit, pastor . . . . That's right, when you voted to accept your pastor you accepted him in that position. That's a biblical position. Then the leaders in the church were accepted when you elected them as leaders of whatever organizations. In this way we recognize that God speaks to each one of us. All of the brains are not behind the pulpit. You can pray to God the same as I, and I encourage you to. As long as we continue to seek the guidance of the Holy Spirit there is hope.

In Mark 9:35 Jesus said that anyone wanting to be in the kingdom of God must be willing to be last and servant of all. If I'm looking to be first in the church, I'll never be first. In Matthew 20:26-28 Jesus is talking about one who wants to be great in the kingdom of God. He says that one must be a servant to be great. Jesus did not come to be served but to serve. In I John we read that if one really loves his brother one would be willing to die for that brother. Is this also telling us that I must be willing to part with ideas I have and allow your ideas to grow?

We must put ourselves second in upholding Christ. Each of us upholding one another can glorify him.

In I Corinthians 12:28 the Bible tells us that in the church God has appointed people with different gifts. Again we see the primary purpose of the church as proclaiming the gospel in the truest and purest sense. We can proclaim the gospel in the type of government we have, in our church, in everything we do. Because as we proclaim the gospel in a Christ-centered church, we are proclaiming the gospel that Jesus Christ is still in control; he is still the head of this church. That's what we have to come to.

You can't join a church and put Christ in the center of that church unless you have him in the center of your life. Because the church is the body of believers who have put Christ in the center of their lives, these have voluntarily joined with others to put Christ at the center of that group so they can work together proclaiming him until the end of time. *Amen.*

Thomas W. McCurdy
Village Meadows Baptist Church
Sierra Vista, Arizona

Sunday
May Thirty-first

Theme: My Peace

Call to Worship: Now may the Lord of peace himself give you peace at all times in all ways. *II Thessalonians 3:16*

Invocation: Leaders of nations talk of peace. Churches talk of peace, but there is no peace. Until we give up our greed and self to the will of God, there will be no peace. Take us, Lord, help us to surrender to your will so that world peace might begin with us. As we honor those who died for our freedom, let us honor them with a world and a people at peace. Your peace, Lord, not ours. We surrender to your peace, your way. *Amen.*

Hymn: "Eternal Father, Strong to Save"

Sermon Presentation: "My Peace I Give to You . . ."

Goals for Today: Memorial Day, or Veteran's Day, or whatever . . . . We do not intend that we should forget those who died in the service of our country so that we might have our freedom. Pay them due honor. The real tribute we intend for these brave men and women is to make this a celebration of peace so that there will be no more war. This is peace day.

This Week in History

June 2—International Mothers' Peace Day—Started in 1872 by Julia Ward Howe: "Those who nurture life on earth are of one mind in their opposition to those who should destroy it.

June 6—D-Day Anniversary—Allied landing in Normandy in 1944 as the beginning of the end to the Second World War.

Announcement for Next Week's Sermon: Are you listening? Most people don't listen. What a shame. We miss so much. Come next Sunday and listen.

Hymn: "Amazing Grace"

Offertory Scripture: Make a joyful noise to God, all the earth; sing the glory of his name; give to him glorious praise!
Psalm 66:1-2

Offertory Prayer: You shower us with gifts. You give us joy and peace. You give us this good earth. You give us life and all its possessions. Lord, never let us forget that all we have is yours. It is a trust, dear Lord, from you. Accept our gifts as a sign of our love. *Amen.*

Prayer: I am alive, not because I take care of myself, not because I am just lucky. I am alive because my God has given me the gift of life. I must be a good steward of my time, my talents, and my life. I must pay honor to all those saints who have gone before, who have sacrificed and even given their lives that I might be here today. No man or woman is an island. We are touched by all that has gone before and we are all a part of the history of tomorrow. How shall we be remembered?

Lord, grant that those who follow might say of us, "They were faithful to the will of God; they kept the faith; they left the world a little better than the one they inherited."

Lord, if we could leave one lasting gift to our children and our children's children, it would be peace. Your perfect peace forever. *Amen.*

Story of the Week: What the world needs is the peace that surpasses all misunderstandings.

MY PEACE I GIVE TO YOU

"These things I have spoken to you, while I am still with you. But the Counselor, the Holy Spirit, whom the Father will send in my name, he will teach you all things, and bring to your remembrance all that I have said to you. Peace I leave with you; my peace I give to you; not as the world gives do I give to you. Let not your hearts be troubled, neither let them be afraid" (John 14:25-27).

The Source of War

Where is the greatest warfare today? The inner turmoil and uneasiness in all of the individuals of the world are greater than

May Thirty-first

the turmoil and tension existing between nations and people of the world. From this turmoil within persons grow the wars between people and nations.

Those who read Adolf Hitler's autobiography before World War II read the prelude to that war. We can't overlook the many economic and political causes of war. Yet even these causes can be traced to the lack of inner peace within the souls of many individuals and to the injustices perpetrated by individuals. Adolf Hitler called his inner turmoil *Mein Kampf*. The German word *kampf* is the verb which means "to fight, to contest, to combat, to battle." The inner turmoil of this one man erupted into a war in which over forty-five million other individuals were killed. The inner lack of a healthy peace—a wholesome, holy, God-given peace—is the source of all warfare between nations.

The Prince of Peace declares the human heart to be the source of human warfare: "From within, out of the heart of man, come evil thoughts, fornication, theft, murder, adultery, coveting, wickedness, deceit, licentiousness, envy, slander, pride, foolishness. All these evil things come from within, and they defile a man" (Mark 7:21-23).

Knowing that the source of warfare is the inner turmoil within the individual person, the Prince of Peace aims at the heart of man when he swings the sword of the spirit—the Word of God. All of our Lord's words about peace are directed at the individual and the heart that needs his peace. In a passage from John's record of the Master's words, we read: "My peace I give to you . . . " (14:27).

If you want to be part of the solution to the world's warring madness, then you must first understand what kind of peace this is. Second, you must by faith receive this peace into your heart. Unless you have his peace within your heart, no matter how many peace rallies you go to, no matter how many protests you lodge against the arms race, no matter how many letters you write to members of congress or to the president, you are part of the world's war problem, not part of God's solution to war.

The Kind of Peace That
Jesus Christ Calls MY Peace

The first priority for anyone concerned with world peace ought to be the proper understanding of just what kind of peace this is which Jesus Christ calls "my" peace. What sort of peace existed in Jesus Christ when he spoke these words to his disciples? What sort of peace was this that enabled him to sleep during a raging storm on the Sea of Galilee? "And a storm of wind came down on the lake, and they were filling with water, and were in danger. And they went and woke him, saying, 'Master, Master, we are perishing!' And he awoke and rebuked the wind and the raging waves; and they ceased, and there was a calm. He said to them, 'Where is your faith?' " (Luke 8:23-25).

Sleeping came easy to our Master! His was sound sleep—deep sleep—that endured even through a raging storm of wind and rain, even in a tossing and seemingly endangered boat! What inner peace there was within his human soul! It is said: "There is no rest for the wicked!" Yet for the righteous, the holy, the guilt-free, the conscience-clean, oh, what heavenly sleep there is! We even sing about his heavenly sleep:

> Silent night, holy night,
> All is calm, all is bright
> Round yon virgin mother and child.
> Holy infant so tender and mild,
> Sleep in heavenly peace.

One of the most important truths about our Lord Jesus Christ is his sinlessness: "He committed no sin; no guile was found on his lips" (I Peter 2:22).

Within the perfectly obedient heart of our Lord Jesus Christ, there existed a perfect peace—a peace that we call heavenly peace—a peace that came from his knowledge about his own righteousness and perfection. No guilt-laden dreams were ever his. No anxious moments because of unconfessed sin were ever his. No bitterness of spirit poisoning his inner life and disturbing his sleep or his peace. Jesus Christ, true man but virgin-born and born without sin—Jesus Christ, true God—he had an inner peace which passes all our understanding.

How Can You Have His Peace in Your Heart?

How can he who was sinless instill into the hearts of guilty sinners that same inner, guilt-free peace which belongs by right only to him? We do not have a right to this deep inner peace of mind, heart, and soul! We do not have a right to this heavenly peace that makes for heavenly sleep!

May Thirty-first

Yet the captain of a slave ship, with a load of slaves below in the filthy belly of the ship, and with a load of guilt in his filthy heart, John Newton, wrote these words about the "how" of gaining this inner peace of Jesus Christ: "Amazing grace! how sweet the sound/That saved a wretch like me!" Although Captain Newton had helped to ruin the lives of countless numbers of human beings and destroyed families by his slave market business, he found that through the amazing grace—the unmerited love, the undeserved love of Jesus Christ—he could have the undeserved, unmerited inner peace of the righteous. Because of Jesus Christ and the death of Christ on the cross, Captain Newton repented and slept well at night. He slept well and deeply in the heavenly peace of the righteous. He received from Jesus Christ the forgiveness and cleansing he needed. He received from Jesus Christ that which Jesus our Lord calls "my peace. . . . "

Some object! Why should so wicked a man be given the inner peace that belongs only to the truly righteous? God's answer to that question is the cross! For it was on that old cross that Jesus suffered and died and for a world of lost sinners was slain. The raging storm of God's wrath against you and me and John Newton was stilled when the Prince of Peace took for us the load of guilt and shame that was really ours. He offers to us this wonderful exchange: His peace for our inner guilty turmoil! All you need do to receive this peace, if you don't already have it in your heart, is to believe in him.

As criminals walk down death row to the electric chair, though they may be justly punished upon earth for their murders, nevertheless, they can enjoy the deep inner peace of those who are assured of going not to hell but to paradise! The thief on the cross knew this peace as he died next to our Savior. Think also of the one named Saul who was made into the Apostle Paul. Paul helped hunt down and execute the followers of Jesus Christ. But then the Prince of Peace attacked Saul on the road to Damascus and aimed at Saul's sinful heart. The persecutor of Christians became the greatest peace warrior for Christ that the world has ever known! Paul's guilty heart is given Christ's peace. The cross of Jesus becomes for Paul the message of world peace. Paul wrote: "Therefore, since we are justified by faith, we have peace with God through our Lord Jesus Christ" (Romans 5:1).

The Greatest Peace Treaty

We have peace with God through Jesus Christ and the covenant, or treaty, he has made for us in his own blood. It is this peace we have with God that makes for the inner peace and it is the blood of Jesus Christ which bought this peace for us. The anger of Almighty God against us was poured out upon himself in the person of his only begotten Son, Jesus Christ. Our Lord Jesus teaches us that the peace treaty is made in his own blood shed for our sins. Our communion with God is through this blood: "For this is my blood of the covenant [treaty or new testament], which is poured out for many for the forgiveness of sins" (Matthew 26:28). The Greek word, which we translate "testament," is *diathēkē* which literally means "full arrangement" and can be translated "covenant" or "agreement"—like a peace treaty that covers all that is needed to bring about complete and eternal peace.

When he offers us his peace, we receive it knowing that it is bought and paid for by his blood—his sacrifice of himself. He who knew no sin and no guilt because of sin, he who had the perfect inner peace of a sinless man, endured for us all the guilty punishment of the wrath of God and of hell on our behalf. There is plenty of testimony given to us in scripture about this wonderful peace treaty in the blood of Jesus Christ: "For in him all the fullness of God was pleased to dwell, and through him to reconcile to himself all things, whether on earth or in heaven, making peace by the blood of his cross" (Colossians 1:19-20).

There are many today who think that this notion of peace with God through the bloody sacrifice of Jesus on the cross is old, stale, and too religious to have anything to say about world peace. The old rugged cross and nuclear warheads? There seems to be a *missile gap* between the blood of Jesus Christ on the cross and the blood that will be vaporized if nuclear weapons are used. Yet it cannot be denied that what goes on in the heads and hearts of those whose fingers are on the buttons of those warheads of destruction is highly relevant to world peace. If our hearts and minds are filled with the peace of Jesus Christ, then the warheads of destruction will become the plowshares of production. How much destruction and killing has not taken place thanks to the peace Jesus has put into our hearts? God only knows, but he does know! And there have been millions spared, I believe, because he has put his peace into our hearts.

May Thirty-first

The great inner peace in the hearts of millions has prevented untold warfare between nations, between families, and between many individuals.

Family and world peace and peace in the church depend ultimately upon faith in the Prince of Peace and receiving his peace won for us on the cross.

Conclusion: He Gives His Peace Forever!

The family with peace that will last forever is the family which has received Jesus Christ as the Prince of Peace. The world family will never be at peace until: "Every knee should bow . . . and every tongue confess that Jesus Christ is Lord" (Philippians 2:10). When the church and the individual Christian make it their primary mission to preach the cross of Jesus Christ and the peace with God that he has won and is able to give to one and all, then the world will see more peace within souls and more peace between people of good will than it has ever before. This peace is a lasting, eternal peace.

When Jesus Christ, our Lord, says he gives peace, yet not like that the world gives, he means that the covenant in his blood is not a temporary cease-fire. It is an eternal treaty between God and you and me. His wrath has been forever satisfied by the blood on the cross. No one need fear hell or be torn by guilt if he or she trusts in the blood of peace. Denying that his blood was shed for your sins is the way of everlasting punishment. Believing that his blood was shed for your sins is the way of everlasting peace.

Ask yourself the question: "Have I received that which Jesus calls 'my' peace?" Do you have faith that he died for your sins and that you have peace with your maker? Are you sure, really sure, that you will spend eternity in heaven thanks to what he has done for you? Or are you trying to win his favor by your good works? Are you trying to win his favor by working for world peace even though you don't have his peace within your heart? If so, stop working for world peace or for your own peace for a moment. Ask him to come into your heart. Ask him to establish his peace within you. Tell him that you really believe he died for your sins and has made peace with God through the blood of his cross. Ask him to come into your heart and surrender to him. Then go forth to be part of God's solution to the world's problem of war. The peace that he will make through you will begin right in your own family and at your place of work as others will receive your humble apologies, your forgiveness, and the kindness that gushes forth from a soul forgiven and at peace with God.

They will want to know what has gotten into you! Tell them: "Jesus and his peace!" *Amen.*

Karl M. Kindt III
Trinity Evangelical United Church of Christ
Lexington, Missouri

Sunday
June Seventh

Theme: Falling in Love

Call to Worship: Husbands, love your wives, as Christ loved the church and gave himself up for her.   *Ephesians 5:25*

Invocation: Help us, O Lord, to look for the good in those whom we love. If we look for love, we see love. Let your love flow through us to all the world, in your name. *Amen.*

Hymn: "More Love to Thee, O Christ"

Sermon Presentation: "Hearing God in Each Other"

Goals for Today: To show how God gives of himself on this Pentecost to all people. If God is love, then he gives himself in love. "For God so loved the world . . ."

This Week in History

June 8-13—National Little League Baseball Week—To honor all those who give their time so that young people can experience sports competition and growth in a positive environment.

June 10—Alcoholics Anonymous—Established June 10, 1935, by William G. Wilson and Dr. Robert Smith. The church has faced the problem of alcohol abuse honestly and can be proud of its contribution.

Announcement for Next Week's Sermon: Can a Christian just sit and pray? If that is all you do, you'd better get moving. Next week, on your feet!

Hymn: "O Perfect Love"

Offertory Scripture: A new commandment I give to you, that you love one another; even as I have loved you, that you also love one another. By this all men will know that you are my disciples, if you have love for one another.   *John 13:34-35*

Greater love has no man than this, that a man lay down his life for his friends. *John 15:13*

Offertory Prayer: If you love someone you have to show it. Lord, we love you. Accept these gifts as a demonstration of our love for you. *Amen.*

Prayer: Lord, it sure is noisy in this your world—cars and trucks on the roads that surround us; planes flying overhead; children laughing and babies crying. Walking through stores and malls we are surrounded by music. Yet you know that there is a great deal of difference between hearing and listening.

In your earthly ministry, the time in which you shared our human experience, you spoke about those who have eyes but see not; those who have ears but hear not. You know that the condition includes those who have minds but think not; have hearts but feel not.

We pray that you would open our eyes that are blinded by apathy. Open our ears that are made deaf by anger and frustration.

Help us not only to hear but to speak as well your healing words of comfort, your strengthening words of hope, your soothing words of healing, your comforting words of peace, your assurance of life in the midst of death and decay.

Be it the booming voice of your prophets or your powerful message that comes to us in a still small voice. Allow us to hear—to respond—to obey. *Amen.*

Story of the Week: The golfer was telling the other members of his foursome about his troubles. "It's my wife," he said. "When I left the house this morning she said that if I didn't stop playing with you fellows four times a week, she was going to divorce me."

"That's terrible," one of his friends said. "What are you going to do?"

"Miss her," the first golfer said.

HEARING GOD IN ONE ANOTHER

A while back, I had occasion to watch a movie called *Tin Man*. It's a story about a young man named Casey, whose treatment for meningitis as an infant affects his ability to hear and leaves him completely deaf and mute into adulthood. Casey, the young adult, is an electronics genius working as an auto mechanic in order to earn enough money to purchase the components necessary to build a machine that will enable him to speak to others by means of a self-styled computer and keyboard.

As the story unfolds, we learn that an operation can now be performed that may restore Casey's hearing through the use of implants in his ears. This surgery is successfully performed, allowing him new opportunity to hear for the first time since very early infancy. He also learns to speak so that others can understand him without the use of his mechanical computer-device. Casey and his speech therapist, Marsha, fall in love; and, for a time, we begin to think that they'll live happily ever after. Some months after the miracle of his restored hearing takes place, we learn that his genius in electronics causes Casey to obtain a certain degree of wealth through the development and marketing of several of his ideas. And just as we think he and Marsha are going to be set for life, we learn that his hearing is fading as his body begins to reject the implants in his ears, and he will inevitably revert to deafness as a way of life.

Then to imagine the mixture of emotions that Casey experiences as he learns of his ultimate situation softened only by his newly acquired ability to speak and read lips. The newly discovered joy of hearing is to be taken from him again, through no fault of his own. And he will now be worse off for having gained a first-hand knowledge of all the sounds he's going to be missing in the world around him—the pouring of liquid into a glass, the screaming siren that he never knew before his surgery had taken place, and now will never again know except in the deep, haunting recesses of his memory.

As in the first portion of this movie, the day of Pentecost celebrates the miracle of restored hearing, for the genuine climax of Luke's account in the book of Acts takes place in knowing that these devout Jews, coming together "from every nation under heaven," were finally able to genuinely HEAR one another! As the text says: "At this sound the multitude came together, and they were bewildered, because each one heard them speaking in his own language. And they were amazed and wondered, saying, 'Are not all these who are speaking

Galileans? And how is it that we hear, each of us in his own native language?' " (Acts 2:6-8).

Perhaps it is futile for us to compare deafness with other disabilities; yet most of us frequently do. Take blindness, for instance. Our immediate instinct is to think of blindness as being more severe than deafness, for to live in a world of complete darkness is a terrifying notion for those of us who can see. We're often overwhelmed by the people like Ray Charles and Tom Sullivan, who professionally entertain us by playing the piano, despite their blindness, while many of the rest of us can barely see our way through a simple rendition of "Chopsticks."

On the other hand, the notion of deafness is often regarded by those of us who can hear as being little more than a nuisance because, unlike the character Casey in the movie, we already know how to speak. Yet, deafness is a deep tragedy as well. Although blindness cuts us off from many of the things around us, deafness uniquely cuts us off from all of the other people around us.

Indeed, the Bible seemingly reckons our inability to hear and understand one another as truly being one of the greatest tragedies of human existence—perhaps surpassed only by our all-too-frequent inability to hear and understand the Word of God for our lives. And each is rooted in our own unwillingness and hardness of heart! It's our tragic unwillingness to genuinely hear one another and to understand one another clearly that prevents us from living out the will of God in our lives each day. You see, it's precisely this disability, that is to say, our unwillingness to hear and understand one another, that God has graciously chosen to miraculously heal at Pentecost, a miracle of healing that each one of us so desperately needs this day!

Is it any wonder that our world continues to ache for a genuine peace between nations and peoples that seems so far from reality in our time? Yet how can there be peace in our time when we refuse to genuinely hear and understand one another? The wife who is frustrated, angry, and abused from neglect cries out to her estranged husband: "You never try to understand my point of view!" An adolescent gropes for a healing word of hope from her parents, and all that she can utter through the bitter anguish of her tears is: "Neither of you understands! You never want to listen to me!" An employee who seeks further recognition for a new idea at work later discovers that the boss will have no time to see him again this week, and hasn't yet bothered even to read his proposal.

If we can't seem to hear and understand one another at home or at work, is it any wonder that whites really never hear blacks and can't understand Hispanics? Is it any wonder that we speak of a conflict between the women of our nation and the Reagan White House? And is it really any wonder that deafness, in all of its "thundering decibles," presently permeates the relationship between America and the Soviet Union, causing each side to freeze on the ladders of life, rather than in the arsenals of death?

O God, how we long for a healing word of hope that will break through the stone-cold barriers of deafness that prevent us from genuinely hearing and understanding each other! How we yearn for a word of life that will shatter the drums of our inner ears with a still, small voice which speaks to us through layers of prejudice, arrogance, pride, age, greed, gender, and hostility that promote the diseases of racism, classism, and sexism among us! How we dream of a just and lasting peace that allows all others an equal access into our lives instead of insisting that they adopt our own values, points of view, and narrow prejudices before we'll honestly have anything to do with them!

"If you love me, you will keep my commandments. And I will pray the Father, and he will give you another Counselor, to be with you for ever, even the Spirit of truth . . . . These things I have spoken to you, while I am still with you. But the Counselor, the Holy Spirit, whom the Father will send in my name, he will teach you all things, and bring to your remembrance all that I have said to you. Peace I leave with you; my peace I give to you; not as the world gives do I give to you" (John 14:15-17*a*, 25-27*a*).

Perhaps we don't really believe in the miracle of Pentecost anymore. Perhaps we've given up believing in the power of God's Holy Spirit to work among and within us. Perhaps we no longer trust that God can somehow enable each one of us to welcome life's strangers into our midst. Instead, we seem all too eager and willing to coerce, punish, and restrain others we do not know and with whom we disagree—"Bring back the death penalty!" "Cut those welfare programs!" "Make the lazy bums work for a change!"—these are but a few of the cries that ring out in our society, and even in our churches today.

It is hard to maintain a Christ-like perspective when crime and interest rates are rising, and our elected leaders continue spending billions of dollars they don't have on new weapons of mass destruction we pray they'll never choose to use. It seems next to impossible to trust in the teachings of Christ as we ship more arms and ammunition to governments in faraway places, whose soldiers slaughter innocent men, women, and children. But as a community of faith whose members have been called out together by the Risen Christ, we have to try, because all that our tough talk and cries of futility really accomplish, in the final analysis, is to keep us from understanding the will of God for our lives, and from hearing the still, small voice of God in each other.

How can we ever hope to honestly hear the voices tell of the socio-economic situations that breed crime over the sound of hot, sizzling human flesh being burned in an electric chair, or over the choking gags of the prisoner in a gas chamber? And how can we ever hope to truly understand the cries of the poor mother in Central America whose husband, sons, and daughters have each been shot with American guns and bullets right before her very eyes, if we can't even bear to listen to the six o'clock news? Indeed, how can peace become a reality in our time if we fail to understand and appreciate that the healing miracle of Pentecost actually means the restoration of hearing for each one of us, that we willingly may come to hear and understand the voice of God in one another? When the Apostle Paul spoke of the gifts of the Holy Spirit to the church at Corinth, he listed many, including wisdom, knowledge, faith, healing, miracles, prophecy, discernment between spirits, speaking in tongues, and interpreting tongues. But he goes on to rightly proclaim that while there are many gifts of the Holy Spirit, "the greatest of these is love. . . . " And how could it possibly be otherwise? For, if God is love, and if God gives of his own Spirit to each one of us by means of the Risen Christ, in whose name we have been called out and baptized, then above all else that gift is a gift of love—which enables us to be open to one another, and to honestly hear and understand each other, despite the many differences among us.

June Seventh

You see, the differences between us won't vanish in the Spirit—indeed, some will always choose vanilla over chocolate—and the poor, as Jesus said, "will always be with us" (Matthew 26:11).

I'm a white, middle-class male who will undoubtedly always remain a white, middle-class male until I die. But if I'm honestly open to the Holy Spirit of God, then I will also be honestly open to the rich differences that can be found in the cultures of other peoples; open to the marvelous differences between women and men; and open to the crushing disparity between myself and the poor, wherein I have even further opportunity and obligation to worship and serve God by working for justice and peace in our time.

If it sounds at all strange to you, it shouldn't: "For by one Spirit we were all baptized into one body—Jews or Greeks, slaves or free [male or female, rich or poor]—and all were made to drink of one Spirit" (I Corinthians 12:13).

And whenever we take time out and really listen for God's love in our lives, isn't this what we hear? After all, it's really the differences between us, and not our sameness, that genuine Christian love appreciates and works among and within us to overcome. And if I fall in love with a woman, as I have, I really fall in love with that which makes her different from all others and from myself—the unique way she finds to put up with my humor; the funny way she "squinches up" her face at me from across a room that signals her displeasure with something I just said; the unique ways she has to tell me of her loving acceptance when I fail; and her equally individual reactions of joy as we succeed in making a baby together with God!

And so it is with the love of God at Pentecost, for with the miraculous gift of the Holy Spirit those who were present that day were, in fact, made even more aware of the differences among them. Yet despite these differences, they were able to hear and to understand one another clearly for the very first time, each in his own native language—not having to change anything about themselves for the others, aside from a willingness to accept and be accepted—perhaps, also, for the very first time.

"And all were amazed and perplexed, saying to one another, 'What does this mean?' But others mocking said, 'They are filled with new wine' " (Acts 2:12-13).

Well, these men were drunk all right, but not with wine. Rather, they were drunk with the staggering possibilities of God's love breaking out all over the place, smashing down the barriers between them, and opening their ears and their hearts to one another for the very first time!

Friends, the good news of the Gospel for each one of us here today, as we come to gather together at the Lord's Table, is that despite the many differences between us, we, too, can know the miraculous healing of Pentecost in our own lives and have our own inner hearing restored in the breaking of the bread, and in the pouring of this new wine. For as we take the Body and Blood of Christ within ourselves, we become the Body of Christ on earth. So that we, too, can begin hearing God in one another, and in all others, through Jesus Christ our Lord and our Redeemer, in whose love there truly is no such thing as a "stranger."

Amen and Amen.

James S. Vuocolo
Wyoming Ministries in Higher Education
Laramie, Wyoming

Sunday
June Fourteenth

Theme: Marching Orders

Call to Worship: Create in me a clean heart, O God, and put a new and right spirit within me. *Psalm 51:10*

Invocation: Lord, let us stand up and be counted. Let us stand up and move forward. We cannot stand still. Your good news must be proclaimed by a church and a people on the move. Move us, Lord. *Amen.*

Hymn: "Rise Up, O Men of God"

Sermon Presentation: "Forth in Thy Name"

Goals for Today: If we are not a church on the move, then we are no longer a church. Christ gave us our marching orders; let's march!

This Week in History

June 14—Children's Sunday—Many Christian churches observe the second Sunday in June as Children's Sunday.

June 15—Magna Carta Day—In 1215 King John of England placed his royal seal on the document. It is regarded as one of the most important documents in the history of political and human freedom.

Announcement for Next Week's Sermon: How big is your God? Does your faith limit the power of your God? How big *is* your God? Next week you will have a chance to measure him.

Hymn: "How Firm a Foundation"

Offertory Scripture: Therefore, if any one is in Christ, he is a new creation; the old has passed away, behold, the new has come. *II Corinthians 5:17*

Offertory Prayer: Lord, move us to a better understanding of your plan for us. Help us to keep moving and keep searching. As we seek to find you, we offer these our gifts. *Amen.*

Prayer: "Mount 'em up and move 'em out." O Lord, so often we watch those old western movies and hear the cavalry officer give this command. "Mount 'em up and move 'em out." That's your command to us, too, this morning—we who are called to be your disciples, your Christian soldiers.

As we move forward in your name, make sure that we are following the path that you would have us, your church, follow. It is so easy for us to get confused, take a wrong turn, and lose our way. Too often our sense of churchmanship is tainted by the passing fads and trends of this world.

Help us to find our way when we wander away from your paths of mission and faithfulness to the Gospel and become concerned instead with attendance figures and treasurer's (financial) reports that would tend to make us more intent on measuring our "success" rather than our faithfulness to your call "to go into all the world and make disciples in your name."

Let us never forget that your gospel "comforts the afflicted *and* afflicts us who are comfortable."

When the world tells us "be still," grant us the boldness to speak your word. Prod us to move forward when we would be satisfied with staying where we are—comfortable and secure.

Let us lift high the cross. Let us boldly proclaim the cross. Let us move out in faith, trust, and confidence, firm in the foundation of our faith in you. *Amen.*

Story of the Week: A golfer's tee shot landed his ball on top of an anthill. His next swing missed the ball but sent several hundred ants flying in every direction. His next swing was the same. As he took his stance for his next try at the ball, one of the ants shouted, "Okay, everybody. The only way to get out of this alive is to get on the ball."

FORTH IN THY NAME

An issue of the magazine *Christianity Today* contained a clever article that called for pastors to re-evaluate their priorities. It seems a clergyman would call a fellow pastor every Monday to inquire how many he had in Sunday school the day before. The number was no sooner out of that pastor's mouth than he was told how many the caller had. Not only that, but he listed the numbers at both services and how much money came in.

June Fourteenth

It is tempting to play the numbers game (especially when you are ahead), but every time I am moved toward that position I am shaken to my senses by the words of Doctor John Mackay. Mackay was a former Scottish missionary to South America, a former president of Princeton Theological Seminary, and one of the church's great saints whose plea was always, "Let the church be the church." In other words, the church can be like no other institution, and when we try to imitate others in mode or mission, we begin to lose our way—our sense of direction. The church must, at all times, *to its own self be true*.

To this end, Helmut Thielicke, a Lutheran pastor who was imprisoned by Hitler, reminds us that the church cannot permit its authority to be defined by people who have no idea of its mission. The church must *not* be shaped by society or any other force. It must be shaped by Jesus Christ, no less than the Lord of the church himself.

Christ leaves little doubt as to the mission of the church as he sees it. As he is about to leave his disciples for the final time, he gives them their charge. "Go therefore and make disciples of all nations, baptizing them in the name of the Father and of the Son and of the Holy Spirit" (Matthew 28:19).

The close of the Gospel according to Saint Matthew sets the tone for the mission of the church. The future is now, Jesus tells them, there is to be no more waiting around. They are to go, and in their going they are to tell others.

Going . . . moving forward . . . how often God calls us to carry on when we would rather stay put.

Jesus' disciples would have loved it if their master had stayed with them. First, they could have continued to enjoy his fellowship. But second, and probably most important, he could continue to bear the burden of proclaiming the gospel message. It is only if Jesus would leave them physically that *their faith could come alive in actions*, giving them the boldness to preach when society said "be quiet," giving them the power to heal when others said it couldn't be done, and giving them the strength to go forward when they would have rather stayed and talked.

Throughout Scripture, God has called men and women of faith to such boldness.

We think of Moses as he stood between the raging waters of the Red Sea and the frustrated complaints of the frightened people while the army of Pharaoh descended upon them.

The people cried to Moses: "Is it because there are graves in Egypt that you have taken us away to die in the wilderness? What have you done to us, in bringing us out of Egypt? Is not this what we said to you in Egypt, 'Let us alone and let us serve the Egyptians'? For it would have been better for us to serve the Egyptians than to die in the wilderness."

"Fear not!" Moses replied. "Stand firm, and see the salvation of the Lord, which he will work for you today. . . . The Lord will fight for you: you have only to be still."

But the Lord said to Moses, "Why do you cry to me? Tell the people of Israel to go forward" (Exodus 14:11-15).

Do you see the conflict? Moses told the people, "Stand firm and keep still." The Lord said, "March on!" *The Living Bible* paraphrase is even stronger: "Then the Lord said to Moses, 'Quit praying and get the people moving. Forward march!' "

That's the way it is, isn't it? The Lord wants us to "march on," "get moving," but we would rather "keep still" and "pray."

The call to the faithful is never keep still and pray, but get moving.

Sometimes our piety can be the greatest obstacle to any acts of faith. If the children of Israel had done what Moses told them, they would have been overrun by Pharaoh's army. It was only when they moved out in faith into the muddy sea bed that God was able to save them. They had to move forward in their faith. Standing still just wouldn't do. The call and command was to carry on, to move forward in faith.

It was the same for the disciples of Jesus. They came to him with the same mixture of doubt and faith that marks all of the resurrection appearances. In return Jesus gives them a command and a promise. They are to go. Not only is he going to leave them, but he also expects *them to leave him*. They are to "march on" and by the music of this march proclaim the gospel's message.

This is a daring plan. The gospel message is placed in their hands; they are to be the stewards of the "Good News." And they are to take that news to the farthest corners of the globe.

Yet there is the promise that they will not go unaided. They will be strengthened and supported by nothing less than the power of God itself. They applied this power to their lives in words and deeds which inspired, healed, and saved. These were the genuine signs of discipleship, not ethereal or

June Fourteenth

supernatural, but real acts and actions which amazed the non-believers.

Jesus' command and promise is just as valid and just as available to us as well. Like it or not our task is clear. We, too, are to bring Christ, the living and powerful Christ, not to just the least and the last but to the most and the mighty as well.

So, while we may sit and pray, the word of the Lord is still clear. *March on*, for it is only when we "march on" that faith can come alive. Then the gospel becomes more than mere words on a printed page, and Jesus becomes more than a figure out of the dark pages of history. When faith is alive Jesus is Lord not only over our lives but also over all of humankind as well. He is present for us, just as he promised.

A couple of years ago one of the saints of the church retired from his pastorate. Doctor Elam Davies was the senior minister at Chicago's Fourth Presbyterian Church. He was a dynamic Welshman and a gifted orator. In 1979 *Time Magazine* named him one of the six great preachers in America.

One day Doctor Davies invited several seminary students to his offices for a discussion about preaching. He astonished them by stating, "I preach from struggle rather than solution." To this end, he was quoted by saying upon his retirement: "I do not come to the end of my formal ministry with any more certainties than I had years ago. But I do come to the end with a deeper certitude about a God in whom I can feel confident."

Davies is right! The truth is that Christ doesn't offer us solutions that we can swallow like placeboes. Christ launches us out into the struggle where we dicover the truth of his promise to "be with us always even to the close of the age."

There is a wonderful hymn, "How Firm a Foundation." This verse sums up the promise of Christ perfectly:

> The soul that on Jesus still leans for repose,
> I will not, I will not desert to his foes;
> That soul, though all hell should endeavor to shake,
> I'll never, no, never, no, never, forsake!

Thanks be to God who, amid our struggles, grants us his promise and gives us the courage to march on. *Amen.*

David C. Nelson
Mt. Pleasant Lutheran Church
Racine, Wisconsin

Sunday
June Twenty-first

Theme: Growing People

Call to Worship: O give thanks to the Lord, for he is good, for his steadfast love endures forever. *Psalm 136:1*

Invocation: O Lord, teach us that the only limits you have on this earth are the ones placed by our lack of faith. If we are willing to trust you fully, all things are possible. *Amen.*

Hymn: "Now Thank We All Our God"

Sermon Presentation: "How Big Is Your God, Daddy?"

Goals for Today: To show the unlimited possibilities God offers to his people, who have the courage to believe he can do all things.

This Week in History

June 21—Father's Day—First observed in 1910. To honor all fathers and to strengthen the family unit in America.

June 27—Helen Keller's Birthday—Blind and deaf from age of nineteen months, she overcame all obstacles to learn to speak and has been an inspiration to millions of handicapped people.

Announcement for Next Week's Sermon: Have we failed God or has he failed us? Now there is a question we had better answer, and quick. How about next Sunday?

Hymn: "I Would Be True"

Offertory Scripture: Or do you presume upon the riches of his kindness and forbearance and patience? Do you not know that God's kindness is meant to lead you to repentance?
Romans 2:4

Offertory Prayer: Father, we thank you for the example you have shown to all fathers. Let us learn to unselfishly give our love to those in our care. Let these gifts be a symbol of our love. *Amen.*

June Twenty-first

Prayer: Lord, Sooo big! That's the only way to describe you. Struggle as we may, we can never hope to know the limits of your power, your mercy, your strength, your wisdom, and your love.

Yet, being human, we wrestle with the question of how big you truly are—of how great you are. We know that you are big enough to know when each and every sparrow falls and still be with each of us who is suffering at home or in the hospital. We know that you are big enough to create each planet and star in space and to control their every movement; yet, you still know when one of your children sheds a single tear.

You are big enough to create the vast variety of birds, fish, animals, trees, and flowers that surround us; yet, you still know each of us by name. We know that you were big enough to be born in a stable in Bethlehem; big enough to be sinless, yet willing to die on the cross outside Jerusalem for the sins of all people of all time; big enough to roll away the stone that men put in front of the tomb and to conquer death once and for all.

O Lord, convince us that you are big enough to protect the weakest and most helpless among us, big enough to forgive our sinfulness. Convince us that with you by our side we are never without hope. May we always realize "How Great Thou Art." Amen.

Story of the Week: A man and his wife invited friends over for dinner. They arrived without their fourteen-year-old son.

"Where's the boy?" the husband asked.

"Oh, he wanted to stay home and fix his own supper," the boy's mother said, "so we let him. Now that he's fourteen years old, and we can begin to stand him, he can't stand us."

HOW BIG IS YOUR GOD, DADDY?

Recently, a friend of mine suffered some financial reverses during a time when his wife was seriously ill. He came home one day, discouraged and despondent. His five-year-old daughter, sensing her father's mood, gave him a hug and said, "Yesterday in Sunday school, my teacher said that God raised Jesus back to life after he had been dead for three days. It takes a great big God to do something like that. Just how big is God, Daddy?"

That five-year-old's question lifted her father out of his depression because he realized that the God who had raised his Son certainly was more than big enough to help his family through the time of crisis. There is a connection between that incident and the prayer of Jacob in the Old Testament. Like my friend, Jacob was a frightened and despondent man. Jacob had deceived his father, Isaac, and had cheated his brother, Esau, out of his inheritance. Jacob went on to make a new life for himself, which culminated in cheating his father-in-law, Laban, out of just about everything he owned. Jacob was the son of Isaac and the grandson of Abraham, two of the godliest men of the Old Testament, but he was also one of the sneakiest, most manipulative characters of the entire Bible.

Jacob was returning home when he received word that his brother Esau was coming with four hundred men to meet him. Suddenly, he was panic-stricken! The Bible says, "Then Jacob was greatly afraid and distressed" (Genesis 32:7). In desperation, Jacob did something that he hadn't done for a long time—he prayed.

Jacob's prayer reveals that he wondered if the God of his forefathers was big enough to help him in his time of distress. God had promised "to do Jacob good," despite the fact that he was a thief and a liar. But in spite of all of God's promises, Jacob wasn't really sure that his father's God was big enough to save him from his brother, Esau.

As we think about Jacob's plight, I wonder how many of our sons and daughters are wondering the same thing about us. I wonder how many of our children are asking, "Just how big is your God, Daddy?" The kind of God in which our children believe is to some extent mirrored in the kind of parents we are. They may not ask us directly, but we can be sure they wonder, and we ought to be willing to answer their questions.

Big Enough to Deliver from Danger

"Daddy, is your God big enough to deliver us from the dangers which confront us daily?" That surely is a question our children are asking today, and it also is implied in Jacob's prayer: "Deliver me, I pray thee, from the hand of my brother, from the hand of Esau, for I fear him, lest he come and slay us all, the mothers with the children" (Genesis 32:11). Jacob knew he was in danger and wondered if his father's God was big enough to deliver him.

June Twenty-first

Our children face many dangers in today's world: kidnapping, child abuse, prostitution, pornography, drugs, nuclear war. The world in which our children live is such a fearsome place that one child psychologist estimates that more that 70 percent of all American children are permanently neurotic. Indeed, all of us live in a fearsome age. The late Elmer Davis once wrote a book entitled *Two Minutes Until Midnight*. The title came from a cover of "The Bulletin of Atomic Scientists," which showed a clock with its hands at various intervals of time. At one time, the hands were at eight minutes until midnight. When the Russians got the atomic bomb, the hands moved to three minutes till twelve. When the Russians developed the hydrogen bomb, the hands moved to two minutes till twelve. No wonder our children are frightened and neurotic. They have every reason to be!

Unless! Unless we parents believe our God is big enough to deliver us from the dangers of the world we live in, and unless we pass that belief on to our children! Most parents believe in the God of the Bible; the Bible makes it perfectly clear that God is big enough to do anything he wants to do. Abraham and Sarah laughed at God when he told them they would have a child. Abraham was one hundred years old and Sarah was ninety, but they had Isaac because God was big enough to make them fertile again. Jesus was able to heal the sick, raise the dead, and conquer his own grave because his Father God was big enough. Paul told the Ephesians that God was "able to do far more abundantly than all that we ask or think" (Ephesians 3:20). We Christian parents believe in a God who is big enough to protect us from anything the world may bring, and we are under obligation to teach our children to believe in that same big God.

One of the most quotable parents of our age is Yogi Berra, the baseball player, who often murders both language and logic, but somehow always makes sense. On one occasion he said, "Ninety percent of baseball is mental. The other half is physical." Yogi can't add, but his observation is correct anyway. Most of life is mental. If you are convinced there is no hope for you, there probably isn't. If you are convinced that you are a failure, then in all likelihood you will fail. If—on the other hand—you believe that God is big enough to save you, and that you are his child by grace through faith, then your life will be good and happy no matter what happens. Psychologists call that kind of living "self-fulfilling prophecy." Christians call that kind of living "salvation through Jesus Christ alone"; and I believe our children ought to believe in a big God like that.

Big Enough to Forgive

"Daddy, is your God big enough to forgive us of our sins and failures?" That is another question our children are silently asking us parents today. It also was a concern which troubled Jacob in his prayer: "I am not worthy of the least of all the steadfast love and all the faithfulness which thou hast shown to thy servant" (Genesis 32:10). Jacob knew that he had been a liar and a cheat; and he wondered if God was big enough to forgive him.

Jacob's concern is that of many children today, even though most of them cannot articulate as Jacob did. Most children are aware that they live in an age which basically has a mean attitude. Very few Americans want to forgive their enemies; they would rather punish them. The record reveals that we put more people in jail and keep them there longer than any other society in history. When prisoners finally get out, we do little to forgive and rehabilitate them. There are few television programs among the top twenty which deal with the Christian approach to forgiveness. Our children watch these programs and cannot help wondering if the God of their parents is big enough to forgive their sins and failures.

A pastor once told of a Sunday school class for eight-year-olds in a United Methodist church. In that class was a little boy who had Down's syndrome. The Sunday school teacher tried to teach those ten boys and girls to love and to forgive one another. On the Sunday after Easter he came to class with a paper bag full of the big plastic eggs which originally contained pantyhose. He gave each child an egg and instructions to go outside, find a symbol of new life, put it in the egg, and then come back and share it with the class. One little girl put a flower in her egg. That symbolized new life; everybody applauded. Another child had a butterfly in her egg; all agreed that was appropriate as a symbol of the Resurrection. The boy with Down's syndrome, however, opened up his egg and there was nothing in it. The other children cried out that he wasn't playing fair. The teacher, however, allowed him to explain. He said, "That egg is empty, Mr. Smith, because Jesus' tomb was empty." When they heard

June Twenty-first

those words, all of the rest of the children became silent. When the boy died four months later, nine eight-year-olds came to the altar of the church where the funeral was held. Each of them brought an empty pantyhose egg because he had taught them that his God was big enough to raise anybody to eternal life—even a little boy with Down's syndrome.

If God is big enough to protect a little boy like that above, and to forgive a scoundrel like Jacob, he is also big enough to forgive us of our sins and failures; our children need to know that God personally.

Big Enough to Keep His Promises

"Daddy, is your God big enough to keep his promises?" I also believe our children are asking that question this morning. Jacob implied it in his prayer when he said, "But thou didst say, 'I will do you good, and make your descendents as the sand of the sea, which cannot be numbered for multitude'" (Genesis 32:12). Jacob knew what God had promised him, but after the kind of life he had lived he wondered if God was big enough to keep his promises.

One of the greatest mistakes any father can make is to promise his children something and then fail to keep that promise. Listen as I tell you of a man who had such an experience. When he was eight years old, the man's father promised to buy him a BB gun when he received his next pay check. This was during the Great Depression, and the father had only a part-time government job. On the day when the check was due, it was raining and the roads were rivers of mud. The check arrived, but with it was a letter ordering the father to go to Atlanta, two hundred miles away, on that same day. The boy knew his father couldn't drive into town, buy the BB gun, come back, and still get to Atlanta on time. To hide his disappointment, he went to his room, sobbing with a broken heart. He heard his parents talking, heard the car door slam, and heard his father drive away. He wept himself to sleep, only to be awakened later by the sound of an automobile horn. He ran to the window and saw his father holding out a new BB gun for him. He ran downstairs and took his gift. He didn't say anything and neither did his father. There was no need for words. His father got back into his old car and drove off to Atlanta. Years later, the boy—now a minister in Georgia—said that when anyone said anything about doubting God's promises, he simply told that story. If an earthly father can keep his promises, how much more can we depend upon our heavenly Father to keep his!

Jacob discovered that God was big enough to keep his promises. God had promised "to do him good," and he did! Jacob was a liar and a thief, but God forgave him, changed him, re-named him "Israel," and made him the father of a mighty nation—because God was big enough to keep his promises. God was big enough to compress himself into a tiny baby born in a Bethlehem cattle stall, a baby who became Jesus who is called Christ. God was big enough to make Jesus the answer to all of the promises of the prophets, all of the prayers of his people, and all of the hopes of humanity. God promised to raise Jesus from the dead, and he kept his promise on Easter Sunday nearly two thousand years ago. God has promised that Jesus is coming again and that he will take all who are faithful to a heavenly city where he will dwell with us, "he will wipe away every tear from their eyes, and death shall be no more, neither shall there be mourning nor crying nor pain any more . . . " (Revelation 21:4), and we know those promises will come true. We can tell our children that our God—the God who was in Christ Jesus—is big enough to keep all of his promises!

"How Great Thou Art" is probably the favorite hymn of more Christians than any other. It tells about a God who is big enough to be found in twinkling stars and soaring mountains, birdsong and windtouch, the Christ on the cross and the empty tomb. That same God was big enough to hear the prayer of a sinner like Jacob and a sinner like me. He is also big enough to protect our children, to forgive their failures, and to keep all of his promises.

"How big is your God, Daddy?"

Any daddy who doesn't know how to answer that question should sing "How Great Thou Art." If you believe it as you sing it, your children will know that God is big enough for them as well as for you—and that's all they need to know. *Amen.*

Raymond W. Gibson, Jr.
Kentucky Conference
of The United Methodist Church
Lexington, Kentucky

Sunday
June Twenty-eighth

Theme: God Forever

Call to Worship: God is faithful, by whom you were called into the fellowship of his Son, Jesus Christ our Lord.
I Corinthians 1:9

Invocation: Lord, we know that you are ever faithful. Help our unbelief. Strengthen us so that we may go through this life and come to spend eternity with you. *Amen.*

Hymn: "My Faith Looks Up to Thee"

Sermon Presentation: "Has Christianity Failed?"

Goals for Today: Has Christianity failed? Impossible! God's promises are forever. We may fail, but God—never!

This Week in History

June 29—Peter and Paul Day—Feast day marking the dual martyrdom of Christian Apostles Peter (by crucifixion) and Paul (by beheading) during persecution by Roman Emperor Nero.

July 4—Independence Day—The Declaration of Independence was signed at Philadelphia in 1776.

Announcement for Next Week's Sermon: Can the church and state work together in this country? That is a very real question. I hope we get some answers next Sunday.

Hymn: "My Hope Is Built"

Offertory Scripture: Know therefore that the Lord your God is God, the faithful God who keeps covenant and steadfast love with those who love him and keep his commandments, to a thousand generations."
Deuteronomy 7:9

Offertory Prayer: We bring our gifts to your altar, not as we should but as we are able. We have failed you so many times but you never stop loving. Accept us and our gifts just as we are. *Amen.*

Prayer: Stupendous! Fabulous! Amazing! Incredible! Extraordinary! Unbelievable! The Best! The Greatest!

Lord, these are words that we hear all around us each and every day of our lives. Words that seek to get our attention and lead us to believe that only the best will do, only that which the world rates as successful should be good enough for us in this life.

There are those who look at you and your church and are quick to apply the label "failure." Some look at the world and see the continuation of war, of suffering, of evil as signs of your weakness and failure. Help us to realize that suffering, war, and illness are not the results of your failure, but of our sinfulness.

Others look at the cross and say, "What a tragedy." But we need to tell them the rest of the story—of the empty tomb—of life where we anticipate death—of victory in the midst of seeming defeat—of the joy of Easter.

May we seek to do your will first, last, and always. And when the world would call you a failure and our work in your name insignificant, remind us again that thine is the glory forever and ever—a glory that you share with us. *Amen.*

Story of the Week: A hunter on safari in Africa almost stumbled on a huge lion at dusk when he was returning to his camp. As the lion leaped at the hunter, the startled man raised his gun and fired—his last shot. Because he was firing at extremely close range, he missed the lion completely. For the same reason, apparently, the lion leaped completely over the hunter. In that brief instant, the hunter ran wildly toward camp, which he reached in safety.

Not to be caught like that again, the hunter went into the woods early next morning to practice shooting at short range. There he found the lion—practicing short jumps.

HAS CHRISTIANITY FAILED?

I would guess some of you will recognize the name of E. Stanley Jones. Perhaps no greater American Christian leader has yet arisen in this century. When he died in 1973 at the age of eighty-nine, he had completed sixty-six years as a Methodist missionary. He spent most of that career in India. E. Stanley Jones, however, became a missionary to all the world, even to his own native America.

I want to recall this morning the greatest venture that possibly ever engaged E. Stanley Jones. Dr. Jones tried to head off Pearl Harbor. From August to December 7, 1941, this American churchman worked to persuade President Roosevelt to cable Japan's Emperor Hirohito with a plan for peace. The cable reached the emperor one day too late, and we know the rest of the story.

It is fascinating to imagine what might have happened had the Japanese ruler received that message from Mr. Roosevelt before December 6, 1941. The whole course of history might have been changed. The lives of billions of people might have been altered. A world might have been spared immense suffering. Dr. Jones, in his autobiography, looks upon this disappointment philosophically—or should we say religiously? He calls it "an adventure in failure." He wrote, "It is not ours to succeed or fail—it is ours to do the highest we know and leave results with God."

Jesus told a story about failure. He reminded people how farmers went about their annual chore of planting (see Matthew 13:3-8; Mark 4:3-9; Luke 8:5-8). In those days no one had the mechanical equipment we have today. Farmers scattered the seed over the ground by hand. This inefficient, but necessary, method meant some seed would be lost.

In his parable our Lord told his hearers what they already knew. Some seed would be lost to hungry, ever-watching birds. Other grain fell on thin soil. There it sprouted rapidly, but soon died because it lacked good roots. Still other seed got choked out by weeds. Not all of the farmer's work, of course, ended in failure; some of the seed produced crops.

We can guess why Christ told this simple tale. In his work, Jesus had begun to encounter resistance to his message. People received his teachings in various ways.

The Lord could not get to some individuals. They had grown into creatures of habit. In many fields hundreds of feet had created hard-packed paths. When seed fell on those paths, nothing could happen to it. Birds saw it immediately and gobbled it up. It was so with many people's hearts. The experiences of life left them hard and callous. No spiritual truth could get through to them; every temptation and distraction took priority. The Pharisees had become hard followers of ritual. The Sadducees clung to wealth and position. Nothing Jesus could say to them got through the hard crusts of their preoccupations.

Others who heard the teacher from Nazareth welcomed his words. In a short time, however, these people disappeared. The Lord thought of farmers' seeds falling on thin, rocky soil. Thin soil allowed no rootage. In the blazing sun tender seedlings could only wither and die. It was so with many who heard Christ. The young Galilean impressed them, but their enthusiasm did not last. The roots of their loyalty did not go deep enough.

And then in some people the truth Jesus taught ran into too much competition. One can think, for example, of the thieves who died with the Savior on Calvary. One can imagine that those men had heard of Christ many times. Those malefactors would be called zealots today. They did not engage in banditry as a simple profession; they stole to get back at the hated Romans. They belonged to those who held that violence would get rid of the outsiders. But whatever their motives, their daily habits stood between them and the gentle good teacher of Galilee. As thorns or weeds in a field, these habits choked out the life of honest labor and love.

All the parables Christ gave grew out of everyday experiences. He took the common events of life and made them serve as means of teaching truth. The account of the farmer who went out to sow was meant for the disciples. Jesus wanted his followers to know that in their work for him they must expect failure as well as success.

The Lord, himself, had not been immune to defeat and frustration. He knew what it meant to be rejected. Even his own family did not accept him. His neighbors turned against him, even tried to lynch him. When he recounted the troubles of the farmer at planting time, the Master simply drew a picture of his own failures and successes.

Permit me to make a bold statement. No person has really become a Christian until he or she has found her or himself seriously asking the question: Has Christianity failed? Has more

June Twenty-eighth

seed of divine truth and love fallen on hard or rocky ground or among pestilent weeds than it has on good soil, bringing forth grain? Has the story of the gospel been the pathetic tale of failure?

As Christians we belong to the next to the oldest major world religion. It has been in existence longer than any other faith except Judaism. Critics will ask what Christianity has to show for its more than nineteen hundred years.

In London one can visit the acreage known as Hyde Park. One part of Hyde Park attracts all kinds of soap-box orators and large crowds of curious listeners. An evangelist spoke there one day about the virtues of religion. A grimy-faced character in the crowd interrupted and shouted, "Christianity has been in the world for two thousand years, and look at the state of the world!" Quick as a flash the orator shot back, "Yes, water has been in the world for two million years, and look at the state of your face!"

We need to be clear about one fact: Christianity never made any claim to be a worldly success. Indeed, the Gospels continually picture Jesus more as a failure than as a success. The Lord did not cultivate friends among the high and mighty. He drew criticism for associating with the down-and-out, the rejects of society. He chose to be poor when he could have been rich. He continually acted in truth rather than in tact when he could not be both truthful and tactful. He elected to be a servant when he could have been a master.

Moreover, many of Christ's followers hardly fit the category of success. Peter denied Jesus. Thomas doubted. Judas betrayed. Ananias and Sapphira lied. Demas quit. Mark ran home to his mother. The Galatians gave in to false teachers. The Corinthians squabbled. The Corinthians could not claim members who had education, political clout, or distinguished ancestors. It seems that all the early Christians knew was tribulation, distress, persecution, famine, nakedness, peril, and death.

Yet when we take an honest look at nineteen centuries of recorded history, we marvel at what we behold. There can be no mistake that Christianity failed, but it also succeeded. The seed of God's truth can fall on good soil and bring forth grain—some a hundredfold, some sixty, some thirty. Our history offers another testimony of the strange mixture of failure and success.

We Americans today find it incredible that this great free country ever permitted slavery. Still even harder to accept is that some Christian people defended this wickedness. In the annals of Christianity, darker days had seldom fallen on the followers of Jesus. Preachers stood in their pulpits quoting Scripture in support of slavery. They completely ignored the Bible's unmistakable teaching about the brotherhood of man under the Fatherhood of God.

We speak of Christian hope. By that we refer to our conviction that in spite of failure God's way will certainly triumph. Nothing in the Scriptures teaches us that God will violate the freedom he has granted his children. Nevertheless, his grace will lead some men to govern their lives according to his purposes.

Now let me add a suggestive illustration. Most of you recall that France endured a pro-German government during World War II. This so-called Vichy régime tried to impose the Nazi way of life upon the French. Two French pastors got into trouble with the authorities because they insisted on taking care of Jewish refugee children. The powers in control threw the pastors into a concentration camp. The government then offered to release the ministers if they would pledge allegiance to it. The two refused.

The concentration camp also housed some Communist prisoners. It fascinated the Communists that anyone in the modern world should refuse to sign a piece of paper if, by signing, he could regain his liberty. The pastors explained to the Communists that they had received a sense of honor from the Bible. This so impressed the Communists they asked if they might sit in with the ministers in their permitted daily Bible study.

After several months one of the Communists told the pastors: "We admit that your religion is superior to ours. This way of life that Jesus taught and lived is the way all men ought to live. It is the way all men will live—after the Revolution. But, of course, it isn't practical now." Christianity does not accept the lie about practicality. When Christ spoke, he did so in the present tense, not in the future: "You are the salt of the earth, . . . You are the light of the world" (Matthew 5:13-14). After the story of the Good Samaritan, Jesus told the lawyer, "Go and do likewise" (Luke 10:37). Five thousand men, women, and children needed

June Twenty-eighth

food. The Master instructed his disciples, "You give them something to eat" (Luke 9:13). And on the mountain, the risen Lord declared, "Go therefore and make disciples of all nations" (Matthew 28:19).

Christ did not stop to worry about practicality. And the whole march of his religion across the ages has confirmed that where people work their faith, it succeeds. That faith, of course, has been in a divine Leader in whom men can put their trust. Where Christianity has succeeded, it has been because human beings have trusted in Jesus Christ. Where it has failed, it owes the failure to a lack of confidence in the divine leader of the ages.

Jesus knew that in the church's being led by humans, there would be failures. He foresaw that Peter would deny him and that Judas would betray him. He understood that ahead of himself lay the cross. The Galilean did not, himself, fail but his immediate mission faced defeat. He accepted this failure. He went to Calvary with his love and faith undiminished. Out of that faithfulness emerged the most stupendous success story ever recorded in human experience.

Nineteen hundred years ago Jesus talked about seeds falling upon the hard, beaten path, on rocky ground, and upon thorns. Some seeds, nevertheless, landed on good soil and a harvest resulted. Our Lord ended his story by saying, "He who has ears, let him hear" (Matthew 13:8). *Amen.*

Charles W. Kern
Grace United Methodist Church
Haverhill, Massachusetts

Sunday
July Fifth

Theme: This Nation Under God

Call to Worship: He shall judge between the nations, and
  decide for many peoples;
and they shall beat their swords into plowshares,
  and their spears into pruning hooks;
nation shall not lift up sword against nation,
  neither shall they learn war any more.
Isaiah 2:4

Invocation: Oh, God, you have kept this nation strong, not by arms, but by the good deeds of good people. Raise up leaders for this time and this place so that your kingdom on earth may prosper and continue to lead all the people of the world to you and your truth. Make us strong to serve you and our beloved nation to your honor and glory. *Amen.*

Hymn: "Battle Hymn of the Republic"

Sermon Presentation: "Let Freedom Ring"

Goals for Today: Today all the parts of the service and sermon are geared to the recognition that this great country is celebrating another birthday in freedom under God. The thrust is to recognize that only with a proper balance of church freedom and state freedom can we maintain the freedom of both partners in this great land.

This Week in History

July 6—John Paul Jones' Birthday—He won the Battle of Lake Erie and was immortalized with the statement, "I have not yet begun to fight." A great example of courage and the will to see a crisis through to a victorious conclusion. Don't give up, fight.

July 8—Declaration of Independence: First Public Reading—John Nixon in Philadelphia. This document served notice on the British King that the American Colonies were going to be

July Fifth

free, even if it meant war. Freedom always costs, perhaps today as much as any time in our history.

Announcement for Next Week's Sermon: "After all I'm only human." That is one of the very well-worn excuses we all use from time to time. We didn't invent it; it started in the Bible. Next week, Clay Feet.

Hymn: "O Beautiful for Spacious Skies"

Offertory Scripture: Render therefore to Caesar the things that are Caesar's, and to God the things that are God's.
Matthew 22:21

Offertory Prayer: For our freedom, we thank you, Lord. For our beloved country, we thank you, Lord. For our leaders, we thank you, Lord. For the blessings which we have received from you we now return these gifts as our way of saying thank you for your great gift of your son. *Amen.*

Prayer: Lord, we live here in this great land surrounded by the abundance of life. Don't let us become so self-satisfied that we lose our vision.

Help us to see those in need at home and all around the world. Where there is hunger, let us feed them. Where they are naked, let us clothe them. Where they do not know the good news of your victory over death, let us spread the good news.

Lord, never let us take our faith or our freedom for granted. Keep us ever vigilant. Bless our country, all its leaders, and all those in authority. Let us live the motto of our land, "In God We Trust." Help us to be part of the great American chorus that cries out across this land and around the world, "Let freedom ring" not just for us but for all God's children wherever they are." Let us go forth into the world and witness so that the world knows us by our love for one another and all people. Amen.

Story of the Week: The visiting preacher had been invited to the big noon "dinner-on-the-ground" before he was to preach the afternoon service at an all-day meeting at the rural church.

One of the ladies of the church offered to fill his plate for him but he stopped her. "I never eat," he said, "before I preach. I find that it keeps me from preaching a good sermon."

After the service was over, a friend asked that same lady what she thought of the sermon. "As far as I was concerned," she said, "he might as well of et."

LET FREEDOM RING

Have you ever had the thrill of visiting the Liberty Bell in historic "old Philadelphia"? If you ever have this opportunity, you will find the bell enshrined in a new setting. You will stop in a pavillion and look at it. You will hear the park ranger give its history, and then, almost as if he were reading your minds, he will say, "You can touch it as you go by."

There is something almost magical about the Liberty Bell. There is something about that bell that seems to mesmerize you. The crack, the bottom where souvenir hunters once chipped away globs of it—not because they wanted to have a piece of the rock, but because they wanted to have a piece of this great symbol for their very own. Then there are the words. Taken from the book of Leviticus, they are imprinted on the side—"Proclaim liberty throughout the land."

We call this day, July 4, Independence Day. Sometimes we call it the birthday of America, but always Independence Day! Over two hundred years ago this week our forefathers decided to make a bold move. As a colony they were ready to attempt to do something that had never been done before—they would declare their independence from the mother country and remain free. July 4 is a day, an annual opportnity, to seek out the soul of America. We look back to a day over two hundred years ago when dedicated men and women gave birth to a nation seeking freedom of conscience—freedom of religion—freedom from fear—the rights of the individual. Is it any wonder that this Bible verse should appear on the symbol of our free nation and that people would sing "Let Freedom Ring"?

So often when we talk about America, a song comes to mind—

> O beautiful for spacious skies,
> For amber waves of grain,
> For purple mountain majesties
> Above the fruited plain!

July Fifth

It's almost as if our nation is in itself alive. The mountains, the Rockies and the Appalachians, are its skeleton. The rivers are its life-blood. The fields of grain and the acres of forest are beautiful skin. But what is the soul of America? What is it that empowered thirteen underdeveloped colonies to become the world's greatest nation? It was their relationship with God, a relationship characterized by faith, fear, and fervor.

We look at our Scripture lessons and we see that miracles never happened until the people demonstrated faith. From the woman who touched the hem of Christ's garment, to the blind, the deaf, the troubled, when they came to our Lord in faith great things happened. When his own hometown rejected him, the Scripture writer recounts that due to the faithlessness of the people, they were denied miracles.

We are told that the fifty-five men who met to draw up the Declaration of Independence, and later the Constitution, had some moments of lively and heated debate. Finally, Ben Franklin asked permission to speak to those assembled. He waited for quiet and then spoke, "We have been assured in the sacred writings that except the Lord build the house, they that build it labor in vain. I move that every morning before we begin our work that we pray to God asking His guidance and blessing." From that day on progress was made. To this day, Congress still opens its sessions with prayer. A strong faith in God; that's why America succeeded then and continues to prosper now.

But we need also to fear God—Not a fear that frightens us, but fear of him in the sense of standing in awe of God, love of God, reverence of our Creator and our Redeemer. When God ceases to be awesome for us, then our future will surely be awful.

When we look around the world we see that God and freedom are closely related. Churches in Russia are closed or attended mostly—almost exclusively—by the elderly. When visiting dignitaries or church leaders, like Billy Graham, visit Russia's churches, the pews are filled with mostly KGB agents. We look at Poland, where the people struggle for their freedom. The labor movement and the churches struggle against unbelievable odds, against terrifying threats like loss of family or exile. Yet because these brave people fear losing God more than they fear the dictators' guns and tanks, the flame of freedom, although at times only a flicker, continues to burn.

These Christians know that it is God's will that liberty be proclaimed throughout the land. In the song we sing "as He died to make men holy, let us live to make men free!" ("Battle Hymn of the Republic"). As Christians, we know the length to which our Father was willing to go to free us from sin and grant us eternal life. On this day after the birthday of our nation, we need to ask ourselves, "How far and to what length will we go to preserve our God-given freedom?"

As well as faith and fear, we must also have fervor. The signers of the Declaration of Independence certainly celebrated the fourth of July with real gusto! Our celebrations are limited only by our imaginations. From pillow-fighting contests to skydiving and stunt flying, to an antique car parade to a supper on the grass overlooking "Old Ironsides" in the harbor and listening to the sounds of the Boston Pops orchestra, from fireworks to family picnics with kids throwing frisbees. These are the sights and sounds of America on the fourth of July. But our fervor for preserving our God-given freedom in the future must be as enthusiastic as our fervor for celebrating our country's birth in the past.

Liberty means responsibility. Those who expect to recapture the blessings of freedom must undergo the fatigue of supporting it. As Teddy Roosevelt once said, "This country will not be a good place for any of us to live in unless we make it a good place for all of us to live in."

For over two hundred years our faith in God, our fear of God, and our fervor to do God's will have made us a great nation. But what about tomorrow? Do we have enough faith, fear, and fervor to do God's will in this, our God blessed nation? Let us continue to proclaim liberty throughout the land in the name of our God forever.

On this July Fourth holiday weekend I would like us to remember our heritage as Americans. We were founded as a nation under God.

In our Declaration of Independence, our forefathers spoke of the laws of nature and nature's God. They spoke of the rights that people are endowed with by their creator.

President Lincoln, in his "Gettysburg Address," expressed the hope that this nation under God shall have a new birth of freedom and that government of the people, by the people and for the people shall not perish from the earth.

July Fifth

In 1829 a prayer room was established in the U.S. Capitol building. This non-denominational room is a place where members of Congress may pray and meditate. It is located off the rotunda under the great dome.

The room is dominated by a stained glass window of George Washington kneeling in prayer at Valley Forge. Beneath it is an altar of white oak on which stands an open Bible. Unfortunately, you and I will never get to see this room because it isn't open to the public.

In 1921 the Tomb of the Unknown Soldier was established. On it is inscribed, "Here Rests in Honored Glory an American Soldier Known Only to God."

Even today both the House and Senate have a full-time chaplain. Each session of Congress is opened with prayer.

I'd like to share with you the fourth verse of our national anthem. This is the verse that recognizes the place of God in our nation and in our lives:

> Oh, thus be it ever when freemen shall stand
> Between their loved homes and the war's desolation!
> Blest with vict'ry and peace, may the heav'n-rescued land
> Praise the Pow'r that hath made and preserved us a nation!
> Then conquer we must, when our cause it is just;
> And this be our motto: "In God is our trust!"
> And the star-spangled banner in triumph shall wave
> O'er the land of the free and the home of the brave.
> *"The Star Spangled Banner"*

Amen.

Thomas E. Richards, Jr.
St. Paul's Lutheran Church
Tannersville, Pennsylvania

Sunday
July Twelfth

Theme: We All Have Problems

Call to Worship: You, therefore, must be perfect, as your heavenly Father is perfect.
Matthew 5:48

Invocation: We struggle for perfection; we seem to want to do it on our own. Lord, show us the way. You are perfection. Let us look to thee and follow thy will. We move closer to you and perfection. *Amen.*

Hymn: "O God, Our Help in Ages Past"

Sermon Presentation: "Clay Feet"

Goals for Today: To give people hope. To know that failure is the time to start a new relationship with God. God continues to love us, warts and all.

This Week in History

July 12-18—Captive Nations Week—Presidential Proclamation calling on all Americans to be thankful for American freedom and to pray that all captive nations might be free.

July 15—Clement C. Moore's Birthday—born in 1779. His "A visit from St. Nicholas" was first published in a newspaper on December 23, 1823. This is still a part of Christmas tradition.

Announcement for Next Week's Sermon: What do you do when trouble comes? No matter how bad things get, there is always a ray of hope. Let's look for that ray next Sunday.

Hymn: "What a Friend We Have in Jesus"

Offertory Scripture: Jesus said to him [the rich young ruler], "If you would be perfect, go, sell what you possess and give to the poor, and you will have treasure in heaven; and come, follow me."
Matthew 19:21

July Twelfth

Offertory Prayer: Lord, I keep trying. I should at least get a little credit for that. I will never be perfect, but do not let me ever give up. Accept these imperfect gifts as I keep on trying. *Amen.*

Prayer: Whew! What a struggle life is these days, O Lord. I say my prayers. I worship you on Sunday. I believe in you and trust you with my life and the lives of my loved ones. But sometimes I wonder, "What am I doing wrong? What am I missing? What can I do to strengthen myself in this struggle we call life?"

I read Scripture and wonder, "Why can't I be like Moses or Paul—so committed, so strong in the face of adversity. What am I lacking, Lord?" What's that you say? I need to open my eyes and read your words again. I need to open my mind and discover how much I have in common with your saints of Scripture. You tell me I will find that they have struggled just as I struggle; they have suffered as I suffer; they have doubted as I have doubted. Their sins are my sins, and most importantly, they are forgiven by your grace just as I am.

I am just like them. Like Abraham and Sarah, I have laughed at your promises; like Moses I have tried to hide from doing what you would ask of me; like Peter I've denied you when those around me pressured me. Just like Paul, I have wondered, "Why do I do things that I know are wrong? Why is it so hard for me to do the right thing?"

Looking at their lives, I see how much I do have in common with the heroes of the faith. They are called saints not because they were perfect, but because they wouldn't give up. They kept on going in your name. And now let me do one more thing just as they have—let me take up your yoke and join with you as we walk through this uncertain life toward the certain glory of everlasting life with you. *Amen.*

Story of the Week: The fourth grade teacher had to leave the room for a few minutes. When she returned, she found the children in perfect order. Everybody was sitting absolutely quiet.

She was shocked and stunned and said, "I've never seen anything like it before. This is wonderful. But, please tell me. What came over all of you? Why are you so well behaved and quiet?"

Finally, after much urging, a little girl said, "Well, one time you said that if you ever came back and found us quiet, you would drop dead."

CLAY FEET

One of the most impressive things about Holy Scripture is its honesty. It is this honesty which makes the Bible so believable. There is a reality about the characters it presents; they are not always painted with a halo neatly in place about their heads, rather they are just like you and me.

Scripture tells us about people who have struggled as we have struggled, have suffered as we have suffered, and have rejoiced in the power of the living God just as we, at times, have rejoiced. Yet, our desire is to romanticize these heroes of the Spirit. We desire to present them with their best and bravest foot forward and then ask the question: "Why can't we be like they were?"

It's like the old question asked by all parents: Why can't our kids be like we were? What's the matter with our children today?

It can be no other way! You see, Scripture is not about characters out of some lost pages of history—it is about us! If it were page after page of men and women who had figured the whole thing out and understood the Living God perfectly, then Scripture would have no meaning for us. It has meaning only when we can see in their struggle our struggle; when we can see our problems in their problems; and when we, like they, discover that we can, with assurance, wait upon the Lord who will renew our strength.

The Scriptures are God's story and they are our story. They tell us about God's dealing in the lives of men and women and their responses to this divine intervention. The danger comes when we see this encounter between God and the biblical humans through rose-colored glasses.

Thankfully, however, Scripture does not allow us this luxury. It opens our eyes, shakes us from our romantic nations, and forces us to look at how things really are for the people of faith.

Almost all of Scripture presents us with men and women who, when they heard the call of God, did not charge headlong

July Twelfth

into the adventure, but who instead responded with a "Hey now, wait just a minute here."

Excuses are plentiful throughout the whole of Scripture. In the Old Testament we find Abraham and Sarah. They were told over and over again that God would make their offspring a "great nation" by whom "all the families of the earth would bless themselves."

But, it is not until Sarah is ninety-one that she is told, by an angel no less, that she is finally going to have that long promised baby.

And what does she do? She laughs. She laughs and says, in effect, "It can't be done." Abraham laughs, too. In fact, they were both laughing so hard that even God took notice. God joins in the joke by suggesting that when the baby boy is born he should be named Isaac, which in Hebrew means *laughter*. Great heroes of the Scriptures laughing at the promises of God.

Or Moses, who came into the presence of the almighty who appeared in the form of a bush which was burning but was not consumed. He is called to leave his shepherding and be God's man to answer the cry from his people in bondage in Egypt. Does he charge off in the direction he has been pointed? No.

Instead he offers excuses: "Who am I to go to, Pharaoh? What if they will not believe me or listen to my words? You know, Lord, I am slow of speech and of a slow tongue."

And God replies: "Now go, and I shall help you to speak and tell you what to say." And so, with God's help, Moses presided over the exodus, the cornerstone event in the foundation of the history of the children of Israel.

In the New Testament, Peter never thought he had the capacity to deny his best friend. "Oh no, Jesus," he cried, "these others may desert you, but not me! I'm prepared to stick with you all the way, even if it means death." He made that oath, only to turn, run, hide, and even lie when times got tough.

James and John wanted to be up in front. They wanted to be Jesus' chief lieutenants when he came into his kingdom—one at his right side and the other on his left. But they, too, were confused and crushed by the crucifixion.

Countless others heard the message of Jesus and embraced it for a time, but then left it by the roadside when it no longer suited their needs.

Scripture tells us many times over of people who discovered that the life of faith was not a luxury, but a call to battle. Perhaps no one knew this better than the Apostle Paul. Paul is seen by so many as the brave saint who sets the standard for Christian courage and who planted churches, even while facing peril, dungeon, and sword. Surely, we tell ourselves, this is one who had his faith all sorted out.

But with beautifully believable honesty, Paul tells us, "No." There are still some things that he is working on. And there is still one thing which leaves him puzzled.

The great saint is troubled by the question that haunts the human condition: "I cannot understand my own behavior," he says. "I fail to carry out the things I want to do, and I find myself doing the very things I hate."

Paul is giving us a glimpse into his very soul. He knows what is right, and he wants to do it, yet somehow he never can. He knows what was wrong and it is the last thing he wants to do, and yet somehow that is what he does.

Paul, before his conversion, was a devout Jew, highly skilled in his study of the law of Moses. Careful adherence to this law was a sign of fellowship with God. Yet, for Paul there was frustration in this fellowship. He could see what was good and knew that doing what was good was pleasing to God. But when it came to practice, Paul always came out on the wrong side of the street.

Certainly, this is a feeling which all of us share when we look at our helplessness in necessary things.

It is part of the human situation that we know the right, yet we do the wrong. Paul labels it correctly, "It is sin." He admits that we are in bondage to this sin. This bondage, like all others, brings with it a frustration, a yearning to be free, and a fearsome struggle to be rid of those forces which hold us back.

Paul sees this battle in such real terms that he uses military imagery to describe his heroic efforts. He describes sin as being "at war with the law of my mind" with the result that he is brought into captivity. He even goes so far as to use the expression employed by soldiers who have been wounded in battle when he asks, "Who will deliver me?" No doubt he feels that he has been grievously wounded in his struggle against sin and is desperately in need of help.

July Twelfth

Paul's response to the issue is as powerful as it is brief, "Thanks be to God through Jesus Christ our Lord!" (Romans 7:25). For, as Paul will tell us one verse later, "There is therefore now no condemnation for those who are in Christ Jesus" (Romans 8:1).

We are no longer captives of sin but captives of Christ. We are free from our own judgmentalism, which would always deem us unworthy. We are free to rely on Christ, who calls us his own, and by so doing, makes us worthy.

By his cross and resurrection, Christ has "led captivity captive." He removes our attention from ourselves and our shortcomings and refocuses our attention on Christ and what he has done for us.

Paul reminds us that in Jesus Christ there is new life. Because Christ lives the Christian is open to a life no longer dominated by his or her own will but by the Spirit of God which fills us with confidence that the penalty for the past is removed and the strength for the future assured.

What Paul told the church in Corinth needs to be reaffirmed in our lives as well. "You are not your own; you were bought with a price" (I Corinthians 6:19-20).

We were paid for by Jesus Christ, in whom there is no condemnation, and who invites us to *yoke* or join ourselves with him to find that our burdens, whatever they may be, are relieved.

Thanks be to God, who through Jesus Christ, makes this so. *Amen.*

David C. Nelson
Mount Pleasant Lutheran Church
Racine, Wisconsin

Sunday
July Nineteenth

Theme: Keep on Trying

Call to Worship: May the God of hope fill you with all joy and peace in believing, so that by the power of the Holy Spirit you may abound in hope. *Romans 15:13*

Invocation: Our hope is built on nothing less than Jesus and his righteousness. That is the only way for our hope to bear fruit in peace and joy. Grant us hope. *Amen.*

Hymn: "My Hope Is Built"

Sermon Presentation: "Harried into Hope"

Goals for Today: Hope starts with understanding. Our job today is to realize that faith in a risen Lord is the only basis for hope.

This Week in History

July 19—First Women's Rights Convention Anniversary—The first national meeting to fight for equal rights for women held in Seneca Falls, New York, in 1848.

July 20—Moon Day—The *Eagle* landed, at 4:17 P.M. EDT, July 20, 1969. Astronauts Armstrong and Aldrin walked and lived on the moon's surface for over twenty-one hours.

Announcement for Next Week's Sermon: You don't have to teach me to pray; I know how to do that. Why don't I do it more often? Next Sunday is all about prayer.

Hymn: "Immortal, Invisible, God Only Wise"

Offertory Scripture: To them God chose to make known how great among the Gentiles are the riches of the glory of this mystery, which is Christ in you, the hope of glory.
Colossians 1:27

July Nineteenth

Offertory Prayer: Lord, we live on hopes and promises. Turn our hope into something that never doubts, but believes. These are my gifts to show my sure hope. *Amen.*

Prayer: I'm afraid, Lord, to pick up the newspaper in the morning. I'm scared to watch the news on T.V. When the news comes on the radio I switch to another station. I'm so worried about the things going on in my world. I'm fearful for my safety and that of my loved ones. The evil around us, and within us, seems to be raging out of control.

In our urban areas we find people who are holding onto life by a thread. The homeless, the poor, the runaways—so often their despair is sandwiched between anger and bitterness.

In our suburban areas the decay is hidden by the abundance of material goods. Yet, the frustration, the doubt, and the hatred of others and of self are shown in divorces, drug and alcohol abuse, family life marked by mistrust and hostility.

Our rural areas find the same problems. Many of the people who live in these areas wonder how long it will be before they lose their present lifestyles, before housing developments replace family farms and our woods are cut down to make way for shopping malls and parking spaces.

To be honest, Lord, sometimes we wonder if you have turned your back on us and that there might not be any hope left for us. What is that you say, Lord? You're glad that you finally got our attention! You say that you have called us to be your people, but we have been so slow in responding. You have offered to guide us by your spirit in truth and righteousness, but we have told you, "Father, please, I'd rather do it myself." You say that it is time for us to get back on your path. The result of doing it ourselves is all this horror that frightens us and causes us to live in fear and tension.

Grant us your hope so that we might live by your promise that we surely will have ruins today, but will experience the resurrection tomorrow; so we can die today but live tomorrow; we realize that today we are victims but tomorrow, victors.

Let us never forget that your love is eternal and in you alone is our hope forever. *Amen.*

Story of the Week: A tourist was watching a man fish from the municipal dock in Miami. The fisherman landed a sea bass that looked to be a four-or-five pounder and threw him back. After a while he landed another big one and threw him back. After a while he landed a small bass and kept him.

"Why did you throw back the big ones?" the tourist asked the man.

"Small frying pan," the fisherman said.

HARRIED INTO HOPE

During the war in the Falkland Islands, we heard a lot about the British *Harrier* jet planes—a reminder of a word seldom heard, but full of meaning. Those jets may well have been a deciding factor in the British victory, but the word harrier, itself, has a message for us in connection with God's Word out of Lamentations.

To harry can mean to torment, to worry another, to harass, or it can mean to force or push along.

The living of our lives often seems to be harried by many pressures and tensions. Peace and justice as God's plan for human society continue to beckon us to be his instruments on behalf of people everywhere. But the harassing horrors of our time hang on. The tensions in the Middle East are hotter than ever. The urban horrors of street life are visible everywhere, reminding us that God calls his people to be always aware of persons suffering and in need. Violent crimes force us into double bolted, barred-window security measures. Yes, it is easy for us to allow these pressures to harry us into constant anxiety. And underneath it all there is the inner anguish of our souls—the soul-harassing horror that makes us cry out with Paul, "For I do not do the good I want, but the evil I do not want is what I do" (Romans 7:19).

The poet who wrote the book of Lamentations certainly knew what it meant to be harried and harassed. Horror lay all around him—he had no tangible reason to face the future with even the slightest bit of hope. His view of the future was grey and numb with horror. Jerusalem and the Temple lay in ruins, with people picking in the rubble for foodscraps or personal treasures. He even saw mothers eating their own children because of famine.

Yet, this poet did not collapse with the paralysis of analysis. To be harried was bad. But to be harried into despair was not his way. He did something very important. He not only talked with

July Nineteenth

God about it, but he also argued with God—he accused God of harrying them beyond the breaking point. He told the Lord how hard it is to live with the feeling that even God is against his people. He had divine anger, accusing God of breaking his bones with bitterness; God had walled him in so tight that his prayers were shut out. God, to him, was now like a bear or lion, just waiting to pounce. Yes, he teetered on the brink of despair in his angry words toward God. He was certainly no blind, "pollyanna" optimist, nor was he a dour pessimist. He was a down-to-earth realist, and the poems we know today as Lamentations were his way of telling it "like it is."

Amazingly, no matter how dark things were, he always found a ray of hope. He was harried into hope, in spite of the prophets of doom all around him. Many Jews had thrown in the towel and worshiped Marduk, the god of the Babylonians. But this man, who may have been Jeremiah, himself, belonged to a remnant of believers who never lost their hope in God. He had no time to sit down and write a reasoned critique of how God was treating Israel. He fairly gasps out his debate with God. Yet, he could look for new mercies every morning. He would not have smiled at the modern bumper sticker that reads: "The end is postponed: No need to repent!" But he believed that God had allowed all those horrors in order to bring the people to repentance and to advance his eternal purposes through this people. God was harrying his people to push them into repentance.

Therefore, Jerusalem in ruins was not so much a lifeless corpse as it was a grieving widow—still stunned by calamity, but holding out hope for new life. No doubt, some of you have gone through the valley of personal horrors. Perhaps your faith in the goodness of God has been sorely tested. If so, then read Lamentations and discover a fellow-sufferer who did not hesitate to argue with God, for in the end, this poet finally caught a comforting vision of a loving God, stooping low over the prostrate forms of his suffering people.

For our own times of near-despair and misery, when harried and harassed by the blows of life, let us then learn something of value from this great poet of the Hebrew exile.

He found at least three reasons to be harried into hope.

First, he never stopped believing that God's love is steadfast. "Great is thy faithfulness" (3:23), he shouted to God even through his tears. There are ruins all around today, but a new day of resurrection coming! We are captive today, but free tomorrow! Tomorrow is a new day, and the Lord's mercy is new every morning.

The writer of Lamentations knew the danger of hope as mere illusion. He knew that people who bring misery on themselves need the cleansing of repentance. He was no flag-waving super-patriot who boasted that his country could do no wrong. He made no attempt to whitewash the nation's sins. He always saw Israel in the white-hot light of her place under God, not just as some self-sufficient human, political grouping. God is always faithful to his part of the covenant made with Abraham so many centuries ago. But also know how rebelliously Israel had pushed God to test his mercy.

And how we today need to remember the Lord's steady, unchanging love for us. Beware of taking his love for granted. Never say, "God will forgive us, that's his business!" Israel's prelude to their horrible exile was to push God off to the fringes of their concern. It is so much easier to enjoy soft living, to promote arrogant nationalism, and to settle for a watered-down religion.

You and I have never known national horror on the scale that Israel knew. We have had great prosperity, in spite of a slowed down economy and the energy crisis. The standard of living allows most of us to pay higher prices in the stores, even though we gripe about them. Our own Civil War is the closest we have come to a national holocaust. Nevertheless, we could be on the verge of horror. A painless religion that merely confirms us in our comforts, perks and privileges is not enough! God never chooses any people just to make them his pets—he always lays upon us great responsibilities as well.

That brings us to the second reason that the poet could be harried into hope. He also cried out, "The Lord is my portion" (3:24). If we are God's own people today, here, everywhere, together, sent out for service and mission—then we must hold tight to God alone as our portion. The prodigal son chose the squandering of an inherited, unearned income as his portion. But it soon ran out and failed to satisfy his need for meaning in his life. And only when he returned to his waiting Father, did he find peace.

July Nineteenth

So it is when we live for our own personal happiness at any cost; it's always just beyond reach. But when we set absolute loyalty to God as our highest goal—even when we are harried and harassed by life—joy comes as an unearned, undeserved, but welcome, by-product. Still, for many people today pleasure is their portion. People scream out in music in defiance of every God-approved life-style, "Be free . . . free in love . . . free in sex . . . and drugs can bring you a bit of heaven right now."

A pharmaceutical company once put an ad in a psychiatric journal. It concerned Handel, the composer of the *Messiah*. Handel was known for his swings from depression to mania. The ad claimed that if he were living today, lithium could probably control his symptoms. The ad went on to say that with lithium Handel would give us his deathless "Bye, Bye Blues." Bluebirds are always singing somewhere over the rainbow. But if we dare to call God our portion, then in the use of our time, talents, and money—in making thoughtful, responsible decisions—and in seeing that bluebirds sing for *all*—this is to call God our portion.

Finally, we learn value of patience: "The Lord is good to those who wait for him. . . . It is good that one should wait quietly for the salvation of the Lord" (3:25).

Who wants to wait for tomorrow? We want instant gratification, to fill the house *today* with instant credit. Yet, we miss the joy of the gradual acquiring of things. The people of Israel, after the fall of Jerusalem they must wait on the Lord. Nothing more possible. We have learned great lessons:

1. We are each accountable for our own sins—no buck-passing to parents, ancestors, or other authority figures;
2. Suffering has great training value;
3. God's justice is absolutely fair; and
4. His life is eternal.

So the only way to be harried into hope is by unshakable faith in God. This learning took place not in peace and prosperity, but in the crucible of national disaster.

The mission of the church today is to seek not just to nourish its own faith, or save its own skin, or to save its own souls! It is to seek the welfare of the common life of all God's people. We should say, "Thus says the Lord," both to personal and national sins.

Let no refugee cry for a haven and us not hear. Fear not to argue with God! He can take it! Nuclear power-pack, mass hunger and brutality, erosion of vibrant faith in God—these are our horrors today. Yet, God calls us (individually and as a congregation) to point the way as harriers into hope. *Amen.*

Harold G. Deal
Luther Place Memorial Church
Washington, D.C.

Sunday
July Twenty-sixth

Theme: You Need to Practice Prayer

Call to Worship: Likewise the Spirit helps us in our weakness; for we do not know how to pray as we ought, but the Spirit himself intercedes for us with sighs too deep for words.
Romans 8:26

Invocation: Prayer is just talking to God. I talk to my friends all the time. God is my very best friend, and I talk to him. Lord, teach me to pray more often. *Amen.*

Hymn: "O Master, Let Me Walk with Thee"

Sermon Presentation: "Teach Me to Pray"

Goals for Today: To look at prayer as an absolute need of the Christian life, not an option for occasional use, but a must.

This Week in History

July 28—Terry Fox Day—This young man, stricken with cancer, inspired the world with his attempt to run across Canada on an artificial leg. He ran 3,328 miles and raised twenty-four million dollars before he was forced to stop. He died soon after.

July 30—Henry Ford's Birthday—A man who put America on wheels. He developed the first assembly line.

Announcement for Next Week's Sermon: How do you handle anger—let it all out or hold it all in? Next week we will deal with anger.

Hymn: "O Jesus, I Have Promised"

Offertory Scripture: Watch and pray that you may not enter into temptation; the spirit indeed is willing, but the flesh is weak.
Matthew 26:41

Offertory Prayer: You taught us in your perfect prayer what to ask for when we pray. Now let us offer these our gifts as a prayer of thanksgiving. *Amen.*

Prayer: "Reach out! Reach out and touch someone." That's what the phone company keeps telling us. O Lord, If we need to communicate more with each other, how much greater is our need to communicate with you, our heavenly Father.

You want so much to hear from us in our own words about the things that concern us, the things that frighten us, the cares and concerns that so often seem to be too big to handle. You already know the things that we want to say. You are that wise and that concerned about each of us. But you want to hear from us so that we will be reassured by speaking directly to you.

To be honest, Lord, so often we feel uncomfortable when we would pray. We wonder if we will have the right words to pray for help in those times when we find life so confusing; for strength in those moments when we are aware of our human limitations, for courage in the face of fear of the known and the unknown, for hope in the face of injustice and death.

Help us to pray not only when we are in need, but also in those times when we have been blessed and owe you our heartfelt thanks. May our prayer be like eating, sleeping, or breathing, that is a natural part of life and a natural expression of our relationship with you. *Amen.*

Story of the Week: The confirmed optimist always said: "Oh, well, it might have been worse."

One day an acquaintance stopped him and said, "I dreamed last night that I died, went to hell, and was doomed to everlasting torment."

"Oh, well," said the optimist, "it might have been worse."

"What do you mean!" cried the man. "How could it have been worse?"

"It might have been true," the optimist said.

TEACH ME TO PRAY

Have you ever noticed how often the people in the Bible had a chance to talk to God and hear the Lord respond? Or how many ways God appears and reveals himself to the people? Ezekiel had an opportunity to listen to God in the wind, an earthquake, a fire, and eventually in the now famous *still small voice.*

James and John, the disciples, sat at our Lord's feet and asked him questions; they, too, waited and listened for his response.

July Twenty-sixth

God is still being plagued with questions, and we still wait for a response. Our conversation with God is simply called prayer. The very dynamic of prayer is communion with God. The goal of prayer is a life of fellowship and friendship with God, cooperating with the Lord's Spirit however it speaks to us and living the Creator's will in the very world in which we find ourselves.

Yet, prayer can be one of the most difficult things for a person to do. Many times, and in various situations, I have heard the request, "Pastor, you pray for me, I don't know how." When those words are uttered, sometimes I am overwhelmed with a feeling of sadness and fright. Why can't we pray? What makes dialogue with God so difficult for us? Why, when life deals us a string of illnesses or misfortunes, do we find it sometimes more difficult to communicate to the one inner source which can see us through; or, why do we often forget to give thanks and praise when the good times come? It should be as easy as talking to your best friend over the phone, relating the day's and week's events, your wants, your dreams, your desires, your emotions, and your expectations. Yet, prayer is something which can frighten us.

When it is my turn to pray and I'm caught unaware, the feelings of inadequacy and fright can come upon me. What words do I use? What formula do I say to make it sound right so it will be accepted? What if I stutter or forget something? Will God understand? Or maybe more importantly at that particular moment, will those listening to my prayer understand and forgive my human weakness and lack of words?

Often, Christians aren't noted for being a praying people. Yet, Scripture, which is very important to us, makes reference to prayer 234 times. Prayer is a discipline and should be a part of life, as natural to us as the very air we breathe.

There is an Indian story of an old man praying by the river. A child comes toward him and asks the old man to teach him to pray. The old man quietly takes the child down by the river and dunks him in, holding his head under water until the boy is fussing and gasping for breath. When the boy is raised from the water, the old man tells him that when his desire to pray is like the desire to breathe, then he will teach the boy to pray.

Most of us are not at points in our lives where we are thirsting and seeking to learn how to pray. Most of the time we treat prayer as a fad, rather than an integral part of our lives.

Often after a retreat experience or a weekend in the wilderness, we come home compelled to keep that mountaintop experience as we walk through the monotony of the day. We vow to take time to smell the roses, to appreciate the sights, sounds, and colors of the world around us, only to be drawn into our old patterns and ruts and forget the communion, the intimacy, and the peace we shared with God.

There is something to be said for spending the weekend outdoors, especially in the country. The out-of-doors attracts not only backpackers and hikers—even poets—but also pray-ers. One of the greatest teachers of prayers seems to have preferred the outdoors for his own personal meditation. We read in the Gospels that Jesus went up to a hill to pray—Jesus went to a lonely place to pray. But Jesus also recommended praying indoors in complete privacy: "Go into your room and shut the door and pray to the Father who is in secret" (Matthew 6:6). Origen, one of the founding church Fathers in the second century, told his congregation: "Any place can be suitable for prayer. . . . But if we want to pray without being disturbed we would do well, if possible, to find a special place in our own home, a consecrated place, so to speak—and pray there."

It's not such a bad idea to have a special place to pray. A private place for prayer has several advantages. For example, one might want to pray lying down, or during the prayer feel moved to lift the arms to the sky. One might want to sigh, cry, or speak out loud. In a public place, any one of us might hesitate to do this. When talking with my best friend, I don't have much hesitation about doing anything or saying anything, unless I am in unfamiliar surroundings with people I don't know or in a public place. When the two of us are alone, I can suddenly break into song or do a two-step; I can play the drums on the kitchen table when a special song comes along—he wouldn't call me crazy or off the wall. More often than not he'd join in and we'd both end up laughing. That kind of freedom in talking and being with a friend is reserved for us in the kitchen, in walks in the woods, or driving down the beach wherever the two of us finally get together.

Doesn't the same principle apply when each of us talks to another very special friend, God? Is it so bad to have that private

July Twenty-sixth

place where we can cry, sigh, sing praises, or yell at the walls when we talk to God? I don't think so. Some of the most popular places for private prayer are the back of the church, your own bedroom, a little-used room in the home, or a secluded spot outdoors. The important thing about a prayer place is that it helps us to pray better. Picking the right place is one of the keys to effective prayer.

In the past years, my prayer place hasn't changed. It depends upon the intensity of my needs and feelings as to where I pray. When I am most desperate and hungering for communion with God, I sit on the steps of the altar; if it's not quite so pressing, but I still have a need for sanctuary, I sit near the back of the church; if I'm home, I find that place in the middle of my bed or kneeling beside it—somehow through the course of my Christian growth these are the places that are most significant to me.

Perhaps more important, or of equal importance, is not having a place to pray and converse with God, but having a specific time.

Ralph Martin, in his book *Hungry for God*, notes that the demands for modern living are such that if we don't have a schedule for prayer, we probably won't pray. Some people don't like scheduling prayer—it's not spontaneous. But think for a moment about the other important activities each of us makes time for—racquetball, eating, business meetings—we don't leave them to chance. They pass from the spontaneous and haphazard events to the scheduled and committed. Martin gives another example: If two people want to become more than mere acquaintances, they need to agree on definite times and places to get together. . . . Romantic ideas about spontaneity are just that, romantic and unrealistic.

But there is still room for spontaneity. Prayer will often surprise us by coming unexpectedly, just as a friend surprises us by showing up unexpectedly, or God, after all the power and strength subsides in the wind, earthquake, and fire, comes before Ezekiel in a still small voice. Unless there is a commitment to a fixed time, there is not likely to be much prayer. That seems to be the way we human beings are made.

Finding the right schedule for daily prayer takes experimentation and dedication. Getting a schedule, maybe even a special place that fits your personal life-style, may take months if you don't already have them, but it is worth the effort. Prayer is that important.

We are in the season of Pentecost. It is a time for spiritual growth and renewal on our parts as Christians—as believers in Jesus as the Christ and our Lord and Saviour. Prayer can be a significant part of that renewal, a very significant part of our own personal, individual relationships and growth of those relationships with God. It is like the seed—once planted, fed, and watered, it becomes rooted, and a very natural part of us.

I haven't mentioned anything about the form or language of prayer, for what and how you converse with God is between you two. The language should be as natural and free-flowing as talking to your best friend, and, unlike talking to my best friend, God's line is never busy.

So I invite you to take up this challenge of finding a time and a place to pray. *Amen.*

Linda C. Beattie
Longview, Washington

Sunday
August Second

Theme: Stay Calm

Call to Worship: Know this, my beloved brethren. Let every man be quick to hear, slow to speak, slow to anger, for the anger of man does not work the righteousness of God. *James 1:19-20*

Invocation: How do you stay calm when the whole world is collapsing around you? Relax on the Lord. He is always ready to enter our lives with his calming presence. Make me a calm Christian. *Amen.*

Hymn: "Lord Jesus, I Love Thee"

Sermon Presentation: "Believe in Yourself"

Goals for Today: Anger can be a constructive or a destructive force in our lives. Our Christian faith should make it always constructive.

This Week in History

August 6—Hiroshima Day—Memorial observances of the first atomic bomb dropped on a populated area, Hiroshima, Japan, August 6, 1945. A day for Christians to remember.

August 7—First picture of Earth from Space Anniversary—The first time man saw a real picture of this planet, not an artist's conception.

Announcement for Next Week's Sermon: Everybody wants something from me; now even God is making demands on me. Next Sunday: What does he want now?

Hymn: "Be Not Dismayed (God Will Take Care of You)"

Offertory Scripture: He who is slow to anger is better than the mighty, and he who rules his spirit than he who takes a city. *Proverbs 16:32*

Offertory Prayer: Lord, we show our love for you by our ability to be calm in the face of provocation. You taught us to turn the other cheek, to be slow to anger. Give us patience to do your will. *Amen.*

Prayer: Give us courage to believe in ourselves. It is the strength that comes from you that gives us self-assurance. Without you we are lost and floundering. With you by our sides we can believe. Give us patience to know your will in our lives. Without your will controlling us, we cannot believe. Grant us the grace to be humble when humility is proper; grant us the courage to be bold when boldness serves your will here on earth. We know our weaknesses; these frailties strip us of our belief in ourselves. Let your Holy Spirit come into our lives, seize control of our lives, and lead us to a faith that lets us say, "Not on my own, but by the grace of God and his presence in my life, I can believe in myself." Grant this unto us all. *Amen.*

Story of the Week: A six-year-old girl was helping her mother do the housework. "Where am I supposed to put this vase?" she asked her mother.

Her mother wanted to teach her to do some thinking of her own so she said, "I want you to pretend that I am not here . . . that I have gone shopping. In that case how would you decide where to put the vase?"

The little girl thought for a moment and then went into her father's den and said, "Daddy, where should I put this vase?"

BELIEVE IN YOURSELF!

Do you believe in yourself? I mean really and truly believe in yourself, to the point where there is no doubt at all in your heart that you are a worthwhile person, a person with special God-given gifts, a person who has a special potential for good to fulfill in this life.

Christianity has long preached the virtues of humility, self-denial, and self-sacrifice. Christianity has taught its followers to avoid like the plague all spiritual pride and self-satisfaction which lead to selfishness and a false, overblown regard for one's own importance. But in so doing, hasn't this emphasis often been overplayed, even to the point where Christians have sometimes been made to feel guilty if they do have a basic love and regard for themselves as persons?

August Second

Of course, it is important to avoid being puffed up with the deceit of self-pride. But isn't there also another side to this issue? Short of callous self-pride, isn't it also important that Christians feel good about themselves as persons?

Long ago, and even up into this century, it was the custom of many Christians to reject any feelings of self-worth. In reading the diaries of our own spiritual ancestors, the Puritans, one often notes a morbid tendency to wallow in feelings of utter worthlessness. A notable, but not uncommon, example of this can be found in the writings of Isaac Watts, the famed English hymnist of the early eighteenth century. You will recall that Watts created such beloved hymns as: "O God, Our Help in Ages Past" and "Jesus Shall Reign Wher'er the Sun."

> Time, like an ever rolling stream,
> Bears all its sons away;
> They fly forgotten as a dream
> Dies at the opening day.
> *"O God, Our Help in Ages Past"*

We can be fairly certain that Watts did not reach this self-deprecating assessment all by himself. Rather it was a prominent theme of the religious climate of his day. Taking the Christian teachings against self-pride to heart, many Christians have carried that denial of self to the extreme. I am reminded here of what Woodrow Wilson once wrote about our spiritual ancestors: "The Puritan was intensely human; but you must remember that he apologized to God as many as three times a day for that fact."

Fortunately in our modern day, we Christians are considerably more knowledgeable about human psychology than our spiritual forbears were. And with that knowledge has come the realization that selfishness and self-regard can and should be distinguished from one another. Whereas selfishness is still considered sinful, self-regard is seen as a basic, even essential, component of any human life which would be both spiritually healthy and morally wholesome. If in the past the great effort was to convince people of their utter worthlessness, today it is recognized that the real need of many people runs in exactly the opposite direction, for instead of loving themselves too much, they love themselves much too little.

Throughout the years of my ministry I have occasionally come into contact with individuals whose egotism is both immense and insufferable. In my own judgment such persons could well benefit from a stiff dose of Christian humility to bring them back in touch with their own humanness. But in my experience such thoroughly prideful persons are relatively rare, for by far the vast majority of people I have known are in a completely different category. The problems they experience in life come not from any overblown regard for themselves, but from not feeling worthy enough. At times their lives are plagued, not by overweening self-pride, but by nagging self-doubts and low self-esteem. For example:

—A woman who was an only child knows much frustration even in her adult years as she repeatedly tries to prove herself to her father, who really wanted a son instead of a daughter.
—A victim of a sagging economy, an unemployed man sits around his home feeling miserable. He is consumed by feelings of his own inadequacy as a bread winner. His enthusiasm and ability to seek a new job are paralyzed.
—A young girl falls in with the wrong crowd, adopting their defiant language and behavior, which eventually leads her into trouble with the police. Somewhere in the course of growing up she became convinced that she was not worthy of a better life, so she chose the path of rebellion and failure as the only one open to her.
—An older woman, recently widowed, sticks very close to her home. Her deceased husband was always the life of the party, so she now avoids old friends and the making of any new ones because of her fear that no one will like her just for herself without her husband.

Such examples may be obvious cases of low self-esteem and low self-image. But isn't it true that such negative, life-inhibiting feelings as these come in a wide variety of forms, many of them far too subtle to be readily recognized? An example is people who chronically over-indulge—whether it be in alcohol, in food, in athletics, in work, or in any other human activity. Although it comes from a very subtle motivation, in many cases isn't such excessive behavior a way of compensating

August Second

for some deep sense of personal inadequacy? Some people brag a great deal about themselves and are almost viciously competitive in their relationships with others. At first one might be inclined to think that such persons are genuinely filled with self-pride. But if we could look beneath the surface and understand them better, isn't it often the case that all their "bravado" is really a cover-up for a deep sense of unworthiness which they harbor within?

More than many of us might realize, feelings of low self-worth are both a serious and a widespread problem in our world. Most people suffer from such feelings at one time or another in their lives. And for many the effect of such negative feelings is devastating. Because of not loving themselves enough, their lives are distorted into patterns of overcompensation. Because of not loving themselves enough, their lives are stripped of enthusiasm and a vital sense of well-being. Because of not loving themselves enough, their lives are wastefully prevented from accomplishing the potential for good which is within them.

At times, in the name of combatting selfishness, Christians have tried to exploit the feelings of unworthiness which people have. Some "hellfire and brimstone" sermons are so harsh that they would make even a saint wince and tremble. But such total condemnation is not only bad psychology, it is also bad Christianity, for as Jesus, himself, seemed to recognize in this ministry, in order to be able to love other people we must first of all be able to love ourselves. If we don't respect ourselves, it is nearly impossible to have a proper respect for others. We shouldn't forget that when Jesus gave us the so-called "Golden Rule" of human relationships, he proposed it in a special way. As you will recall, he said, "You shall love your neighbor as yourself" (Matthew 19:19). I would call your attention to those last two words, *as yourself*.

From time to time I hear people enter into philosophical discussions, asking whether it is possible for a person to be totally selfless. Invariably in such a discussion, someone will insist that a good deed really becomes a selfish act if the person performing it derives even the slightest bit of pleasure or self-satisfaction from this act. This is both an untenable and an unrealistic position, for no matter how hard we might try we can never completely separate our own personal feelings from our acts. But even if such a separation were possible we should not desire it, for it is precisely out of our good feelings that our good deeds are both inspired and given value. It is the glad heart which can and will do the most to love others. Feeling good about helping another person does not make the deed a selfish one. What makes a deed selfish is doing it primarily to please ourselves and not to benefit the other person.

By way of analogy, consider the craftsman. Because the craftsman takes pride in his work there is no reason to discount the value of his work. In fact, we would much prefer the work of a craftsman, who took pride in his effort, to that of a laborer who did not have any such positive feelings. So it is with the Christian life; basic, positive feelings of self-pride and self-worth are essential to all the good we would hope to accomplish as Christians.

In the Gospels, Jesus certainly had his sharp moments when he upbraided certain Pharisees for their overblown pride. But let us not forget the major impetus of his ministry, for as the Gospels recount in story after story, Jesus came to save the lost, the downtrodden, and those who suffered from their own sense of unworthiness. You will recall Jesus' parable of the prodigal son (Luke 15:11-32). When the son finally returned home, deeply remorseful for his wasteful spree of loose-living, the father did not make his son bow and scrape in abject self-deprecation. Instead, he honored his son by killing the fatted calf for a banquet and outfitting his son with the best robe and a ring for his hand, which symbolized his full restoration to the family. The father consciously sought to restore the boy's self-esteem, and in so doing he effectively freed the boy to be both the son and the loving person that he could be.

You will recall Peter, who denied Jesus three times. In the aftermath of the crucifixion, Peter was crushed by his own sense of unworthiness. But as John's Gospel tells us, in a resurrection appearance Jesus came to Peter on the shores of Galilee (John 21). It was a poignant encounter which tore at Peter's heart. But the result was that Jesus restored Peter's faith in his own basic goodness as a person; thus, Peter was enabled to become an effective leader in the early Christian church. As you will recall, Paul, the great persecutor of Christians, had a similar experience on the road to Damascus, the result of which was

August Second

that he became the foremost Christian missionary to the Gentiles and the inspired Christian author whose letters make up a major part of our New Testament.

Just for the sake of argument, suppose Jesus had allowed Peter and Paul to wallow in their feelings of unworthiness. Would they have been any use at all to the Christian cause? I think not. But then this was characteristic of Jesus. Whether it was the fraudulent tax-collector Zacchaeus, the prostitute Mary Magdalene, or even the man who lay paralyzed by the pool for thirty-eight years, Jesus prompted these people to believe in themselves once again.

Buoyed up by his new self-confidence, the Apostle Paul exuberantly proclaimed to the Christians at Rome, "There is therefore now no condemnation for those who are in Christ Jesus . . . . For all who are led by the Spirit of God are sons of God. For you did not receive the spirit of slavery to fall back into fear, but you have received the spirit of sonship" (Romans 8:1, 14:15).

As Christians, it is essential that we believe in God. But along with that belief, there also comes another one which we should not ignore. Truly believing in God, we can and should believe in ourselves, for if we are so worthless as persons as we sometimes might think—

Would God have created us in his image?
Would God have sent us his son as a human being, flesh of our flesh?
Would God have allowed his son to suffer on the cross to atone for the sins of each and every one of us?
Would God have raised up his son on the third day to teach us that we also can be victorious over sin and death?

Of course, none of us is perfect. We have our individual flaws for which we should feel a deep sense of humility before God. But even this does not alter the basic truth that each and every one of us is a worthwhile person. We are infinitely precious to God, so we should also be precious to ourselves. At times, when feelings of unworthiness plague us, we may be inclined to forget it; nonetheless, the simple truth, bluntly stated is this: our God, our Creator, does not make junk! God has blessed each of us with certain gifts and abilities. And he has given to each of us a special potential for good to fulfill in this life.

The Christian gospel would have us believe in ourselves. Also it would have us believe in the essential worth of others. But here is the problem: in the midst of personal crisis, we tend to stop listening to this gospel. Too often we hear only the voice of our own misgivings or the voices of those who reject us. We measure our personal worth only by the circumstances of our lives, which often rise and fall as arbitrarily as the thermometer. Instead, we should be measuring our worth by the love and grace of our Creator who never relaxes his belief in us.

Feelings of low self-worth are both a serious and widespread problem in our world. But they needn't be if we would both realize our own value as persons and follow the example Jesus set for us—the example of building up the self-esteem of others. The Gospel message concerning human self-worth is powerful. But the magnitude of that power is increased manifold when we add to that message our own personal touch, such as Jesus did. In short, believe in yourself, but also believe in others. Look for those special God-given gifts which others possess. And when you find those gifts, affirm them openly. Clearly and often, tell others that you believe in them, and then watch to see what a difference those affirmations will make in their lives. As you and your neighbor discover the truth of self-worth, our whole world will become a better place in which to live. *Amen.*

Douglas K. Showalter
The First Church in Belfast
Belfast, Maine

Sunday
August Ninth

Theme: What Now, Lord?

Call to Worship: If thou, O Lord, shouldst mark iniquities, Lord, who could stand? But there is forgiveness with thee, that thou mayest be feared. *Psalm 130:3-4*

Invocation: Make us ready, Lord, to be equal to every demand or request that you make of us. Let us be willing to give of ourselves until we know that we are acceptable in your sight. Bless us as we work for thee. *Amen.*

Hymn: "Jesus, Savior, Pilot Me"

Sermon Presentation: "Meeting God's Demands"

Goals for Today: Life is not always easy, and neither is the Christian way of life. God expects us to live according to his rules. No *ands*, *ifs*, or *buts*; his way only.

This Week in History

August 13—Berlin Wall Anniversary—The East German government closed the border between East and West Berlin. Then came the wall, proof of Communism's greatest failure.

August 15—National Failure's Day—To honor the failure in the pursuit of all noble dreams, ideals, and impossible goals. We all need a day like this.

Announcement for Next Week's Sermon: What do I do now? It seems I ask myself that question a dozen times a day. The sermon next Sunday may offer us some answers.

Hymn: "A Charge to Keep I Have"

Offertory Scripture: Have mercy on me, O God, according to thy steadfast love; according to thy abundant mercy blot out my transgressions. Wash me thoroughly from my iniquity, and cleanse me from my sin. *Psalm 51:1-2*

Offertory Prayer: Lord, show us what you want us to do: to serve, to witness, to teach, to listen, or to give. Accept these gifts as our response to your demand. *Amen.*

Prayer: What do I owe you? Every day we ask this question of so many people, be it clerks in the store, the person pumping gas, the UPS delivery man, the youngster who delivers our newspaper each day. But, "What do I owe you?" is a question that we should be asking you, too, Lord. But too often we don't.

You, who have given to us the gift of life, the promise of the forgiveness of sins, and eternal life in our baptism, call on us to strive for perfection. By perfection, you mean that we should treat those around us and relate to them in the most godly manner possible.

We know that all of us have fallen short of your expectations and are in need of your forgiveness. It is only through your mercy and grace and the work of our Lord, Jesus Christ, that we are counted as righteous and are at peace with you.

In response to the privilege of being called your people, you would have us live out our calling by being responsible in our actions and our relationships. You call on us to be caring about those in any need, to be as concerned about our enemies as we are about our friends and to work toward reconciliation with those with whom we disagree. You even call on us to pray for those who would make our lives miserable and cause us pain. Help us to love the unlovely and the unloving.

Help us always to remember that in this, your world, it is people who are to be loved and the objects to be used, and let us never forget that we can never repay to you the debt we owe. *Amen.*

Story of the Week: The conductor of the community orchestra was almost out of his mind because at every rehearsal at least one member would be missing. At the last rehearsal, he called for attention and said, "I wish to thank publicly the first violinist for being the only member of the orchestra to attend every rehearsal."

"It seemed the least I could do," the violinist said humbly, "since I won't be at the concert tonight."

August Ninth

MEETING GOD'S DEMANDS

It would seem that anyone interested in any kind of relationship with God would also be interested in meeting God's expectations. Any relationship imposes demands upon the parties involved, and this seems to be the reason that many people try to avoid relationships with other persons; they fear the demands that may be placed upon them.

Many people, however, take the attitude that God's demands cannot be very great. A popular song a few years ago stated it: "Though it makes him sad to see the way we live, we always know he'll forgive." Or as another put it: "It's God's business to forgive." For such persons, the demands of God do not weigh very heavily.

On the opposite extreme is the Apostle Paul. For him, God's demands were so high that he could not possibly meet them. Paul came from a background of living under the Jewish law, which he tried to do perfectly. Paul was a Pharisee of Pharisees, trying very hard to meet every expectation of God. Out of his despair in trying to meet the law, he came to the concept of justification by grace through faith. Through the work of Jesus Christ, we are "counted as righteous," and have peace with God.

But those who heard Paul preach this countered with, "But what then? Are we to keep on sinning that grace might abound the more?"

"By no means!" Paul replied. "Sin must not be your master."

Still, the demand is there. We are not condemned by our failure to successfully keep the law in every detail; we are justified, counted righteous, through the work of Christ, but still we are to live as near as possible to the demands of God.

Where can we find help? Perhaps Jesus can give us the answer. What does Jesus say? "You must be perfect, just as your heavenly father is" (Matthew 5:48). Now that didn't help much at all! We are again driven to despair. How can any of us be perfect?

When ministers are about to be received into The United Methodist Church, they are asked a question which has been asked of Methodist ministers for over two hundred years: "Are you going on to perfection?" Now, that is a hard question. What does *going on to perfection* mean? It does not mean perfect in the sense of being faultless, "without defect or omission, flawless, completely correct or accurate" as the dictionary defines perfect. It is not the same as scoring 100 percent on a true-false test, or making a perfect copy of a piece of printed material. It is not the same as a corn plant which has received all the necessary moisture and plant food and has become a perfect corn plant. No one could be perfect in judgment, knowledge, or insight.

To be perfect is to share the nature of God. It has been called "perfection in love." If you want to be perfect, treat people the way God does. People are to be loved, treated with good will. This kind of love is more than emotion, for we can love people we don't personally like. "People are to be loved, and objects used." So often we love objects and use people. Love causes us to treat people responsibly, with good will. Nor does this mean that love is soft and sentimental; love can be firm when necessary. Jesus summarized God's expectations in his summary of the law: "You shall love the Lord your God with all your heart . . . soul . . . mind . . . . You shall love your neighbor as yourself" (Matthew 22:37-39).

All people are to be loved, treated with good will, for this is the way God does. God has no favorites! As Jesus says: "He make his sun rise on the evil and on the good and sends rain on the just and on the unjust" (Matthew 5:45). Sometimes during summer drought someone will say, "You're not paying the preacher enough." I hope no one thinks now that the preacher is getting paid too much! At any rate, Jesus tells us that God treats us all alike. God loves people no more because they are good, no less because they are wicked. A bad man and a good man out on the golf course have an equal chance of being struck by lightning if a sudden rain storm comes up. Pope John Paul II, the target of an assassination attempt, has traveled over the world preaching goodwill, peace, and nonviolence; yet, this has not spared him from experiencing violence himself.

This has been a difficult lesson for the human race to learn. In much of the Old Testament there is the concept that one is rewarded in accordance with one's behavior. One of the most forceful and dramatic challenges to this position is found in the book of Job. Job is suffering greatly and his friends come to comfort him. They tell him they are concerned about him and don't like to see him suffering the way he is. "Some sin has caused this," they say. "Repent of your sin and all will be well."

August Ninth

To this Job replies that he cannot believe that his sin has caused all the suffering to come upon him. Likewise, Jesus was confronted with the same thought. When he was asked if those upon whom a tower fell were worse sinners than others, or if a sick young man or his parents were guilty of sin, to each Jesus denied that sin was the cause of the trouble.

On the other side of the picture, a song in the play *Sound of Music* deals with the reward side. The song tells us that nothing comes from nothing, nothing ever could. So, somewhere in our pasts we must have done something good.

But, where's the justice in this? Why be good if you're not going to be rewarded for it? The best reward of all is the reward which is the natural outgrowth of the goodness itself. Tithing is sometimes practiced as a way of getting other benefits, but I think the best satisfaction comes from knowing you've done what you thought was right and the feeling of having invested in the Lord's work in the world.

Punishment, likewise, is not something added on to actions, but an inevitable result of those actions. Even though the wicked seem to prosper, our sins do find us out; wrong actions inevitably lead to bad consequences somewhere along the line.

But the most staggering thought is that God loves the good and the bad equally. To be perfect is to do the same, to treat people the way God does. Just being friendly to our friends and loving those who love us is not enough. Jesus called his followers to surpass the experts in goodness. "Unless your righteousness exceeds that of the scribes and Pharisees, you will never enter the kingdom of heaven" (Matthew 5:20). If we restrict our love to our friends, we are still novices; we have not yet begun the race. To surpass the scribes and Pharisees is to treat others as God does, treating all with goodwill. The farmer who doesn't go to church gets just the same weather as the one who does; we are to treat all with goodwill.

But how can we do it? It seems almost a mockery to ask it of us. It is impossible on our own. It can only happen through the grace of God. As Albert Outler puts it, in speaking of the church: "On balance, the church's record for relatively selfless service is at least a shade better than that of any other human institution I know. This, of course, is no matter of merit nor any ground for pride. It is the work of grace, turning human hearts from self-love to the love of God and neighbor." The command that Jesus gives to love God and our neighbor as ourselves is possible through grace.

It also helps for us to remember that we are all sinners. None of us has any claim upon God's love. None of us deserves any special blessing. But even though we are sinners, Christ died for us all. The graciousness of God is nowhere more tellingly revealed than in the parable of the prodigal father. No, I didn't make a mistake. The parable is more about a prodigal father than it is about a prodigal son. It is the story of a father who "foolishly" continues to love a son who has wished him dead, who has wasted everything in foolish living, and who then comes back home. Why, common sense would tell you not to give that kind of son anything more. Yet, here is a father who not only let him come home but also kills the fatted calf and has a party in his son's honor. What a prodigal father, a spendthrift with love! But, says Jesus, this is what God is like.

Meeting God's demands is possible as we share the nature of God, which is love. In this way we become the sons and daughters of God. Since "God is love," love becomes our nature also. We are reminded in I John that he who loves God loves his brother also.

If we are to meet God's demands, if we are to be perfect, we will learn to care about people, all people, good and bad alike, friends, strangers, enemies. To the extent that we can't feel this, we will know we are still "on the way" to perfection; we haven't arrived yet. As a teacher said, in asking this question of one class of entering ministers, "If you aren't going on to perfection, where are you going?" It isn't a question of having arrived, but of being on the right road.

God's demands are that we love one another. Jesus said: "This is my commandment, that you love one another." If you would be perfect, if you would meet God's demands, seek God's help, God's grace, God's strength to be able to practice love and goodwill toward others. *Amen.*

Richard A. Chrisman
First United Methodist Church
Mason City, Illinois

Sunday
August Sixteenth

Theme: What Will I Do?

Call to Worship: And this is the confidence which we have in him, that if we ask anything according to his will he hears us.
I John 5:14

Invocation: O God, we need you to direct our lives. This old world is so confusing. We just do not know what to do or which way to go. Lead us, direct us, give us confidence in your guidance. *Amen.*

Hymn: "Abide with Me"

Sermon Presentation: "On Knowing What to Do"

Goals for Today: With all the confusion in the world today, the church had better have an answer for us all. If it doesn't, all is hopeless. Let us have a very clear direction today.

This Week in History

August 19—National Aviation Day—Observed each year on the birthday of Orville Wright, who piloted the first self-powered flight in history, December 17, 1903.

August 22—Archibald M. Willard's Birthday—Best known for his painting *The Spirit of '76.* I bet you didn't know that, did you?

Announcement for Next Week's Sermon: Are you afraid to love? It's a gamble you could lose, and that hurts. Next Sunday, God knows how it hurts to lose in love.

Hymn: "I Am Thine, O Lord"

Offertory Scripture: Hence we can confidently say, "The Lord is my helper, I will not be afraid; what can man do to me?"
Hebrews 13:6

Offertory Prayer: Sometimes I feel like a child playing that game where they blindfold you and turn you around and around. You try to walk; you can't; you are lost. Take my hand; take my gift; be my guide, or I am lost. *Amen.*

Prayer: We're in a fish bowl, Lord. All of the world looks at us and wonders, "What are those Christians all about?" It is frightening sometimes when we realize that the way we speak, the manner in which we respond to the people around us, the way we act say more about you than all of the books ever written. We truly are your representatives in this your world. People hear your word and judge its truthfulness by our actions. But like Paul, we continue to do the things that we would not do while doing the things that we should not.

Forgive us when we go astray and lead others likewise. Return us to your path of righteousness and truth. Make us worthy of our calling to be your disciples. Keep us from compromising your teachings and our values and ethics. May we always seek your kingdom first. May our light shine before others, casting out darkness and showing others your way. Let us never intentionally do anything that would bring you anything other than praise and adoration in the eyes of the world's people.

Don't allow us to be imposters. May the words of my mouth, the actions of my body, and the thoughts of my mind be acceptable in your sight and well-pleasing to your will. *Amen.*

Story of the Week: The banker was telling a friend how he got started in the business.

"I was out of work," he said, "so to keep busy, I rented an empty store, painted the word 'Bank' on the window. The same day, a man came in and deposited $300. Next day, another fellow came in and put in $250. Well, sir, by the third day I'd got so much confidence in the venture that I put in $50 of my own money."

ON KNOWING WHAT TO DO

What does the Lord require of you, but to do justice, to love kindness, and to walk humbly with your God?

A lion, according to a fable, strutted through the forest asking all, "Who is the king of the jungle?" "You are, sir," said a little

August Sixteenth

mouse. "You are, sir," said an excited monkey. When the lion roared up to an elephant and asked, "Who is the king of the jungle?" the elephant simply wrapped his trunk around the lion, whirled him around his head, and crashed him to the ground fifty feet away. The lion, dizzy and dazed, hobbled to his feet and complained to the elephant, "You don't have to get sore just because you don't know the right answer."

Sometimes we do know what to do, but we are too busy with the lesser things of life.

Baroness Isak Dinesen, who lived on a lovely farm in the highlands of Nairobi, wrote a classic entitled *Out of Africa*. She told about her houseboy, named Kitau. After three months he asked her one day to give him a letter of recommendation to his old friend, Sheik Ali Ben Salim. She did not want Kitau to leave just when he had learned the routine of the house, so she said that she would raise his pay. He said he was not leaving to get more money, but that he had made up his mind that he would become either a Christian or a Muslim, only he did not know which yet. For this reason he had come to work for three months in the baroness' house, to see the ways and habits of Christians. From here he would go for three months to Sheik Ali in Mombassa to study the ways and habits of the Mohammedans. Then he would decide.

"My heavens," exclaimed the Baroness as she contemplated all of her obvious imperfections. "Why didn't you tell me?"

Can you put yourself in the Baroness' place for a moment? Suppose a stranger came into your house to live for three months. Would he or she conclude after three months with you that the life of a Christian is the best?

Do you remember the story that we call "The Rich Young Ruler" (Luke 18:18-25)? This young man came to Jesus and asked: "What shall I do to inherit eternal life?" Jesus said: "You know the commandments: Do not kill, Do not steal. . . ." The young man replied, "All these I have observed from my youth." Then Jesus hit him where it hurt—his pocketbook. "One thing you still lack. Sell all that you have and distribute to the poor . . . and come, follow me."

Jesus told him what to do. He really knew what he ought to do. But he wasn't willing to do it—not yet!

How often we know what we should do. But do we do it? Paul

said "The things that I should do, I don't, and the things that I shouldn't do, I do."

One of my favorite stories is one from colonial Connecticut. Maybe you know it. On May 19, 1780, in Hartford, at noon, a terrifying storm arose. The sky became dark as night. People became frightened. Believing it was the Judgment Day and that the world was coming to an end, some people ran here and there; others knelt down in the street to pray. The Connecticut House of Representatives was in session. The Speaker of the House, Colonel Davenport, stood up in the middle of the fear-filled chamber and said: "Gentlemen, I do not know whether this is the end of the world or not. If it is not, it would be a waste of time for us to quit our tasks. If it is Judgment Day, I, for one, want to be found doing my duty. Therefore, let candles be brought and let us be found continuing our tasks!"

The Bible tells us many things we are to do. Certainly as Christians, we are to witness, worship, wait, and work. When Psalm 96 tells us to sing a new song to the Lord, these should be part of our song, and part of what we are doing for Christ.

I ran across a bit of humor this week that will make you either laugh or cry. It seems a man was reading the paper one morning and said to his wife, "Hey, listen to this. The cashier down at the bank has absconded with $100,000. Not only that, he stole one of the bank's executive limousines, and then ran off with the bank president's wife."

"My, that's awful," said his wife. "I wonder who they will get to teach his Sunday school class next week?"

That's meant to be a joke, of course. But there is a bit of truth there. We live in an atmosphere of compromise, and in this society of moral ambiguity it is often difficult to tell just who is a true follower of Jesus Christ and who is not!

"Let your light so shine before men, that they may see your good works and give glory to your Father who is in heaven" (Matthew 5:16).

We read once again the story in Luke 24 of the two followers of Jesus on their walk to Emmaus. They were discouraged, just as you and I often are. Then Jesus joined them. He made sense for them of the events that had happened. It is only in Jesus that, even in bewildering times, we can learn what life means.

The story tells that these two, when they realized who it was that had been with them, knew immediately what to do. They

August Sixteenth

turned around and walked the seven miles back to Jerusalem, in the dark, that same night. They could not keep the good news to themselves; they had to share it. The Christian message is never fully ours until we share it with someone else. That is knowing what to do.

In a kindergarten class, it was time for art period. Young Paul drew a stagecoach. The teacher was encouraging: "That's well done, Paul, but I don't see any wheels. What holds up the stagecoach?" Explained Paul, "Bad men."

What holds up the kingdom of God? Not bad men or women, but folks like us who know what to do—witnessing, worshiping, waiting, and working!

In the year 1492 a German author produced a book entitled *The Nuremberg Chronicle*. It is a compendium of all the calamities that had befallen the human family up to that time. With a climax of dejection, the author invited the reader to use blank pages at the end of the book to record any further catastrophes that would occur before the not-too-distant end of the world.

The very next year there sailed into the harbor of Lisbon a battered little sailing ship. It had come through storms in the Atlantic. At the helm was a man whose story was too amazing to be true. He spoke, not about the end of the world, but about a new world of endless possibilities. Of course, you know his name—Christopher Columbus. Just when things looked their worst, something happened which changed despair to hope.

That's what Jesus' Resurrection did for the disciples and does for us.

We sometimes forget just how popular Jesus was when he first began his ministry. Remember his visit to the house of Simon Peter. Jesus healed Simon's mother-in-law. But notice what Mark tells us next: "That evening, at sundown, they brought to him all who were sick or possessed with demons. And the whole city was gathered together about the door" (Mark 1:32-33).

A little further on we read, "And in the morning, a great while before day, he rose and went out to a lonely place, and there he prayed. And Simon and those who were with him pursued him, and they found him and said to him, 'Every one is searching for you'" (1:35-37).

All men and women do seek Christ. They may not even know his name, and they might use symbols and terminology far different from what you or I would use. But they are searching for Christ. He is the way, the truth, the life. All persons, everywhere, need what Christ can offer.

We need to believe that life does make sense. On a December morning in 1944 somthing happened that almost affected the course of the Second World War. The Allied offensive, begun six months before, had rolled across Western Europe. Suddenly, on that December day, a major portion of the mighty army ground to a halt. A counter-offensive had been launched, and a great bulge in the battle lines became apparent. It was a critical day for the Allied forces. If the counter-offensive had succeeded, the end of the war might have been indefinitely delayed. The drive almost did succeed.

A few days before, German soldiers, dressed in American uniforms, together with American jeeps, had been parachuted behind American lines. These "soldiers from the sky" carried no weapons. Their mission was to drive over the roads on which reinforcing Allied armies might travel and change all the signs pointing to strategic towns and villages. Their task of turning the signposts to give wrong directions had deadly consequences. The defenders in the "Battle of the Bulge" called for help, but much of the needed help never arrived. Whole battalions were lost trying to find their ways across a countryside where the signposts were either down or wrong.

Of couse, the point is that we live in a time when many of life's signposts have been torn down—moral, ethical, and religious. An epitaph on the tombstone of a three-week-old child says it for all of us, regardless of our age:

> It is so soon that I am done for,
> I wonder what I was begun for.

The years pass so fast and many of us have no idea what we were begun for. Thus we turn to Jesus and we see in him what we were created to do—to be—sons and daughters of the Divine.

But sometimes, when we don't know what to do, we just lash out! You know that great philosopher of the comic strips, Charlie Brown. Lucy says to him, "Life is a mystery, Charlie Brown. Do you know the answer?" Charlie Brown answers, "Be kind. Don't smoke. Be prompt. Smile a lot. Eat sensibly. Avoid cavities, and mark your ballot carefully. Avoid too much sun.

August Sixteenth

Insure your belongings and try to keep the ball low. . . ." Before he can get out another platitude, Lucy interrupts: "Hold real still," she says, "because I am going to hit you a very sharp blow upon the nose." We can appreciate her frustration, can't we?

In the midst of daily life, with its ups and downs, its spring mildness and its winter blizzards, do we know what to do?

We need to ask God's forgiveness for our past failures. We need to pray for God's grace for today and tomorrow. And, yes, we need to ask God for a greater sensitivity to others.

In the fifth verse, and following, of Isaiah 58, the prophet asks what kind of action (or fasting, if you like) is pleasing to the Lord. The answer Isaiah gives us on behalf of God is to tell us that the only kind of fasting that God chooses is "to loose the bonds of wickedness"—apartheid in Africa—"let the oppressed go free"—Central American refugees seeking sanctuary in our country—"share your bread with the hungry"—food pantries—and "bring the homeless poor into your homes."

Or as Micah puts it:

> He has showed you, O man, what is good;
> and what does the Lord require of you
> But to do justice, and to love kindness,
> and to walk humbly with your God?

Amen.

Carl Armin Viehe
United Church of Christ
Buffalo, New York

Sunday
August Twenty-third

Theme: The Courage to Dare

Call to Worship: But by the grace of God I am what I am, and his grace toward me was not in vain. On the contrary, I worked harder than any of them, though it was not I, but the grace of God which is with me. *I Corinthians 15:10*

Invocation: Give us the sheer nerve to take chances. Let our faith and trust in you be so sure that the world may see us as gamblers, but we know, because of your grace, life is no gamble. *Amen.*

Hymn: "Make Me a Captive, Lord"

Sermon Presentation: "God's Gambling Grace"

Goals for Today: Life is a sure thing for those who love the Lord. Using the word *gambling* may be a strange way to describe an action of God, but people will understand what we are saying very well.

This Week in History

- August 23-29—Freedom of Enterprise Week—To focus attention on the contributions made to our way of life by the free enterprise system in this country.
- August 29—Beheading of St. John the Baptist—Honors the martyrdom of John, who was beheaded by King Herod about A.D. 29.

Announcement for Next Week's Sermon: Is religion always just? Next Sunday we try to find the fine balance between religion and justice.

Hymn: "Where Cross the Crowded Ways of Life"

Offertory Scripture: And from his fullness have we all received, grace upon grace. For the law was given through Moses; grace and truth came through Jesus Christ.
John 1:16-17

August Twenty-third

Offertory Prayer: Lord, it is a risky business living in this world. We are tempted on all sides to believe in ourselves instead of you. Teach us to give all that we have in full trust to you, starting now. Amen.

Prayer: Love, love, love—that's what it's all about. Love God—love your neighbor—smile, God loves you—love is all you need—love is in the air! Well, Lord, with all this talk about love, we wonder why there seems to be so much hatred and anger in our world. Nations continue to take up the sword against nations. Husbands and wives begin their relationships in love, but too often end up in the bitterness of divorce. Too often children who were born of their parents' love become victims of sexual or physical abuse. We speak often of love, but to be honest, too often we aren't really sure of what we speak. We confuse love with sex, a cheery smile, or a pat on the back.

It is only by turning to you that we can find the source of perfect love. You loved us as we were conceived in our mothers' wombs. In the waters of baptism, you pledged your unfailing love and forgiveness. In the bread and wine of communion, you restore that loving relationship that was begun in our baptism but broken by our sinfulness. You love us not only in this life, but also beyond the grave and to eternity.

Guide us as we seek to learn the manner and meaning of loving each other as God loves us. Strengthen our response to your love for us so that we can love you, not just as we are able, but as we move each day toward loving you as we ought. Encourage us to refine our love for you and for each other until we can follow your commandment to "Love the Lord your God with all your heart, all your mind, and all of your soul and love your neighbor as you love yourself." Focus our hearts, our minds, our eyes on the cross so that when we ask "if" or wonder "how much" God loves us we see in the cross the power, the depth, and the extent of God's love.

He who was sinless died so that we could be treated as righteous. He died so that we could live.

"Love, love, love, that's what it's all about!" Amen.

Story of the Week: The class had been told to write an essay on the care of the teeth. One essay was short and to the point:

Care of the Teeth:
1. See your dentist twice a year.
2. Brush your teeth after every meal.
3. Watch out for kids who push and shove at the drinking fountain.

GOD'S GAMBLING GRACE

To love is to risk! Loving is a risky business. It is a gamble. Some people have been so burned by love that they have lost their courage to ever, ever love again. Psychologically, emotionally, and socially they have been so hurt by a love relationship that they have turned bitter, so bitter that they are "burned out." They have been so intimidated, so smashed, that they are fearful of ever loving again. They don't love! They can't love! They avoid it like poison.

To really love takes courage. When Uncle Abraham heard that nephew Lot was in trouble, he equipped his men, went in pursuit of Lot's captors, and rescued Lot—instant courage powered by love. When God, their Father, saw that his people were in trouble (the poison from those snakes was as though their blood had turned to fire!), immediately through Moses, God prepared a way of healing, so that by looking at that brazen serpent the fire went out and they were healed—divine courage powered by divine love and grace.

Nicodemus, an old, super-religious Pharisee, and Jesus were visiting. It was a cool evening with a gentle breeze blowing. As a ruler of the Jews, Nicodemus was saturated with the history of his people—their grumblings in the wilderness, their rebellions against Moses, their rejections, even murders of God's prophets. All this sordid history was like a hot fire under his conscience so that, in essence, old Nicodemus was asking Jesus, "How can I be saved? With all the fiery guilt in my Jewish blood, how can I ever hope to enter the kingdom of God?" The gist of Jesus' answer was that flesh born to flesh has to become spirit born of spirit, a spiritual rebirth. In other words, a completely spiritual person.

Well, old Nicodemus, ignorant of spiritual things but a genius on religious matters, couldn't quite figure Jesus out. He

August Twenty-third

wondered how this could be. Jesus jabs him a little about being a teacher in Israel, yet not being able to understand heavenly things. He goes on to give him a very vital lesson! In John 3:14, Jesus says, "As Moses lifted up the serpent in the wilderness, so must the Son of man be lifted up, that whoever believes in him may have eternal life—may inherit the kingdom of God, to get back to Nicodemus' original phrase.

Now, that must have been a bundle for Nicodemus' mind to thresh out. He could understand about Moses and the serpent in the wilderness; his people had sinned. They had betrayed God and Moses and deserved to perish. The lifted-up serpent was God's gracious gamble to save them. This Nicodemus understood. But now Jesus was applying this gracious gambling act of God to himself, to the people now and in the New Testament! As Moses did it then, so God, through his Son, Jesus, is doing it now.

The Son of man would be stretched out like a nailed-down criminal. Yes, Jesus, too, would be lifted up for all people to look at and by their looking the fire of guilt in our veins, too, goes out. We are saved. We inherit the kingdom of God; we do not perish! This is what had old Nicodemus stumped. It is an act of pure, divine, gambling grace powered by love. Yes, God did take a dangerous gamble in his acting out of grace rather than of punishment and judgment. "For by grace you have been saved through faith; and this is not your own doing, it is the gift of God" (Ephesians 2:8).

In our credits and debits way of human thinking, we are like old Nicodemus. We cannot understand God's gracious gamble. How could God have let those guilty, grumbling Jews off by their looking at the bronze serpent? Why didn't he at least demand an initial change of attitude, or some evidence of it? Shouldn't he have required them to set their lives straight before they could be saved? But Jesus told Nicodemus instead that God did not send his Son into the world with the purpose of condemning it. No, but that the world might hopefully be saved through him—God's gracious gambling love!

Thank God that no, he is not really interested in the punishment or destruction of the sinner. His primary concern is that sinners be saved, that they not perish but have eternal life! Well then, if that is the purpose and object of God's gracious gamble, then his salvation is going to have to mean more to us than just his rescuing us from the mess and terror of our sins (like just healing the snake bite). It is going to have to mean a new life of fellowship with God. We must enter into a child-parent relationship with God, which he longs to have with all his children, so that we can become so motivated by God's daring, gambling love that we in turn love others with that same kind of love. If this is God's goal, could any other method have achieved it other than the one God chose? For the Jews in the wilderness, the threat of death by snake bite would be a powerful motivation for them to see their sin, confess it, and make some amends and reforms. God could have put them under an intense pressure, like our modern defense weapons, and really tightened down the screws so that he could bargain from strength. But for God to have done that any change or reform would have been purely fear and self-preservation motivated not by a love for God and for each other. Fear and a human desire to escape punishment do wonders for changing our outward behavior, but they cannot and do not change the inner motivations of the heart.

Therefore, that method would not have brought about the kind of salvation, the personal wholeness, that God wanted. So, there is no bargaining on God's part with his people. Instead he effected his gambling grace. That bronze serpent became a physical symbol of his forgiving love. And you can be sure there were those, many in fact, who interpreted God's grace as a license to continue grumbling, to keep on being ungrateful to God, and to be unloving to others. Yes, that fact, that possibility was a part of God's gambling grace, and still is today.

Some people did turn and repent. They became faithful believers of God's gracious act, and it is the same today. God's gambling grace, as we hear it described in John 3:16, "For God so loved . . . that he gave," still does not enjoy universal success. Far from it! There are many who hear of it and even see it, but few accept it. God is taking a dangerous gamble by acting with grace rather than with punishment and judgment. But the point of this lesson is that, although grace through faith may not always succeed, there is no other way than by faith through

August Twenty-third

Jesus Christ; thus, we must be saved. So God continues with his gambling grace. *Amen.*

Virgil R. Anderson
Wallingford Lutheran Church
Wallingford, Iowa

Sunday
August Thirtieth

Theme: Justice for All

Call to Worship: He saved us, not because of deeds done by us in righteousness, but in virtue of his own mercy, by the washing of regeneration and renewal in the Holy Spirit.   *Titus 3:5*

Invocation: Lord, call us to be just to all people. We find it so easy to make excuses for injustice when we see it. It is so comfortable to just let things be the way they always have been. Shake us up. Make us angry every time we see injustice so that we cannot rest until justice is done to all people. Do not let us settle for burnt offerings when action is needed. Make us fearless in fighting the good fight for you here in this place. Amen.

Hymn: "God of Our Fathers"

Sermon Presentation: "Religion and Justice"

Goals for Today: We want our people to look out with pride at this great world that God has created. We want them to realize that they have a responsibility to be God's strong right hand. To smite injustice wherever it appears, here in this church, in this town, in the state or nation. Injustice to my brother is an injustice to me for I am diminished if he is not free. Let this church be an Amos to this community, in a call for justice for all.

This Week in History

September 1—Korean Air Lines Flight 007 Disaster Anniversary—Shot down by a Soviet interceptor plane killing 269 people in 1983. Excessive national pride and national fear are two deadly sins that can do great harm to the peace of the world.

September 5—Anniversary of First Continental Congress Assembly—This meeting in Philadelphia in 1776 led to the Declaration of Independence and the birth of this nation.

August Thirtieth

Announcement for Next Week's Sermon: Sure I am a Christian, but what difference does that really make in my life? Next Sunday you can find a real meaning for your life.

Hymn: "God the Omnipotent"

Offertory Scripture: Do not lay up for yourselves treasures on earth, where moth and rust consume and where thieves break in and steal. *Matthew 6:19*

Offertory Prayer: For religion and justice, Lord, we thank you. We know that if there is justice, it is a gift from you. If there is salvation it is a gift from you. We cannot earn our salvation, but we can fight for justice. May this be our way of saying thank you for your many blessings and gifts to us. *Amen.*

Prayer: Lord, we know what creates injustice. It is the misuse of power. It is greed on the part of a few at the expense of many. It is my personal fear that I must build up treasures so that I will have a future without want. It is the worship of false gods, money, property, power, and possessions. Lord, we are always planning to build a new barn to store our goods; we know this is foolish but we do it anyway. Help us to heed Amos' call to fight injustice so that we may still be saved and we may not hear in the midst of our striving for possessions, "Today your soul is required of you."

Give us time to catch the vision. Give us courage to strike at injustice wherever it may be and that we refuse to give up until the victory is won. God demands justice from us all and for us all. He will accept nothing less. There is no true religion without true justice. Only with your help can I become a fearless fighter for justice. Be with us today; let this day be the beginning of a new awareness that we are all free or no one of us is free. Help us to reach out in your holy name and for your sake. *Amen.*

Story of the Week: The little girl had been told about democracy and elections and voting. When her mother went to the polls she took the little girl along. As the little girl watched her mother mark her ballot she said: "Do you always vote for the man you love the most?"

"What makes you think that?" her mother asked.

"Because I saw you put a kiss by his name," the little girl said.

Minister's Annual

RELIGION AND JUSTICE

Not long ago in Detroit a storefront church met for Sunday worship. The minister believed that people should take part in worship. At the conclusion of his sermon he asked if anyone in the congregation had anything to say. No one responded.

The pastor noticed two young men who had come to church late that morning. "Maybe these two young men have something to say," the minister said encouragingly. One of the young men shook his head. The other stood up, indicating he had something to say. He announced, "This is a stick-up!" and he pulled out a gun.

The two visitors then cleaned out seventy dollars from the collection plate and ten more from the pastor's wallet. The two then left without waiting for the benediction.

Perhaps some of you may be speculating now as to just what that little story illustrates. Certainly the church should be no place for a holdup! It goes without saying that we expect from worshipers a level of conduct that fits the occasion. We look for a certain consistency between religious acts and the ones performing those acts.

Now, of course, we learn that from the Bible. Jesus, for example, made that very clear. How often we have heard his words from the Sermon on the Mount: "If you are offering your gift at the altar, and there remember that your brother has something against you, leave your gift there before the altar and go; first be reconciled to your brother, and then come and offer your gift" (Matthew 5:22-24).

Long before Christ, however, people had begun to be concerned about the connection between worship and everyday life. Among the Lord's ancestors religion took time to grow and to develop. The Israelites did not come to their faith in one step. Their beliefs and practices developed and grew. Many obstacles had to be overcome. Religion involved trial and error.

This explains a good deal of what we read in the Old Testament. We may be puzzled by what we find, for example, in the prophets. It may distress us that the prophets seemed so critical of their own brethren. Scripture portrays the Israelites as God's Chosen People; he called them to be his own special nation. Out of all the human family the Creator selected Israel to represent him on earth. The Almighty guided and supported

August Thirtieth

the Israelites. He rescued them out of slavery. He led them through the wilderness. He brought them to the Promised Land.

Yet, in all the accounts we have, the Chosen People never seemed to satisfy their God. Their history makes up most of the Old Testament. That record never moves along smoothly. Israel does not present an unblemished reputation; for every success there seemed to be at least one failure. The leaders of the nation had a hard time satisfying heaven. Every step forward led to at least one step backward.

Take David as an illustration. A humble shepherd boy rose to be his people's king—David's career almost follows the rags-to-riches scenario. To this day the Jews honor no greater hero. David remains the model for every Israelite.

Yet, the Old Testament does not hide from us the truth about this great leader. He did not go to his grave a paragon of perfection, or, as the French say, the crème de la crème. We see David not only in the glory of goodness, but also in the depths of failure, fault, and folly.

And so for Israel as a whole. A prophet had blown the whistle on King David. A whole company of prophets called the nation to account. The first to do so was Amos. Amos bore down on God's people because of the inconsistency between their worship and their attitude toward their neighbors.

To understand Amos we must remember some history. Eight hundred years before Christ, Israel experienced unusually good times. The country knew peace and prosperity unheard of since the days of Solomon. Invasions by the Assyrian Empire had reached an end. The long war with Syria concluded in victory for Israel. The Israelites had enlarged their boundaries as never before. Everyone enjoyed an era of luxury, trade had increased, and money was plentiful. Few better examples of successful free enterprise can be found in ancient times.

I said that everyone enjoyed an era of luxury. That statement, however, stretches the truth. Most of the plentiful cash found its way into the pockets of only a few. As a consequence, poverty rubbed shoulders with affluence.

The Bible recognizes poverty as a plain fact of the human condition. Jesus, himself, declared that "you always have the poor with you." Scripture, therefore, reminds us continually of the obligation of those who have to those who do not have. But poverty inevitably seems to involve injustice. Wherever wealth exists, it represents power. Power always fills the vacuum of weakness and want to the detriment of the needy.

Amos saw this in Israel eight hundred years before Christ. He witnessed the well-to-do trampling upon the poor. For example, he observed merchants cheating the people when they came to buy food. Sellers measured out grain in undersized bushels. The buyers paid for their purchases by the weight of their silver. The dealers used oversized weights in their scales. Therefore, common people paid more and got less in such dishonest dealings.

The exploitation of the underprivileged not only implicated merchants. In order to buy life's necessities the poor sank deeper and deeper in debt. Their creditors then foreclosed, often for trifling amounts. Amos referred to this when he declared "They sell the righteous for silver, and the needy for a pair of shoes!" (Amos 2:6). He meant that creditors sold human beings into slavery. The rich showed callous disregard for the bitter hardships forced upon simple folk by the greed of the well-to-do.

No one has ever been able to show that Amos overstated the conditions. Centuries of research have confirmed his charges. But Amos and other prophets saw a day of reckoning ahead. They warned that Israel would be punished for her injustice and wrongdoing.

And, indeed, the Old Testament leaves us little choice but to see that judgment taking shape in the Exile. The proud, prosperous land of Israel went down before her invaders. Outsiders destroyed the nation. The enemy marched most of the population into captivity. By the waters of Babylon the Jews sat down and wept as they remembered their homeland.

But these grim details of history may lead us away from our point. The word of the Lord came to Amos, and Amos uttered it to his fellow Jews. God told Israel,

> I hate, I despise your feasts, and I take no delight in your solemn assemblies. Even though you offer me your burnt offerings and cereal offerings, I will not accept them, and the peace offerings of your fatted beasts I will not look upon. Take away from me the noise of your sons; to the melody of your harps I will not listen. But let justice roll down like waters, and righteousness like an ever-flowing stream. (Amos 5:21-24)

August Thirtieth

These words from the Almighty indicate he had a grievance other than Israel's injustice; God had a complaint about Israel's religion.

In mid-eighth-century Palestine people at least went to temple. In America today the best "guestimates" put churchgoing somewhere around only 40 percent of the entire population. We have no comparable figures for temple-going in Israel 2,800 years ago.

The Old Testament gives us the impression, nevertheless, that Israelites visited the shrines in great numbers. They offered sacrifices freely. They paid tithes even more frequently than the law commanded. Worship involved much music by both voices and instruments. The people scrupulously kept the holy days. All in all, they seemed to be religious.

It amazes us, then, that Amos lashed out against such piety. One would think a man of God would be grateful for such a display of devotion. But the prophet understood worship not as an end in itself, but only as a means to an end. People entered the Lord's gates with thanksgiving, they came into his courts with praise. That act one performs not for the sake of a reward; faithful souls go to public prayer because they simply love their Creator. One has no other way of showing gratitude for his love toward them and for all their fellowmen.

This God to whom they gave burnt offerings and peace offerings, to whom they sang anthems and played harps, however, wanted far more than ceremonies and ritual. Men must publicly witness to their faith. God desires his children to assemble to pray and to hear his Word. But his worship must be offered him with a clean heart and a new and right spirit.

The psalmist asked, "O Lord, who shall sojourn in thy tent? Who shall dwell on thy holy hill?" (15:1). And then the psalmist answers his own questions of what God expects. The worshiper must be an individual who loves and honors his neighbor. Jesus emphasized the love of neighbor as being just as important as one's love for God. We recall the story Christ told of two citizens who went to the Temple to pray. The visit of one accomplished nothing because he lacked humility. It impresses us that along with his pride the Pharisee lacked compassion for his fellow-worshiper.

Someone has put it this way: "Sin is not a failure to worship in the right way; it is a failure to do what is right in daily living"—namely, showing unfailing justice in one's dealings with his fellow-man.

We Americans ought to remember the Preamble to our great Constitution. There it lists justice before it says anything about the blessings of liberty. The Declaration of Independence states that all men are born equal. Yet, good American Christians once used the Bible to justify human slavery. Can we complain about becoming upset when we read the writing of ancient prophets?

If the Bible ended with the book of Amos, we would have reason to despair. But the Bible does not conclude with Amos or even the Old Testament. God spoke to and through Amos and the other prophets. Those spokesmen only paved the way for God himself to come to earth. Incarnate in Jesus of Nazareth, the Almighty lived, taught, and in the end died for justice. You and I have come here today to witness to all the world that we believe in a God who wills right relationships among his human children. May we never be found unfaithful to that divine will. *Amen.*

Charles W. Kern
Grace United Methodist Church
Haverhill, Massachusetts

Sunday
September Sixth

Theme: Looking for Meaning

Call to Worship: My son, do not despise the Lord's discipline or be weary of his reproof, for the Lord reproves him whom he loves, as a father the son in whom he delights.
Proverbs 3:11-12

Invocation: Lord, I can take the good and the bad. You don't have to give me all good days. The cloudy days help me appreciate the bright days all the more. Just stay with me and give meaning to my life. *Amen.*

Hymn: "Be Not Dismayed"

Sermon Presentation: "What Is the Meaning of Life?"

Goals for Today: We are all experts at living our lives. Today we should find some help in finding some meaning in our lives.

This Week in History

September 7—National Neighborhood Day—To recognize the neighborhood as a vital national asset.

September 8—International Literacy Day—Sponsored by the United Nations to encourage literacy around the world.

Announcement for Next Week's Sermon: There is more to life than possessions. You may want to take it with you, but you can't. Let's face it next Sunday.

Hymn: "If Thou But Suffer God to Guide Thee"

Offertory Scripture: He said to me, "My grace is sufficient for you, for my power is made perfect in weakness." I will all the more gladly boast of my weakness, that the power of Christ may rest upon me. *II Corinthians 12:9*

Offertory Prayer: Lord, show me a better way. My life has meaning when it is in touch with you. Take these my gifts as an offering of thanks for your showing me your way. *Amen.*

Prayer: There are so many wasted lives that just drift aimlessly with no direction. Not me, Lord, not me. You have shown us the way through the example of your son. We do not have to search for meaning in our lives; all we have to do is follow your example. To love the unlovely; to serve and feed the poor; to be a friend to the friendless; to visit the lonely; to be servants to all mankind—all we have to do is know where we came from and where we are going—that gives us direction and meaning to our lives. Make us sure of our faith because we have tested our faith. We have called on you and you have never failed. That's it, Lord. It is just that simple. You own me; I am a child of God. That is all the meaning my life wil ever need. Be my father; be my guide for ever and ever. *Amen.*

Story of the Week: Because of a snowstorm, a little boy missed school for a week. When he did show up for school, his teacher said he would have to bring a written excuse saying why he had been absent.

His mother was irked at the teacher and wrote this note: "Dear teacher: Our little boy's legs are 20 inches long and the snow was 30 inches deep. Now you know why he didn't get to school last week."

WHAT IS THE MEANING OF LIFE?

I decided to do some research on a few of my friends. When I telephoned them I said, "I'd like to ask you a question, if you don't mind."

"Sure, Pastor, what would you like to ask?"

"What is the meaning of life?" I asked in return. Then I was quiet and listened.

There was a long pause on the other end of the line. Then I heard giggling and laughing and before very long gasping for breath. They were so carried away by my question that they couldn't carry on a conversation. Try that with some of your friends. Call them up and ask in a serious way, "What is the

September Sixth

meaning of life?" You will be surprised at the kind of response you get.

Some years ago an advertising slogan said, "Ask us." If you wanted to ask directions, you could stop at a gas station and ask for directions. A popular magazine had a cartoon that showed a driver asking a station attendant, "What is the meaning of life?" All of us have laughed at jokes having to do with gurus on mountaintops giving absurd answers to the question, "What is the meaning of life?" You may have seen a T-shirt which says, "You live awhile and then you die." There's another slogan which says, "Life is a game in which, when you die, the one with the most toys wins."

What does your T-shirt say? What do you believe is the meaning of life?

Christians do not believe that question is either laughable or incredible. They know what the meaning of life is, not because they have rationally and intellectually figured it out, but because it has been revealed to them in the life, death, and resurrection of Jesus Christ. If they want to know about life, they know they can look to the example and the illustration that is Jesus.

John 13:3-4 is a tremendously insightful passage that tells us clearly and concisely the Christian answer to the question, *What is the meaning of life?* "Jesus, knowing that the Father had given all things into his hands, and that he had come from God and was going to God, rose from supper, laid aside his garments and girded himself with a towel."

It's appropriate that this text, which talks about the meaning of life, begins with the word *Jesus* because for Christians, Jesus is the standard. Jesus, Christians believe, is the revelation of God. But he's not just the revelation of God. He is also a revelation of the meaning of human existence. For Christians, Jesus is the standard. It is important to have a standard. In Washington, D.C., there's a building called the Bureau of Standards. If you were to go into that building, you would actually find there a piece of metal that is a measure of a pound. Another standard measures a pint, one measures a quart, and one measures a ton. There are other measuring standards for an inch and a yard. Jesus is our standard! We also have a thing such as standard time. But did you know that until 1887 there was no standard time? There was only local time.

One town might decide that it's four o'clock now, and the town right next door would decide that it was 10:30. There was only local time, and it didn't seem to make much difference until the invention of the continental railroad and the requirement for schedules. When the railroad started operating around all the local times it was chaos. So, a man by the name of Peter Fleming, who worked for the Canadian Pacific Railroad, invented standard time. He used as a base Greenwich, England. You've all heard the term "Greenwich mean time." In 1886 the leaders of sixty-six nations came together and agreed that in July of 1887 they would all begin to use standard time. And that's when it began.

Jesus is our standard of time. All of history has been measured—B.C. and A.D.—around his birth. Jesus is our standard of values, our standard of time, our standard of life, of what it means to be a human being. So our text begins with the word *Jesus*.

The verse goes on to say, "Jesus, knowing that the father had put all things into his hands . . ." It doesn't say, "Jesus, guessing," or "Jesus, believing," or "Jesus, hoping." It says that "Jesus, *knowing* that the Father had done a particular thing." Do you know anybody who knows about the reality of God? This text is suggesting that Jesus knew. He didn't just guess, or believe, or hope, or think. He knew about the reality of his heavenly Father. God was a reality to him; he knew about his presence and power just as much as he knew that he was talking to a friend or eating a meal. Do you know people who have such faith, such an intimate relationship with God, that they know about God? God isn't something about which they guess, or believe or think, or hope. They know God. Do you know people like that? Carl Jung, the psychiatrist, said that he knew. He didn't believe—he *knew*. This passage tells us that Jesus knows; it is telling us not only about Jesus but about you and me, that it is possible for you and me to know God. This passage is talking about our lives. It's revealing the nature of human existence, that we can know God. The passage says, *Jesus, knowing*.

What did he know? "Knowing that the Father had put all things into his hands." Jesus had the world in his hands. You know that old song, "He's Got the Whole World in His Hands." We believe that, don't we? That finally God is the Lord of life, of

September Sixth

all being. But this passage is also telling us about our lives, that God has put all things into our hands. God has made us responsible for his world, not only for the natural world, but also for our fellow human beings. God is there helping us, guiding us, and finally he will be there to decide. But he's given us real freedom now. He has put all things, this world, into our hands. We are responsible. If we want a world of peace, we have to work for peace. If we want a world of justice, we have to work for justice. If we want to live in a loving, caring family, we have to work and accept responsibility for creating that kind of family or that kind of church. God said that we are responsible. "Jesus, knowing that the Father had put all things into his hands . . ."

Then the text goes on to say, "And knowing . . . that he had come from God and was going to God." That is also an illustration of our identities. It is not just of Jesus. But what it means to be a human being is to be someone who has come from God and whose destiny is to return to God. We don't live in a vacuum. We didn't suddenly appear out of nothing. We come from God. "Jesus, knowing that the Father had put all things into his hands, that he had come from God and was going to God." What a context!

You want to know what is the meaning of life? The meaning of life is that you are one of God's children. You were sprung from the womb of God. God has put all things in this world in your hands. When your life is over, when this is all done, then you return to be with God once again. God is the source of your life and the destiny of your pilgrimage.

"Jesus, knowing that the Father had put all things into his hands, that he had come from God and was going to God, rose from supper, laid aside his garments and girded himself with a towel." In this context, he accepted the role of being a servant. You remember that it was then that he began to wash the feet of his disciples. He was a servant who was radically committed to charity, radically committed to serving and loving the world, because he knew that the Father had put it all in his hands, that he was responsible for creating a world of compassion, care, love, and sensitivity.

An important passage is that which says he "laid aside his garments." Our garments are symbols of the way in which we try to hide from our fellow human beings. Our garments are the ways in which we assume all the pretentiousness of human society. We say, "Clothes make the man." Women know about clothes, too, don't they? I've always wanted to have an expensive suit. Do you know an expensive suit in the world of clothing is like a Rolls Royce? You may not realize how our statures in the world rise when we wear expensive clothes. How difficult it is not to take that seriously. But isn't it true that when we wear uniforms we also proclaim to the world who we are, how important we are, and how the world needs to take us seriously? We wear military uniforms and the insignia are all there with the ribbons and all the rest telling everyone how important we are. The police are the same way. Those who work downtown, those who work anywhere, wear their uniforms. Someone might say to me, "Who are you?" and I'll open up my coat and say, "Read my label. That's who I am!" Our cars are another way in which we clothe ourselves. Or our homes. All these are pretentions that separate us and establish our stature and our status before other people.

Jesus took off his expensive suit. He girded himself with a towel. It's an invitation for you and me to be servants of Christ. It's an invitation for us to go to our fellow human beings and to be simple, ordinary, mortal, human beings, to be vulnerable, filled with pain, insecurities, and limitations as well as all kinds of gifts and strengths and powers just the way we are. We must humble ourselves in order to be a friend, in order to be a servant. That's the meaning of life—freedom to be a servant.

It's also the meaning of the Christian church. The purpose of the church is to increase in the love of God and neighbor in Jesus Christ through sharing, caring, outreach and worship. It's a reflection of our understanding of the purpose and the meaning of human existence.

What's the meaning of life? Here it is, my friends—"Jesus, knowing that the Father had put all things into his hands, that he had come from God and was going to God, rose from supper, laid aside his garments, and girded himself with a towel." Amen.

James L. Kidd
Asylum Hill Congregational Church
Hartford, Connecticut

Sunday
September Thirteenth

Theme: You Can't Do It

Call to Worship: Let us consider how to stir up one another to love and good works. *Hebrews 10:24*

Invocation: Lord, sometimes it just does not seem fair that good works do not count for more. Why is it always tied to faith or love—so we do not become too proud of our works and neglect faith and love? That's it, isn't it, Lord? *Amen.*

Hymn: "Faith of Our Fathers"

Sermon Presentation: "You Want to Take It with You?"

Goals for Today: To help people to understand the fine balance between faith and works. You can't have one without the other.

This Week in History

September 13-19—National Singles Week—To promote a positive image of being single. The church needs to find the role for the single persons in what is usually a family-oriented setting.

September 17—Citizenship Day—To appreciate the value of citizenship in this great land of ours.

Announcement for Next Week's Sermon: Someone is always trying to take advantage of us. Jesus did, too, but for our own good. Next Sunday, the secret.

Hymn: "Are Ye Able"

Offertory Scripture: [The purpose of scripture is] that the man of God may be complete, equipped for every good work.
II Timothy 3:17

Offertory Prayer: Lord, I know I can't take it with me; I just have it to use while I am here. Let me use it wisely. Let me share it with you and all people. *Amen.*

Prayer: I never really, I mean really, thought about it that much, O Lord. Everytime we say the Creed, we confess that we believe in the Resurrection. On Easter Sunday we celebrate the fact that you rose from the tomb. I know that someday I'm going to experience the Resurrection thanks to you. But I've never given it a whole lot of thought. It's like death; I know it will happen someday, but I don't want to dwell on it too much. Perhaps it's because it's such a hard thing to comprehend. It's beyond my imagination. Death will certainly rob me of the loving relationships I have with my family and friends. I won't be able to cheer the home team on. I won't be able to enjoy the freshness of spring, the purity of a new snow, the soothing sensation of a cold drink on a hot day, my child's hug, or the joy of a good putt.

I know you'll forgive me, Lord, for prizing these things so highly, but these are the things that I know about—the things that mean a great deal to me right now. It's difficult to imagine seeing you face to face. It's difficult to imagine meeting all those saints in heaven. It's even more difficult to imagine, to experience your forgiveness and to never sin again—ever.

It's difficult to imagine a healing that will mean I will never be sick again. I can't wait for the day when the broken will be made whole again, when hatred will cease and love will abound, when war's final victim will have found eternal life, and peace will become a way of life forever.

I look forward to the day when life will be good—no, better than good—great—greater than I could ever imagine. *Amen.*

Story of the Week: "All right," said the manager of the store, "I'll hire you. Here, take this broom and sweep up."

"But I'm a college graduate," the young man said.

"That's all right," the store manager said, "I'll show you how."

YOU WANT TO TAKE IT WITH YOU?

The question of whether there is life after death is not dead! Not only does it offer grist for college student midnight discussions (the sexist term is "bull sessions!"), but it also has intrigued folks who are bored with the topic as they've heard of the out-of-body experiences of persons pronounced clinically dead being brought back to life. Somewhere along the way, most of us realize the question—and its answer—makes a difference because we are going to die. We realize that we have a personal stake in the truth, in what really happens.

We haven't been the first to ask this question. A religious group of Jews, called the Saducees, presented Jesus with a dilemma they thought disproved resurrection; it was a kind of logical impossibility for resurrection. If a Jewish man died leaving behind a wife, it was his living brother's duty to take this woman as his wife—and then for her to bear children by this second husband, naming the first one after the dead brother, so that the name of the dead brother might live on in this child. Immortality was achieved through family which lived on after one had died. Now the problem presented to Jesus by the Saducees was more a riddle, perhaps, than a real-life situation: what if a woman ended up being married to seven brothers because they each, in turn, died before any children were born? Whose wife will she be in the afterlife? To the Saducees, the answer was ridiculous enough, they supposed, that along with it resurrection itself was ridiculous!

Now it seems that Jesus might have proposed a logical solution. How might it have been if, when raised from the dead, each of these men might have been able to spend one day a week with her as wife? A few frequently married celebrities of our time might resonate with that one! Or how about the solution of Brigham Young, the nineteenth-century Morman leader, who found polygamy quite acceptable, and whose followers today still claim that everyone is married for eternity? Surely Jesus, too, could have found a logical solution which would have satisfied everyone! Surely he could have negotiated, for instance, a shared-time agreement whereby everyone would have been reasonably happy! But he doesn't! And there's the key!

Resurrection is radical! It means a real change! It doesn't mean just "more of the same"! So, in the resurrection, people don't struggle with the self-centered, logical question of "How can she be his wife—and mine, too?" But instead, as Jesus says, "All live to God!" There's no longer marrying and being given in marriage, no longer fights for property and custody, no longer stigmas connected with being divorced or married or single, but there's a new way of living in which the focus of life is God! No longer will we be caught up shouting out the devil's three favorite words, "Me, Myself, and I!" No longer will there exist that snarling spirit of "What's mine is mine and what's yours is, too!" Instead, there will exist a new community where we all exist for the praise of God! If you recall that in Jesus' day, wives were ordinarily regarded as the property of their husbands—in other words, wives existed for their husbands—you'll glimpse how radical Jesus is! He is saying: In the new life, in the resurrection, nobody owns anybody; we all are alive for the sake of God!

As I hear the words of Luke 20:27-28, two points are made powerfully through the words of Jesus: First, that there is without doubt a resurrection of the dead; and second, that this resurrection will not be simply more of the same from this life.

Of course, if resurrection is simply more of the same, who wants it! I don't—and I suspect you don't either. Yet, we are a strange people, as I am reminded of a line from a little book I have. It says that millions of people long for immortality who do not know what to do with themselves on a rainy Sunday afternoon. Oh, yes indeed! If that's what resurrection means, may the Lord not be so cruel! Then there's that old cliché we're so good at using but probably not so effective in believing, "You can't take it with you!" Of course, you can't take your house or your new car, your cash or your American Express Card, but maybe that's not so bad. Maybe what is good and hopeful about the resurrection is that we don't simply get raised in the next life with all the attachments of this life, for that would mean, then, that what goes with us includes not only that house but the fights that we thought we'd forgotten, not only the cash we've accumulated, but also the people who've gotten hurt because we thought that was so important! So the question really becomes, "But do you want to take it with you?" Honesty compels us to say, "Some things, yes—and some things, no!" And the truth is we do not decide what goes with us!

And there is the Good News! God decides! How many parents have thought their kids, most of all, wanted things—new things, more things—only to find out too late that these kids didn't want things, but them, their love, their time, their attention! That's why it's good that God decides what we "take

September Thirteenth

with us," so to speak. We are poor judges. We'd simply get more of the same in the next life, too! God decides—and in his mercy, he's already given us a hint of what it will be. That hint is the Resurrection of Jesus. Look to Jesus' life for a glimpse into the future, for God raised Jesus—and with his Resurrection, speaks a resounding "Yes!" to all the loves and longings that were part of his life! What we take with us, then, are the loves and longings that are Christly, the parts of us that loved the neighbor and praised our God. What we will look like then, I don't know! I suspect there shall be lots of surprises, both for ourselves and for one another. Resurrection is radical! Thank God it's radical! Thank God we don't take everything with us!

Once, so goes the story, someone asked the American evangelist Dwight Moody if we would know each other in the after life. "Of course," came Moody's answer, "we won't be the fools we were in this life." So it shall be, but, of course, there are hints of that radical change in this life, too, if we'll but see them for what they are! Most of the time, we miss resurrection clues because we're convinced that we're pretty good folks who just need a tiny sin washed off here and a nice, new virtue pasted on there. We pray, "God, make me less selfish" and then think that prayer is answered when we increase our pledge to the church a bit. Trouble is, this human being goes on about everything as if unchanged. Our cage, so to speak, hasn't even been rattled a little bit! But resurrection really changes us—and a little quotation from C. S. Lewis reminds us how it's so:

> When I was a child I often had a toothache. . . . And I knew those dentists; I knew they started fiddling about with all sorts of other teeth which had not yet begun to ache. They would not let sleeping dogs lie.
>
> Now, if I may put it that way, Our Lord is like the dentists. If you give him an inch he will take an ell. Dozens of people go to him to be cured of some one particular sin. Well, he will cure it all right, but he will not stop there. That may be all you asked, but if you once call him in, he will give you the full treatment.

Resurrection is the full treatment. In its completeness we shall know it only beyond the grace where the brokenness, the hurts, and the hates of this life will be radically removed from who we are. But already, here and now, there are hints of that resurrection which makes us new people.

—There's a hint in our experience of being forgiven by someone; for not only is a particular sin dealt with, but from head to toe we feel a new freedom for living. That's resurrection!

—There's a hint in our experiences of being sick, of being so ornery or passive we'd rather be dead. But healing comes! It's not that just one part of or body feels better, but all of life is good again. That's resurrection!

—There's a hint in our experience of no longer nursing our bitterness or hurt feelings, when suddenly being with people feels good again. That's resurrection!

In all of this there's a kind of bad news/good news word. The bad news is that you can't take it with you; the good news is that much of it you wouldn't want to take anyway. The good news that's the very best and the truest is what we have in Jesus: that all live to God! Because that's only partly true of us now, in this life, we shall be changed! Thank God for that—and for all foretastes of things to come! *Amen.*

Glenn L. Borreson
First Lutheran Church
Decorah, Iowa

Sunday
September Twentieth

Theme: I Know, It's Always to My Advantage

Call to Worship: God is faithful, by whom you were called into the fellowship of his Son, Jesus Christ our Lord.
I Corinthians 1:9

Invocation: Lord, let us trust in thee. When you said, "I must go away," your disciples were afraid. The Holy Spirit came and wiped away all fear. Fill us with the Holy Spirit and remove all our fear. *Amen.*

Hymn: "Praise to the Lord, the Almighty"

Sermon Presentation: "To Your Advantage"

Goals for Today: God never leaves us alone; he is always near, ready to help. You need never be alone. Never.

This Week in History

September 22—National Good Neighbor Day—To build a nation and world that cares. To increase understanding of all people.

September 25—First American Newspaper Anniversary—*Publicke Occurrences Both Foreign and Domestick* was published in Boston, Massachusetts, in 1690.

Announcement for Next Week's Sermon: No two people are alike. If that is true, why are we so upset when someone is different? I hope we can get an answer next week.

Hymn: "Breathe on Me, Breath of God"

Offertory Scripture: The steadfast love of the Lord never ceases, his mercies never come to an end; they are new every morning; great is thy faithfulness. Lamentations 3:22-23

Offertory Prayer: Lord, don't let us be afraid of change. You left us and that change frightened us. You never really left us; it was all in our minds. Accept us and our gifts as we accept your unchanging love. *Amen.*

Prayer: "A bird in the hand is worth two in the bush." That's the attitude we seem to have in our relationship with you, O Lord. It's probably because you are so good in a world that often seems so bad. You are the one truth we find in a world full of lies. You are the life in a world that teems with decay and death.

Like most people in our world, we mourn what we don't have instead of being thankful for what we have received. Some of us here today wish that you lived among us today instead of two thousand years ago. We would have found comfort in touching your hand, hearing your voice. But you have given us the privilege of knowing you in God's Holy Spirit. We know that flesh and blood will not live forever—ashes to ashes, dust to dust. But your spirit, which was present at the time of creation and was the moving force behind the establishment of your church, is your gift to us today.

May we always be open to your spirit which offers us your guidance, touching us at our deepest levels where we feel, where we think, where our creative impulses begin, and where our most important decisions are made.

May we always be open to your Holy Spirit which brings to our often confused, troubled, and sorrowful lives your peace and comfort. May we always be open to your Holy Spirit which, as our counselor, offers us the gift of your wisdom.

May we lead Spirit-filled, Spirit-directed, and Spirit-responsive lives in your name, O Lord. *Amen.*

Story of the Week: The little boy went to church with his aunt. When the collection plate was passed, he put his dime in with all the other loose change and quite a large pile of dollar bills.

"I can't understand," he said to his mother when he arrived at home, "why some people paid a dollar in church. I had a real good seat right down front for only a dime."

TO YOUR ADVANTAGE

It's somewhat strange, but it was by his absence more than his presence that Jesus had a deeper influence on his followers.

September Twentieth

With his absence, the Holy Spirit came—the church was born—those individual gifts were given to build up the Body of Christ. With his absence, therefore, we were given an advantage. In the Gospel according to John, this was Jesus' intention, "It is to your advantage that I go away, for if I do not go away, the Counselor will not come to you; but if I go, I will send him to you" (John 16:7).

Of course, the human Jesus couldn't stay—the flesh and bones Jesus—the Jesus who was born . . . suffered . . . crucified . . . and buried. Therefore, his ascension was the early church's graphic portrayal of what happened to him—he ascended into heaven and was seated at the right hand of God the Father Almighty. However, it was the Comforter, the Holy Spirit, who carried on. It was his coming that created the church. The book of Acts states it graphically, "When the day of Pentecost had come, they were all together in one place. And suddenly a sound came from heaven like the rush of a mighty wind, and it filled all the house where they were sitting. And there appeared to them tongues as of fire, distributed and resting on each of them" (Acts 2:1-3).

Now, this event occurred just fifty days after the Resurrection. There were one hundred twenty people present to celebrate an old Jewish festival called Pentecost. It was a festival associated with the giving of the Law to Moses at Mount Sinai. With this event, some three thousand persons were made converts to the faith; the Church was born. "It is to your advantage that I go away, for if I do not . . . the Counselor will not come to you; but if I go, I will send him to you."

To our advantage, then, the Counselor did come. It's just another name—and an important name—for the Holy Spirit, the living God at work in our time, in the church, and in our personal lives. The Counselor isn't someone different from God, nor from the living Christ; the Counselor, the Holy Spirit, is the living God.

Is God really present today? By his Holy Spirit, does he enter into your life and mine? Here, the Korean Creed helps point the direction of our response: "We believe in the Holy Spirit, God present with us for guidance, for comfort, and for strength." He is present for guidance. So the God of eternity, present also to the people of the Old Testament, is the very same God of whom the psalmist could affirm—"If I take the wings of the morning and dwell in the uttermost parts of the sea, even there thy hand shall lead me, and thy right hand shall hold me" (Psalm 139:9-10).

The guidance of God is its most effective at the level of our unconscious selves. An artist states that by the time the creative process becomes conscious, it is already under way. That is, by the time the artist becomes aware that something is going on, it has been going on for a while. The crucial question for the Christian experience of God is whether, by his Holy Spirit, he can reach us at this deepest level. It's whether, in our emotional lives, our intellectual lives, our spiritual lives, including all our creative insights, the Comforter comes to touch us there. With others, I am convinced that he can and that he does. I am also convinced that it is there that he does his most effective work, and not on the level of helping to decide which suit to wear. That trivializes God.

The Holy Spirit is also present for comfort. Beyond all human aid, but often using human beings, he comes as the comforter in our battles as well as in our sorrows. Then, he's also with us for strength. Undoubtedly, more of us need to be waiting upon him more often than we do, recognizing our petulant, sometimes mixed-up lives. However, like a good father, the Counselor doesn't do for us what we, as sons and daughters, must do for ourselves. Our waiting upon him isn't for the purpose of turning everything over to him to control. I didn't turn over the control of my human life completely to my biological father, and I didn't expect my son to turn over the control of his life completely to me! To be sons and daughters is to share a mature sense of independence in life, never denying the importance of the parental relationship. In our relationship to God, it seems that the strength we seek is in love! So to wait upon him we must go back into life and our relationships with our human powers strengthened.

It was for this advantage—the coming of his Holy Spirit, the Counselor—that our Lord left us. In his book *Reaching Out*, Henri Nouwen, a great, present-day spiritual leader, looks at this on the human scene. He says, "A few times in my life I had the seemingly strange sensation that I felt closer to my friends in their absence than in their presence." Or, if not from him, then take it from Gibran, who writes, "When you part from your friend, you grieve not: For that which you love most in him may

September Twentieth

be clearer in his absence, as the mountain to the climber is clearer from the plain."

Of course, the other basic advantage we gained with the absence of our Lord was that the church was born. Pentecost is the birthday of the church.

Now, the church has been compared to many relationships—household, Temple of the Spirit, Colony of Heaven. But the most familiar, and deeply significant, is the Body of Christ. "Just as the body is one and has many members, and all the members of the body, though many, are one body, so it is with Christ. For by one Spirit we were all baptized into one body" (I Corinthians 12:12-13).

We do, indeed, need to come to terms with the church as the Body of Christ. It's amazing how, through the ages, her life has ebbed and flowed. One of the basic reasons to hold her precious among relationships is how, within herself, she has that amazing capacity for renewal. Or we could say that God loves her so much because he created her—that his Spirit continually renews his church. To be sure, we have sad chapters in our history. To be sure, there are those counterfeits around of the real thing. But there also are those places without limit, and those times without end, where the church is faithful to the living center of her life.

Now, as we reflect on the challenges to our lives, it seems that one of our greatest isn't from some alien force out there someplace. It's that battle which goes on, or needs to go on until it's won, right within the individual soul. Every now and then I ponder that famous thirteenth chapter of I Corinthians. How we melt as we hear that hymn to love! However, if this is all we hear, we miss the struggle inherent in what the love of God involves. In that passage Paul says that he be a big giver, but if his inner motive is "look at me," rather than "what can I do to help?" he gains nothing. He can be big on faith, known as a spiritual person, but if his faith is unrelated to the heights and depths of what God's love is accomplishing, he is nothing. One might have been given the gift of speaking in tongues. But if that gift becomes self-indulgent; if it becomes an exercise in self-display, unrelated to God's loving concerns, "I am a noisy gong or a clanging cymbal."

You see that love is the living God, the living Holy Spirit at work in us, wooing us, prompting us, guiding us. To be sure, the Holy Spirit is more than such love. In fact, at this lovely season, we are again aware of how, in continuing creation, he's got the whole world in his hands.

Nevertheless, the Counselor's deepest intention for creation, for his church, and for you and me, is our richest, fullest life. "God is love" says the New Testament, "And he who loves is born of God, and knows God." So during this Pentecost season—though really, all through the year—we can claim the advantage which is ours. So we sing, as we have, both for ourselves and for the church:

> Breathe on me, Breath of God,
> Fill me with life anew
> That I may love what thou dost love,
> And do what thou wouldst do.
> *"Breathe on Me, Breath of God"*

Amen.

Warren A. Nyberg
Minnetonka, Minnesota

Sunday
September Twenty-seventh

Theme: Differences Can Be a Blessing

Call to Worship: These things I have spoken to you, that my joy may be in you, and that your joy may be full.　　*John 15:11*

Invocation: We all want to belong, to be part of the crowd, to be accepted, but not at the cost of our souls. There are times when we must be different, stand for all that is good and Godly. Give us the courage to be different. *Amen.*

Hymn: "The Son of God Goes Forth to War"

Sermon Presentation: "On Being Different"

Goals for Today: Difference is what keeps life interesting. If we can learn to handle being different, life will be very much worth living.

This Week in History

September 27—Gold Star Mother's Day—To honor all women who have lost men in the service, giving their lives to protect our freedom.

October 2—Charlie Brown's and Snoopy's Birthday—The "Peanuts" gang, created by Charles Schulz, first appeared October 2, 1950. Some of the best sermon material you can find.

Announcement for Next Week's Sermon: How often have we said, "How come God punishes the good and the bad alike?" God never said it would be easy. Next Sunday, he never promised you a rose garden.

Hymn: "When We Walk with the Lord"

Offertory Scripture: Just so, I tell you, there will be more joy in heaven over one sinner who repents than over ninety-nine righteous persons who need no repentance.　　*Luke 15:7*

Offertory Prayer: Make me different. Make my Christian life stand out for all to see. Not so people will say, "Isn't he good," but that they might see you shining through me. Make me different. *Amen.*

Prayer: . . . Like a big box of crayons. All the colors of the rainbow and every shade and hue in between. That's what we are like.

. . . Like snow flakes . . . similar to one another, yet each unique in itself. That's us, the church of Christ!

It's been said that variety is the spice of life, but so often we feel threatened and uncomfortable with the great diversity that we find in this world.

Some are quiet; others seem as if they were "vaccinated with a phonograph needle." Some are tall, others short; some like loud music, while others enjoy the sound of a soft melody; some like baseball and others enjoy golf. Some can work with their hands and sit next to those who work best when they are thinking up innovative and creative ways to tackle old problems.

We thank you for the great diversity of gifts that you have given to us your people. We thank you for the unique person that you have made each of us. But we also thank you for the oneness we share. Each of us, a child of God, stands at the foot of the cross, having fallen short of our Father's expectations and in need of the forgiveness that comes from your sacrifice on the cross for our sins.

Many, yet one. Different, yet so similar, but all called by you to be children of the one Heavenly Father. *Amen.*

Story of the Week: The clever young man with lots of experience in the ways of girls, said to his girl friend on their first date, "I heard a real good one the other day. Do you know the difference between a single hamburger and a seven course dinner?"

"No," said the girl, "I'm sure I don't."

"In that case," the young man said, "we'll stop in the drive-in after the movie and have a hamburger."

ON BEING DIFFERENT

The acceptance of being different poses quite a problem for all of us. Being different is not simply associated with the extremes

September Twenty-seventh

and the obvious, but it is everything we are as we live out our lives. We find that difference appearing in our marriage relationships, our families, and, believe it or not, we even find differences in attitudes within churches (horrors!). Our problem is, and always has been, how we deal with differences in human beings, a fact all of us have to face—no, not once in a life time, but in that day to day person to person relationship. How do we manage? How do we adjust? How do we accept, if we can accept at all?

Look at those obvious differences—some people are tall; some people are short; some are quite heavy; and some quite thin; some people have a different color in the pigment of their skin; different temperaments; different personalities; different skills; different talents; gifts; attitudes; opinions—so, being different is a basic fact of life.

I don't know about you, but many Saturday evenings I sit with my wife and watch T.V. We Americans still like to live in a romantic era, you know. After all the high mountain peaks are crossed, all the ferocious dragons disposed of, and all the barriers broken down the gallant knight rides up on his white stallion, and sweeps up his fair lady. As they ride off into the forest, we are left with the feeling that they will live happily ever after. In the Western version, we see the rustic cowboy and his romantic heroine riding out together into the sunset. We are led to assume that they, too, will live happily ever after. But you know it—I know it—that is not real life; that is a fantasy, for in real life, once the knot is tied the honeymoon comes to an end. Differences enter and stick out their supposedly unwanted virtues. In so many cases, our choice in marriage is thought out objectively. There are times when we are not that certain about our method of selectivity. It is like the old adage, "opposites attract," and that has quite a bit of truth connected with it. It could very well be that we admire and respect the qualities in others which we ourselves are not free to admit were once or have not been present within ourselves. You know the consequences: The quiet person settles down with the talkative one; the overweight with the thin; the scatterbrained with the methodical; the athlete with the feminist; the atheist with the pious; the withdrawn with the extrovert—so, before we decide to tie the knot, we look at the differences as being quite complementary to ourselves, and then things begin to happen.

After we are involved for a time, we quickly discover that those qualities which we at one time admired in the other person are really not that complementary—they are becoming irritations—so we begin to think, "Why don't I stay at home anymore? Do you have to sit through all those boring football games every Sunday afternoon?"

Every couple seems to have instilled in them the myth that their marriage will become enriched if they both like the same things. If we really loved one another, we would always do the same things, agree about the same things, so what we are really saying is this: "If you really love me you will do precisely what I want you to do!" Now we all have a little bit of that in us, don't we? Being different at times becomes quite unacceptable for us. In that marriage covenant, much that we have been taught leaves no room for being different. The "in" thing for many weddings today is the Unity Candle; it looks great and wonderful and beautiful as the two people take their candles and light the one in the center. All of the wedding guests oooh and ahhh and sigh . . . "how lovely" . . . but when the couple takes the individual candle and blows out that light, something happens. It's almost as though they cease to be individuals anymore; some new sort of organism is being formed, and they pass out of existence as humans. Strange, isn't it, how quickly Bill discovers that he is still Bill after the wedding ceremony, and Alice is still Alice. Bill loved Chinese food before he was married. Alice has a favorite color of blue, and you had better believe that their home will have plenty of blue colored decorations. So part of the responsibility that goes hand in hand with the building of a good marriage is how well we all learn to appreciate and respect differences.

But differences do not begin and end in marriage or family relationships. Somehow they enter right into that loving, caring, sharing relationship we call church families. Some prefer soft organ music; some like it loud. Some would like guitars; some would not. Some like small discussion groups, while others prefer the traditional lecture method. Some think that Jesus will return quickly, while others seem to feel he will in God's own time, and others just don't seem to care. Some think that you need to know precisely the day and the hour when you made your first commitment to Jesus Christ, while others feel that it is a long growing process, and there is really never a need

September Twenty-seventh

to know the precise time. Some feel that the central thrust of the Church is always how well the Evangelism Committee functions, while there are others who disagree—it really should be how well the Social Ministry Committee does its job. Some live out their lives with a remarkable degree of conservatism, while others prefer to work through the creative group decision process. Some live out their lives with a passive and silent faith, while others show that faith by word and by deed. Some feel that they are quite committed to God in the assurance that he will do everything, and that they can do nothing without him. Others believe that God helps those who help themselves. Some seem quite willing to accept leadership roles in the congregation; others would not dare to consent to such a move. Some love to have coffee and conversation, while others would never dare to profane their bodies with such inadequacies.

Now our real question is this: Why do we always consider these differences to be threats? Why does being different bother us so much? We have some difficulty in remembering the differences, which were remarkable, present in the early formation of the church. Each one of those leaders was in his own way a rugged individualist; how different they were. Their leadership was characterized by the variety and the uniqueness they could offer to the group. Who were they?

We would have to call one a collaborator . . . one a system man . . . one a traitor . . . there was an extreme nationalist . . . an anarchist . . . a fisherman . . . a first-class well-to-do society man . . . a blue collar man . . . a scientific believer . . . and yes, an unbeliever. An innocent like Nathaniel. A Peter, but also a Thomas. A Judas, but also a John. A James, but also a Bartholomew. So, if there were ever a motley bunch assembled together to form God's mission, this crowd was it, and the church flourished!

Later on, when Paul began to assemble the churches of Asia Minor, there was nothing which would even come close to resembling our standards of uniformity. You name the race, the creed, the color, and it was there! How much God must love differences and variety, for there is so much of both.

I Corinthians 12:12-21 speaks quite plainly about differences and what a blessing they can become. The body does not consist of just one member, but of many different and varied parts. How well Paul seems to explain that no one part can ever become the whole and do the whole thing; each one of us has a place and a function, and each member adds balance. Put this all together and we have a vital, vibrant, and functioning body.

There is a decided difference between unity and uniformity. Genuine organic unity encourages and thrives upon individual differences; it never seeks to press people, persons, into a similar mold. If there is anything which is precisely clear in the New Testament teachings, it is that the church is not what you and I would say, a cookie cutter!

So, we admit that there are differences within the body, but how does all that work? Most certainly we cannot function effectively as a unit when things do not go our way, as we violently oppose anything that seems to be happening. No body can function effectively with that sort of attitude. I like to look at it as a self-respect which comes from knowing that you are a vital part of God's intricate design. It is your God-given uniqueness being put to work, as you take on the form of servanthood to minister to others in what you can best do. That develops your capacity for being part of God's kingdom!

It is only in the form of understanding our freedom that we can rejoice in the awareness of knowing and accepting the good news that we are the people of God! Uniformity is doing everything the same. Unity is that unique individual relationship we all have in Christ Jesus! Look again at how we fear being different. Do we not still have bred within us that idea that being different could divide us? Paul asked the people of Corinth the very same question: Is Christ divided? The response he gave to that question was an emphatic and resounding NO! We are one, because of, and in spite of, being different. We love, not because we think alike, but simply because we know we are one in Christ. So we can love—because we are not interested in the same thing—God forbid that to happen; what a boring, lifeless group of people we would be! Jesus came, not to take away our differences, but to bring all of those differences which men feel could divide into a clear and better perspective. When he speaks about his church the words hostility, mistrust, prejudice, and hate are not in his vocabulary. Instead, he brings with him new dimensions of peace, hope, faith, love, and joy! And that is why the words of scripture never change. . . . There is still *one body* . . . *one Lord* . . . *one faith* . . . *one baptism* . . . because God, himself, did it, and God is the ultimate!

September Twenty-seventh

I have that inner desire to someday write a book. If I ever do, I would preface and dedicate that book to my wife, who at times hardly seems to agree with me on anything, but all at times is my wife, lover, companion, and friend in everything. That is the Good News we seek to celebrate—on being different—it has been for us a blessing and a gift from God.

Our problem is this: can we accept what Scripture speaks about, of all members being a part and functioning well together to make the body work as it was originally designed? God felt that it was good when, in our creation, we were made to be different. Now, why cannot we feel the same and build up the Body of Christ?

Are we still in that process of learning to love? *Amen.*

D. Timothy Robinson
St. Mark's Lutheran Church
Isle of Palms, South Carolina

Sunday
October Fourth

Theme: God's Promises

Call to Worship: If one member suffers, all suffer together; if one member is honoured, all rejoice together.
I Corinthians 12:26

Invocation: Lord, your promises are good and you are faithful to those who love you. We are always hoping to find a promise of special treatment; there is none, just continued patience and love as we struggle to please you. *Amen.*

Hymn: "What a Friend We Have in Jesus"

Sermon Presentation: "God Promises No Rose Gardens"

Goals for Today: God never deserts you. You just have to know where to look for him. Too often we want him at our time and on our terms. Wait on the Lord.

This Week in History

October 4-10—Fire Prevention Week—To promote fire safety in all places. Do you have a fire safety program and plan for your church?

October 5—Child Health Day—To promote higher health standards for all children.

Announcement for Next Week's Sermon: I hear about grace in church all the time, but I'm not sure just what it is or how it works. Next Sunday you will get the answers.

Hymn: "I Need Thee Every Hour"

Offertory Scripture: [Paul and Barnabas] Strengthening the souls of the disciples, exhorting them to continue in the faith, and saying that through many tribulations we must enter the kingdom of God.
Acts 14:22

Offertory Prayer: We bring these gifts to you and expect nothing in return. You loved us first; you promised us salvation. That is enough for us. *Amen.*

Prayer: "Hang in there!" "Keep the faith baby!" These are the popular phrases of the day. We turn on the T.V. and hear a so-called minister of the gospel telling us "You can't lose, lose, lose, with the stuff I use!" But let's be honest, Lord, life is much like a rose, beautiful, but beware of the thorns.

So often we find that the expectations we have for life are soured by life's experiences. We look to you, Lord, to save us from all of the trials and troubles that make up life's journey. We expect that by simply saying, "Lord, Lord," we will be kept safe from the pain, sorrow, guilt, fear, and depression that surround us and threaten to make us the next victim.

We have confused you, Lord, with a good luck charm or some witch doctor who has the power to cast magic spells that will protect us from suffering and tragedy.

You have promised to care for us and to see us through the dark moments of life, even the valley of the shadow of death. You have promised to stay by our sides, offering your strength and guidance. We look to your word and realize that being one of your disciples means that, like Paul, we will suffer for the sake of your kingdom and the privilege of calling you our Father.

May we always trust in your power to help us overcome our problems. Grant us the wisdom to find solutions to our troubling situations. But most of all, grant us the strength to endure until the day that will come again and end all suffering and pain in our lives.

Let us never wallow in defeat but be sustained by Christ our Lord's victory over sin and death; a victory he has promised to share with us some day. *Amen.*

Story of the Week: The minister's five-year-old daughter was put to bed early because she had a slight fever. As her mother left the bedroom, the little girl said, "Mommy, I want to see daddy."

"Your daddy is too busy right now," her mother said. "You go on to sleep."

"But I want to see my daddy," the little one said.

"I told you no," her mother said. "Go to sleep."

"I'm a sick woman," the child said, "and I want to see my minister."

GOD PROMISES NO ROSE GARDENS

"Are they servants of Christ? I am a better one—I am talking like a madman—with far greater labors, far more imprisonments, with countless beatings, and often near death. Five times I have received, at the hands of the Jews, the forty lashes less one. Three times I have been beaten with rods; once I was stoned. Three times I have been shipwrecked; a night and a day I have been adrift at sea. I have been on frequent journeys, in danger from rivers, from robbers, from my own people, in danger from Gentiles, danger in the city, danger in the wilderness, danger at sea, danger from false brethren; in toil and hardship, through many a sleepless night, in hunger and thirst, often without food, in cold and exposure."

It is a well-known fact that human beings have their share of tragedy. A man was at a banquet when the subject of a recent earthquake in South America came up. A guest seated next to him inquired, "Did you know that a much lower percentage of Christians died in that earthquake than non-Christians?" The man responded with, "What about the Christians who were killed? What had they done to deserve such a fate?"

Hidden behind the guests' conversation is the magical belief that God will protect us from suffering and tragedy. Of course, the key to this protection is our faith and moral characters. How many T.V. speakers have promised, "God is going to bless you, to heal you, to take care of that financial problem, that marital situation when you give to God's cause."?

"Pastor, you mean to tell me that my faith, my Bible studying, my church going, my money giving, does not entitle me to God's protection and blessings?"

Our hardest lesson to learn is that God promises no rose gardens.

God has not promised to solve our problems. You say, "Well, that is not what I have been taught. I've always heard that if you are close to the Lord and you've got enough faith, then God is

October Fourth

going to answer your prayers, thus taking away and solving your problems."

Would you say that the Apostle Paul was close to God? Why didn't God spare Paul the heartaches and pain he suffered? Note his experiences in II Corinthians 11:23-27:

—He was in jail several times and beaten half-to-death;
—He was beaten by Jewish brothers who were once his friends;
—He was stoned, then shipwrecked, spending a whole day and night just hanging onto a piece of wood in the ocean;
—His lifestyle was as dangerous as that of James Bond;
—He states that he had been to bed cold, naked, and without a morsel of food. He knew what it was to be so hungry that the stomach ties itself into knots.

Why didn't God get Paul out of jail? Why did he allow him to be beaten half-to-death? Is a horse-whipping God's way of taking care of his servants? Who wants to serve a God who is going to let you starve?

God has not promised to be your miracle worker in the sense of taking away your problems. No matter what kind of faith you have, he is not going to take away your marital problems. He is not going to take away unemployment or financial strain.

I remember reading an article about unemployment—a frightening condition to be in. An executive lost his job. He prayed about it, trusting the Lord, and nothing happened. It was over a year before he got a break. My mind began to ask, "If God cannot solve my problems, what good is he?" Or maybe you are thinking, "Doesn't the Bible teach that if you ask anything in his name, he'll do it?" At this point many folks begin to yank out several verses of Scripture to prove their points. What about these verses and promises of God? Are they outdated to this present generation? Isn't faith the only thing we need to have these promises granted?

There are promises by which we twist God's arm.

Have you ever had someone in an armlock? You can push up on that arm and he'll cry "uncle" right fast. Sometimes we try to do this with God. John 14:13-14 is a passage we use to twist God's arm: "Whatever you ask in my name, I will do it, that the

Father may be glorified in the Son; if you ask anything in my name, I will do it." Basically, the verse says "Ask whatsoever you desire, and I'll do it."

Doesn't this passage teach that God will solve my marital and financial problems if I ask? Isn't it saying, "Just believe and your loneliness, your guilt, your depression, and your worries will be taken care of?"

Yet, how does this deal with the teenager who dies of leukemia despite all types of prayers? The truth of the matter is that this passage, and others, apply to the mission of the kingdom. These verses speak of the power and resources to carry out God's redemptive cause in the world. From a practical standpoint, this means that if you have a ministry for the Lord, then ask for whatever you need to implement that ministry in the world.

Does it work? I can only say that you must respond to God's calling in your life, find your particular ministry, and then experiment with this promise. People testify that while being on mission for the Lord, their problems have been healed. It seems that by being a blessing to the unchurched, God's children find the healing that they need so badly.

Our problem is that we want to see this promise outside the context of God's assignment for us. We are like the little man who pounded on the desk, "Don't disturb me with the facts!" We do not want to hear about being servants who are called to minister in the world. We want worship to substitute for service. We want a God who solves our problems, a God who serves us, rather than us serving him! At times we are looking for a magical daddy.

How does one cope with personal struggles?

You can cope effectively with your difficulties through prayer and the community of believers. When a person has a struggle in the areas of work, marriage, kids, and just life itself, negative feelings are created. The result is an overload. The danger of overloading your circuits with negative voltage is that it short-circuits your ability to cope with life. You feel helpless to handle these trouble spots.

What happens when too much electrical current goes into an appliance? It blows. When too much negative energy overloads

October Fourth

our personalities, we develop physical and relational problems hosted by emotional burnout. Guilt, anxiety, fear, and depression are signs of overloading. Prayer—not formula prayers, but real prayers—is a way of fully expressing this negative build-up to the Lord. King David did this when he fasted, prayed, and cried all night long for the life of his child. The Apostle Paul calls it "inward groaning," which is expressing fully before the Lord what is bottled up. An example of this is the experiencing of grief. To hide the pain and hurt only overloads the system. To remember the loved one's birthday, anniversary, the good times, and the resentments allow the pain to express itself and allows God to love you.

The release of this negative energy creates inward peace. More importantly, you become aware of the power of the Holy Spirit. With this awareness you develop the inner assurance that you have inward power to cope with your situation. Herein is the promise of God; God has promised you the power to cope with whatever comes your way, to cope not in a defeated spirit, but with the power to overcome all the difficulties you face. You will have power to cope with your marital difficulties, your finances, your job, and your broken relationships. This is the promise of God manifested by his Spirit.

Another way of coping with your personal struggles is through the Body of Christ—the community of believers. Jesus said that where two or three are gathered in his name, he will be there. This is the power of the community of God. Within this community is the power to heal and to impart the strength to cope effectively with our difficulties.

But it involves a risk. The risk is sharing your personal struggles. It means allowing someone else to know what your feelings, thoughts, and fears are concerning your difficulty. Without this type of honest sharing, the community of God cannot be of real assistance to you. You will find that most pastors are willing to hear your struggles and help you to discover the power of Holy Spirit within you to cope. Bible study groups are also designed to be places to unload your hurts and to find the power to cope. You will find that they also have problems and hurts and collect negative nervous energy around their problems. Yet, in the midst of their problems they are calling forth the power within to cope with life, for God has not promised us a rose garden, but he has promised the power to cope with the thorns we experience in life. *Amen.*

Dan Phipps
Westwood Baptist Church
Roxboro, North Carolina

Sunday
October Eleventh

Theme: My Grace

Call to Worship: But grow in the grace and knowledge of our Lord and Savior Jesus Christ. To him be the glory both now and to the day of eternity. *Amen.* *II Peter 3:18*

Invocation: Your grace is sufficient for all things and for all times, even unto death. That is your promise. Lord, help my unbelief; strengthen my faith so that I may fully accept your promises. *Amen.*

Hymn: "O Master, Let Me Walk with Thee"

Sermon Presentation: "Grace"

Goals for Today: Make grace real to your people. Help them understand that it is a free gift from God and there is no way to earn it.

This Week in History

October 12—The White House's Birthday—The Presidential residence at 1600 Pennsylvania Avenue in Washington, D.C. The cornerstone was laid in 1792. It is the oldest building in Washington.

October 16—World Food Day—To heighten public awareness of the world food problem. To encourage the elimination of hunger from all the world.

Announcement for Next Week's Sermon: On a dark night, did you ever take a step and not know where your foot would come down? God asks us to do that all the time. I wonder why? The answer is next Sunday.

Hymn: "Amazing Grace! How Sweet the Sound"

Offertory Scripture: [Because Jesus can sympathize with our weaknesses] let us then with confidence draw near to the throne of grace, that we may receive mercy and find grace to help in time of need. *Hebrews 4:16*

Offertory Prayer: By your grace I am what I am. All that I have is by your grace. Grant that I might show the joy and freedom your grace gives through these gifts which I now return to you. *Amen.*

Prayer: I can't believe it. It sounds too good to be true. It seems like a dream. I'm afraid I'll wake up and find out that I'm back in the real world—a world in which you reap what you sow; a world in which each of us "gets" what we deserve; a world in which each of us is on our own and we "make it or break it."

I like to believe that I could do it on my own. But let's be honest, Lord. Everytime I carry the ball I make some yardage, but then I fumble the ball. When I'm alone I can admit to myself, and to you, that I am less than perfect. I am a coward when I should be bold. I'm selfish when I should be selfless. I doubt when the moment calls for faith. But then I hear the "good news" that has excited and given hope to men, women and children for two thousand years.

I hear about your grace that overcomes my apathy, my rebelliousness, my focus on myself, and my destructive and rash impulses. When I should have been condemned, you pronounced me "not guilty." You pronounced me "free" when I was a slave to sin. When I was blinded by worldly desires and ambitions, you gave me a vision of your kingdom. When I was your enemy, you sent your Son to turn me into your friend. When I was dead, you showed me that death can take my body but not my life. Now that I live under your grace, I am free—free from fear of punishment; free from fear of rejection; free from fear of death. By your grace, I live as your child, beloved, forgiven, secure in the promise of your love.

You promised me, "My grace is sufficient for you." Grace. Amazing Grace, how sweet the sound in this believer's ear. *Amen.*

Story of the Week: The woman had received a beautiful skunk coat for Christmas—a gift from her husband.

"My," she said with excitement. "I just can't understand how a beautiful coat like that could possibly come from such a miserable evil-smelling little beast."

"Well," said her husband, "I didn't exactly expect any gratitude from you, but I do think I deserve a little bit more respect."

October Eleventh

GRACE

I'm like a zombie when I get up in the morning. But when I take a shower it revives me, invigorates, and wakes me up. Other people splash cold water (or warm water) on their faces, or belt down a cup of coffee to achieve the same effect.

Sometimes words are like that—they wake you up—they just jump out at you, leap off the page and grab your attention. What Paul wrote in Ephesians 2:1 is like that. He says some great things about how he prays and gets carried away in his thoughts about Jesus. Paul says:

> "Having the eyes of your hearts enlightened that you may know what is the hope to which he has called you, what are the riches of his glorious inheritance in the saints, and what is the immeasurable greatness of his power in us who believe, according to the working of his great might which he accomplished in Christ when he raised him from the dead and made him sit at his right hand in the heavenly places, far above all rule and authority and power and dominion, and above every name that is named, not only in this age but also in that which is to come; and he has put all things under his feet and has made him the head over all things for the church, which is his body, the fulness of him who fills all in all. And you he made alive, when you were dead through the trespasses and sins" (1:18–2:1).

WHAT? Yes! Dead! Not sleeping, needing only to be awakened. Dead—beyond all reasonable hope, beyond all human help. The penalty for our lapses and shortcomings, our apathy or rebellion towards God, our transgressions and sins is . . . death (Romans 6:23).

Like electric kitchen appliances without cords or plugs, we had no power, no life. In the things that really matter most in life we were inert, stiff, locked in rigor mortis. We were utterly unable to meet God's requirements because the most vital part of our personality—our spirit—was dead to the most important factor in life—God. We were powerless even to turn to Christ in repentance and faith. Paul declared, "The unspiritual man does not receive the gifts of the Spirit of God, for they are folly to him, and he is not able to understand them because they are spiritually discerned" (I Corinthians 2:14). We were in a state of moral and spiritual ruin!

Paul continues to explain the dimensions of this disaster. "For I decided to know nothing among you except Jesus Christ and him crucified. And I was with you in weakness and in much fear and trembling" (I Corinthians 2:2-3). We are all chips off the same block! Natural man is altogether at the mercy of the tyrant self and its rash impulses. We have a natural bent toward doing evil. Our entire posture of life, our heart attitude, was "hostile to God" (Romans 8:7).

We were condemned, defiled, enslaved, blind, dead, and under God's wrath. We were without excuse, with no possible defense. None of us were innocent! We deseved to be "[punished with] eternal destruction and exclusion from the presence of the Lord and from the glory of his might" (II Thessalonians 1:9). That could have been us!

That way we act sometimes, you'd think the song began "Amazing grace how sweet the sound, that saved a wretch like YOU!" We think we're all right because we compare favorably with certain people. "Hey, I've never murdered, raped, or robbed; in fact, since I became a Christian I'm a rather likable, good guy!" Well, that's not how God sees it. He says that our righteous deeds, our best achievements, and even our greatest moments are as filthy, dirty, bloody, repulsive rags in his sight (Isaiah 64:6).

Two men were trying to jump across a thirty-foot chasm. Beneath ran a roaring, foaming river, dashing pell-mell over the rocks. One man jumped ten feet and the other jumped twenty. The second did better than the first, but neither made it to the other side. We can compare ourselves against others all we want. But against the backdrop of God's holiness, we all come far short!

I Corinthians 2:1-3 speaks in the past tense. Is it possible that something could have actually changed the situation? What happened? "And my speech and my message were not in plausible words of wisdom, but in demonstration of the Spirit and power, that your faith might not rest in the wisdom of men but in the power of God" (I Corinthians 2:4-5). God has given us a position of favor and privilege, secure and unchanging, out of the corrupting reach of evil. Peter wrote, "His divine power has granted to us all things that pertain to life and godliness,

October Eleventh

through the knowledge of him who called us to his own glory and excellence" (II Peter 1:3).

This means we are free from the fear of the future. We know that nothing can separate us from the love of God in Christ, and that nothing can happen to us that is not for our long-term good.

Or as Romans 8:32 puts it, "He who did not spare his own Son, but gave him up for us all, will he not also give us all things with him?" God's grace frees us from fear of rejection and from the fear of the unknown future. All this is "through faith." Faith is turning from self to Christ in trust and dependence, committing our minds, emotions, and wills to him. We are not saved by faith—faith does not save us, God does. We are not saved on account of faith—as if God said, "Oh, I see Peter has faith, so let's give him salvation." No! We are saved through faith; it is only the means.

Faith is not something we can produce. Even faith is a gift from God. Paul says "not by works," and comprehensively rules out any kind of human effort. We owe our salvation entirely to God's grace!

Grace is not the result of works, but the power that enables works . . . as Paul goes on to say in I Corinthians 2:10: "God has revealed to us through the Spirit. For the Spirit searches everything, even the depths of God."

As grace sets God in action for our good, so it should set us in action for the good of others. In II Corinthians 9:8, Paul explains that "God is able to provide you with every blessing in abundance, so that you may always have enough of everything and may provide in abundance for every good work." As Jesus said, "You did not choose me, but I chose you . . . [to] go and bear fruit" (John 15:16). As Christians, we are called not only to be recipients of God's grace, but we are also called to be channels of that grace.

We must come to terms with how completely unable we are to do anything good in our own strength. Even the good we now do has its source in God, who made it possible. Paul used himself as an example in I Corinthians 15:10 when he said, "But by the grace of God I am what I am, and his grace toward me was not in vain. On the contrary, I worked harder than any of them, though it was not I, but the grace of God which is with me" (cf. Colossians 1:29).

Someone once observed that if we do not believe that the matter of grace is at root, if we are doing the work, we will give up. We will be swamped by trials, demands, and problems unless we have a clear sense of God's continuing grace. The weaker we are, relying solely on grace, the stronger God is. Grace produces confidence! Look at what Paul wrote in II Corinthians 12:9-10: "But he said to me, 'My grace is sufficient for you, for my power is made perfect in weakness.' I will all the more gladly boast of my weaknesses, that the power of Christ may rest upon me. For the sake of Christ, then, I am content with weaknesses, insults, hardships, persecutions, and calamities; for when I am weak, then I am strong."

At one time, we who are Christians were dead—morally and spiritually dead! If God had decided to destroy us, he would have been entirely justified. It is simply staggering to realize that God has offered us, *us*, his undeserved love and mercy in Jesus Christ! But God didn't just save us. He has blessed us with everything we need to grow spiritually. And by grace he has given us every resource with which to serve him. He has given us the power to share the pain and hurts of others without being destroyed ourselves. In grace he has broken our stubborn pride toward those who are not saved yet (I Corinthians 1:26-31, 4:7).

And he has given us the commission to take to them the good news of his saving grace in Jesus.

John Newton, the old converted sea captain, understood well the grace of God. After years of rebellion and debauchery as a slave trader commited to a cruel and vicious way of life, he became a believer. Newton went on to become an Anglican minister. Until his death at eighty-two, he never ceased to marvel at God's mercy and grace that had so dramatically changed his life. He is best remembered for the hymn "Amazing Grace."

> The Lord has promised good to me,
> His word my hope secures;
> He will my shield and portion be
> As long as life endures.

Amen.

Peter D. Hardt
Castro Valley, California

Sunday
October Eighteenth

Theme: That First Step Can Kill You

Call to Worship: And Jesus said to him, " . . . All things are possible to him who believes." Immediately the father of the child cried out and said, "I believe; help my unbelief!"
Mark 9:23-24

Invocation: How many times have we come to you and said, "Help my unbelief"? We know of your great patience, and I am sure we try it often enough. Again today we ask, "Lord, give me faith and help me through those moments of doubt." *Amen.*

Hymn: "Blessed Assurance, Jesus Is Mine"

Sermon Presentation: "The Leap in the Dark"

Goals for Today: To be sure that everyone understands God's unlimited patience. He will never give up on his children.

This Week in History

October 20—National Shut-In Day—To renew concern for the sick, the incapacitated, and the incarcerated. This is a day worthy of special Christian concern.

October 24—United Nations Day—Commemorates the founding of the United Nations in 1945.

Announcement for Next Week's Sermon: Next Sunday's sermon could be called, *Not One of My Better Days*. That was the day Martin Luther stood up to the Pope and said, No, and made it stick.

Hymn: "How Firm a Foundation"

Offertory Scripture: And Jesus answered them, "Have faith in God . . . I tell you, whatever you ask in prayer, believe that you have received it, and it will be yours."
Mark 11:22, 24

Offertory Prayer: Lord, your church grows and moves forward only when people are willing to take a stand of faith for you. Let these gifts be a sign of our faith and that we stand with you. Amen.

Prayer: It's like standing at the door of an airplane—the light changes from red and flashes to green. The parachute is on my back. The reserve chute is in front of me. My teacher tells me to count to five and pull. I've got the chute. I've got the backup. I've had the training. But now the moment of truth has arrived. It's time to leap, but do I have the faith?

Not many of us jump out of planes, Lord. But each of us has a life to lead, and that, too, requires a great deal of faith. We grope through life looking for a way that involves minimal risks but maximum results, maximum security, and "a piece of the rock."

Lord, I look at Scripture and I see how the fishermen put away their nets in response to your call and risked everything so that by your grace they might become fishers of men. How many of us have that kind of faith that would allow us to give up what we are for what we can become?

I see how Paul surrendered the security of his life as a Pharisee in order to become your apostle. How did he survive jail, beatings, people saying bad things about him, even a shipwreck? It must have been his faith in you. He believed your promises. May I believe like him. He must have trusted you. May I, too. Lord, I believe; help my unbelief. In the midst of darkness, grant me your light; in the midst of things I don't know, grant me your wisdom; in the midst of things I do not understand, grant me patience; in the midst of things that would overwhelm me, consume me, devour me, grant me your protection; in the midst of turmoil, grant me your peace; and in the midst of the shadow of death, grant me your promise of life, eternal life.

I know that with you as my shield and defender, I need not fear anything. Well, here I come, Lord, "Ready or not!" But, of course, I know you are always ready. *Amen.*

Story of the Week: The American diplomat was traveling through several of the new countries of Africa. He had planned to speak at a number of meetings of the natives and had been assigned one of the best interpreters from the American Embassy. At his first stop he began his speech with a rather long, funny story. At the end of the anecdote, the native interpreter said five words to the audience and they burst out with screams of laughter.

The diplomat was amazed and said to the interpreter, "How were you able to tell that long story to these people in only five words?"

"Oh," said the interpreter, "story too long. I just say, 'He tell joke, everybody laugh.'"

THE LEAP IN THE DARK

Imagine that you are climbing around in a mountainous place. Night sets in, and it becomes totally dark around you. You grope ahead, constantly making sure of the ground before you. Suddenly you stop dead. There is nothing ahead. You know that you have reached a sharp drop-off. What do you do? Do you give up your climb and stay put? Do you jump? If you jump, you know that one of two things will happen. Either you will jump over a narrow break in the ground safely to the other side, or you will jump to your death. You are taking the ultimate risk by making this leap in the dark.

In the nineteenth century, the Danish philosopher Kierkegaard described faith as such a leap in the dark. He did not see faith as a hesitant commitment to God. He did not try to protect himself from the radical demands of faith by believing and still having all sorts of reservations. Rather, he saw faith as the ultimate risk, the leap of faith that either destroys the meaning of a person's life or lands that person safely in the hands of God.

Is this Christianity business really that serious? Do we have to take that kind of risk? I thought that our modern society had made risks minimal in our lives. Much of what we do seems directed at giving us maximum security. Our material goods are protected from catastrophes; if they are destroyed by fire, theft, accidents, or floods, insurance will pay for the loss. After all, "you're in good hands with Allstate," or your insurance company "gives you a piece of the rock." Of course, the other insurance companies have their own ways of stressing the security you have with them.

Also, retirement is no longer the risk it once was. We provide for a secure retirement well in advance with pension plans and Social Security. Our country is secure from invasion. We continue to take part in the arms race rather than seriously trying to stop it in all countries of the world.

Of course, I am not suggesting that we not use insurance, pensions, and Social Security. I am simply trying to bring to your attention the amount of effort that we expend on security. Do we still place our faith in God or do we rely on our own efforts for all of our security?

The Old Testament stresses the faith of Abraham. If anyone ever knew that faith meant taking a risk, Abraham did. He started his life as a Mesopotamian. He could have had a secure life with his family in his homeland, but Abraham experienced God. God offered Abraham great advantages if he would take a risk. The risk was leaving his homeland and going half-way across his world to Canaan. The advantages were that he would become father of a great nation and that Canaan would be its home land. So, Abraham took the risk.

The stories of Abraham are ones of jeopardy. That is, Abraham's promised advantages are repeatedly placed into jeopardy. But God always manages to remove the jeopardy and keep the promises alive. For example, the promise of the land becomes questionable when Abraham and his nephew, Lot, decide to split the land between them. Lot chooses the best part of the land, and it seems that Abraham's promise is not going to be worth very much. But Lot's choice doesn't take into account the moral corruption of the land he has chosen and that corruption leads to the destruction of that region. So, Abraham has the better land in the end.

Most often, however, the promise of a great nation is placed into jeopardy. Abraham is over seventy-five years old, and he still does not have a child. In the text, God tells Abraham that he will have a child, yet. In fact, he will have as many descendants as there are stars. As unbelievable as that sounds, Abraham believes; he trusts God to carry through on his promise (Genesis 15:1-6).

Abraham's risk turns out to be worthwhile because he has a faithful God. He has a son, Isaac, and becomes the father of a great nation, Israel. Also, God gives this nation Canaan as its land.

October Eighteenth

Does Christian faith involve that kind of risk today? Yes, real faith does. But that is not necessarily the same as what passes for church membership in many people's minds. A common attitude toward faith was expressed already by the French philosopher Pascal in the seventeenth century. According to him, faith was a wager. If a person believed in God and there were a God, the person won. If there were no God, faith cost nothing, so there was no real loss. It was more to a person's advantage to believe in God than not to. Many people live according to Pascal's wager. Church membership is not really a risk for them; it only involves attending church somewhat regularly and keeping up contributions. The church does not have much impact on their daily lives, so the wager is worthwhile to them. Christianity costs little and has big promises of eventual gain.

But is that faith? Faith is a leap in the dark. Faith is leaving behind our calculations and our self-made security and jumping out into the unknown. There we cannot protect ourselves. There either God catches us or we fall.

Living by faith is different, then, from living by Pascal's wager. It involves risks. As we set life goals, our faith affects them. We try to use our lives more in the service of others than in self-service. That involves a risk. We will have less time and effort to expend on our own financial security. We shall be using time and effort we might have spent on ourselves on other people instead. Living by faith may mean turning down a job with a higher salary to take a job with greater opportunities for service.

Also, living by faith may mean making some ethical choices that are risky. If our employer expects us to be somewhat dishonest in our business practices, do we dare show a smaller profit because we are honest? Would we take the risk of quitting a job and looking for a new one because we could not square the first job with our Christianity? And it is a risky thing to use time and energy for the service of Christ's church. The more we become involved with committees and jobs around the church, the more demanding they become. The more we forget ourselves and use ourselves in service, the greater risk we take. We are leaping out into space, believing that there is a God to catch us there.

As we live like this, we are living like disciples of Jesus. Jesus lived by a risk-taking faith in the Father. His ministry was a time of constant self-giving. He expended himself in healing the sick, preaching to the crowds, and seeing to the needs of people around him. His faith showed most strongly at the close of his career. He freely went to Jerusalem knowing that his greatest danger lay there. For the sake of our salvation, he gave himself up to death. He let his enemies crucify him. He took the ultimate risk—death, with faith in the Father.

That was Jesus' leap in the dark. He did not fall into nothingness. The Father was there in the dark and made Jesus victorious. He raised Jesus from the dead.

That is the model for our leap in the dark, too. God receives us and makes us victorious. A life of faith is not a dismal prospect. A life of faith is a fuller life. Jesus said, "Whoever would save his life will lose it; and whoever loses his life for my sake and the gospel's will save it" (Mark 8:35). One reason why a life of faith is a fuller life is that it is freed from calculation. We no longer have to worry about how much we are going to preserve ourselves before we give of ourselves to others. God cares for us. We can give of ourselves without concern. Then, with the burden of calculation gone, we can live with greater openness and joy.

A remarkable thing is that when we are no longer consumed with providing for our own security, God provides us with a truer sort of security. He told Abraham "Fear not, Abram, I am your shield" (Genesis 15:1). I have found it to be true in my life that when I have planned and worked to provide some advantage for myself, often nothing has come of it. Some of the biggest blessings I have received have been totally unexpected. They have reminded me once again that I am not in charge of myself, but that a much wiser giver is in charge.

We stand before the chasm now. The old temptation is to stay put there and insure our security. But leap boldly. God awaits you. *Amen.*

Bruce V. Malchow
Sacred Heart School of Theology
Hales Corners, Wisconsin

Sunday
October Twenty-fifth

Theme: A Continuing Reformation

Call to Worship: Now faith is the assurance of things hoped for, the conviction of things not seen. *Hebrews 11:1*

Invocation: Today we celebrate the day the Bible was set free. No more was the common man denied the word of God. Now all may hear and read. Thank you, Lord, for this freedom to know thee. *Amen.*

Hymn: "A Mighty Fortress Is Our God"

Sermon Presentation: "Raising a Tudor Rose"

Goals for Today: To create an awareness of the word of God, freed from the tyranny of the few church leaders so all people might be able to meet God face to face as a personal Savior.

This Week in History

October 25—Mother-in-Law's Day—We all have them; we all love them. This day we forget all the bad jokes and honor them by saying how much we love them.

October 31—Reformation Day—Commemorating Martin Luther's signing of the Theses in 1517.

Announcement for Next Week's Sermon: "I think the pastor should never preach about politics." Next Sunday find out not just why he should, but why he must.

Hymn: "Now Thank We All Our God"

Offertory Scripture: You see that faith was active along with his works, and faith was completed by works . . . . For as the body apart from the spirit is dead, so faith apart from works is dead. *James 2:22, 26*

Offertory Prayer: Your word guides our lives and assures us of the final victory. Let your word rule our lives today and may these gifts be pleasing in your sight. *Amen.*

Prayer: "A small boat in a big sea," that is the image we have not only for our individual lives, but also for our life together as your people of God, called together in the church. We hear the story about you and your disciples traveling across the Sea of Galilee in a small boat. It is a story that we can easily identify with: the storm, the fear, the uncertainty, the doubt. We're all in the same boat. As we journey through this life, let us make sure of the sturdiness of the vessel in which we will travel. Is our rudder firmly set in the word of God? Since it is our rudder which will give us direction and keep us on course, we must be certain that your way is our way.

May our sails be powered by your Holy Spirit, giving us the strength and faith to reach not only our final goal, but to minister to all of the people we meet and in the places we travel. And in those moments when our lives would be driven off course by the waves of complexity; when we are at the mercy of the winds of doubt and the waves of despair, Lord, serve as our anchor to steady us and keep us safe.

Lord, in your church, you have provided us with a fine vessel with the strong oars of your word and sacraments with which to navigate this vast sea we call life. For your church, for our place in the communion of saints, and for the faith that gives meaning, direction, hope, and guidance for our lives, we give you our thanks, not as we ought, but as we are able. *Amen.*

Story of the Week: A patent medicine salesman at the fair was shouting his claims for his Rejuvenation Elixir. "If you don't believe the label, just look at me," he shouted. "I take it and I'm 250 years old."

"Is he really that old?" asked a farmer of the salesman's young assistant.

"I really don't know," said the young man. "You see, I've only been with him for 120 years."

RAISING A TUDOR ROSE

Paul writes: "But by the free gift of God's grace all are put right with him through Christ Jesus, who sets them free."

October Twenty-fifth

For 437 years the *Mary Rose*, a seven hundred ton, four-masted flagship of the navy of Henry VIII moldered in the chilly waters of the Solent, near the historic town of Portsmouth. She had capsized and sunk on July 19, 1545, one year before Martin Luther's death. Six hundred sixty-five seamen went to the forty-foot-deep sea with her.

Not long ago she was brought to the surface and then to shore. Prince Charles was there to watch the ship being lifted out of its watery grave, just as King Henry VIII watched her capsize and sink 437 years earlier. At the time it was the most expensive underwater archaeological salvage operation in history.

Perhaps, rather than haul up this old warship of the sixteenth century and continue the battles of the Reformation by firing a weak volley of ammunition at the Roman Catholics, we would do better to examine what sank the ship and the pre-Reformation church in the first place, and to examine how we can avoid such a disaster again!

During the Reformation, clergy, theologians, and lay Christians were taking too much credit for themselves. There were all kinds of ways you could earn God's salvation—you could buy indulgences and masses; icons and relics were worshiped. All this perversion made the church top-heavy with an emphasis on works, and the once-unified Catholic church sank in waters of denominationalism, sectism, nationalism, and divisions.

Paul had been so very clear about it all. He said that all we have is a gift from God. We don't have to deserve it, but by the free gift of God's grace all are put right with him.

It's called grace—amazing grace, when we sing it—all-encompassing and covering grace—a charming, attractive gift of salvation, forgiveness, and a new life in Christ. Paul pointed it out first in the New Testament. Wycliff, Huss, and Luther lifted it up again from the depths of theology and study of Scripture. They held it high: *Sola Graticia,* meaning "by grace alone." When all Christians take seriously that we are sinners and God gives us the gift anyway, we will surely have to relate differently to each other and to God.

Paul and Martin Luther called attention to grace. You need not earn it—God gives it as a gift. I recently heard a story of a certain man who died and approached Saint Peter. Peter said, "It'll take one thousand points for you to be admitted."

"I attended church every Sunday and sang in the choir," said the man.

Saint Peter said, "Fifty points."

"I gave very generously," said the man.

Saint Peter said, "Twenty-five more points."

"Sometimes I taught Sunday school," said the man.

"Twenty-five more points," said St. Peter. "That makes one hundred. You need nine hundred more."

Frantic and in utter panic, the man blurted, "At this rate, the only way I'm going to get into heaven is by the grace of God!"

Saint Peter smiled, "That's nine hundred more points. Come on in."

God chose to grant us a gift—one of grace. It's the heart and soul of what we believe God is!

Another danger that wrecked the ship of the church back in the sixteenth century was an emphasis on the church organization and supremacy of the church. Luther pointed to Paul, who taught that all are put right with God through Christ Jesus. It isn't, then, through popes, councils, vestments, incense, robes, and candles, but by Jesus Christ. What Christ did and who he became are what is essential to us. "Now, there," Paul and Luther would say, "is the one who makes things right between God and us again."

It is my firm conviction that a Reformation celebration should call all God's people together. It should never widen the differences between us. It should never be a time to dredge up old differences and battles with Roman Catholics, Baptists, or Fundamentalists. Rather, it is this kind of unbending, "I'm always right," sort of attitude which caused the Reformation of the sixteenth century to sink the once unified church of Jesus Christ and force it to splinters.

A Reformation in our day should be a call for joining hands with all the baptized people of God. It should call to everyone of good will to do the great work of the kingdom together, unified, to confront sin and injustice, to work for compassion and mercy, and to make a great witness to the Good News which we share. Don't use this day to dredge up old prejudices and hate. If you must, don't call me your pastor or this your church!

October Twenty-fifth

The writer of Hebrews teaches us that all religion is access to God. He said that we rebel and tear apart our relationship with our Creator God and with each other. That's why God had to send his Son to the cross—to make things all right again. "But God . . . made us alive together with Christ (by grace you have been saved), and raised us up . . . in Christ Jesus" (Ephesians 2:4-6).

There are many ways we try to make things up to one we have offended:

a parent we disappointed

a spouse to whom we were untrue,

a friend we let down.

This affects our lives and our relationships for years. But not so with Christ. We don't have to go tippy-toeing around, wondering if he likes us. We can dump the guilt here. We can throw out the shame. We can rid ourselves of that nagging in the pit of our stomachs. As the prodigal son came back home, confident the father would completely forgive him, so can we come home to our God.

If you have been seeking a peace and blessed assurance; if you have strayed and want to come home again, here it is: *all are put right with him through Christ Jesus.*

We see that we can't earn salvation with God—it's a gift of grace. We see that the church and all its paraphernalia will not make us right again with God; Jesus Christ does that.

John Huss was a Bohemian reformer who was burned at the stake one hundred years before Luther for holding up before the rigid, unwilling-to-change church this idea: God gives us salvation as a gift from him.

At Drew Theological Seminary, there is a tradition that when the late, beloved Samuel F. Upham was dying, friends and relatives gathered at his bedside. Someone, wondering if his life had come to a close, advised, "Feel his feet. No one ever died with warm feet." Upham opened his eyes slowly and said, "John Huss did."

Another thing that made that church go down was the idea that religion had to be a burden rather than a joy. The Mary Rose sank because it was top-heavy while trying to fight off the French forces. The Reformation came because the church in the sixteenth century was trying to load more on top of people, instead of unpacking their loads.

Paul said that by the free gift of God's grace all are put right with God through Christ Jesus, who sets them free. Before that, Jesus had told the people he came to make their loads light, not heavy. "Come to me, all who labor and are heavy laden, and I will give you rest. . . . For my yoke is easy, and my burden is light" (Matthew 11:28-30).

True Christianity is not to further weigh us down, but to lift us up. All of our religion is a practice of response to God's gift. It is not based on fear, but on response to love. It is not "in order to;" but "because we already have."

Our religion should set us free from worry over death, from the fear of being alone, and from concern about our things and our possessions to be the full person God created us to be, striking out boldly with love for others and confident of God's love for us.

By the free gift of God's grace all are put right with him through Christ Jesus, who sets them free.

In Tampa Bay on January 13, 1982, a large ship began to list. Three tugs were brought against the side of it while the ballast was shifted. It had seemed safe in the harbor. But according to the T.V. news, it suddenly began to list badly. So, they needed those three tugs to go against its side to right it. Well, the ship of the church started to list badly in the sixteenth century. Tugs like Huss, Martin Luther, Calvin, and Zwingli churned against her side while the ballast was shifted to even keel again. Tugs like grace instead of works, Christ instead of the institutional church, and joy instead of burdens, contributed to righting her on course again.

What we will do with our reformed church, our freedom, our right relationship with God, our gift of salvation and grace, still remains to be seen! Some prefer to try to preserve it and keep it just the way it is. Others like to dig it up once a year and start the war over again. Still others want to ignore it altogether. It's up to us. What shall we do with the dynamite of freedom, grace, and right relationships? Let's share it with all who will listen, and let's live it out in every area of our life-styles: let's thank God for it over and over again.

We have talked about the Reformation for many years. Again, today, we raise it up and renew our thrill in its magnificent view of Christ and his church. The rest is up to us. It can be in a museum beside other great events in history, or it can be an

October Twenty-fifth

alive and vital force in all of our lives and the lives of our community. We raise from the depths of the sea today, again, a Tudor rose.

But by the free gift of God's grace all are put right with him through Christ Jesus, who sets them free. Amen.

Jerry L. Schmalenberger
St. Johns Lutheran Church
Des Moines, Iowa

Sunday
November First

Theme: Politics and God

Call to Worship: God is faithful, and he will not let you be tempted beyond your strength, but with the temptation will also provide the way of escape, that you may be able to endure it.
I Corinthians 10:13

Invocation: Lord, don't let us stand off to the side while others make the decisions. If you are to have a voice in politics, it must be my voice. Let me speak up loud and clear for the Christian way. *Amen.*

Hymn: "A Charge to Keep I Have"

Sermon Presentation: "The Politics of Faith"

Goals for Today: To let all your people know that they, as Christians, can and must make a difference. Do it!

This Week in History

November 1—All Saints' Day—In the Protestant church it is the day we remember all the saints of this congregation who have died in the last year.

November 1—World Community Day—Focuses on prayer for the establishment of a just and lasting peace.

Announcement for Next Week's Sermon: Were you born miserable, or do you make yourself miserable? The sermon next Sunday says you make yourself miserable. Do you think that is true with you?

Hymn: "O Jesus, I Have Promised"

Offertory Scripture: He who is faithful in a very little is faithful also in much; and he who is dishonest in a very little is dishonest also in much.
Luke 16:10

November First

Offertory Prayer: Lord, be a good thief for me. Strip me of all my phony pretense. Make me real. Accept me and my gifts just as I am. *Amen.*

Prayer: "Vote for this one! Vote for that one! It's time for a change! Let's have more of a good thing!" Lord, it's election time again in America. It's the time each year that we become painfully aware of the things that remind us of our differences and the things that divide us. We divide ourselves into parties and labels like Democrats and Republicans. We characterize ourselves as being conservative, moderate, or liberal.

It is time that we are reminded of our common bond. The fact that all of us, not just in this country, but people all around the world, are children of the Heavenly Father. It is time that we remember our calling. As your ambassadors in this world we are Christians first and Americans second. We are to rise above party affiliations and personal ambitions.

Grant us the courage and the will to work to insure that the best interests of your people are always our top priority and that in all we do, we work to and for life, liberty, and justice for all. May our prayer that "Thy will be done" be a goal that we strive for each day of our lives.

And when we hear people try to divide your world into the so-called sacred and the secular, remind us that this is a man-made division. This whole world was created by you and, as your children, we are responsible for every corner of this world of yours.

As we cast our votes, may we elect government leaders and officials who will bring us closer to the day when "justice rolls down like water and righteousness like an everflowing stream for all God's children." *Amen.*

Story of the Week: A young fellow, studying political science, asked his father, "Dad, what is a traitor in politics?"

"Any man who leaves our party," said his father, "and goes over to the other one is a traitor."

"Well, what about a man who leaves his party and comes over to yours?" asked the young man.

"He'd be a convert, son," said his father, "a real convert."

Minister's Annual

THE POLITICS OF FAITH

November is usually election month in the United States. Win or lose, we are all a good deal richer for having experienced the electoral process, for it helps put our lives into perspective once again, knowing that we're each a part of something far greater than ourselves, called "America."

Yet, even as Americans, we're simply a subsection of the almost 4.5 billion people who presently inhabit the "global village" known as earth, and together, all 4.5 billion of us; we're each children of the One Creator-God. White, black, Asian, and red; rich and poor, young and old; male and female; healthy and ill—we have each been created *Imago Dei* (in the Image of God).

All too often we seem to forget this basic fact. We allow ourselves to get too caught up in our own ideologies and in the everydayness of human existence, so much so, that it seems to take the magnitude of a famine in Ethiopia; an assassination in India; or an election in America to remind us that beneath the arbitrary boundaries of time zones, languages, and political ideologies, we are but one with our human brothers and sisters throughout the earth.

Several months ago, I was reminded again of this basic fact, as a friend called in order to respond to a sermon I had sent her to read. Her reaction was one of concern for my well-being as she said: "Why do you insist on preaching about political issues? Don't you realize most people don't like it? Why can't you just say what people want to hear, the way most other preachers do?"

Well, believe me, I know where she was coming from, and I also honestly appreciated the concern for my well-being implied in her remarks. Yet, I equally realized that she was merely voicing the same kinds of questions that so many credible scholars, journalists, theologians, and others have posed during the course of an election year in America, namely: "What is the proper role of religion in politics, if indeed, it has any role at all?" Now, that's truly a "loaded question" amid an intentionally pluralistic and representative democracy like ours.

But, if nothing else, I'd like for each of us to bear in mind that the role of religion in politics has been an inherent part of our Judeo-Christian tradition since its very beginning, not in the sense of a "civil religion" as was employed by the so-called founding fathers of our nation, that led to having American flags placed in Christian sanctuaries; tax-exempt status for religious organizations; patriotic "high holy days" like July 4th and Veteran's Day; or catch-phrases like "In God we Trust" on our coins and "One nation under God" in our pledge of allegiance to the flag. Indeed, "civil religion" necessarily leads to what Thomas Jefferson called "a wall of separation between Church and State"; a separation of authority, not of cooperation, between these two powers. Yet, to find the phrase "separation of Church and State" constitutionally, one has to look at the Soviet constitution, and not our own, for in the Soviet Union it is true that no member of a church can be a card-carrying member of the Communist Party. Yet, in America, no such "separation" exists, as evidenced by the fact that so many of you who are members of this congregation fully participated in our representative democracy. Our American Constitution, in the First Amendment, merely asserts that the State "shall not establish any religion, or prohibit the practice thereof."

In fact, many of our founding fathers were Deists, not Christians, who believed in and affirmed a Supreme Deity, but did not adhere to the ethics or imperatives of the Christian gospel. A brief look at virtually every Presidential Inaugural Address since the time of George Washington, shows this to be true, for, while *God* is evoked time and again in conjunction with the nation, the name of Jesus Christ is noticeably absent! Thus, we question the realism and truth of a Jerry Falwell, who repeatedly calls for a return to "Christianity," that America may, once again, become a "Christian nation." In truth, America has never, in its entire history, been any more or less of a "Christian nation" than any other sovereign state, including the Soviet Union, where there are presently at least thirty million practicing Christians in Orthodox churches!

So, while "civil religion" leans toward a "wall of separation" between church and state, it is a separation that has no place in our Judeo-Christian tradition! Rather, as a people of faith, we need to recognize and appreciate the truly prophetic role that religion has necessarily played in politics for our tradition, ever since Yahweh commanded Moses to return to everything he had sought to escape from in Egypt (including an indictment for murder!), and declare unto Pharaoh, "Let my people go!"

Therefore, it really shouldn't surprise anyone in our tradition to witness men and women of faith, and/or their pastors and priests, becoming involved in the political sphere of life, but it does! It really shouldn't surprise us when people go on a hunger strike for days in our nation's capital, and risk their own lives in order to draw attention to the plight of the homeless poor in America, but it does! Nor should any be surprised to learn that ordinary people of faith risk civil disobedience, from Texas to Washington State, by non-violently positioning themselves along the path of the so-called "White Train" which hauls nuclear warheads of death from production to deployment, but surprised we are!

Each of these actions, and more, points in its own way toward the redemptive will of Almighty God for humanity, and declares to the oppressive powers and principalities of our world, "Let my people go!"

The plain truth of the matter remains that as long as the redemptive will of God is kept from becoming a reality for all of God's children on the earth; as long as the active shalom of God is being effectively undermined by the fallen powers and principalities of the world; and as long as people of genuine faith, from whatever tradition, continue having to pray, "Thy kingdom come, thy will be done on earth," because it isn't yet being done; as long as it takes, people of genuine faith will continue to play an active role in the political arenas of life, until that day wherein the prophetic vision of Amos is truly fulfilled, and "justice rolls down like waters, and righteousness like an everflowing stream" for all of God's children!

When we stop whatever we're doing long enough to really think about it, isn't this the way it honestly should be; perhaps especially so for those of us who affirm Jesus Christ as Lord and Redeemer of human existence.

Indeed, it is our Lord's own example, and his own willingness to engage the powers and principalities of the world—even to the point of his own death at the hands of the State—that we, who call ourselves his disciples, seek to emulate, for if nothing else, in human terms, Jesus suffered from the injustice of capital punishment as it was carried forth in his own day!

November First

He is the one who tells us "as you did it [or failed to do it] to one of the least of these my brethren, you did it [or failed to do it] to me" (Matthew 25:40).

History tells us about Martin of Tours, a Roman soldier who, when riding into a small village one cold winter's day, was met by a beggar who badgered him through the streets. Despite the soldier's best efforts to avoid him, the beggar persisted until, finally, Martin desperately tore his own red cloak in half and gave one portion to the man. Later that night, in a dream, Martin was granted a heavenly vision of Jesus Christ, draped in half of a Roman soldier's old red cloak. An angel inquired, "Lord, why are you wearing that ragged old cloak?" Jesus replied, "Because my friend, Martin, saw fit to give it to me earlier today."

"Inasmuch as ye have done it unto one of the least of these my brethren, ye have done it unto me."

Where do we actually see Jesus Christ, our Incarnate Lord? Probably in as many different places as there are people with genuine physical, psychological, emotional, and spiritual needs.

Perhaps in the face of the smaller-than-life Ethiopian child, near death, on the six o'clock news.

Perhaps in the expressions of the three soldiers depicted on the statue that was added to the Viet Nam Memorial in Washington, D.C.

Perhaps in the rooms at a hospial.

Or in the struggle of students for new values with meaning and purpose.

But always, always, I think, in the midst of hardship, suffering, and pain!

Is it foolish to think of God as being actively at work in the political sphere of life? Not really, for the politics of faith is such that we know our God is present amid the individual and corporate decisions of our world that shape the quality of life for all of God's children. America has no special claims upon the God of human history, who judges all the nations equally.

None of us can be Christians in isolation, for Christianity, by definition, is being in a right relationship with God and with each other through Jesus Christ!

That's why we gather together, and not alone, to worship the Prince of Peace.

That's why I need to be here today, with you, as a community of faith, and that's why we each can affirm, with absolute certainty, that the Prince of Peace is present with us, in power, this very moment!

The kingdom of God—is here and now! It's in you, and in me, and in our struggle together to become more fully human each day, after the example of Jesus Christ!

Even those who have "fallen asleep"—that is, the dead—cannot be separated from the heart and mind of their Creator and ours!

As a people of faith who affirm Jesus Christ as the Sovereign Lord and Redeemer of the entire created order, our primary allegiance is to God alone! The Christian is one who must never forget this amid the task of being prophetic in the heated rhetoric of politics, for it's precisely our ultimate allegiance to God, in Jesus Christ, that lies as the basis of our involvement in the political realm! That's why so many of us actively engage in the politics of faith, and why so many more of us should do so.

We are people of the covenant; our absolute fidelity is to the God of the covenant, regardless of which parties, personalities, or ideologies rule in any given nation for a particular period of time.

Our God is the sovereign of all the nations. The politics of faith is but one way that we're called to serve Almighty God on behalf of God's children throughout the earth.

As you seek to faithfully do so, may the God of the patriarchs, prophets, apostles, and martyrs grant each of you "Shalom"; through Jesus Christ our Lord and our Redeemer.

Amen and Amen.

James S. Vuocolo
Wyoming Ministries in Higher Education
Laramie, Wyoming

Sunday
November Eighth

Theme: Be Happy, Not Miserable

Call to Worship: This is the day which the Lord has made; let us rejoice and be glad in it. *Psalm 118:24*

Invocation: If we had a choice to be miserable or filled with joy, we would all pick joy. If we have faith in you, our joy will be full. Love is the greatest source of joy, and we are certain of your love forever. *Amen.*

Hymn: "All People That on Earth Do Dwell"

Sermon Presentation: "Making Yourself Miserable"

Goals for Today: To show that life does offer choices. We can find joy even in the face of sadness. Job knew it would all end some day, and so do we. Keep the faith.

This Week in History

November 10—Martin Luther's Birthday—Leader of the Reformation. On October 31, 1517, Luther nailed his ninety-five theses on the door of Wittenburg's castle, asserting that the Bible was the sole authority of the church.

November 11—Veteran's Day—To honor all veterans, living and dead, of all wars. There has been a special emphasis to honor hospitalized veterans for their valor and suffering they have endured.

Announcement for Next Week's Sermon: Can you believe in God but not love him? I doubt it, but let's find out together next Sunday.

Hymn: "He Leadeth Me: O Blessed Thought"

Offertory Scripture: These things I have spoken to you, that my joy may be in you, and that your joy may be full.
John 15:11

Offertory Prayer: There is so much misery in the world today. As Christians we should be instruments of joy, not misery. Make us live joyfully and give joyfully. *Amen.*

Prayer: A great football coach once told his players, "Winning isn't everything, but wanting to is." Lord, we work so hard trying to be a winner in life. Yet, even when we get our raises, receive our promotions, purchase our new cars, or move to the better neighborhoods and bigger houses, we still feel sort of hollow. The more we have, the more we seem to feel that something is missing from our lives. Perhaps the problem for us is that we want to "win," but we don't know what "winning" means.

You have told us, the people who are called by your name, that in this life we are to "seek first the kingdom of God." You warned us that unless we realize that we must begin with having a right relationship with you, then all else is meaningless.

You have given us the responsibility of making this world a better place. You have told us that being successful in your name means that we are to love you first and then love our neighbors as much, if not more, than we love ourselves. In this life, let us set our priorities: God first, others second, and myself third. *Amen.*

Story of the Week: The Sunday school teacher said to her class, "It is our duty to make someone happy during the week. Have you done it?" she asked the little boy.

"Yes," he said without a moment's hesitation.

"That's fine. And what did you do?" asked the teacher.

"I went to see my Aunt Jane, and she was happy when I came home," he said.

MAKING YOURSELF MISERABLE

Have you ever made yourself miserable? Most people believe that it is others who create misery for us. The reality is that we cultivate our own misery.

Johnny, a second-grader, is determined to aggravate his teacher. Sitting at the back of the class, Johnny begins to

November Eighth

snicker. Mrs. Smith responds by moving him to the front of the class. When Mrs. Smith turns her back to write on the board, Johnny turns and makes faces at the class. Then the class begins to snicker. This time, Mrs. Smith puts Johnny on the stool in the corner. After being quite for a minute, Johnny does the "Elvis Presley" wiggle and falls onto the floor. Johnny thinks he is having fun by irritating the teacher, but how is this scene going to end? Who is creating his coming misery?

I have a suspicion that even in our relationship with God we make ourselves miserable. I have decided, out of pastoral love, to tell you how you can make yourself miserable.

Many spiritually minded people will die without making the world any better off, primarily because Christians substitute worship for service. Ask the average congregation, "What is it that God wants you to do?" The answer will be, "Worship the Lord."

A young preacher by the name of Isaiah entered a congregation speaking these words, "People of Israel, God is not excited that you came to church. God is not excited about your offering. God is not excited about your prayer meetings and Bible studies. And above all, God despises your fasting."

The congregation was greatly offended: "What right does Isaiah have to condemn our worship?"

Isaiah continued, "God wants to know why you are not sharing your bread with the hungry. Why are you not bringing the homeless and poor into your homes? Why are you not providing shelters for unwed mothers who are considering abortion? Why are you allowing the court system to punish the innocent and set the guilty free?" When Isaiah had finished, the congregation was in a state of silent misery.

Have you substituted worship for service? When you die, will you have left the world any better off?

See the greed but not the human need. Bill, a trustee, was the church's self-appointed watchdog over the budget. Every month Bill called the treasurer wanting a detailed explanation about certain items. The treasurer felt so badgered that he told his wife, "This is my last year as treasurer. I love the Lord and his church, but I'm not putting up with this."

One month, Bill decided to go over to the treasurer's house to discuss the budget. Well, he was not home but his wife was. She lit into Bill like a hound dog chasing a rabbit. "Bill, I know why you are here and I want you to know that if you spent half the time in witnessing for the Lord as you do being a watchdog over this dumb budget, our church would change overnight. You could hear the heavenly choir sing, 'Hallelujah! Hallelujah!'"

Just then someone came to the door. Guess who? The pastor; talk about bad timing! Bill confronted the pastor, who replied, "Bill, I appreciate your concern over where the church is spending its money, but the lady is right. You are focusing upon money rather than ministry."

Bill swore he would never attend church again. Bill is like Peter in Luke 9:28-36. On the Mount of Transfiguration, Peter wants to build three churches—one for Jesus, one for Moses the lawgiver, one for Elijah the prophet. The motivation is right, but the direction is misguided. For months Bill did not attend church. Upon leaving, he took his large annual donation, placing a burden on the church. But God blessed this church, and it grew both spiritually and financially. After a year or so of being miserable, Bill came back a changed man. Today he is chairman of the deacons, guiding them in a prison ministry.

If you want to be miserable, focus on money and property rather than ministry as our Lord has called us to do.

The common understanding is that the cross is your sickness, your personal burden, your marital problem, or some other setback of life. People say, "God has laid this tremendous burden upon my shoulders. Why? I don't know. Maybe this is my cross to bear."

This is nonsense. God's purpose is to redeem, not to inflict suffering upon mankind. The Apostle Paul, who had this severe problem, did not conceive of it as his cross. Paul's cross, which is God's will, was to be a missionary to the Gentiles.

The cross is whatever mission God has called you to do now. There is a middle-aged mother with a crippling form of arthritis. Sometimes the pain is so severe that she cannot close her left hand. During her morning devotions she once read the passage, "If any man would come after me, let him deny himself and take up his cross" (Luke 9:23). Being a mature Christian, she knew her arthritis was not her cross. So she prayed, "Lord, what are you calling me to do?" The word *soup* kept popping into her mind. For a week she meditated upon this verse, and the response was the word *soup*. She did not understand.

November Eighth

The next Sunday her class was informed that the director of the soup kitchen, a ministry to the needy, was leaving. She knew God was calling her to this volunteer ministry. Today she is the director, feeding soup to the poor and sharing her faith.

If you want to be miserable and aggravating to God, turn the cross into your personal and private burden.

The difference between winners and losers is how they handle their problems. Winners solve their problems by coping effectively with the situation. Losers don't solve problems and "feel" they cannot cope.

In marriage a winning couple solves relational problems as they arise. They cope effectively with such interpersonal dynamics as resentments and anger, intimacy and independence. The miserable couple never solves the problem and creates an unhappy home life. The winning couple does not have greater love, but a strong determination to cope effectively with any marital problem.

In the church world a winning church is one in which problems are solved and goals are accomplished. A losing church is one that chooses not to solve the issues and does not complete its goals. Thus they end up going nowhere.

A winner follows Christ in obedience and a loser comes up with excuses, like the man who wanted to stay home and wait until his father died before following Jesus. You can make yourself quite miserable by seeing your problems as unsolvable and by not obeying the Lord.

Dance to your own music rather than listening to the voice of the Lord. On the Mount of Transfiguration, God speaks from a cloud, "This is my son, my Chosen; listen to him!" (Luke 9:35).

A medical doctor, who was a member of the Church of the Savior in Washington, D.C., had to make a decision between an offer to join the faculty of a prestigious university center or to spend an additional year establishing a medical ministry to the poor. Which road would you have taken? Would you jump at the chance to further your career? Or risk the possibility of losing prime offers to be a healer to the poor? I wonder what you think the doctor decided? Did he dance to his own music or to the Lord's? Mom, what would you have told your son to do?

Concerning your journey through life, are you dancing to your own music or to the Lord's? Jesus strongly stated, "What good is it if you have a nice job, a good family, and live to see your grandchildren, and yet, you lose your very soul?" *Amen.*

Dan Phipps
Westwood Baptist Church
Roxboro, North Carolina

Sunday
November Fifteenth

Theme: Love Conquers All

Call to Worship: Trust in the Lord, and do good; so you will dwell in the land, and enjoy security. Take delight in the Lord, and he will give you the desires of your heart. Commit your way to the Lord; trust in him, and he will act. *Psalm 37:3-5*

Invocation: Lord, keep us humble. It is so easy for us to become self-righteous with our own importance in the church here on earth, that we forget we are on our way to a higher calling. Make us gentle Christians. *Amen.*

Hymn: "Pass Me Not, O Gentle Savior"

Sermon Presentation: "Faith Without Love"

Goals for Today: Our goal in this life is to show we are Christians by our love. Keep us humble and gentle as we work here in this church.

This Week in History

November 15-21—American Education Week—To build public support for American public schools. It is the Christian's responsibility to work for better education for all.

November 19—Lincoln's Gettysburg Address Anniversary—One of the greatest speeches ever delivered.

Announcement for Next Week's Sermon: Anger can be a dangerous thing, if it is out of control. It can kill you if you keep it all inside. Next Sunday learn to deal with anger.

Hymn: "There's a Wideness in God's Mercy"

Offertory Scripture: The Lord is my rock, and my fortress, and my deliverer, my God, my rock, in whom I take refuge, my shield, and the horn of my salvation, my stronghold.
Psalm 18:2

Offertory Prayer: Give us loving hearts that can feel and understand the pain that others may be suffering. Give us the gift of grace as we give you our gifts today. *Amen.*

Prayer: Another notch on our "gospel gun!" Another scalp of an unbeliever to show off to the faithful! We'll show 'em, won't we, Lord?

Just like the Pharisees of your day, Lord, there are many of us who confuse religiosity and correctness of doctrine with being faithful to our calling as your disciples who are charged with bringing the "goodness" to those in need.

May we always remember that our Father in heaven sent you, his Son, into this world not to condemn, but to console; not to put people down, but to lift them up; not to judge, but to save. If we cannot extend support, strength, and hope to those we meet, then remind us to be silent.

May we always treat those we meet with the same tenderness, the same sensitivity, the same unjudgmental attitude, the same compassion; in short, the same loving kindness as you did. You are our perfect example in all the things that we do, but most of all, in our relationships with those around us.

Love is said to be the identifying characteristic of your people. May our faith in you be shown in our love for others. *Amen.*

Story of the Week: Girl's father: "What reason do you have, young man, for wanting to marry my daughter?"

Young man: "I haven't any reason. I'm in love."

FAITH WITHOUT LOVE

A friend once told me of a funeral he had attended. The deceased was a young man who had suffered an untimely death in an automobile accident. The funeral home was packed with people, both young and old, who were nearly consumed with grief over this tragedy of a young life wasted. The boy's parents were so stricken that they could barely control their tears. The service began with uplifting words from the Scriptures. But then as it continued, a disturbing thing happened, for instead of the expected eulogy, the minister launched into an extended harangue. Citing the fact that this young man had never joined a church, the minister used his death as an opportunity to admonish all who were assembled there. As the minister said, in effect, because of his lack of Christian commitment, this young man might not make it to heaven. However, it was not too late for those in the room to learn from his example. It was not too late for them to confess Christ and make their eternal peace with God.

Apparently this minister was quite pleased with his homily, for after the service he circulated among the mourners, shaking hands, trying to make both himself and his church known to as many strangers as possible. In sharp contrast, my friend was disgusted with this self-righteous performance.

A woman was in the hospital recovering from surgery. A minister from her town, whom she knew only slightly, came into her room and plunked himself down on the bed. Still exhausted from her surgery, this woman didn't want any company. Even so, she tried to be polite to this man of the cloth. Totally ignoring the woman's need for rest, the minister read her passage after passage from the Scriptures, in between which he repeatedly asked her if she were spiritually prepared to meet her maker. Before leaving, the minister asked if he might say prayers over her. Summoning all her courage, the woman said no, she didn't really want his prayers. But ignoring her answer, the minister went ahead and said his prayers anyway—for her health and particularly for the conversion of her lost soul. After he finally left, the woman was shaken and frightened to the point where the nurses had to console her. Later the woman's husband angrily confronted this minister. But as the minister explained, he was only doing his Christian duty, bringing the Gospel to those in need.

Another woman spent long hours over several months caring for a woman friend who was terminally ill. It was a very difficult experience requiring a great deal of personal sacrifice and understanding. Even so, the woman, in her loyalty, persisted in trying to make her friend's last days on earth as comfortable and as peaceful as possible. Eventually her friend did pass away. At the funeral service, all the emotions that this woman had bravely put aside during the past few months swept over her at once and she began to cry. The next day the minister who had conducted the service came to this woman's home, even though she was not one of his parishioners. The minister's message was a simple one. He said it was wrong for this woman to grieve. In fact, if she were truly a Christian she would be filled with joy that her friend had passed on to a better life with God.

Needless to say, this woman was stunned. Having both her feelings and her faith called into question, her already heavy burden was increased considerably as she now wrestled with the deep pangs of guilt and self-doubt.

Medical doctors follow the rule of the ancient Hippocratic oath; that is, if they cannot bring healing, they will at least be cautious lest they inflict any more harm. Shouldn't Christians be guided by a similar rule? If they cannot bring spiritual healing, shouldn't they at least be careful lest they add to the burdens other people already carry? Unfortunately, the three incidents related above are far from unique. More often than many of us might realize, such incidents occur time and time again within the Christian religion. Time and again, overly zealous Christians impose upon others their own pale caricatures of the Christian faith, which are woefully lacking in love.

It may seem strange to suggest that there can be a Christian faith without love, but isn't it such loveless faiths that have hindered Christianity through the ages? Isn't it such loveless faiths that have led Christianity into such excesses as the burning of heretics, the hanging of witches, and the waging of wars, ostensibly fought over religious differences? The sad fact of the matter is that many Christians care much more about being "right" in their own eyes than they care about being kind. They care much more about their own rigid religious doctrines than they care about the welfare of people. They approach other people not as persons who are inherently precious, but as objects to be manipulated in accord with their own religious convictions.

We might call to mind here that robber in ancient Greek legend who was known as Procrustes. Procrustes was infamous for an iron bed that he owned. After capturing his victims, he would carefully fit them to this iron bed. If a victim was too short for the bed, Procrustes would stretch him. If the legs of the victim hung over the end of the bed, Procrustes would cut them off. Unfortunately, many Christians have a Procrustean view of their faith. Ignoring human needs, they try to fit everyone to the

November Fifteenth

unyielding iron frame of their own personal dogmas. Denying the personhood of others, they treat them as though they are merely objects; objects who may be preached at, judged, and even emotionally coerced when necessary—supposedly "for their own good."

The minister at the young man's funeral—did he care that this bereaved family and community desperately needed a word of hope and not condemnation in the midst of their tragedy? Did the minister see that at this moment the healing of their pain was much more important than the effort to build up his own church through conversions?

The minister at the hospital—did he care that this woman needed rest and peace of mind, and not an aggressive, unwelcomed intrusion into her life? Did he see that the fear which he needlessly planted in her mind could only undermine and not enhance her recovery? Did he truly respect this woman as a person, or did he treat her only as an object to be subjected to his own religious zeal?

The minister at the woman's home—did he care that this woman needed to unburden herself of the deep feelings accumulated over the months of loyal service to her dying friend? Did the minister really care about this woman's well-being, or was he more concerned about appearances and his own need to press home a theological point to her?

And I might add, a theological point which has little or no Scriptural backing. After all, when Jesus' good friend Lazarus died, didn't Jesus himself feel moved to weep the tears of grief at his tomb? Jesus even knew that it was within his divine power to bring Lazarus back to life. But even so, he still wept at this earthly parting. Contrary to what this particular minister insisted, can we who are only human be expected to be any less moved than Jesus was by the death of a loved one?

It is true that Christians need to have certain religious principles by which to guide their lives. It is true that at times they will need both to defend their faith and to share its strength with others; after all, Christianity is a religion of deeply held convictions. It is also a missionary religion which seeks to reach out and inspire the lives of others. But in all of these things, can our Christianity ever afford to ignore the purposes of love? Can it ever afford to ignore the personhood of those to whom it would minister?

Many Christians, who zealously impose their beliefs upon others, claim justification for their actions from our Holy Scriptures. But the model to which they aspire is less that of Christ than it is of certain pious Pharisees who provoked Jesus to anger because of their hard-hearted faith. You will recall two instances in which certain Pharisees were highly critical of Jesus and his disciples for their behavior on the holy sabbath.

In Mark 2:23-28, Jesus' disciples were hungry, so as they traveled through grain fields they plucked heads of grain to satisfy their hunger. According to the Pharisees, this act of plucking grain was a serious transgression of their religious laws, which forbade any kind of work on the sabbath. Cleverly, Jesus countered their criticism by referring to a time, recorded in Scripture, when King David was so hungry on the sabbath that he went so far as to eat the holy bread in the Temple.

In Mark 3:1-6, Jesus entered a synagogue on the Sabbath, and while there he healed a man's withered hand. The Pharisees were also very critical of this sabbath work, even though it benefited this poor man who had the deformity. They left the synagogue, seeking a way to destroy Jesus. But as Mark's Gospel relates, before these Pharisees left, Jesus "looked around at them with anger, grieved at their hardness of heart" (3:5).

Both of these instances illustrate human need in direct conflict with religious dogma, and to both of these instances Jesus declared, "The sabbath was made for man, not man for the sabbath" (Mark 2:27). The Pharisees wanted to deny these legitimate human needs in favor of enforcing their own religious presumptions. But not Jesus. He restored human need back to its rightful place of priority, ahead of their religious dogmas.

Jesus had a gospel to proclaim. He hoped to influence people into accepting that gospel. But the fact of the matter is that Jesus was not willing to use that gospel as a pretext for denying people their own inherent rights as persons. At one time the disciples wanted permission from Jesus to call down fire from heaven to punish a village which had rejected their ministry. Not only did Jesus refuse to consent to this act, but he also rebuked his disciples. Jesus often taught his followers that even their enemies and those who rejected them were still worthy of love as persons.

November Fifteenth

It was characteristic of Jesus that he respected and honored people for their individualities. He treated people not as objects to be manipulated spiritually, but as precious individuals, precious individuals who, with all their flaws, their anxieties, and their personal needs were worthy of his consideration and care. Typically, Jesus did not impose his religion on people like a thick, smothering blanket of do's and don'ts. Instead, Jesus met people where they were in life. From that basic starting point of listening to their needs and looking into their hearts, Jesus both ministered to them and encouraged them to seek first the kingdom of God.

You will recall:

—how tenderly Jesus dealt with the Samaritan woman at the well who had had five husbands and was now living with another man.

—how sensitive Jesus was to the woman who washed his feet with precious ointment using her own hair, while certain disciples were in the background griping at the extravagance of her act.

—how unjudgmental Jesus was in calling the hated tax-collector, Zacchaeus, down from his tree perch so that they might share a meal and fellowship together.

—how compassionate Jesus was in ministering to blind Bartimaeus who sat alone at the road's edge, and to the strange woman with a hemorrhage who, in the midst of the crowd, touched Jesus' garment for healing.

—and yes, how considerate Jesus was even of Judas by including him in the fellowship of the Last Supper, even though Jesus knew that Judas would soon betray him.

The New Testament is full of such stories of Jesus' meeting people where they were and respecting their individualities. It is these many stories which stand forever in judgment of all who would use their Christian faith like an unfeeling club to coerce others.

The Apostle Paul said it well, "If I have prophetic powers, and understand all mysteries and all knowledge, and if I have all faith, so as to remove mountains, but have not love, I am nothing" (I Corinthians 13:2). Paul's words are right on the mark, for as Jesus told his disciples at their last supper together, there was one thing above all others which should characterize their discipleship—one thing above all others by which people should be able to identify them as followers of Jesus. That one thing, that one essential Christian characteristic, was none other than their love for one another.

Faith is important, but even more important is faith's willingness to be loving. Without love, Christian faith becomes a mere caricature of itself. Drained of its vitality, its humility, and its deep sensitivity to others, Christian faith without love becomes just a hardened shell of self-righteous piety which does far more to hinder the cause of Christ than to help it.

The deep grief of parents exploited as an opportunity to win converts; a woman lying vulnerable in her hospital bed frightened to the point that her nurses need to console her; another woman told to deny her spontaneous, honest feelings of loss for the sake of her Christianity—can any such incidents truly be called victories for Christ? If we would be ambassadors for Christ, if we would be faithful to his teachings, then let us first of all be sure that we treat others with the respect, the kindness, and the consideration which their God-given humanity deserves. *Amen.*

Douglas K. Showalter
The First Church in Belfast
Belfast, Maine

Sunday
November Twenty-second

Theme: Stay Cool

Call to Worship: The Lord is merciful and gracious, slow to anger and abounding in steadfast love. He will not always chide, nor will he keep his anger for ever. *Psalm 103:8-9*

Invocation: Lord, teach us to be patient, slow to anger, but not afraid to show our wrath when evil is around. We need to be ready to act in love, not anger, and to be firm for right and justice. *Amen.*

Hymn: "He Leadeth Me: O Blessed Thought"

Sermon Presentation: "On Dealing with Our Anger"

Goals for Today: It is the inner anger that gives us ulcers and heart attacks. God's love can replace that anger. Let it happen.

This Week in History

November 22-28—National Bible Week—An interfaith campaign to promote reading of the Bible.

November 22-28—National Family Week—To highlight the role of strong families in the strengthening of the nation.

Announcement for Next Week's Sermon: God chooses some of the strangest people to carry on his work on earth. Next Sunday meet some real strange ones.

Hymn: "This Is My Father's World"

Offertory Scripture: He who is slow to anger is better than the mighty, and he who rules his spirit than he who takes a city. *Proverbs 16:32*

Offertory Prayer: Let me be angry when anger is required. Let me be loving when love is required. Let me be generous with my gifts always. *Amen.*

Prayer: Lord, this morning we would speak to you about what for many of us is the unspeakable—anger.

We are told "Nice people don't get angry." To be honest with you, Lord, Proverbs 16:32 makes us feel rather uncomfortable. You see, we're "nice people." We don't like to admit to getting angry with our families, our friends, our fellow church members, even with ourselves. Then when we hear about your anger we become confused. So often we picture you as being meek, mild, compassionate, and caring. We're comfortable with a loving, forgiving God. To hear of your anger makes us wonder, "Will God ever lose his patience with me?"

Help me to realize that being a Christian does not mean I cannot get angry. Help me to be angry about the right things. Like you, I want to pity the unfortunate and to get angry when people are taken advantage of. Like you, I want to be angry when people and institutions lack compassion. Like you, I want to become angry when those in authority abuse their powers.

But being angry is only the beginning. Guide me in my angry moments so that I might be able to use my anger constructively instead of destructively. And when the time for anger is past, let me then work just as hard to be a peace-maker. *Amen.*

Story of the Week: A man had been trying to reach his home by phone for over an hour, but kept getting a busy signal. Finally, he asked the operator if she could cut in on the line. She told him that she could do it only in a case of life or death.

"Well," said the man. "I can tell you this much. If that's my teenage daughter on the phone, there's going to be a murder."

ON DEALING WITH OUR ANGER

It might surprise us to recognize that Jesus could, and did, become angry. That's a fundamental dimension to the familiar cleansing of the temple. In this incident, recounted in all four Gospels with some variations, Jesus drove money-changers out of the temple. To do something like this, he must have been moved to the depths of his being. His vigorous protest was directed toward a misuse of the temple. It was to be a house of prayer; the money-changers had made it a house of trade.

One New Testament scholar has said it was Jesus' overt attack on their financial interest that was the real cause of the later

November Twenty-second

accusation brought against him by the priests. Or, as one has said it in a more vivid way, Jesus wasn't crucified for saying, "Behold the lilies of the field, how they grow." He was put to death because he said, "Behold the Pharisees, the crooks, the exploiters of widows, how they steal!" It's this anger of Jesus with which we must reckon, in his life as the unique Son of God, and in our own lives as those who are branded with his name. If one of the evidences of Jesus' humanity is that he was tempted, then yet another is the fact that he could become angry.

But isn't this also an evidence of his divinity? Indeed it is. In the First Epistle of John, the ending is this: "We know that the Son of God has come, and has given us an understanding, to know who is true. . . . This is the true God and eternal life." To be sure, Jesus was gentle, meek, and mild. However, he wasn't so flabbily good-natured that he overlooked the demonic in our sins, and all that was a violation of God's will.

Today, then, let's confront our own anger, and with him, deal with it. That's not easy for many of us to do. Though we were branded with the name of Christ, and though we are Christian, we feel that the expression of anger is almost a betrayal of our discipleship. We were among those who were brought up with that fundamental teaching: *Nice people don't get angry.*

Yet, all of us do get angry! And when we do—many of us—we take a big risk. The risk is that we might lose our feeling of belonging. That feeling of belonging means three things: I like myself as I am; I like you as you are; and I feel that you like me. But when I become angry, I risk losing those feelings—the risk that you won't like me anymore; the risk that I will feel guilty and lose self-respect. So, I tend to hold back on expressing my anger.

However, something else comes into play. We violate Jesus' teaching that we must come to a proper love for ourselves. When we refuse to acknowledge our anger, and to express it in appropriate ways, the end result is for us to become depressed. What this points us to is that our refusing to be angry doesn't necessarily mean we are well-balanced. It doesn't even mean, on this issue, that we are the most striking example of the Christian life—if indeed we grant that anger, unexpressed, can sour our relationships with people, and can drive us to self-hate. To be sure, our own good is involved in how we handle this emotion. After all, Jesus came that we might have life deep inside, and have it abundantly. It involves learning a proper love for ourselves, both for our good and for the health of our relationships.

Of course, just as in our friendships and in the husband/wife relationship, this has powerful significance. If, in the midst of such relationships, you feel depressed, could it be from an anger toward those you love, which you have never found possible to express? It's a question worth raising. In his *Trouble Book*, Eugene Kennedy says, "We are sometimes angry at persons we love but we cannot face this. . . . It violates what we want to feel toward them all the time and we are afraid that even a small deviation from this positive emotion would be disastrous."

What we need to understand—we who live in relationships as those branded with the name of Christ—is that if we refuse to deal with our anger, we are engaging in one of the most unloving things we can do. Why so? For the fact that it can kill a warm and close relationship, we must deal with our anger, and we must do that in constructive ways. In a workshop on this matter, three rules for expressing our anger are explored: (1) Don't hurt yourself; (2) Don't hurt the other; (3) Don't smash things up.

However, what are we going to do about the anger of another person, expressed or unexpressed? What about those times when we are the objects of such anger? Fae Moog used this illustration: A husband comes home for lunch, slams the door shut, and tramps hard through the house. At lunch, he takes big bites of his sandwich and says nothing. Of course, a less aware wife would think to herself, "Now what have I done?" But the more aware wife says to him, "Do you want to tell me why you feel so angry? You slammed the door shut and tramped hard all over the house. Now, you're eating angrily, and are very quiet."

The husband says, "I'm not angry!"

Then, as a way of maintaining her own spiritual, emotional balance, she says, "Well, super! I was about to put that inside of me. I thought maybe I did something to make you mad. I'm going to have myself a good day. I thought you were angry. If you discover that you are, and want to talk about it later, just let me know." Baptized in Christ, you and I can come to face the shadows in our lives as well as the lights. We can face anger,

November Twenty-second

both our own and that directed toward us. In the living Christ, we find grace to deal with it.

Go further with me, then, to see that the anger of Jesus had something else distinctive about it. That is, according to the records, his was an anger directed at wrong done to another person. Many of us tend to get angry at something done to us. With Jesus, it always involved a wrong to another. In the incident where, out of compassion, Jesus sought to heal a man, he "looked around (at the Pharisees) with anger, grieved at their hardness of heart." I like the way one writer has put it—"[Jesus,] wrath is the negative electricity at one end of his life, caused by the positive electricity of his love at the other end." Consequently, because he pities the unfortunate, he has profound indignation when he sees widows being robbed of their property. Because he has compassion for the woman caught in adultery, we can almost breathe his anger as he says, "Let those who are without sin among you cast the first stone." Yes, because of abuses of the temple, his prophetic anger is poured out on those who were trading there. That is, both positive and negative poles of the current of life were at work in him; the ability to love deeply meaning also the ability to show deep indignation when people were being harmed. Someone said it this way, "Anger is one of the sinews of the soul; he who lacks it has a maimed mind." Before he was president, Abraham Lincoln traveled down the Mississippi to New Orleans. After disposing of the cargo, Lincoln and a fellow boatman wandered about the city. There they came upon the first slave market Lincoln had ever seen. He saw people being sold to the highest bidders, families being broken apart, humans being treated like animals. He said to his companion, "If I ever get a chance to hit that thing, I'll hit it hard!"

You and I come into a most significant relationship when we are branded in baptism, and then live out the meaning of it within and through the household of God. Within that relationship we face our temptations, knowing that, even if we fall, we are sustained by him with eternal grace. Within that relationship we deal with our anger—knowing that we must do so for our own good, and for the good of our relationships. After all, the love of God is really a many-splendored thing. Often it is gentle, a "joy of heaven to earth come down." At other times, it is filled with indignation whenever and wherever his creatures are debased, degraded, and denied their places as his children.

Our anger at injustice is proper as a means of bringing about change so that all of God's children participate equally in life, so that all "might have life and have it abundantly." *Amen.*

Warren Nyberg
Minnetonka, Minnesota

Sunday
November Twenty-ninth

Theme: God Has Some Strange Friends

Call to Worship: Preach the word, be urgent in season and out of season, convince, rebuke, and exhort, be unfailing in patience and in teaching. *II Timothy 4:2*

Invocation: Lord, give us the grace to see ourselves as others see us. We are so quick to see others as a little strange, but to see only perfection in ourselves. Help me see the real me. *Amen.*

Hymn: "Dear Lord and Father of Mankind"

Sermon Presentation: "In Praise of Unlikely Apostles"

Goals for Today: We are a diverse group of people right here in this congregation. But we are the people of God; individually and corporately, we are the people of God.

This Week in History

November 29—First Sunday in Advent—The first of four Sundays before Christmas. A time of preparation for the coming of the Christ Child.

November 30—Mark Twain's Birthday (Samuel L. Clemens)— One of America's most celebrated authors. He wrote *Tom Sawyer*, *Huckleberry Finn*, and so forth.

Announcement for Next Week's Sermon: Did you ever think of Jesus as a thief? Next Sunday we will talk about Jesus as a thief.

Hymn: "Savior, Again to Thy Dear Name"

Offertory Scripture: My son, do not despise the Lord's discipline or be weary of his reproof, for the Lord reproves him whom he loves, as a father the son in whom he delights. *Proverbs 3:11-12*

Offertory Prayer: Lord, you have given us the charge to go out into all the world and proclaim the good news to all people. We offer our gifts and our lives to your cause. *Amen.*

Prayer: Who me? Do you mean me, Lord? You've got to be kidding! I'm not the material saints are made of. Or am I?

So many of us have the image that all of your followers in Scripture and all of the saints we commemorate were "perfect" people. We call them models for righteous living. But when we study your word, and read history, we find that we have more in common with your disciples than we had first believed.

There was the great King David, who was the finest leader your people ever had. But like us, he, too, could fall victim to his desires and lusts. Thomas was one of your chosen disciples, but like us, he had his moments of uncertainty and doubt. Peter, the one whom you called the rock, his faith was great, but like us, he knew moments in which he became frightened—so scared that he even denied knowing you. And then there's Mary Magdalene, who, like many of us here today, had to take a hard look at her life and make some radical changes so that the life she led might be closer to your will.

You, who are perfect, call us, who are imperfect. You, who are sinless, call us, who are sinful. You, who are good, call us . . . well, you know us better than we know ourselves.

Remind us, Lord, that being a child of God is not a matter of our doing, but is a response to your call of discipleship to us. You look at what we are and know what we can become. As Christians, we aren't perfect, but we are forgiven.

Let us never forget that with God, the best is always yet to come. *Amen.*

Story of the Week: The famous Civil War general's great-grandson was visiting the small town in which his famous ancestor was born and raised. Strangers were scarce in the town, and as he walked down the street, several people were staring at him.

"I wonder who that fellow is," one of them asked.

"You don't know who he is?" the other said. "He's the great-grandson of that statue down in the city park."

IN PRAISE OF UNLIKELY APOSTLES

Perhaps it is no wonder that the women were first at the Cradle and last at the Cross. They had never known a man

November Twenty-ninth

like this man—there never has been such another. A prophet and teacher who never nagged at them, never flattered or coaxed or patronized; who never made arch jokes about them—never treated them either as *the women, God help us!* or, *the ladies, God bless them!*; who rebuked without being peevish, and praised without condescension; who took their questions and arguments seriously; who never mapped out their sphere *for* them, never urged them to be feminine or jeered at them for being female; who had no axe to grind and no uneasy male dignity to defend; who took them as he found them and was completely unself-conscious. There is no act, no sermon, no parable in the whole gospel that borrows its pungency from female perversity; nobody could guess from the words and deeds of Jesus that there was anything 'funny!' about woman's nature.

Those words were written by the British writer and theologian, Dorothy Sayers. They demonstrate perfectly why Mary of Magdala followed Jesus; why, throughout his ministry, there was such a solid, loyal core of women in his company; and why this Mary, whom we commemorate, was the first human witness of the Resurrection. Indeed, because she was first to the tomb, she became the earliest herald of the Resurrection to the disciples, still hiding in Jerusalem after the tragedy of the previous Friday. This is probably also why this Mary is almost always named first in any Gospel list of the women around Jesus.

The company of Jesus was indeed a diverse mixture of all sorts of men and women. There were some Galilean fishermen, subject to ridicule because they talked funny; a Jewish revolutionary traveling incognito; another in charge of supplies, who found Jesus' way of feeding the five thousand embarrassing; a former taxman; one bothered by both his intellectual density and his doubts; several who weren't quite sure of Jesus' strategy; some rather ordinary men who just went along; and then, the women. Certainly this was no "Rainbow Coalition," but it was indeed a motley group of human beings.

None of them would have been candidates for sainthood during those hectic years with Jesus! Especially not this Mary of Magdala! We don't know much about her personal history, but theories abound. Some think she was the woman Luke tells us about who washed Jesus' feet with her hair, to the horror of

Simon the Pharisee. Others believe she was one of a group of women out of whom he had cast demons, and that this Mary was possessed of not just one, but seven evil spirits. Tradition also has it that Mary, before she came into the company of Jesus, was the kind of woman we see standing on the street corners around town. Whoever she was in her uncertain past—demon-possessed prostitute or something else—the Gospels tell us that she had one great redeeming trait—her unswerving loyalty to Jesus during his ministry, at the cross of his dying, and beyond death to the garden of his resurrection.

Last summer, in a group discussion of Rahab, the participants learned that Rahab was the prostitute who sheltered the Hebrew spies who had gone to scout out the city before Joshua and his army could enter it. It was also discovered that Rahab is the name of a great sea monster, mentioned several times in the Old Testament.

The Bible will never let us forget the unlikeliness, the seediness, the downright unsaintliness of so many of its heroines and heroes. We men have to admit that we tend to be far harder on the Rahabs and the Marys than we are on drunken Noah, adulterous King David, cowardly Peter, or bigoted Paul!

It is, indeed, timely that the lesson from John 20:1-18 holds high before us two women as role models of faith and faithfulness. Ruth was a Moabite woman whose love and loyalty to her Hebrew mother-in-law's family and religion led her to marry two sons of that extended Hebrew family. In her marriage to Boaz, she entered, through their children, the direct line of descent of Jesus, himself, as well as being the great-grandmother of King David.

Today we really need to get rid of every false or chauvinistic idea of what saintliness means! In the Bible, saintliness is what God does with the persons he chooses, rather than what those people do for him! A biblical saint is given that honor *not* because she or he had some special piety or character trait, but because God wants that person to do something that partakes of his holy will and purposes in the world! A saint is, therefore, one who participates in God's work and becomes a willing carrier of his love and justice. Peter wrote to all who have experienced being chosen, through baptism, into Christ: Once you were no people, but now you are God's people. As a popular slogan goes, "God is not through with me yet!"

November Twenty-ninth

Everyone of us can rightfully say the same! Or, "We are always in the process of becoming Christian." So, arriving at sainthood is when a nobody becomes a somebody because the Lord God puts her to his righteous and loving use!

All of this is not to imply that the seediest of the saints just retain their seediness even after God uses them for holy purposes. Jesus said to the woman, about to be stoned for adultery, "Go, and sin no more!" Rahab had sense and insight enough to say to those Hebrew spies, "The Lord your God is he who is God in heaven above and on earth beneath." The author of Hebrews, centuries later, included Rahab in his "great cloud of witnesses": "By faith Rahab the harlot did not perish . . . because she had given friendly welcome to the spies" (Hebrew 11:31). Ruth looked at her mother-in-law and said, "Your God will be my God." Mary left the streets of degradation behind! And we celebrate today that she left the garden of recognition and ran to tell the men that she had, indeed, seen and talked with the risen Jesus.

God works against male chauvinism in mysterious ways! Because in her society women were not counted for much, it was safe for Mary to go to Jesus' tomb early in the morning! The male disciples had to hide for fear of the authorities! And so it was a locked-out, looked-down-upon woman whom God used as the first reporter of the resurrection!

Rahab, Ruth, and Mary were all tough, courageous survivors. The books of Ruth and Esther were not put in the Bible just because Ruth helps explain that Jesus' bloodline is full of questionable characters! Esther is not there just because the Hebrew Festival of Purim goes back to her story. Those two books really belong in the mainstream of God's story through the Bible! Ruth and Esther were women who in their own times became primary carriers of God's saving grace.

So a saint's day is not to help fill up some Christian pantheon with larger-than-life or holier-than-others semi-gods to be worshiped alongside our God! The ancient Romans did that, and all that is left today is ruins of their statues and buildings! It is also interesting that only twenty-two of the 194 individuals we now commemorate throughout the church year were women! I suspect that number would be much, much larger except for the male bias of most of our fore fathers in the faith, not to mention the lingering bias of those who selected those

194 persons just a few years ago! In spite of his own residue of chauvinism, the Apostle Paul put it so well: "There is neither male nor female in Christ Jesus" (Galatians 3:28).

All of these true saints of God become for us role models of redemptive living and witnessing. Our world says, "God has decreased so that human beings may increase!" If God seems to have gone into eclipse in the thinking and attitudes of so many people today, unlikely apostles, such as Mary, are the means God uses to let the Son shine again! Through the Ruths, Rahabs, Esthers, and Marys of his choosing, God proves that he is not in hiding! One of the primary ways we can know today that God is alive, active, and in control is through the steady, persistent, often unrecognized witness of the saints in embryo among us today! Fifty or one hundred years from now, our grandchildren and great-grandchildren in the faith will be remembering and commemorating people we know—the women and men who are helping bring God out of hiding for us! I dare to believe that such a future list of commemorations in the worship of the church will be far more evenly balanced between male and female!

If that happens, it will be because all of us—men, women, and children alike—will come to accept more completely than is true today the amazing grace of a risen Lord who taught his followers never to put people in slots according to age, sex, race, or class!

Finally, the lesson Mary learned in Joseph's garden is one that we so deperately need to learn in a time when sexism and age discrimination are so prevalent among us! According to John's account, Mary wanted to touch Jesus, as if to be sure he was not an apparition. But he said, "Do not hold onto me!" In other words, the eternal God will no longer be plain to women and men in the earthly figure of Jesus of Nazareth. He is no longer visible to us in the flesh, and he certainly did not remain in the tomb! But from the first Easter right down to this moment, the risen Christ is God's guarantee that he is visible to the world now through witnesses, such as Mary, who learned that eternal reality goes far deeper than what one can touch or embrace! Now, through the eyes of our Resurrection faith—and through the lives of a great cloud of witnessing women and men—we know and see God alive, working in his world still today, and still busy making saints!—often out of the most unlikely

November Twenty-ninth

material. As we start this Advent season, you, too, can be one of the saints created out of this most unlikely material. *Amen.*

Harold G. Deal
Luther Peace Memorial Church
Washington, D.C.

Sunday
December Sixth

Theme: Jesus Stole My Heart

Call to Worship: We know that in everything God works for good with those who love him, who are called according to his purpose. *Romans 8:28*

Invocation: Lord, you have stolen our hearts. Now complete your way with us and steal our lives so that they may be yours. Take us and make us what you would have us be and do for your kingdom on earth. *Amen.*

Hymn: "Take My Life, and Let It Be Consecrated"

Sermon Presentation: "The Good Thief"

Goals for Today: To help your people understand God's mysterious way of stealing our lives for his glory and our salvation.

This Week in History

December 6—St. Nicholas' Day—The Bishop of Myra in the fourth century, noted for his charity. Santa Claus and the giving of gifts are said to derive from St. Nicholas.

December 10—Human Rights Day—To proclaim the basic rights and fundamental freedoms to which all men and women are entitled.

Announcement for Next Week's Sermon: Is Jesus just a symbol, or is he a reality? Next Sunday we have a definite answer to that question.

Hymn: "O God, Our Help in Ages Past"

Offertory Scripture: Work out your own salvation with fear and trembling; for God is at work in you, both to will and to work for his good pleasure. *Philippians 2:12-13*

Offertory Prayer: As we talk about stealing we are forced to face the question, "Would a man rob God?" No, we would say, never me. Lord, here are our gifts; you be the judge. *Amen.*

December Sixth

Prayer: Linus was so right when he said, "The struggle for security knows no season." Each and every day of our lives we look to become more secure in our lives. In this Advent season, we remember that you came into our world two thousand years ago and you will come again someday.

It is not for us to know the day or the time, but it is for us to prepare ourselves for your arrival.

Help us to sort through our lives to rid ourselves of those things that would provide us with false hope and pseudo-security.

May we never follow the path of the rich fool who spent his whole life building his business and putting all of his efforts into building his security in his bank account. Then when his life was taken from him, he found that all he had was a false security.

Remind us always that we are constantly in danger of mistaking his gifts for God. You promised to come to us so that we might have life and have it more abundantly.

Let us realize that our real security will never be found in material things that wear out, in relationships that deteriorate or are terminated by death, or in life itself, which one day will come to an end. Abide with us, O Lord. Hold our hands. Let us feel your presence so that we might live secure in our relationship with you.

Let us never forget that without you as the foundation of our lives, we can never have the hope that endures, the trust of living under your grace, and the faith in the living Lord. *Amen.*

Story of the Week: A man's wife was storming mad and said to her husband, "That new cleaning woman must have stolen two of our towels."

"Well, some people are like that," her husband said. "Which towels were they?"

"The new ones," she said. "The ones we brought back from the hotel in Miami Beach."

THE GOOD THIEF

The title of the sermon may not be the best. It certainly does need some explaining! I tried it out on the church secretary. I asked her what it meant to her. She said, "Robin Hood." That's not exactly what I had in mind! However, her reaction was faithful to the selection.

It wasn't my intention to forward some economic point of view, in which the rich are to be robbed in order to give to the poor. Since my level of wealth is roughly equivalent—more or less—to the wealth of many of you, I recognize how much I dwell within a community of wealth. Now, the biblical text which triggered all this is from that awesome epistle, II Peter, "The day of the Lord will come like a thief, and then the heavens will pass away with a loud noise, and the elements will be dissolved with fire, and the earth and the works that are upon it will be burned up" (3:10).

That almost sounds like a forecast of nuclear disaster, doesn't it? But it isn't, for, in this account, the holocaust is understood as intended and initiated by God. Now, whatever people may say, the horror of unleashing nuclear weapons will be initiated by human beings, not by God.

Well, the biblical writer was wrong—both about the intention of God for his world and about the second coming of the Lord, which was to bring about the fiery holocaust. However, that biblical writer is right about something else; he's right about the fact that when the day of the living Lord comes—which can be at any moment and at any time—our false securities will be held up for what they are. It's that day, whenever it comes, when we will be pushed to place our securities where they properly belong, to live with them—and through them—in faith and by faith in God. So, the writer ends his letter with that powerful benediction, which even John Calvin called a "remarkable passage." "To him be the glory both now and to the day of eternity" (II Peter 3:18).

So, then, moving from the biblical text, and to some extent away from it—but surely influenced by it—this sermon is about our securities. It's about the *Good Thief*, Christ our Lord, who unmasks our securities for what they are and who, with the gift of faith, plants our feet on steady ground.

In one "Peanuts" cartoon, Linus sits contentedly, thumb in mouth, clutching his blanket. Snoopy races by and snatches the blanket. But Linus holds on. Out the door they go. The next four scenes show a royal battle for the possession of that blanket. Finally, Linus stands at the door—the winner—blanket still in hand. He merely says, "Whew!" Lucy says to him: "Are you

December Sixth

crazy? It's cold outside! You could catch pneumonia rolling around out there in the snow." The strip ends with Linus warming his hands before the fire, saying, "The struggle for security knows no season."

Now that helps to make the point of the sermon, for a good case may be made for Snoopy's being "a little Christ." In the book *The Gospel According to Peanuts*, Charlie Brown describes him as one who has the wonderful qualities of love, loyalty, watchfulness, and courage. But, being a dog, he has his other traits, also. As his name implies, among those traits is the tendency to pry and to snoop. None of the popular false gods of the Peanuts patch are secure when he's around, not even the blanket which Linus holds so closely.

I wonder if this sermon might not be better entitled "Creative Insecurity," for, at every point, isn't life insecure? Physical life is insecure; the tragedy of poison gas leakage in Bhopal, India, makes us aware, again, of how fleeting life can be. Among his many insights, Gibran, the poet/philosopher, said about sorrow and joy, "Remember that when one sits alone with you at your board, the other is asleep upon your bed. Verily, you are suspended like scales between your sorrow and your joy."

The inner life, also, is insecure. Perhaps far more people than we ever can know are fighting huge inner battles just to keep from becoming unglued. In his classic *Understanding and Counseling the Alcoholic*, Dr. Howard Clinebell refers to alcoholics, and to alcohol as their security blanket, as being "God in a bottle." Or take the breakdown of mental illness. I still recall a young parishioner who was on the road to recovery. She laughingly said she wanted to take her psychiatrist home with her. He was her security blanket.

Then, take our material possessions. For most of us, they are not only necessary, but they are also security blankets of the first order. We should accept them and live with them as part of what God intends for our lives in his world. That means our physical bodies, our salaries and pensions, our houses and food, our agriculture, and gasoline for our cars. After all, this is the season when we recall that "the word became flesh and dwelt among us, full of grace and truth" (John 1:14). That word did not remain pure spirit, nor did he come among us as spirit only. Moreover, right from the beginning of creation, in

Genesis, it's recorded how God saw everything he had made, and beheld that it was very good.

Take also our precious human relationships—our close ones, especially—how we cling to them, and how important they are for the life which God intends! But they are fleeting; they cannot fulfill some of the demands we place on them, and, in the end, they, too, give way.

This, then, is to point out the obvious, but important. All of us have our security blankets—physical life, inner life, material possessions, and close human relationships. There's a deep tradition within the Christian faith which affirms these needs and views them as part of the intention of God. However, that same tradition is painfully aware of the fleeting nature of each one. Furthermore, these gifts being from God, we tend—while we have them—to depend upon them and to live with them, as though they were God, himself. Rather than living life outward from the divine center, we live it out from one of his fragile creations. When the day of the Lord comes, then, it comes like a good thief, to snatch away our false sense of security that we might find that security on a more enduring basis.

It could well be that the substitute sermon title—Creative Insecurity—is just another way of affirming the nature of the good thief. In another "Peanuts" cartoon, Charlie Brown and Peppermint Patty are resting under a big tree. Patty asks, "What do you think security is, Chuck?"

"Security?" responds Charlie Brown. "Security is sleeping in the back seat of the car when you're a little kid. You've been somewhere with your mom and dad. It's night; you're riding home in the dark, and you can sleep in the back seat. You don't have to worry about anything. Your mom and dad are in the front seat, and they do all the worrying. They take care of everything."

In the next scene, Patty has a great big smile on her face. She says, "That's real neat!"

Then Chuck continues, "But it doesn't last! Suddenly, you're grown up, and it can never be that way again! Suddenly, it's over, and you'll never get to sleep in the back seat again! Never!"

"Never?" says Peppermint Patty, a look of dismay crossing her face.

"Absolutely never!" replies Charlie Brown.

December Sixth

The last scene shows both of them with dismal looks. In desperation, Patty says "Hold my hand, Chuck!"

Well, amid all the insecurities of life, there's a good deal to be said for the significance—indeed, the God-reference, involved in "holding hands." In a deep sense, Linus is right in saying, "The struggle for security knows no season." But isn't *holding hands* what we are doing, across the seas, when we respond to our World Hunger Appeal for the starving? Isn't *holding hands* what prayer does when pressing needs are presented to us? And, isn't that what we are doing when, all unwelcomed, death comes, and we hold hands by sending a hot dish to a friend who's engulfed by the loss?

At whatever time and in whatever place the day of the Lord comes as a kind of good thief. He does not seek to take away what the Lord of life has said is good. What he does take away, what he seeks to steal from us, is that undue reliance on his gifts, as if they were the ultimate and the lasting. After all, Jesus said, "I came that they may have life, and have it abundantly" (John 10:10). That's a cornerstone of faith in every single generation, but that faith can't come to its greatest heights until we learn to live in faith, and by faith, in him who lifts life up, who, as he does so, gives a kind of security the world cannot give nor take away.

We don't often sing that old hymn, "Abide with Me." If we can see through what that hymn is trying to communicate, then we see that it speaks to the whole range of life, and not just to the time of death. Yes, it speaks not to denigrate the securities to which we all cling, but to point us beyond them to the one without whom they are woefully incomplete:

> Swift to its close ebbs out life's little day;
> Earth's joys grow dim; it's glories pass away;
> Change and decay in all around I see;
> O thou who changest not, abide with me.

My reference to this hymn is meant to be taken as an affirmation of faith in him. Though that faith doesn't come easily—and sometimes has to be hammered out by experience to become deeper through the years—it's a faith which touches both our securities and our insecurities. It's a faith which has come *like a thief,* taking from us all false reliances, raising questions about all our sources of security, forcing us to place those sources within their proper limits. That faith forms the background of our lives, where we believe it properly should be. Except at those times when it comes into the foreground, on occasions such as this hour of worship. And on those many occasions in the common life when, as Emerson said, "What you are speaks so loudly, I cannot hear what you are saying."

We are now in that glorious season when the day of the Lord is focused upon a Bethlehem manger. For the person of faith, every day is a day of the Lord. So, because of what once occurred—all the way from the crib to the cross—we can affirm with the psalmist; "This is the day which the Lord has made; let us rejoice and be glad in it" (Psalm 118:24).

That's the moving faith which the Good Thief seeks in us, and that's the moving faith available to each of us. In the midst of all our securities and insecurities, our joys and our sorrows, we affirm him as Savior and as Lord. Then, as our ultimate security, we affirm, with the psalmist, and we so live:

> The Lord is my light and my salvation;
> whom shall I fear?
> The Lord is the stronghold of my life;
> of whom shall I be afraid? (Psalm 27:1)

Amen.

Warren A. Nyberg
Minnetonka, Minnesota

Sunday
December Thirteenth

Theme: Is God Real?

Call to Worship: And the Word became flesh and dwelt among us, [and we beheld his glory, the glory as of the only begotten of the Father] full of grace and truth. *John 1:14*

Invocation: Lord, make your presence real in my life. I cannot settle for a God who *probably* exists. Touch my life so that I can feel your presence. Come into my life and possess me; then I will know the reality of God. *Amen.*

Hymn: "Once to Every Man and Nation"

Sermon Presentation: "The Presence of Jesus: Symbol or Reality?"

Goals for Today: Life is filled with experiences that give God a chance to touch us: the birth of a baby, a clear spring morning, the illness and recovery of a loved one. At all these times, God seems so real. Learn to trust, and God will be real.

This Week in History

December 13—Phillip Brooks' Birthday—Clergyman and composer, remembered for his Christmas carol "O Little Town of Bethlehem."

December 15—Bill of Rights Day—The first ten Amendments to the Constitution, ratified December 15, 1791. To guarantee freedom to all people in America.

Announcement for Next Week's Sermon: Do you like surprises? Everyone does. Would it sound strange if I told you all of life is one big surprise? Next week: Surprise!

Hymn: "Blessed Assurance, Jesus is Mine"

Offertory Scripture: For God so loved the world that he gave his only Son, that whoever believes in him should not perish but have eternal life. For God sent the Son into the world not to

condemn the world, but that the world might be saved through him.
John 3:16-17

Offertory Prayer: Don't ever leave me, Lord. I need you by my side because without you I am scared to death. Be my God and let me be your servant. Accept these gifts as a token of my confidence in your reality in my life. *Amen.*

Prayer: The pace of this world is so fast I just can't keep up with it. The wonders of science have revealed more of your wonders to us in the last twenty-five years than in all the previous time. How are we to keep up? How do we know what is real and what is fake? There are wars and rumors of war; terror stalks people everywhere. Murder and accidents kill people every day. All this is so new to us it just makes us look in a confused way and say, "Is God real?" That is the same question the Jews asked two thousand years ago. They, too, were confused about the answer. We are not confused. I know that my redeemer lives. You sent your Son; he died; he rose again, and now we know he lives.

Is Jesus a reality or a symbol? He is a reality in my life. He owns me and I serve him with joy. He is real; he is real; he is real! Amen.

Story of the Week: The minister had announced that he was going to read that day from The New English Bible. When the service was over, and he was greeting people at the door, a little lady said to him, "I didn't like it. If the King James version of the Bible was good enough for Paul and Silas, then it's good enough for me."

THE PRESENCE OF JESUS: SYMBOL OR REALITY?

On the evening of that day, the first day of the week, the doors being shut where the disciples were, for fears of the Jews, Jesus came and stood among them and said to them, "Peace be with you." When he had said this, he showed them his hands and his side. Then the disciples were glad when they saw the Lord. Jesus said to them again, "Peace be with you. As the Father has sent me, even so I send you."

December Thirteenth

And when he had said this, he breathed on them, and said to them, "Receive the Holy Spirit. If you forgive the sins of any, they are forgiven; if you retain the sins of any, they are retained." (John 20:19-23)

The above text is a rather well-known one, but one which many people have often misinterpreted. The disciples had gathered in a room somewhere in Jerusalem, having fearfully locked the doors. Their leader, Jesus, had been crucified. All their hopes had been dashed. They were crippled with fear. It is very human that they reacted in this way. They had placed all their hopes in this man over a period of three years, during which they followed him on his preaching and teaching missions. They had grown fond of this man; they liked him as a person. But more importantly, they attached to him those hopes of expecting a messiah, which had grown out of the Jewish tradition and which had gained a special flavor during the time of the late Roman occupation of Israel. Jesus had been not only a religious figure, because of the status of the Jews as a subdued power, but Jesus had also attained political significance. The Jews had exploited in a clever way this political aspect of Jesus' mission, which made it possible ultimately for Jesus to be nailed to the cross.

In this situation it was incriminating to have been associated with Jesus. The sign of the cross was the sign of punishment of a criminal. It was a human reaction to attempt to shake off this incriminating tinge. The disciples had acted in that general way even during the last days of Jesus' life. They had disowned him; most especially Peter had done so, that one of the disciples who had sworn eternal loyalty. But we must understand what it meant for them, psychologically, to have had their esteemed leader taken from them. They were in a state of shock and grief when Jesus was nailed to the cross. Grief, uncertainty, and personal insecurity set in when we experience a dramatic change in our lives, but they do so especially when a member of our family or a close friend dies. Grief is necessary, so modern psychology tells us, for us to get over the loss and to learn to adapt to the real world of those with whom we have to continue our lives. The disciples were in this state of shock and grief, and in addition they believed they have to hide themselves for political reasons. They sat quietly and inertly in the room behind locked doors.

There is also a theological reason, beside the human one, which is significant here. The Swiss theologian Karl Barth has made a distinction between religiosity and Christianity. Barth's distinction is now somewhat disputed, but he based it only on an Old Testament theme which cannot be overlooked. Already the old prophets had warned of false religion, a type of religion which man invariably establishes as a prop to hold up his faltering self. Feeling isolated and helpless, distant from the real God, so the Old Testament prophets have told us, man creates idols to which he becomes attached. That is the old story of religion, or rather pseudo-religion, with which Christianity must not be confused. Karl Barth spent most of his considerable theological intelligence in the service of Christianity combatting religiosity.

But Barth has pointed to someone before him as a source of his thought: Ludwig Feuerbach. Feuerbach became famous for his book *Essence of Christianity* in the nineteenth century, in which he put forth those ideas which are in large part still the foundations of contemporary Communistic atheism. The insight which Feuerbach had is that men find themselves, generally, in a state of misery. To become conscious of this misery is the first step to rising above it, but the one who becomes conscious of it frequently commits a drastic error. Instead of turning against the misery itself, man projects a symbol of perfection onto the screen of the universe and bathes himself in the glory of this pseudo-world. The real misery is not changed at all in this process. On the contrary, the constant gazing at the imagined world of perfection perpetuates and solidifies the real world of imperfection. So Feuerbach polemicized admirably against these symbols of perfection which become barricades against enlightening social action. He polemicized against pseudo-religion and insisted that man should make only one thing the object of all his adoration, man himself. Feuerbach identified Christianity as that type of pseudo-religion which is in need of destruction if man is to become freed from socially repressive ideologies.

Barth understood the significant aspect of this critique of religion. He did not go with Feuerbach's contention that the real object of belief and adoration should be man himself. On the contrary, he insisted that man becomes himself only if empowered to become so by God, himself, in whose image man

December Thirteenth

is made. But Barth understood that a good part of Christianity—cultural, historically grown Christianity—indeed conformed to the self-made ideology model which Feuerbach attacked.

Marxism also inherited this understanding of religion, and the sad thing is that modern Marxist societies have a completely warped understanding of "religion." Religion is only to be discarded, and Marxism has no creativity to distinguish the right from the wrong kind of religion, as Barth had done. There is a museum famous for its large collection of ancient icons. The most famous one is of the face of Christ. This icon is famous for the almost other-worldly smile on the face of Jesus. So beautiful is the face, that tradition has come to believe that the image was not painted by human hand at all, but by God, himself. The Communists believe man does not need religion. Religion is not opposed by the state, but by those who are unenlightened, who can brush it aside as an unnecessary encumbrance. You cannot help detecting a great pride in all the Russian achievements of man. The sensitive person also has to observe how forced everything is, how little grace there is in everything, and how the complete reliance on mere human achievements also betrays an essential and deep insecurity.

Of course modern Russian atheism is right in one point, as had been Feuerbach and Karl Barth; that the balloon of manmade religious illusion has to pop some time. When that time comes, a great disillusionment and passivity cannot help but settle on the heart. That kind of disillusionment stifled the disciples. It is a disillusionment that is basically necessary for the life of the church. Jesus knew that there was something wrong in the allegiance of his friends, but he could do nothing about it. He knew that he had to take that false faith with him into the grave. Theologically, the discontinuity between human religion and God-given Christian faith is just as necessary as Christian faith also builds on the human yearning for God.

At the point of disillusionment, when the followers of Jesus sat fearfully and quietly in the locked room, at just that point Jesus enters the room—the text does not say where he came from; the intimation is that he simply walked through the wall. Then we have a strange, mysterious statement: "He breathed on them, and said to them, 'Receive the Holy Spirit' " (John

20:22). The theological point is obvious, the young church had to be cleansed of all impurities, all human passion, zest for achievement, hopes, and accomplishments had to die before God could start his work. Before the young church could start to be active, all human endeavor had to become passive.

When we read this passage in John 20, another passage from the Bible comes to mind. It is the second creation narrative in Genesis 2, in which the Jahwist, in his typically anthropological vein, describes the manner in which God creates man. This new creature is related to the ground from the very beginning. The ground, the earth, needs man just as man needs the earth. Without human cultivation, the earth is barren and chaotic. But man needs the earth as his source of livelihood. In fact, the human frame is made of earth. Then we read the passage which is so similar to the one in John 20—God, having formed the frame from clay, breathes life into it. We can envision that passive frame—there is no life in it at all, just like there is no life in a lump of clay. The disciples were as passive as that lump of clay, Adam, before God breathed life into him. The breath of God's life is quickening, and when John alludes to that passage in Genesis 2, he does so with good reason: the saving event of Christ's presence can become active in human lives and in God's history only if human religiosity has come to an end, only if the human zest to secure life has been overcome. The secret of God's death in Christ is this, that this quest for human security, the barricade to real religiosity, can be overcome only if God makes himself available as an object of human adoration and kills it by taking it with himself to the cross. Once that is accomplished, God can start his work all over again, his redeeming work, which now takes place in Christian history every day and every hour.

Karl Barth loved United States history, and especially church history. But he was in this country only once. When he lectured and worshiped with Americans, he astounded his hosts with his astute knowledge of American history. Once, after a service in which the famous all-American church hymn, "Stand up, Ye Men of God, Be done with lesser things," was sung, he said to his hosts: That hymn should really be called, "Sit Down, Ye Men of God, Ye Cannot Do a Thing!" It is not that God does not use human initiative and energy, not that mere moralism is of little

December Thirteenth

value, not that man should not strive to be good or follow the ten commandments. These natural religious forms, given with God's creation, are of inestimable value in ordinary life, but man inadvertently corrupts them and forgets that there is little salvation in knowing that one has conformed to a law. Luther once said that the ten commandments can be fulfilled. But the *law* of the New Testament, as we find it in the twenty-fifth chapter of Matthew, is impossible to be fulfilled. What shall the good Christian, who tries to live by the *new* law, do then? In despair he is driven into the arms of Christ, who has already fulfilled this law for him. Therefore, the Christian is free from the bondage of the law, knowing that in Christ, into whom he is grafted, has already fulfilled it.

The fourth movement of Beethoven's Ninth Symphony contains the famous choral part in which the great composer immortalized the *"Ode to Joy"* by Schiller. In part of that ode there appears the statement that there must be a dear Father above the heavens. I have always wondered about those words. Is Schiller not certain that a dear Father lives above the heavens? The mere assertion, however insistent it may be made, that there must be a dear Father somewhere is of no consolation to me. I want to know for certain. The religious type invariably builds his faith on such a diluted insistence that man must be religious, that he must strive onward and upward to reach God. To mistake Christianity for this type of religiosity is to make a fatal mistake, for God came to man in Jesus Christ and therewith crossed out all misleading attempts to reach God with imposing towers of religiosity. Christians, in the United States and abroad, were once again affirmed in their problematic understanding of the Christian faith in the song, "The Impossible Dream," from the musical *Man from La Mancha*. There is nothing impossible in Christ's coming. We have in him God before us, indisputable, historically certain. We need not strive anymore for the impossible. We need no longer yearn for the beyond.

All attempts to explain away this historically certain presence of God must lead astray. What type of presence do we find, then, among the disciples who locked themselves in the room? It is certainly more than a mere physical presence. John indicated this with the hint that Jesus did not need to break any locks or walls. He was simply there, the presence of the

Resurrected Christ in the resurrected body of the earthly Christ, but nonetheless more than that old body. The mere physical body of Jesus of Nazareth would not help us very much, for he could not be with us always and at every place. Is the presence of Christ, then, merely symbolic, perhaps an imagination or representation of the ingenuity of the human intellect? The biblical testimony rules out this alternative. Christ was more than a mere possibility. Christ was really present among his friends. Of what nature then, was, his presence? It was spiritual, for Jesus says to them: "Receive the Holy Spirit."
Amen.

Rolf Ahlers
Russell Sage College
Troy, New York

Sunday
December Twentieth

Theme: Life Is Just Full of Them

Call to Worship: Let us consider how to stir up one another to love and good works. *Hebrews 10:24*

Invocation: How we all love a surprise, but Lord, not from you. Be that steady force in our lives that adds stability, so that when the surprises of life overtake us we can handle them. You are always there—yesterday, today, and forever. *Amen.*

Hymn: "Jesus Calls Us O'er the Tumult"

Sermon Presentation: "Surprise"

Goals for Today: Life is filled with surprises. How we cope with the surprises in our lives is the key to a happy one or one lived in fear. Face all the surprises with faith and you will live a joy-filled life.

This Week in History

December 24—"Silent Night, Holy Night"—Oberndorf, Hellein and Wagrain, Salzburg, Austria. Commemorating the creation of the Christmas carol in 1818.

December 25—Christmas—What else can I say? A blessed Christmas to you all.

Announcement for Next Week's Sermon: If you have had a new baby in your house recently, you know how everything can change. Wait until you see the changes the baby in next week's sermon makes in the whole world.

Hymn: "Have Thine Own Way, Lord"

Offertory Scripture: Be kind to one another, tenderhearted, forgiving one another, as God in Christ forgave you. *Ephesians 4:32*

Offertory Prayer: We give these our gifts joyfully; that comes as a surprise to me. Until I gave a sacrificial gift, I did not know the true joy of giving. How you can keep on loving me, imperfect as I am, is a constant surprise to me. Keep on loving me, Lord. *Amen.*

Prayer: Surprise! Lord, that is a word we hear so often in our lives. Sometimes it is good news—a party and a gathering of friends to share a good time and an important event. Other times surprises come in the form of an accident or a tragedy.

Even your relationship with us can be called a surprise. It surprises us that you, who are so good, could love us, who are so sinful; that you, who are so mighty, could care for us, who are so weak; that you, who are so wise, would care for us, who are so ignorant.

You come to us in so many surprising ways—in a pillar of fire, a burning bush, the mighty words of a prophet, in a whirlwind, in a still small voice, in the waters of baptism, in the bread and wine of communion, in a small baby named Jesus, in an empty tomb from which you rolled away the stone. You even come to us on a cross.

But let us never forget, O Lord, that even in the midst of all the surprises of life, there is one thing of which we can be sure—that is our relationship with you.

Remind us always, in the words of Paul, "Nothing can separate us from the love of God which is ours in Jesus Christ our Lord." *Amen.*

Story of the Week: A woman had been taking tranquilizers and her friend was asking her about them.

"There are times when I get nervous," the first woman said. "I have thought of taking a tranquilizer now and then, but I am afraid they are habit forming. Are they?"

"Habit forming?" her friend said. "Certainly not. Not if you take them regularly."

SURPRISE

Indulge me for a moment while I make a sweeping generalization. It seems that just about every momentous human event takes place as a surprise. With that said, let's see if I can defend it.

December Twentieth

Marriage is a surprise. I don't really know of anyone who out to get married. The relationship simply evolves.

Birth is a surprise. Even if a woman is trying to get pregnant, when it finally happens, it's a surprise. The actual birth is a surprise—it's a boy! Or a girl! Or one of each!

Death is also a surprise. Death often catches us unsuspecting and unexpecting. Even when we get the news that our cancer is terminal, death is still a surprise.

Illness is a surprise. No one intentionally sets out to catch the worst case of flu, but after it's over, it is remembered as a momentous event.

Humor catches us by surprise; otherwise it wouldn't be humorous.

A legal firm once sent flowers to an associate upon the opening of its new offices. Through some mixup, the ribbon which bedecked the floral piece read "Deepest Sympathy." When the florist was informed of his mistake, he let out a cry of alarm. "Good heavens," he exclaimed, "then the flowers that went to the funeral said, "Congratulations on your new location!"

death / Resurn

Within the church experience, the conversion event is a surprise. To use a colloquialism, no one walks out of the house in the morning with the notion of going out and "getting saved." That event, which has many different shapes and forms, happens unexpectedly and is always a surprise. The first time I publically confessed Jesus Christ as my savior, I sort of shook my head when it was all over and said, "Whew! I wonder what made me say that?" It had not been my intention for that day's business.

Let me take us one step further and say that most of our religion is a surprise. Let me read portions of the seventy-third psalm:

> Truly God is good to the upright,
>   to those who are pure in heart.
> But as for me, my feet had almost stumbled,
>   my steps had well nigh slipped.
> For I was envious of the arrogant,
>   when I saw the prosperity of the wicked.
>
> For they have no pangs;
>   their bodies are sound and sleek.

They are not in trouble as other men are;
   they are not stricken like other men.
Therefore pride is their necklace;
   violence covers them as a garment.
Their eyes swell out with fatness,
   their hearts overflow with follies.
They scoff and speak with malice;
   loftily they threaten oppression.
They set their mouths against the heavens,
   and their tongue struts through the earth.

Therefore the people turn and praise them;
   and find no fault in them.
And they say, "How can God know?
   Is there knowledge in the Most High?"
Behold, these are the wicked;
   always at ease, they increase in riches.
All in vain have I kept my heart clean
   and washed my hands in innocence.
For all the day long I have been stricken,
   and chastened every morning.

If I had said, "I will speak thus,"
   I would have been untrue to the
      generation of thy children.
   But when I thought how to understand this,
      it seemed to me a wearisome task,
   until I went into the sanctuary of God;
      then I perceived their end.

When my soul was embittered,
   when I was pricked in heart,
I was stupid and ignorant,
   I was like a beast toward thee.
Nevertheless I am continually with thee;
   thou dost hold my right hand.
Thou dost guide me with thy counsel,
   and afterward thou wilt receive me to glory.
                              (Psalm 73:1-17, 21-24)

Here we find a discouraged person. One who feels beaten and angry with God, one who is almost ready to denounce God for the world's injustice. This looked to him to be a tiring task;

December Twentieth

so, for whatever reason, he went to the temple to collect his thoughts, and maybe even prepare to begin his maligning of God.

Something happened—we don't know what—but somehow he came out with a different attitude. One of his discoveries was a big surprise to him; that through his darkest hours, God had been there, offering strength, and perseverance for life.

There is a lovely bit of prose that has as its theme this same sense of God's support. It's called "Footprints."

> One night a man had a dream. He dreamed he was walking along the beach with the Lord. Across the sky flashed scenes from his life. For each scene, he noticed two sets of footprints in the same; one belonging to him, and the other to the Lord.
>
> When the last scene of his life flashed before him, he looked back at the footprints in the sand. He noticed that many times along the path of his life there was only one set of footprints. He also noticed that it happened at the very lowest and saddest times in his life.
>
> This really bothered him and he questioned the Lord about it. "Lord, you said that once I decided to follow you, you'd walk with me all the way. But I have noticed that during the most troublesome times in my life, there is only one set of footprints. I don't understand why when I needed you most you would leave me."
>
> The Lord replied, "My son, my precious child, I love you and would never leave you. During your times of trial and suffering, when you see only one set of footprints, it was then that I carried you."
>
> (Author unknown)

It is a surprise when we look back on life and discover for the first time that we have been carried through some of our toughest times because of our faith in God through Christ. That's quite a revelation, quite a surprise.

There is much about our religion that catches us by surprise.

Some time ago, old Methodist churches were called "Meeting Houses." The understanding of the term has changed over the years, but its original intent was this: When old-time Methodists gathered to meet, it wasn't to be entertained, or to have worthy discussions—although this did happen—it was to meet. Not to meet each other, but to meet the risen Christ. The church gathers together expecting the risen Christ to be present among us and known by those who hear the word and share the bread and cup at communion time.

Dull services result when we never really intend to meet.

Yet, the very presence of God is always a surprise!

We come expecting to meet Jesus Christ; we expect the Holy Spirit to have influence over our lives, and still, when it happens, it's a surprise. And it's a wonderful surprise.

Frederick Buechner, a theologian and author from Vermont, recently wrote abook entitled *Wishful Thinking*. It's a kind of dictionary of random thought. Under the heading of "Magic" he says some interesting things about religion and its quality of surprise, without actually calling it by that name. He states that magic is saying *Abracadabra* and pulling the rabbit out of the hat, stepping on a crack to break your mother's back, a dashboard Jesus to prevent smash-ups. It is going to church so you will get to heaven. It is using Listerine so everybody will love you. Magic is the technique of controlling unseen powers—it will always work if you do it by the book. Magic is manipulation; it says *My will be done*. Religion is propitiation and says *Thy will be done*.

Religion is praying; maybe the prayer will be answered and maybe it won't—at least not the way you want, or when you want, and maybe not at all. Even if you do it by the book, religion doesn't always work, as Jesus pointed out in one of his more somber utterances, "Not everyone who says to me, 'Lord, Lord,' shall enter the kingdom of heaven" (Matthew 7:21). The corollary to this statement would appear to be, "Not everyone who wouldn't be caught dead saying 'Lord, Lord,' shall be blackballed from the kingdom of heaven." He softened the blow somewhat, then, by adding that the way to enter the kingdom of heaven is to do the will of his Father in heaven. When religion claims that it's always sure what that will is, it's only bluffing. Magic is always sure.

If security's what you're after, try magic. If adventure is what you're after, try religion. The line between them is notoriously fuzzy.

The outcome is always a surprise.

In Luke 24:13-25, two disciples on the road to Emmaus

December Twentieth

happen across a stranger who shares their company, conversation, and food. He unexpectedly opens to them greater understanding of Scripture and has their hearts burning with enthusiasm. When they share their meal with this stranger, they recognize him as Jesus of Nazareth, the risen Christ. They were so surprised, that they immediately rushed back to Jerusalem to tell the rest.

The very presence of God is always a surprise. *Amen.*

Terrence M. O'Neill
First United Methodist Church
Ticonderoga, New York

Sunday
December Twenty-seventh

Theme: I Was There; I Saw It

Call to Worship: But you shall receive power when the Holy Spirit has come upon you; and you shall be my witnesses in Jerusalem and in all Judea and Samaria and to the end of the earth. *Acts 1:8*

Invocation: Lord, we are surrounded by a host of witnesses, all of whom testify to your divine birth. Let me be part of that great host in saying, "I believe; I believe it all." *Amen.*

Hymn: "Come, Thou Almighty King"

Sermon Presentation: "A Boy, a Baby, and Bethlehem"

Goals for Today: To make the miracle of Christmas an experience that lasts all year. We are all witnesses to this earth-shattering event.

This Week in History

December 28—Holy Innocents Day—Commemoration of the massacre of the children in Bethlehem by King Herod after the birth of Christ.

January 1—New Year's Day—The earth begins another orbit of the sun. In the next 365 days we, and the earth, will travel 583,416,000 miles.

Hymn: "We've a Story to Tell to the Nations"

Offertory Scripture: But when the Counselor comes, whom I shall send to you from the Father, even the Spirit of truth, who proceeds from the Father, he will bear witness to me; and you also are witnesses, because you have been with me from the beginning. *John 15:26-27*

Offertory Prayer: Lord, as we close this year, may we draw closer to thee. Accept these gifts as a thanks-offering for all thy blessings this year. *Amen.*

Prayer: The ribbons and bows, the wrapping, and tissue paper have all been made ready for the trashman's next visit. The gifts

December Twenty-seventh

on this Sunday after Christmas are placed under the tree. Some will become our favorites. Others will remind us of the people who gave them; some will never be used, soon to be forgotten.

Now that all of the hustle and bustle is over, it's a time in which many people believe, "Well, that's it for another year." But Christians remember that on that night two thousand years ago, in the back corner of the stable in Bethlehem, you gave us the greatest gift ever given—your Son, Jesus Christ, our Lord, our Savior, our Messiah.

You sent your Son into the world to be blood of our blood and flesh of our flesh. he began his life on earth in the humblest surroundings, but from this simple beginning came the "Lord of lords and King of kings." This was the sign that we had waited for, for it was in this tiny baby that God kept his promises. God heard our cry "O Come, O Come, Immanuel"; "God be with us." It was in Jesus that we saw what it meant for God to answer the prayers of the sick who prayed for healing, of the suffering who cried out for comfort, of those enslaved by sin and guilt for freedom, of the dying for eternal life.

You are very kind to us and we are grateful. Let us follow the example of the shepherds who came to the stable that night. Let us awaken the people with the good news "Christ is among us. God is with us. This is what makes Christmas merry." *Amen.*

Story of the Week: The little lady in the witness box had been getting the best of the lawyer.

"You claim to have had no education," he said sarcastically, "yet you have been able to answer my questions all right."

"You don't have to be educated," she said, "to answer a lot of silly questions."

A BOY, A BABY, AND BETHLEHEM

"And she gave birth to her first-born son . . . because there was no place for them in the inn " (Luke 2:7).

History has a way of being unintentionally garbled and distorted. The case in point concerns the birth of a baby, a boy in Bethlehem, and the events of that day. I know my good friend, Luke, has given an accurate account of those who witnessed and participated in that evening's events, but he didn't imagine that the innkeeper and guardian would end up in the limelight. You have heard his version of the story, now I would like for you to give ear to mine.

I am sure that over the years you, too, have assumed it was the innkeeper who provided a place to lodge Mary and Joseph for the evening, although that is not exactly what took place.

But let me backtrack and tell you a bit about myself. My name is Stephen. I am told that my father wanted that name, since his native country was Greece and my name in his land means *the crowned one*. I don't remember my father, for after I was born he left my mother. It was while I was still quite young that my mother died, but before her death she asked the rabbi if he would find a suitable home for me. It was his choice that brought me to the home of the innkeeper, Jacob, and his wife, Sarah. They are the only real parents that I can remember.

I guess it was a wise choice, at least one that I have never regretted. Oh, they are not wealthy people or learned like the rabbi, but I have always felt they loved me and included me as a part of the family. I guess the best part of the situation is that I love animals. No one has had to take care of more animals than I, except for maybe the shepherds. There were cows and goats to be milked daily; once in a while there was a horse to be groomed; and when the shepherds herded their flocks in from the hills, there was wool to be sheared and cuts and bruises to be tended. Then there were oxen that came in from the fields at night tired, hungry, and grateful for stalls with fresh straw and water to quench their thirst.

I never felt that my life was hard, though looking back, I suppose it was. It was good training, though. If I had it to do over there is nothing that I would change. The hardest things to endure were the taunts and jeers of the other boys who learned that Jacob and Sarah were not really my father and mother. It was pretty hard to listen to them shout, "Hey, Stephen, where did you get that silly name? Are you really the crowned one? We'll crown you all right." The one that hurt the most was when they would ask, "Why didn't your father ever come back after you were born? Was he ashamed of you?" Many times I would come home from the synagogue with tears streaming down my cheeks and anger in my heart. It always helped to go out to the stable where I could pick up the pitchfork and toss hay until the air was filled with dust and chaff, which would start me coughing and sneezing.

Even as I could sense the weariness of the animals after a long day in the fields, they seemed to notice my hurt. They would look at me with sympathetic eyes which seemed to say, "We understand."

The time about which Luke wrote was a particularly busy one for us at the inn. People seemed to be coming from everywhere. Jacob said it was because someone in Rome had given an order that everybody had to go back to the place where he or she was born. We were lucky, since Bethlehem has always been our home, but if the number of travelers was any indication, many people must have left our city over the years. Where they came from, I don't know, but it sure kept us hustling just to keep up with the continual crowds. I could hear Jacob once in a while mutter something about, "If they keep coming tomorrow like they did today, we're gonna run out of space."

We worked far into the night. As I said, I was used to working hard, but the hours became longer and longer. Sarah would protest that no growing boy should be expected to work so hard and long without proper rest. I know that it bothered Jacob, too, but there wasn't much he could do except to hope that in a few days the rush would be over. Why, we even cleaned out some animal stalls and used them. Some travelers turned up their noses at staying in a place where animals had lived; I guess they must have taken it as a personal insult, but it seems to me that animals seem to treat each other with more consideration than do some people. I wouldn't say that to just anybody, but, then, you know what I mean, don't you?

It was the third or fourth day of this rush, and we had been working long before sunup. By mid-afternoon we were again starting to turn people away. We did everything we could to squeeze as many people into what space we had, but in a short time we had to start saying, "Sorry, we just don't have a place that isn't filled." You could see the despair in the eyes of some; their bodies sort of slumped when we told them. I know it was especially hard on those who had been traveling for days, and it often hurt us even more than it did them. For some, it seemed to be the straw that broke the camel's back. Several times tempers flared as if we were to blame for the overcrowding and the order from Rome, but what could we do?

At about dusk, a man and woman arrived, she on a donkey and he walking. If anybody could use a good night's rest, they sure did. I heard them ask Jacob if there was a place in which they might stay and saw him shake his head. The man seemed to be pleading that if we might be saving a room for someone who hadn't arrived, would Jacob consider giving them the room. It was no use, though; there just wasn't any space . . . except . . . just maybe . . . there was a bit of space back in the stable. Maybe Jacob had forgotten, or possibly I didn't tell them that I had earlier in the day gotten it ready for some sheep, which are often herded in from the hills, but for some reason they hadn't come in for the night.

The couple started to leave, and I ran up to the man. "Sir, maybe I could help you. If you don't mind, there is a place in the stable which you can use. I know it isn't much." He dropped his head as if this was the final insult, but his wife said softly, "Joseph, it's not that bad and it's only for one night."

"But Mary," he protested, "what if . . ."

But she put her hand to his mouth and wouldn't let him finish. Turning to me, she said, "It will be fine, I'm sure. Would you show us where it is?" When she looked at me, I thought to myself that this must be how my mother looked and talked. It was her face and voice that sort of tugged at my memory, as if it were my mother speaking. I knew right then that I would do anything for her.

I motioned for them to follow me and led them back to the stable. Her husband lifted her off the donkey, and she breathed a sigh of relief as she reclined on the fresh straw. I ran back to the inn to see if I could find extra blankets so that they might be protected from the chill night air. Jacob wanted to know what I was doing; I told them that I had found a place out in the stable for some travelers and needed some blankets. He just shook his head as if to say, "What do you expect from a boy?" I did manage to find some blankets, along with a lantern and a bit of cheese and dates, which we always seemed to have in abundance.

As I came back into the stable, I heard Mary and Joseph talking softly and saw her grimace now and again as if she were in some pain. I asked if there was anything else that I might do for them, but was assured that they were comfortable.

December Twenty-seventh

Joseph said, in an accent I had learned to detect, for it betrayed those from Galilee every time, "You are very kind to us, and we are grateful. Without your hospitality this night, I don't know what we would have done."

I felt good inside. I wanted to stay near to them, but there were chores to do. I took care of their donkey, milked the cows and goats, fed and watered the oxen, and tended to the needs and wants of all our other guests. By the time I finished, it was late in the evening. Though it was dark out, there seemed to be an unusual amount of light; in fact, it seemed to me that it was centered over our city. Some had said that the stars were an omen of a great event which was to take place soon.

The cattle were quieted for the night, and I thought it best to check back on the couple. When I did, I found Mary asleep, with her husband keeping watch as though he expected something to happen. As I came near the stall he put his finger to his lips, and I whispered a good night and went to my room.

I was so tired that my head had no more than hit the mat than I was asleep. How long I had slept, I don't know, but I was awakened by loud voices. I could tell that it was Jacob and Sarah; they seemed to be arguing with some men. I rubbed my eyes, yawned, and was about to go back to sleep when I heard one of the men say, "Angels told us a baby was born here tonight." Then I was awake! A baby born here? When? Who? That was all it took for me to run out of my room to join the group outside.

"Stephen, what are you doing up at an hour like this?" said Sarah.

"Well, I heard all this noise. Is it true what they say—that there is a baby born here tonight? Can I see it?"

"Now, see what you've done," said Sarah. "You've awakened my son and heaven knows how many others. Now be gone, all of you!"

But the men, whom I now realized were shepherds, insisted that they were not going to leave until they could see the baby. Finally, I guess in order to get rid of them, Sarah went into the stable to see if it would be all right, and pretty soon she came back out.

"You can go in, but mind you, don't stay more than a minute."

This was my chance to see the baby, so I mixed in among the shepherds and went in with them. There had been two, but now there were three, a new baby. I listened as the shepherds told Mary and Joseph their story of how messengers of God had spoken to them while they were out on the hillside. They said that this baby was the Messiah that our people had long been awaiting.

I couldn't see how a baby could be much of a Messiah. Now, years later, I have come to know that he was the Messiah. That baby born in our stable in Bethlehem was God's gift and promise to our people and to the world, for he was my Messiah. For these many years, I, like Luke, have been one of his followers.

Outside the walls of Jerusalem, near the gate that was ever after to be called "St. Stephen's Gate," a man was being stoned to death. But the pain of the pelting stones was now gone. He could no longer feel their hurt, nor could he hear the cries and shouts of hatred. His mind went back to that inn-scene of years ago, a time when he, as a boy in Bethlehem, helped find an earthly home for the King of heaven. He remembered the after-years when the King had come out of Galilee to establish God's rule and reign. He recalled the wonder of his ministry; how, because of his humble birth, the common people heard him gladly and he summoned them to join him in bringing about God's will on earth. How he healed the sick, touched the suffering, befriended the outcast, and freed man from his guilt and sin. Stephen remembered the horror of the Crucifixion, the glory of the Resurrection, and the overwhelming joy of Pentecost. He recalled the day when the church grew and flourished, how he was chosen as a deacon—one whose duty it was to look after the needy, to tend the sick, to distribute alms, and to prepare the table when the disciples gathered round to break bread.

Now the enemies of this King of heaven had taken him, Stephen, and condemned him to death. Then, like his Lord, he prayed for those who were taking his earthly life, "Lord, do not lay this sin to their charge." When he had said this, Stephen's earthly journey had come to an end.

He, first of all the followers of the Christ-child, had won the crown of martyrdom. Stephen had fulfilled the promise of his name. Possibly that is why Christians for centuries have

December Twenty-seventh

celebrated the Feast of St. Stephen on the day following the birth of the Christ-child in Bethlehem. So this day we invite you, too, to follow this same one born as Lord and Savior of all humanity. *Amen.*

James M. Logan
Catalina Baptist Church
Tucson, Arizona

SPECIAL SEASONS
SPECIAL SERMONS
SPECIAL SERIES

SPECIAL SEASONS

DEATH IS THE BEGINNING

Ash Wednesday

After a recent funeral, a woman stayed at the graveside of her loved one long after the other mourners had started to return to their cars. The pastor walked over to where she was standing, and she said to him, "It's so hard to believe she is gone. I read the obituary. I went to the viewing. I sat through the funeral. I'm here at the graveside, and the whole situation became real to me only when you said the words 'We commit her body to the ground. Earth to earth, ashes to ashes, dust to dust.' "

The pastor hesitated for a moment and then said, "Did you hear the rest of what I said after that? 'Ashes to ashes, dust to dust, in sure and certain hope of the Resurrection of Jesus Christ our Lord.' "

So often in life we find ourselves listening to, or getting only half of, the story. When I tune in the evening news on T.V., I know that the announcer will probably tell me that the big story tonight is a fire in center city or uptown or downtown. He fills in the details of how severe the fire was; what kind of building was burned, whether a house or a factory or a store; how many people were killed or injured; and how extensive the damage was. We see dramatic pictures of the blaze, the firefighters, and the victims. It's a horrible thing to experience and to witness. A family's whole life's efforts, everything they have worked for gone up in smoke and flame, and in the end reduced to ashes. I'm waiting for the evening to come when the announcer fills us in on what happened to the family after the fire. Where did they relocate? How are they doing, emotionally? But there is never any follow-up. The next night there is another story about another fire and another set of ashes.

Today we begin the Lenten season, and we gather together on a day called Ash Wednesday. This particular day received its name in A.D. 1099 from the practice of the priests' taking the left-over palms from Palm Sunday, burning them until only ashes remained, and then marking the foreheads of the faithful with the words "Remember thou art dust and to dust thou shalt return."

We live in a world that doesn't spend much time talking about ashes anymore. The Lenten season and Ash Wednesday seem to have diminished in importance in most people's lives. We live in a world that tells us, "You owe it to yourself. Enjoy!

Ash Wednesday

Enjoy! Let yourself go! Live it up!" The ideas of self-denial and penitence are looked upon as being out of date.

Some have said, "Lent is too solemn." But how do we take seriously the fact that during Lent we remember how our Savior traveled to Jerusalem and the cross to die for our sakes? It's quite a dilemma in our modern age. We seem to be giving less emphasis to Ash Wednesday and more and more emphasis to the phenomenon of burn out.

We hear so much about burn out these days; people who simply give and give until they have nothing left. The fire in them has gone out. Their whole lives are reduced to smoldering ashes.

We find the perfect cure for burn out in the Gospels.

One of the hardest things even we Christians have to accept is God's grace. In the Gospels we find examples of how not to gain a right relationship with God.

The basic question we must all answer is: "Where is my heart?" Is it really caring about how we get along with God? Is it in how other people view us or what they think of us? In the eighteenth chapter of Luke, Jesus told the story about two men who went up to the temple to pray. One was a Pharisee, the other a poor sinner.

The Pharisee prayed with a loud voice in the synagogue, "Oh, Lord, I'm so glad that I'm not like others. I'm especially glad that I'm not like that sinner over there. I know, Lord, that you realize how righteous I am."

The other man simply prayed, "Lord, have mercy on me a sinner."

The first man made an issue of his own goodness. He must have been aware of his faults, but he was going to make darn sure no one else knew. He even tried to fool God.

Isn't it interesting that Jesus didn't choose twelve boastful disciples? Each seemed almost to be taken by surprise when they were called to discipleship. There were fishermen, a tax collector, and so forth. They were humble, honest men who realized that their sinfulness could not be overcome by their own efforts, but only by God's grace.

If we try to win God's love and acceptance, we will only burn ourselves out. It's useless. It's hopeless. We'll end up in a pile of ashes, and in the end all we will do is return to ashes and dust.

If we expect to rise from the ashes of life to a newness of life with Christ on Easter, then we first have to die with him during Lent; we must die to selfishness and self-centeredness.

God gives each of us a chance to rise out of the ashes of life. To do so, we will have to stop making excuses and take responsibility for our lives and actions. That means no more shifting of blame; no more trying to look good at someone else's expense. We are going to have to stop accusing others and deal humbly and thoughtfully with our own selves. Someone once said that Christians aren't perfect, but they *are* forgiven. Christ gives us the freedom to say, "I blew it. I was wrong. I made a mistake. I'm sorry." We also need to be honest and conscious of that for which we need to be forgiven. What stands between us and God? Where have we disappointed him? Where have we fallen short of his expectations? When have we loved someone or something more than God?

Out of the ashes God says, "Let me show you how to be born anew."

As we come to the Lord's table today, Christ says, "This is my body given for you. Don't worry about being good enough. My goodness I will gladly share with you. This is my blood shed for you. I love you in spite of your short-comings. Bring them to my table. Leave them here. I'll take your sins and your old self. You take my body and blood, and out of the ashes you will rise to a newness of life based wholly on my love for you. Eat and drink unto eternal life."

As Paul says,

> We beseech you on behalf of Christ, be reconciled to God. For our sake he made him to be sin who knew no sin, so that in him we might become the righteousness of God. Working together with him, then, we entreat you not to accept the grace of God in vain. For he says, "At the acceptable time I have listened to you, and helped you on the day of salvation." Behold, now is the acceptable time; behold, now is the day of salvation. (II Corinthians 5:20*b*–6:2)

Let God change you from an enemy to a friend. Don't waste God's grace. Do it now and rise from the ashes of life to share in his heavenly glory. *Amen.*

Thomas E. Richards, Jr.
St. Paul's Lutheran Church
Tannersville, Pennsylvania

COMPLICITY

Good Friday

Complicity is a strange phenomenon among human beings, having to do with our personal association in a wrongful event. It's something that potentially affects us all; yet, it's also something we usually fail to acknowledge when it actually happens in our lives.

Take, for example, Pontius Pilate in John 19:1-24. As Roman procurator in Palestine during the time of Jesus, he could have saved our Lord from death; yet, he didn't because of his own complicity with the Jewish leaders. Every bit of evidence we glean from the Gospels points to the fact that Pilate inwardly wanted to save Jesus. Yet, Pilate never attempted to do so for fear that the Jews would turn against him and against the authority of Rome, even as their leaders had coerced the people to turn against the man of Nazareth during the course of a week we now call "holy."

Now this isn't to say that Pilate wasn't a man of conscience, for, time and again, he had said to the chief priests and Pharisees, "I find no crime in this man."

Yet, he could have done more. He could have uttered a simple word of comfort to our Lord when there was nobody else in a position to do so—perhaps he could have given just a hand-shake, indicating some form of human compassion and feeling. He could have spared Jesus the scourging and the cat-calls from the soldiers in his command. The least he could have done would be to resist the pressures placed upon him, and tell the Jewish leaders to enter into a hell of their own making. He could have done any of these things—*but he didn't!*

Instead, the long, slow, and painful walk to Calvary's hill took place, culminating in the morbid sound of nails ripping into flesh that was all too human! Perhaps Pilate actually washed his hands in an effort to cleanse himself from what he hadn't done for Jesus while he had the chance, perhaps not. But, now, the damage was done, and although God would be able to forgive Pilate's complicity in the murder of Jesus, how could Pilate ever begin to forgive himself for allowing the Jewish leaders to use him as a "pawn" in their murderous game?

With each dull, *thud . . . thud . . . thud* of the hammer striking against the nails, more and more of the world's sinful complicity was being driven deeply into our Lord's body—Pilate's, and yours, and mine!

Why yours and mine? Because we, too, have opportunities to make a difference for those around us. We, too, have a daily responsibility to make gestures of compassion and human feeling to others whom we meet. And we, too, have been introduced to the man of Nazareth as a people of faith, who are commanded to love exactly the way that he loved. But it seems that each time we fail to demonstrate his love for one another, or for others—no matter who they are—we inadvertently and irresponsibly place our Lord back on a cross and drive new nails of sin into his Body, the Christian church. To make matters worse, we do so in full view of the world he died to save!

Complicity is a strangely subtle thing. As we think about our own contemporary responsibilities for the death of our Lord—or, at least, our daily negation of the life he died to give—let us meditate upon the following anonymous text pertaining to complicity:

> When they arrested the poor and the young, I did not protest, because they were criminals. When they arrested the blacks, I did not protest, because they were revolutionaries and lawbreakers. When they arrested the anti-war activists, I did not protest, because they were opposing the government and helping our enemies. When they arrested Puerto Ricans, Native Americans, and Chicanos, I did not protest, because they weren't really Americans, and were influenced by outside agitators. When they arrested the socialists and radicals, I did not protest, because they were Communist-influenced. When they arrested tax-resisters, I did not protest, because the law must be upheld! And when they finally came to arrest me and my loved ones, there was nobody left to protest!

So there he hangs, like a side of slaughtered beef, suspended between heaven and earth, with only a small sign hanging above his head to hint at the heinous human complicity that placed him there.

In Hebrew, Latin, and Greek, it read:

Jesus of Nazareth, the King of the Jews

Good Friday

We know better, don't we? As Christians, we realize that the person hanging there was actually the King of kings and Lord of lords, the Christ, the Son of the living God! And we also know who put him there . . .
AMEN AND AMEN.

James S. Vuocolo
Wyoming Ministries in Higher Education
Laramie, Wyoming

LET IT BE

Christmas

Christmas is a family time, as most of us would readily recognize and acknowledge. Reunions take place; it's always a heartwarming experience to go down to the bus station or to the airports and watch people as they greet arriving family members. How wonderfully exciting it is to see people hugging one another with squeals of delight, tears of relief, and sighs of profound satisfaction. Parents, children, grandparents, uncles, aunts, lovers, friends. . . . Christmas is a family time.

Ogden Nash has defined the family as "a unit consisting of children, a man and/or a woman, occasional animals and the common cold." It is appropriate that Christmas should be a family time because on the first Christmas, Mary was, as we say, in a family way, and the Holy Family was about to get its start. The angel Gabriel had come to Mary and said these famous words, "Hail, O favored one, the Lord is with you. . . . you will conceive . . . and bear a son, and you shall call his name Jesus" (Luke 1:28-31). Then the angel added, "Blessed are you among women, and blessed is the fruit of your womb [Jesus]" (Luke 1:42).

Now this was not good news to Mary. She was not married. She had not planned to have a child at this point in her life. Most of us know that pregnancy is always a time of intense personal crisis. Almost never do babies come when we plan to have them. Pregnancy is a crisis for people, but the absence of a pregnancy for young couples today is an equally great crisis.

When people learn that the Lord has something in mind for them that does not fit into their plans, almost always they respond by saying, "Oh no, no, no, no!" But Mary didn't respond that way. The angel came and told Mary that the Lord had something in mind for her that didn't fit into her plans, but Mary responded with these wonderfully profound words, "I am the handmaid of the Lord; let it be to me according to your word" (Luke 1:38). *Let it be.*

Paul McCartney wrote a popular song some years ago which included these words, "When I find myself in times of trouble, Mother Mary comes to me speaking words of wisdom. Let it be."

Christmas

We have an AA group in this town that meets every week. It's probably the biggest group in the area—one, two, sometimes as many as three hundred people meet in this group. It's probably one of the most important ministries that goes on in this town. Lives are literally changed by that AA group. The parking lots are full of cars. Notice the bumper stickers on those cars. One of the bumper stickers that is on at least fifty percent of the cars in the parking lot says, "Nice and Easy." Nice and easy.

One of the characteristics of the type of individual who becomes an alcoholic is that he or she finds it very difficult to deal with messages from the angels. That person resists dealing with reality and gets all excited and upset. This behavior is not confined to alcoholics. But that's why it's so important for them to remember to take it nice and easy, not to get excited and allow themselves to become upset by the message the angel brings to their lives. Nice and easy, that's what Mary said. Nice and easy, let it be. Let it be. That's not like saying "Uncle"; it's not like giving up. It is Kierkegaard's "infinite resignation," a way of dealing with reality, and the changes in our plans that God brings about. It is coming to terms, making peace, with the new realities.

But it's not so easy to respond that way. We become distracted so easily, so quickly by many things. That is especially true at Christmas time. People are not really interested in what the preacher has to say. Many people are thinking, "I hope he makes the sermon short."

What is on your mind? Are you thinking about gifts that you've given or received, or gifts that you didn't give and didn't receive? Are you thinking about how tired you are and things you have to do—the turkey that has to be put into the oven—or miles to travel this afternoon? You may be thinking about heated words that have been exchanged with your spouse, your children, your parents, a friend, or a neighbor. We get so excited at this time of the year, and can get angry very easily, especially with drivers, other drivers. Some of you are thinking about poor people; you've gotten so much that you have become aware of the fact that there are many who have little while we have much. Some of us really worry about that and feel badly because we have so very much at Christmas time.

Still others worry about nuclear war. It has been claimed that forty percent of the population said they expect the world to be annihilated by nuclear war before the end of this century, before the year 2000. Maybe you're worrying about that. Or maybe you're worrying about some personal tragedy in your own life or in the life of a friend.

There was a philosophy professor who was acquainted with tragedy. When he was a young man, his brother was killed. After he was married, he lost two sons in the Second World War. He had a tragic sense of life, but he was a man who was present and sensitive. He wrote many marvelous prayers, and I want to share one of those prayers with you this morning.

> Mighty and merciful God, born into this flesh, and in this flesh living in this world, we seek the support and refuge of every earthly thing and power, and though life brutally and forcibly forces us to drop one thing after another, we return again and again to put our trust in things obvious to sense and use, although there is no hope but in thee and no lasting joy save in thy kingdom.

Do you believe that? It's true. But most don't believe, so we get excited and distracted. But Christmas day is the time to say, with Mother Mary, "Let it be." Let it be. Let go of all that other stuff, all the other things on your agenda, and let it be; let it be. Now is the time to worship the Holy Child in our midst. Everybody who shared in that first Christmas had to do that. The shepherds had to leave their flocks; the kings had to leave their kingdoms in order to come and pay attention. They had to leave all those other things that were so distracting in order to come and pay attention to Jesus. Let it be. Let it be.

On Christmas day, we become worried and anxious about so many things, but Christ has come into our homes, and into our lives. One time, Jesus went into the home of his friends in Bethany, Mary and Martha. Mary came and sat down at his feet and listened to him, but Martha became anxious and concerned about being a good hostess. She was worried about getting the turkey into the oven on time, about the stuffing, about the neighbors, about all the things that had happened, the things that people had said to one another, and how Mary was out there not helping with all the things that had to be done. In her home was Christ; yet, she paid no attention to him!

My friends, let it be. Let go of all those other things, all those other distractions—at least for a few minutes—and let us come

Christmas

and worship the Christ who is in our midst. Christmas invites us to kneel in thanksgiving at his cradle and receive him into our lives. The angel of God has come and told us the good news. Let us respond as did Mary, let go of our plans for five minutes and say, "Let it be. Let it be." *Amen.*

James L. Kidd
Asylum Hill Congregational Church
Hartford, Connecticut

THE CHRISTMAS STAR

Christmas (Short Message)

"Now when Jesus was born in Bethlehem of Judea in the days of Herod, the king, behold, wise men from the East came to Jerusalem, saying, 'Where is he who has been born king of the Jews? For we have seen his star in the East, and have come to worship him.' . . . When they had heard the king they went their way; and lo, the star which they had seen in the East went before them, till it came to rest over the place where the child was. When they saw the star, they rejoiced exceedingly with great joy; and going into the house they saw the child with Mary his mother, and they fell down and worshiped him" (Matthew 2:1-2, 9-11a).

A star appeared, and suddenly it moved in the sky and stopped directly over the spot where its Creator was living on the earth. The Magi saw it. They came and worshiped the Lord of starlight!

How can we believe this report? Is this literally true? In the past, I have had trouble believing that this actually happened. Stars are gigantic balls of burning gases, that are supposed to be many times larger than the earth and very far away from the earth. We are told to believe that suddenly one day one of these gigantic fireballs appeared in the sky and moved until its light shone through the night onto the house where a baby named Jesus was living in a small town named Bethlehem.

Yet, is it more difficult to believe than what we are told about this child? We are told that this little baby was the great Creator of the stars and of the earth. We are told that the star the Magi followed was directed and guided in its path by the baby upon whom it shined its light. We are told that this spotlight in the heavens was planned by the infant whom the Magi came to worship. This is the heart of the Christmas news from the first century: the God who created the stars came to earth and took upon himself the flesh and blood of a human child—in fact the Creator joined himself to our human nature—he became a man who was and remained God! The Scripture puts it this way: "All things were made through him, and without him, was not anything made that was made. In him was life, and the life was the light of men. The light shines in the darkness . . . " (John 1:3-5).

Christmas

The star he made, by his will and plan, shined its light down upon him at precisely the moment he had predetermined. He created the Christmas star. He dictated that it would draw not only the wise men to him, so that they might worship him, but also that that same star might attract our attention to him. We see that star through the faithful words written by Matthew.

Why did he come down into his creation? He answers that question: "I lay my life down. . . ." This was his purpose in coming at Christmas, so that he might die for us on Good Friday and rise for us on that first Easter Sunday. He came to die in our place for our sins that we might all have the assurance of eternal life and his forgiveness. All he demands of us is that we receive him! Receive him who is the Creator of the stars, and his light will lighten up your life with his love!! "To all who received him, who believed in his name, he gave power to become children of God; who were born, not of blood nor of the will of the flesh nor of the will of man, but of God" (John 1:12-13).

So the star that shone down on him reminds us of the light that he will make shine in those of us who receive him. *Amen.*

Karl Kindt
Trinity United Church of Christ
Lexington, Missouri

SPECIAL SERMONS

WEDDING SERMON

(A MIXED OR ECUMENICAL MARRIAGE)

All marriages are mixed marriages—the couple being joined always brings together a variety of social, cultural, and personal attitudes. The religious mixed marriage often has the added dimension of a variety of life-styles which strike at the heart of one's basic approach to life. Whether real, imagined, or myth, there are often feelings which far outweigh any facts, and which tend to imply that such a marriage is somehow less than a real union.

Recognizing, of course, that differences do in fact exist, we must also recognize that the factors present in such a union are constant in all marital unions. These must be lifted up in order that the singleness of purpose, which brings the two together as one, can be clearly seen. In so doing, the unity of mankind will be affirmed and the teachings of the faith, concerning one God, one Lord, and one baptism, will become instruments enabling the couple and the concerned family members to celebrate a true and complete bond in love.

> And he made from one every nation of men to live on all the face of the earth (Acts 17:26a).
>
> Yet for us there is one God, the Father, from whom are all things and for whom we exist, and one Lord, Jesus Christ, through whom are all things and through whom we exist.(I Corinthians 8:6)

You will leave this place as one, but so it is that you have come—one in love, one in hope, one in the joy of each other. You are both equally loved of the one God who made you, who calls you his own, and who now blesses your marriage. It is this same God who calls himself Father and who calls you his children. Your love for each other is held as precious to him as you have each been individually held precious. He who made you loves you both.

You are one in the Father because you are one in the Lord. You know the same Lord, Christ Jesus, and are known by him. United in him, you are already united with each other in many ways; you are members of the household of God, redeemed by his love in Christ, seeking Christian perfection and living under grace.

Wedding

Your marriage today affirms your singleness of purpose as it affirms your love and your common faith. Affirmed, too, is the fatherhood of God, under whom you live, move, and have your being. Let this affirmation be the moving spirit of your life; let it give your love a rich depth which is founded in the God of love, and let it keep you united before the Lord who blesses this marriage.

Your lives may reflect your faith, your hopes, and your expectations in a variety of ways. Never confuse this with essential differences, and do not allow the rich variety within your lives to cause you to walk separate paths. You belong one to another and you belong to God. You hold your love dear and your love is precious to him. In this you are one in the spirit and you are one in the Lord.

As a body has many members and each differs from the others in a variety of ways, yet belong to the others and complement them in complete unions, so let it be with you. Rejoice together; share together; love together; hope together; struggle through the creative tensions of life together, and know that in all things and in all ways the one Lord who made you is with you as you enter into marriage and now commence your life together. *Amen.*

Charles Chakour
North Illinois Conference of
The United Methodist Church
Chicago, Illinois

THE LORD BLESS YOU AND KEEP YOU

Wedding

One of the most triumphant notes in the marriage service comes when the ceremony is concluded and, having embraced with the kiss of peace, the couple prepares to leave the chancel as husband and wife. What we term the recessional is not a recessional at all—not in terms of the marriage! It is the beginning of a new life; the first steps in a wondrous journey; the first steps taken together!

There is need, today, for the Word to be spoken to those who set out into this changed and changing world. At this magnificent moment, cannot the church do more than to simply "recess" the couple to the accompaniment of organ music and to the stereotyped clichés of well-wishers?

It is fitting that the minister, at this point, at the very end of the service and as a part of the benediction, offers a spiritual compass which can bring the couple to peace amid the chaos and the uncertainty of the days ahead:

> Therefore, since we are surrounded by so great a cloud of witnesses, let us also lay aside every weight, and sin which clings so closely, and let us run with perseverance the race that is set before us, looking to Jesus the pioneer and perfector of our faith. (Hebrews 12:1-2*a*)

And so you are married! Together you now set out upon your journey through life. What a journey that will be as you enter upon life, love, and hope—side by side!

You will move together into this last part of the twentieth century. These are the days to which you are called. There is one who can tell you what these days hold for you, for the shore to which you are heading is beyond an uncharted sea. Old pathways are being undone; new ways have not yet been developed. The old is rapidly dissolving, the new has not yet come, and today is filled with the troubles and upheavals of our social and cultural order.

Somehow, you must find your way and your place in this society. You must find meaning for life, and you must find your peace as your wind your way through the uncertainties of the day.

Wedding

You will search together, but you will not search alone. While you are moving into the unknown future, and while your faces are set to the new day, you have a rich tradition which will support you. You have a family who loves you, and who has nourished and fed you of itself. What a rich heritage this is!

You have a church, and the Lord of the church, who have set out on uncharted courses before, and who have won great victories of joy amid doubt, fear, and uncertainty.

And you have a Father—one who loves you, cherishes you, and now blesses this marriage. You are held in his hand. In his hand, too, he holds the future. As he has been God of the past and is God of the present, so, too, is he God of the future. He will walk with you in your coming journey.

He takes your love seriously; take each other the same way. Love completely; communicate honestly and share fully. By so doing, you will be able to face any onslaught which may rise against you, and you will be enabled to fully celebrate the many joys which await you.

You will have problems, but with such strength, never more problems than you are able to bear. And you will have joys. With such a heritage, your joy will be full. *Amen.*

Charles Chakour
North Illinois Conference of
The United Methodist Church
Chicago, Illinois

A FUNERAL SERMON

Funeral

What can we say at a time like this? This isn't a new question. Two thousand years ago the church in Rome asked of the teacher, Paul, this same question.

Faced with the pain, the injustice, the insecurity, the often tragic quality of life, they were filled with many of the emotions that we share today, feelings of anger, guilt, disbelief, anxiety; feelings of pain and protest—it's so hard for us to believe that _____ is dead.

As we search for the *why*, we come to the realization that so often life is unjust, and we feel so terribly insecure. We come face to face with the reality that someone we love can be with us one minute and gone the next.

Like the people in the church of first-century Rome, we look and say, "There are so many things that threaten to steal the God-given gift of love from us." They worried about disease. They feared persecution by the government. They were filled with superstitions. Today we find so many things still threatening us and our young people: drugs, alcohol, illness, fear of nuclear war, and feelings of despair that tear hope from our hearts and drive us to suicide. Now, just as then, there is the unexpected—the accident that barges into our lives.

We hope that we can learn from our mistakes—that's a part of education—but then there are those mistakes in judgment or action that we or others make that end up not in our acquiring knowledge, but in our losing our lives. Like the Romans, we ask "Where is our security? Where is our hope? Who can we turn to in the midst of the trials and tragedies of life? Who will bind up our wounds and wipe away our tears?" The answer is God.

Perhaps some of you came to the church today angry at God. We know he is present with us now, and we ask, "How can you let this happen?" God would respond by saying, "There is no place where earth's sorrows are felt more than up in heaven." From looking at Scripture, we see that God's people did suffer. But God sent his Son into the world to let people know that pain, sickness, tragedy, and death are contrary to God's will for his people.

_____ died on _____. It was a Friday afternoon two thousand years ago that the life of God's child came to a tragic

Funeral

end on a cross. It, too, seemed so senseless, so unfair. But we know that on Easter God set things right. The question each of us must face is what do we really believe in? A popular phrase among kids today is "Life is hard and then you die." If that's your philosophy, then life is just a cruel joke. Jesus would say to you, "Let not your hearts be troubled; believe in God, believe also in me. . . . I am the resurrection and the life."

The one who rose from the dead on Easter has shown us that he is stronger than sin and death. He has shown us that God can overrule the grave.

Instead of tragedy, we can find triumph. Instead of being victims, God allows us to share his victory. Standing on the other side of the Resurrection, _____ says to us, "Because my Lord lives, I live. God has shown me that death can take my body but not my life."

But what about us who are left behind? _____ would say, "Take your life seriously. Life is full of uncertainty and we shouldn't waste a moment or an opportunity to grow in some way, to help another person, to express love and gratitude to the people around us.

God loves _____. God loves you and me. There isn't anything that can take our heavenly Father's love and care from us.

May God's care and love, his triumph over sin and death bring peace and hope to your lives.

Amen.

Thomas E. Richards, Jr.
St. Paul's Lutheran Church
Tannersville, Pennsylvania

GIVE THANKS—THE TITHE

Stewardship

Today we're going to talk about money. "Wait a minute," you say. "This wasn't announced as Stewardship Sunday!"

You're right. I wanted you here this morning, not taking the day off. But don't get too excited; I don't make it my business to jump on your "guilt button." I'm not interested in seeing several long faces leaving this morning, feeling badly about how they do or do not support the church. And I'm certainly not interested in hearing anyone say anything about the preacher's delivering a poor sermon.

I make no apologies about speaking of money in church. Money is what keeps us afloat, and regardless of what your mystical feelings toward the church may be, that remains the reality of the situation. Our collective bills need to be paid just as our personal bills must be paid.

Well, this is supposed to be a sermon, right? You can't have a sermon without making a biblical theme come alive and made real. To that end, let me tell a tale.

Once upon a time there was a millionaire. He made his millions by keeping everyone around him poor. He ran a sardine cannery and paid everyone as little as possible. In the winter when the factory closed, he spoke often with his employees about "better times," and how the cannery would soon reopen. He kept everyone's hopes up; so, they never looked for work elsewhere. The cannery opened, but not soon. Only after a long, hard winter, and only after all the workers were very hungry, very eager, and very grateful to return to work did it open.

Our millionaire—who lives in a great white mansion with a four-car garage and an indoor heated swimming pool, surrounded literally by tarpaper shacks which housed his people—was also the church treasurer. He was the treasurer because he felt that none of the people could be trusted with the church money. He always told the people they had no money. They worked very hard, and they gave their little church-with-the-falling-down-steeple all they could; still, according to the millionaire treasurer, it was not enough.

One evening, during a dark and stormy night, the cellar of the little church flooded and the old furnace exploded. A new

Stewardship

furnace had to be installed at a cost of fifteen hundred dollars! Where would they get that much money?

The millionaire treasurer told the people not to worry, that he would have a new furnace installed. The people of the little church sighed a breath of relief, thanked the millionaire, but despised him for his arrogance.

A new minister came to the church and heard this story of generosity, but thought it curious that the people knew nothing of their own finances, and certainly never saw any business transacted. The new minister could get no information from the millionaire treasurer because "ministers just want to spend money."

So, the minister went to the bank. The branch officer in the little village refused to give him the information because the bank feared the millionaire treasurer. But the bank had a home office, in the big city, which knew nothing of the millionaire treasurer and was happy to tell the new minister what the financial picture of his church was.

The minister discovered a curious thing. The little church had many small deposits over the years and one fifteen hundred dollar withdrawal. Still, there was much money left in the account. The people of the little church had purchased their own furnace. The people of the little church, who were made to feel as though they could do nothing without the millionaire treasurer, had cared for all their own needs, and the millionaire had indeed contributed nothing except deceit, mistrust, and dread among the people.

The people of the little church, once informed by their new minister, were able to take some pride in themselves. They had cared for their house of worship; they were responsible people acting on behalf of God; and they had reason to thank God for delivering them out of the hands of their millionaire treasurer tyrant to continue to worship and work for God. The people of the little church got together and voted the millionaire treasurer out of office, secured the books through the courts, and lived happily ever after working for the kingdom of God.

That's a nice success story of a church family. It centers upon attitude, and that is what the prophet Malachi centers upon.

The custom of *tithing*, or the giving of "first fruits," is a matter of attitude. When the ancients gave the temple their first fruits to ensure that the work of the temple would carry on and that the hungry would be fed, they did not know whether there would be any second fruits. When a farmer makes his first cutting of hay, he has no idea just what his second cutting will be like. So the giving of first fruits, the tithe, is indeed a matter of attitude; it is an act of faith.

For twentieth century men and women, first fruits, or tithe giving, amounts to giving the church ten percent off the top of our incomes. This is what the Bible tells us is an appropriate gift—an appropriate sacrifice.

There are very few things in this life as equitable as a tithe. It's a matter of attitude.

Every now and again someone will hold up the Mormon church as an example of fine people—united, dedicated, making valid points on T.V. with their commercials. Then that person will ask, "Why aren't we doing the same?"

It's a matter of attitude. We've become lazy and complacent as a people. We do not require enough from our brothers and sisters. If you were a Mormon, it would simply be expected that you would donate one tenth of your income to the church, and that you would actively solicit new members. If you didn't, you'd be asked, "Why?"

Malachi 3:6-12 shows us that the Israelites had begun to take their tithes for granted, too. He perceived that God was angry over that. God had felt cheated, and, through Malachi, tells us so in no uncertain terms.

Now I can stand before you and tell you this: There was a time when I was personally responsible for cheating God. I did not tithe, but I made up my mind that I would tithe because that was expected of me by God. I made a plan, so that over a three year period I brought up the level of my giving. It was surprisingly easy. It was, and is, simply a matter of attitude.

I believe that the Christian church is most responsive to the call of God in America. That's why I became a Christian. I believe that this church is the most responsive and responsible church to the call of God in our area. I want nothing to stand in her way.

Jesus, through his parable of the talents, tells us this tithe is not to be a matter of pride. It must not be. It can certainly be a source of satisfaction, so long as we do not become self-satisfied.

Stewardship

When speaking of the finances of the church, while knowing that hundreds of thousands throw their money away in casinos, and that millions buy daily and weekly state lottery tickets, I make no apologies seeking your tithe on behalf of the church of Jesus Christ.

I've made no attempt to find your guilt button. Your decision is between you and your God. Pray about it; examine your own finances; prepare yourself to make your pledge; pray for your church; and I will pray for you. *Amen.*

Terrence M. O'Neill
First United Methodist Church
Ticonderoga, New York

THE CITY OF GOD

Confirmation

Imagine the grandest object built by human hands.
What do you see in your mind's eye? A machine? A monument? A building?

Some contemporary architects take a larger view, and say the grandest thing built by men and women is the city. The city is a relatively modern product of civilization, but its origins go back to a time when kings built cities as monuments to themselves: Babylon, Jerusalem, Athens, Rome, Paris. Some modern cities have been built as monuments: Brazilia, Sao Paulo, Washington, D.C.

But, usually, a city is built as an unplanned accumulation of houses, streets, and factories. A problem of our time is the rehabilitation of our cities. What if you could plan a city, a pleasant city? Not Denver, Albuquerque, or Washington, D.C., or any city of people, but a city of God.

I don't mind saying that I stole my title and theme from a book written almost sixteen hundred years ago by Augustine, a bishop of the Christian church in North Africa. His book, *The City of God*, compares society and civilization founded upon pagan beliefs with a society founded upon faith in the true God, and shows that life in harmony with God is superior. So we are both using the term *city* allegorically. I want you to think of your mind as a city.

A city could conceivably be the grandest man-made thing, the finest product of our art, philosophy, and technology. First of all, a city is a living thing, a group of people. A city can be ugly or graceful, dirty or clean, orderly or confused, planned or random. It makes a good figure of speech for a human personality.

Youth confirmation traditionally takes place during adolescence; it recognizes the difficult period between childhood and adult maturity. We recognize the fact of growth, and take note of the young persons' entering into adult society. It's a good time to emphasize Christian priorities and goals. Pentecost is an appropriate time to hold confirmation because we know that our minds can be influenced by the Spirit of God.

Now imagine the perfect, the ideal city. It is beautiful. It has

Confirmation

graceful buildings, clean streets, trees, parks, flowers, comfortable houses, prosperous industries, and commerce based on using the products of farms, mines, and animals. There is order, peace, goodwill, and justice. There are institutions. There is no order without institutions. There can be no order without government; no prosperity without business and industry; no religion without organized churches; no loving families without marriage.

Compare the institutions of society with water pipes. Water flowing across the land is called a flood; it is destructive. But water flowing through an irrigation ditch, or through a pipeline into a turbine is doing beneficial work. So your city will have institutions of government and business to channel the energies of its people.

Also, the forces in your personality must be contained and channeled. Just as a riot in a city is a sign of social disease, confusion, hatred, and fear are signs of spiritual illness. Information we take in needs to be organized. The laws of an orderly personality are well known; they are called virtues. The word *virtue* is from a Latin word meaning "strength." The virtues, or strengths, of your personality it doesn't matter what are honesty, self-respect, courtesy and kindness, trustworthiness and respect for others, and reverence for God. Psychiatrists have names for the "government" of the personality; they are called, we know there are contradictory forces at work in us.

Young persons are often more sharply aware of these forces because they seem new and difficult to control. We know there are strong desires in us; some we approve of, and some seem harmful. We seem to have very little control over our own emotions. Sometimes a force is released in us that is beyond our control, such as a fire or flood in a city. We don't need to feel embarrassed to ask for help from others when emotions seem too strong for us to control.

Closely related to a city's government are its parks and gardens. Recreation, art, sports, music, beauty—these are not just accessories to a city, they are essential aspects of our living together. We ornament our houses and cities just as we make our appearances pleasant to others. The ornaments of a pleasant personality are our acts of kindness. People quickly see through an appearance which is deceiving; a smile that is phoney, a nice-looking person who is contemptuous of others.

A personality is lacking in something essentially human if it lacks the capacity for friendship, generosity, and compassion. These are expressions of emotions that are constructively channeled and make us beautiful to others.

A hermit doesn't need friends, but hermits aren't normal. Most of us are social beings and need the love of parents and friends as much as we need nourishment and physical comfort.

A city is, first of all, a collection of people who come together for their common good. Every person has a contribution to make. But what is the smallest component of a city? In an old high school science text, I read that the atom is the smallest component of matter. There can be nothing smaller. Now, we know that an atom can be broken into smaller particles, but doing so changes the nature of matter. In the same way, the smallest social unit of a city is a family. Like the atom, a family can be broken. But to do so changes each of the members.

People have a place in society as members of a family. We begin life as children in a family. We come to feel a need to break away from the embrace of our families, but then we want to make new families of our own.

A once-popular song has the line, "You're nobody 'till somebody loves you." The church teaches this. The family is the basic unit of society. It is the source of our strength.

So build your city. Take charge of your own personal growth. Let the Spirit of God guide and organize your mind and personality: your looks, your talents, your brain power, your health, your knowledge, and your skills. Let the church advise you about the channels and outlets for your strong feelings, and for your desire to be loved and respected. Let your Christian friends share your need to do and to be something worthwhile, not just a hodgepodge of urges, but a beautiful and orderly structure.

You've heard of self-made men—usually a less-than-expert job. Don't do-it-yourself; let the Spirit of God guide your growth and be the head of your government, reflecting his power in your beautiful personality. *Amen.*

Robert M. Belles
St. Mark's Lutheran Church
Roswell, New Mexico

JOHN CALVIN—
SERVANT OF THE WORD

Few people who have lived since biblical times have influenced what you and I believe more than John Calvin. He was born in France in 1509 and proved to be a very bright boy. Indeed, he became a cleric, a chaplain, in Paris at the age of twelve. Calvin studied law and earned the equivalent of a doctoral degree at the age of nineteen. A biographer called him "the most learned man in Europe."

Calvin was converted at the age of twenty-one as a result of studying the Greek New Testament—he was attempting to defend the Roman Catholic Church against the teachings of Martin Luther! Interestingly, Calvin and Loyola, the Catholic scholar, were both students at the University of Paris at the same time.

John Calvin was a shy scholar of iron self-discipline. Each morning he repeated what he had learned the day before. He carried a heavy work load all his life and suffered constantly from poor health.

Calvin wrote the *Institutes of the Christian Religion* when he was in his early twenties. Having written it in Latin, he later translated it into French. It is a basic statement of Protestant doctrine.

Leaving Paris, Calvin stayed overnight in Geneva. The Swiss reformer, Farel, persuaded him to stay. He remained there twenty-two years. On one occasion, Calvin participated in a debate in Lausanne. He debated on the church fathers and New Testament doctrine—from memory. Two hundred priests were won over to the Protestant point of view.

Geneva was a theocratic city-state and a fortress with a population of fifteen thousand. There was no separation of church and state, and there was no tolerance. Persons swore allegiance to Protestantism, or they were banished from the city. Calvin opposed radical Protestants as he did the church of Rome. He consented to the drowning of Anabaptists in Lake Geneva. Anabaptists were a group who wanted to take the Reformation to its logical conclusion. For one thing, they intended to restore the New Testament pattern of the church. This included the baptism of believers by immersion. Hence, their name, Anabaptists—those who baptize again. (The populace had all been baptized at infancy.)

Calvin preached to overflowing crowds in the Cathedral of St. Peter. He began as assistant pastor to Farel and later became the official pastor. He preached there four times a week and lectured on the New Testament six days a week.

At the age of twenty-nine, Calvin married Idelette, the widow of an Anabaptist who had been converted under his preaching. She had two children from that previous marriage. She and Calvin had three children, all of whom died in infancy. Idelette was in poor health and lived only nine years after their wedding.

John Calvin was not a well man, either. He suffered from arthritis, bronchitis, kidney stones, gallstones, tuberculosis, and other ailments.

John Calvin was an intellectual giant and a spiritual prince in Protestantism.

John Knox and other Protestants were banished from Scotland by Mary, Queen of Scots, who was Roman Catholic. They settled for a time in Geneva, where they came under the powerful influence of Calvin. During this time, they translated the Bible into English. It is called the Geneva Bible and nicknamed the "Breeches Bible"—in Genesis, when Adam and Eve were driven from the Garden of Eden, the translation says God made them "breeches of fig leaves." English Baptists long preferred the Geneva Bible to the King James Version, which did not translate baptize as immerse.

In 1559, John Calvin founded the University of Geneva with contributions from wealthy merchants and common people as well. It had nine hundred students enrolled the first year. Geneva was a city of sober, thrifty, industrious citizens. It personified the Protestant work ethic.

Calvin was a man of slight build. He had large brown eyes and a long slender beard. He wore a robe with a fur collar, for it was cold in the cathedral. In the pulpit, Calvin wore a hat with a brim. This was not a symbol of impiety—there were pigeons in the rafters.

Calvin preached enthusiastically without notes. He called the sermon "the audible Eucharist." He contended that the preaching of the gospel is the Word of God. His last will and testament was begun with the words, "John Calvin, Servant of the Word in the Church of Geneva."

John Calvin

When Calvin was dying of tuberculosis, he was taken to the cathedral on Easter Sunday, 1564. He joined the congregation in singing, "Lord, now let thy servant depart in peace." At his death, the body lay in state in the cathedral. Such huge crowds appeared, that officials feared the development of a cult. Calvin's funeral was held hurriedly, without a eulogy or hymn. He was buried in an unmarked grave. Several months later, some students asked to visit Calvin's grave. No one could identify it among the mounds of fresh earth in the cemetary. The epitaph of John Calvin would be: "Soli Deo Gloria"—for the glory of God only!

In Geneva today, one may visit the Cathedral of St. Peter, which has been recently renovated. Across the street is the John Knox Chapel, which holds Calvin's chair. Another place well worth visiting is the Reformation Wall, opposite the University of Geneva. There are statues and quotations from such Reformation leaders as John Calvin, Farel, John Knox, and others. One will also find the statue of Roger Williams, founder of the colony of Rhode Island and the First Baptist Church of Providence (the oldest Baptist congregation in America).

When we think of John Calvin, we recall his emphasis on the sovereignty of God and predestination. His teachings have influenced all churches of the Reformed tradition, including the Baptists. Calvin's emphasis on predestination is a denial of works salvation and an emphasis on the grace of God in electing (choosing) believers for salvation. Predestination was taught by the Apostle Paul in the letters to the Romans and Ephesians. The doctrine was also emphasized by Augustine in the fourth century. However, it finds classical expression in the teachings of John Calvin.

Baptists are Calvinists. They believe in salvation by grace and the fore-knowledge of God. Because God certainly knows the future, he could elect to salvation those who would believe. Those whom he chose were called to faith. They have been justified or made right with God, and one day they will be glorified. When we are with him, we shall be like him (see Romans 8:29-30).

There are those who go farther than Calvin. That means that just as some are elected to salvation, others are predestined to damnation. They hold a view of the "limited atonement"—Christ died only for the elect. Some "hyper-Calvinists" contend that what is to be will be. Such a view may border on fatalism, which is more akin to Islam than to Christianity.

God's fore-knowledge does not interfere with my free will. He simply knows ahead of time what my response to his Son's atoning death will be.

An interesting understanding of predestination is the combining of it with Einstein's physics. We live in time and space, a temporal existence. God is not limited by time and space. He is eternal. Einstein contended that time is relative to motion. The faster we travel, the more slowly time passes. If we could travel at the speed of light—186,000 miles per second—there would be no passing of time. We would live in the "eternal now." God lives in the "eternal now" and is not subject to time. The Scripture indicates that a day with the Lord is as a thousand years, and a thousand years as a day (Psalm 90:4). Christ is the Alpha and the Omega—the beginning and the end. He was before the beginning and will be after the end. When God revealed his name to Moses as Yahweh, it meant, "I am that I am." Some translate Yahweh as *the Eternal*. Jesus said, "Before Abraham was, I am" (John 8:58). He is the eternal cosmic Christ, in flesh. God lives in the eternal now, and that is the realm we enter at death, "away from the body and at home with the Lord" (II Corinthians 5:8).

Predestination is looking at salvation from God's point of view, in the eternal now. Belief is looking at salvation from man's point of view, our faith response to God's grace.

We are not saved by good works. We cannot earn, deserve, or be good enough to be worthy of salvation. We are saved by grace, divine favor, for a life of good works. Predestination and election mean we have been chosen by God, and salvation is all of grace. John Calvin was right about that.

We encounter God in time and in the eternal now. Yesterday is gone. We cannot recall a moment of its mistakes or its joys. Tomorrow is not yet, and we have no promise that it ever will be. Now is the time to decide for Christ and his church. "[Today] is the day of salvation" (II Corinthians 6:2). *Amen.*

Alton H. McEachern
First Baptist Church
Greensboro, North Carolina

MONETARY MESSIAHS

Electronic Preachers

"I am the vine, you are the branches. He who abides in me, and I in him, he it is that bears much fruit, for apart from me you can do nothing" (John 15:5). The president of a large business gave a speech to a very affluent group. One woman, dripping with diamonds, came up to tell about her hobby, the stock market. "It's just so wonderful to watch God work. The other night about 3:00 A.M. God woke me up and told me to buy Johnson & Johnson at thirty-five." This was during the Tylenol scare. "Do you know it's now at fifty dollars a share?" Like many other people, she believes God promises her financial wealth.

Monetary Messiahs (TV preachers, and the like) teach this idea. Their message is—through prayer and faith, God will give you your heart's desires. They even quote Scripture to back up their claims. Let's take a look at these passages they insist create financial blessings.

Before we do this, let me remind you that the scientific and logical way to interpret Scripture is to interpret the verse within the historical context of the passage. For example, in Timothy 5:23 the Apostle Paul urges Timothy to drink wine instead of water for his stomach ailments. If the verse is jerked out of its context, one can teach that Christians should drink wine instead of water, or that drinking wine heals stomach disorders. So, now, let us examine the belief that God promises us financial blessings through faithful giving.

"Give, and it will be given to you" (Luke 6:38)

Here, the Monetary Messiahs translate Scripture to mean that if you become a faith partner, committing one hundred dollars a month, God will reward you tenfold (one thousand dollars). Or God will give you the right job, career promotion, or heal you in some special way.

But in context, Scripture is not promising financial rewards. Our Lord warns, "Woe to you that are rich" (Luke 6:24). So if you give to a religious dynasty, God is not going to make you prosper financially. What God promises is that if you give to the needy, he will bless you. Is there a difference between giving to a religious dynasty and giving to the naked and hungry?

"I pray that all may go well with you" (III John 1:2)

Here the Monetary Messiahs would have us to believe that God wants us to be financially prosperous. The key to God's bank is, "Brothers and sisters in the Lord, just send your twenty-five dollars a month to help us build our empire, and God will make you prosper. Pray, believe, ask and it will be yours."

Of course, in context the Apostle John really says, "I pray that you may enjoy good health and that all may go well with you." Is this a far cry from receiving a financial dividend from God?

"He who sows sparingly will also reap sparingly, and he who sows bountifully will also reap bountifully. . . . You will be made rich" (II Corinthians 9:6, 11)

Again, the Monetary Messiahs contend that if you will help spread the gospel by increasing their budgets from forty million dollars to fifty million dollars a year, God will reward you. If you sow two thousand dollars, then the gates of heaven will release showers of financial blessings.

Incidentally, you need to ask, "How much of that forty million dollars is going to feed the hungry, clothe the naked, make disciples, and how much is constructing a religious dynasty?"

When we look at the passage in context, we see that Paul is seeking a financial gift from the Corinthians for the needy people in the Jerusalem church, for the people are without jobs and food due to a recession. The Apostle Paul is urging folks to make a very generous gift to these people. He promises that if they do respond with generosity, God will surely bless them both spiritually and materially. What will they reap for giving to those in need? Note verse 13, "you will glorify God" with gifts of love to the needy.

Beloved, recognize that the Bible does not support the belief that if you give to a religious dynasty, God will reward you financially. These Monetary Messiahs are fleecing the sheep.

They are creating a religious dynasty in the name of the Lord—their own private kingdoms.

Compare these religious directors with the biblical models of faith. Do you recall the poor woman who gave all she had? She gave her two mites and was praised by the Lord. Yet she still does not escape her poverty.

One of the apostles suffered financial calamity. The Apostle Paul, who sowed and sowed, ended up not financially blessed, but in jail. His last days were spent as a poor jailbird needing the material assistance of others.

And then last, but not least, is our Lord. He ended up not only financially broke, but also naked upon a cross. As you can see for yourself, the Bible does not promise a Heavenly Stock System, whereby God gives you financial dividends. God's will is not that you become rich, but that you obey his will for your life, which means bringing your desires, dreams, hopes, and money into his will. Listen to the words of our Lord, "Not every one who says to me, 'Lord, Lord,' shall enter the kingdom of heaven, but he who does the will of my Father" (Matthew 7:21). *Amen.*

Dan Phipps
Westwood Baptist Church
Roxboro, North Carolina

CHRISTIANS AND GOVERNMENT

Patriotic

We are proud of our country. We are grateful to be Americans, and feel privileged to live in a democracy. Notice what the Bible teaches about Christians and government.

God and Caesar—Jesus (Matthew 22:17-21)

> "Tell us, then, what you think. Is it lawful to pay taxes to Caesar, or not?" But Jesus, aware of their malice, said, "Why put me to the test, you hypocrites? Show me the money for the tax." And they brought him a coin. And Jesus said to them, "Whose likeness and inscription is this?" They said, "Caesar's." Then he said to them, "Render therefore to Caesar the things that are Caesar's, and to God the things that are God's." (Matthew 22:15-22)

The Pharisees and Herodians hatched a plot to trap Jesus. Politics has always made strange bedfellows. Those groups were enemies.

Jews of the first century considered their nation a theocracy (God-rule). Therefore, paying taxes to Rome was a burning issue. In order to support the occupation troops, the Romans levied a head tax—one denarius for each Jewish male over the age of fourteen and each female over twelve. That was equal to a day's pay. It was a very unpopular tax, added to property taxes and customs duties. The denarius bore the image of Caesar; it was considered a form of idolatry and was forbidden by Jewish religious laws.

Jesus' opponents complimented him, but he saw through their hypocrisy. Their question put him on the horns of a dilemma: "Tell us, what do you think? Is it right to pay taxes to the Roman Emperor or not?" If Jesus said yes, the people would no longer listen to him. If he said no, the Roman authorities would come down on him as a rebel.

Jesus asked for one of the silver coins used to pay the head tax. It bore the inscription "Tiberiou Kaisaros." Tiberius was the Emperor of Rome between the years A.D. 14 and 37. Jesus asked whose image was on the coin. The people replied, "Caesar's." "Well then," said the Master, "pay to Caesar what belongs to the Emperor, and give God what belongs to God."

Patriotic

A Christian has obligations to both government and God. Without government we would have anarchy, no law and order. The government protects our lives and properties, and provides services. Therefore, the state has a right to collect taxes. Our coins and currency bear the image of the state. But mankind is made in the image of God. We owe our ultimate loyalty to him.

Honor the Emperor—Simon Peter

> Be subject for the Lord's sake to every human institution, whether it be to the emperor as supreme, or to governors as sent by him to punish those who do wrong and to praise those who do right. For it is God's will that by doing right you should put to silence the ignorance of foolish men. Live as free men, yet without using your freedom as a pretext for evil; but live as servants of God. Honor all men. Love the brotherhood. Fear God. Honor the emperor. (I Peter 2:13-17)

Simon Peter wrote about civil obedience. He admonished believers to be law-abiding citizens. Obviously, Rome was not yet persecuting the church. Christians had the protection of Roman courts.

Simon Peter contended that the proper function of government is to punish evildoers and praise those who do good. He gives a motto in verse 17: "Respect everyone; love fellow-believers; have reverence for God; honor the Emperor." We should support good government, for its authority is derived from God (Romans 13:1).

When God and Government are In Conflict

> So they called them and charged them not to speak or teach at all in the name of Jesus. But Peter and John answered them, "Whether it is right in the sight of God to listen to you rather than to God, you must judge; for we cannot but speak of what we have seen and heard." (Acts 4:18-20)

What happens when the Christian conscience is in conflict with the demands of the state?

On the day of Pentecost there were three thousand converts. Later, Peter and John preached in the temple courtyard. They were promptly arrested and brought before the council. The authorities forbade them to preach about the Resurrection of Jesus. Peter responded, "We must obey God, rather than men."

A modern example of such a conflict is the experience of Martin Niemoller, who died at the age of ninety-two. Niemoller was a U-boat captain in World War I. By the 1930s, when Hitler came to power in Germany, he had become pastor of a prominent Lutheran church in Berlin. Niemoller resisted the policies of the Nazi regime. He said, "God is my Furher!" The pastor was arrested by the Gestapo and remained in prison from 1937 until he was freed by the Allies in 1945. In later years he was honored in West Germany, the Soviet Union, and the United States.

Patriotism is appropriate, but when it is made the ultimate good, patriotism becomes a sin. Christians are "citizens of heaven" as well as citizens of their nations (Philippians 3:20).

Application

Christians have been champions of religious liberty and the separation of church and state. In 1639 Roger Williams founded the colony of Rhode Island. It was the first civil government on earth to grant religious liberty to all. People went to prison in Virginia rather than pay taxes in support of an established church. John Leland influenced the adoption of the First Amendment to the U.S. Constitution: "Congress shall make no law respecting an establishment of religion or prohibiting the free exercise thereof."

We believe in the separation of church and state—a free church within a free state. Neither should seek to control the other. The Moral Majority is in danger of becoming a political action group—imposing its will on the state.

A prominent national religious leader said recently that the idea of separation of church and state originated with the founder of the American Civil Liberties Union, and that the term came from the Soviet constitution. Such an idea is like a person born without an umbilical cord—no sense of heritage. The separation of church and state has been a grand American experiment for over two hundred years.

A legal requirement to establish prayer in the public schools is a violation of the separation of church and state. The public schools are supported by taxes and should not be made the instruments of churches to indoctrinate children. Tax credits for parents who send their children to church schools is also a violation of the separation of church and state.

Religious liberty and the separation of church and state work for the good of the state. It is fair to all in our pluralistic society. It also works for the good of the churches. Religious faith is more vigorous when it is voluntary and not established by law. It tends to be from the heart and is supported with voluntary gifts, not tax money.

In a democracy, such as we enjoy in America, citizens are called on to participate in the political process. We are to pay our taxes, register, vote, and encourage worthy men and women to seek public office.

Our church shies away from partisan politics, but helps to register people and encourages them to vote. There are sincere Christians in both political parties. We have a duty to pray for those who govern us.

Civil religion has its appropriate place. It finds expression in such things as prayers at inaugurals and at opening sessions of Congress and legislatures. The national motto is an expression of civil religion: "In God We Trust." So is the pledge of allegiance to the U.S. flag; it includes the phrase, "One nation under God."

Remember, we have a dual loyalty—to the nation and to God. But we worship God, not America.

Happy Birthday, America! You're looking great! We promise to help keep the torch of liberty burning brightly. *Amen.*

Alton H. McEachern
First Baptist Church
Greensboro, North Carolina

SPECIAL SERIES

THE ALMIGHTY TROUBLETH ME

Job 23

We want to start a series of sermons, looking at some of the insights found in the book of Job that are not traditionally emphasized. For the next few Sundays, I want to lift up some great statements made by Job and his friends as we journey forward.

In chapter 23, verses 15 through 16, Job says, "Therefore I am terrified at his presence; when I consider, I am in dread of him. God has made my heart faint; the Almighty has terrified me."

"The Almighty has terrfiied me." When we look at all of the pain and suffering in the world, we are troubled by the Almighty. Phillip Yancey, in his book *Where is God When It Hurts?* says a problem that won't go away—and he quotes C. S. Lewis from *A Grief Observed*—is one of the most disquieting symptoms. When we're happy, so happy that we have no sense of needing him, if we turn to him with praise, we'll be welcomed with open arms. But if we go to him when our needs are desperate, when all other help is vain, what do we find? A door slammed in our faces, the sound of bolting and double-bolting on the inside. After that—silence. We may as well turn away.

There are no easy answers to the problem of pain and suffering. The Bible itself does not give us a clear answer to why some people suffer, and others do not suffer. Why do some suffer more than others? The Bible does not give us a consistent answer. The only thing the Bible assures us is that we will suffer in this life.

Job is a clear example of one who suffered mightily, who was upright and perfect, says the Bible; yet, this man suffered mightily. In response to Eliphaz's argument that Job was sinful, Job launches out with a bitter denunciation of Eliphaz's position. Job says,

> Today also my complaint is bitter; [God's] hand is heavy in spite of my groaning. Oh, that I knew where I might find him, that I might come even to his seat! I would lay my case before him and fill my mouth with arguments. I would learn what he would answer me, and understand what he would say to me. Would he contend with me in the greatness of his power? No; he would give heed to me. There an upright man could reason with him, and I should be acquitted for ever by my judge. (23:2-7)

The Almighty Troubleth Me

Job wants to find God, and pain and suffering will make us search for him as well. Pain and suffering will do one of two things to us. It will either make us turn to God, or we will turn away from him. Job was troubled by trouble. He had done nothing wrong; yet, trouble came. That seems to be a part of life. We don't have to do anything; just be in this world, and trouble will come. We can sit in our houses, and someone will break in—and murder us or rob us. Job had lived an exemplary life. He prayed sometimes five times a day. He was a deeply devout man; yet, trouble came. Trouble will come in your life. Trouble will come in my life. The point is, how will we handle trouble? How do we control trouble? Do we control trouble or does trouble control us? Do we become frustrated, confused and befuddled, exasperated, or desperate when trouble comes into our lives? What do you do? How do you handle it?

Job goes looking for God. He says, "O, if I knew where I could find him. If I knew where I could find him, I'd stand before his throne and I'd argue my own case. I'd be my own lawyer." Job is so confident of his integrity that he feels he could be his own mouthpiece at the throne of God. "And I know that when I get through presenting him my arguments, he will vindicate me because I'm pure; I'm righteous."

Many times most of us are like that; we feel that God is unjust in his dealings with us. God ought not do that to us; therefore, we question Almighty God. When Job uses the word *Almighty* here, he is doing something that is germane to the whole structure of the Bible. This is one of the words—the Almighty-ness of God—that shows that God can handle any situation which comes into our lives.

The same idea is found in Genesis. God says to Abraham, "I am God Almighty" (17:1). Then God tells Abraham about how he's going to bless him and how many nations will come from his seed, out of his loins; and how Sarah, his wife, will conceive. Abraham can't believe that his wife, at ninety, would conceive, or that he would be the one responsible for the heir at one hundred. But the Lord God Almighty can do anything. God is saying, "I can do anything. I am in control of every situation that comes into the lives of my children."

So when Job says, "The Almighty has terrified me," the Almighty, Job implies, could have prevented his trouble. He could have stopped his children's death. God could have stopped the destruction of houses and barns, his cattle and asses. God could have stopped it, Job is saying. He is Almighty. He is All-wise. He is All-knowing. God could have stopped it, but he didn't.

Haven't you raised that same question? Could not God have prevented this? Haven't you been troubled by the Almighty? Is your faith so sound and so solid that you never questioned the Almighty?

Job was not only troubled by trouble, but also by the extent of his trouble. He could understand some hardships, but the trouble in Job's life escalated. There was an escalation of tragedy in Job's life. One after another, as we read that first and second chapter, we see that tragedy fell on Job; it just kept falling. You remember the song they used to sing, "Into each life, some rain must fall?" Down there, somewhere, the writer must have said, "But too much is falling in mine." Job could have been saying that, too. Why? His children are gone. His livestock is gone. His money is gone. Then his wife starts acting stupid. And God finally tells Satan, "I want you to take him, attack him!" And Job becomes sore from the top of his head to the bottoms of his feet. One after another come trouble, trials, and tribulations. Job can't understand the extent of his troubles.

Have you ever experienced tragedy on top of tragedy? Trouble on top of trouble? *Why is my child born with a defective heart? Why did I lose my job at this time, with a house note of one thousand dollars a month? Why is my heart going bad? Why do my kidneys not function properly? Why has my husband filed for a divorce? Why are my children making F's in school and other folks' children are making A's? Why is it that this man is driving a Cadillac, and I'm walking? Why is it that this man's house is happy, when my home is full of sorrow? Why is it that I can't get myself together? Why is it that my mind won't act right? There is no logical way I can approach life. My mind is confused and frustrated. I'm messed up! Why is it that I am disturbed emotionally? Why can't my nerves settle down? Why is it that others have peace, and I don't have any peace? Is God unjust? Is God there? Is God available? Is God real? Why doesn't he answer me? I'm troubled by the Almighty. He doesn't seem to be just.* That is the final reason Job is so troubled. Job discovers the direction from whence the trouble comes; it comes from God. Now this is not to say that all trouble comes from God. Some we bring on ourselves. If you go out there and jump on the corner bully, you

The Almighty Troubleth Me

brought that trouble on yourself. If you indulge too much in some drinks, you drive, and you kill somebody, you brought that trouble on yourself!

Yancey claims that one of the things we've done in the Christian church is to take a fatalistic attitude, which is unChristian toward trouble. The fatalist says, "This is the will of the Lord." We don't know that. That's fatalism. As Christians, we cannot believe that everything that happens to us is the will of God. We ought to re-evaluate ourselves when we say, "Well, that's the will of God for my life."

Job was troubled by the direction from whence the trouble came. It came from God. When Satan said to God, "The only reason Job is so loyal and faithful is that you've got a hedge about him. If you move that hedge and let me get to him, I'll make Job curse you to your face." God did not ask, "Job, can I try you? Can I test you?" He didn't say anything to Job. He made the bargain with Satan. He didn't get Job's permission. He was bargaining with Satan. That seems contradictory, but it's there in the Bible.

God removed the hedge, and told Satan, "I'll move the hedge." What would happen if God removed your hedge? What would happen if you went home and your house was on fire? What would happen if you went to your job tomorrow morning and the boss said, "Well I can't use you anymore?" What would happen if, on your way back home, you heard on the radio that your child was run over by a car and killed? What would happen if, when you got home, your spouse said, "I am going to leave you." What would happen if you woke up the next morning and your child had a gun at your head and was going to blow your brains out? What would you do? Trouble! How would you act?

God has a hedge around all of us. It's not because of our goodness that these things do not happen to us. It is because God has a hedge about us. We are not worthy of God's mercies and tender compassion, but God has built a barrier around all of us. It is by God's grace that we stand wherever we stand with whatever degree of security we have. It is God's grace and God's mercy.

Would you still sing the Lord's songs in a strange land when all of your supporting systems were knocked from under you? Would you still be faithful, loyal, and committed? Where would you stand? I don't know where I would stand if all that happened in one day, but I'm hoping that I would trust in the Lord. It has never happened to me like that, but if it does happen to me, I hope that I can stand like Job, with faith, loyalty, and fidelity.

Job is deep in the pit of depression and despondency, but out of his bowels, he says, "He will slay me . . . yet I will defend my ways to his face" (13:15). God is misusing him and abusing him, has gotten him to stand when waves of affliction have swept over his soul. Can you stand? Will you stand?

Several things that suffering will do for us are: it will refine our faith; it will make us mature; it will allow an opportunity for God to display his work in our lives; it will make us conform to the image of Christ Jesus; and it will produce in us perseverance and Christian character.

Let us trust in the Lord. Even as the Almighty troubles us, let us trust in the Lord. When there is nothing but dark clouds in the sky, trust in him. Stand firm in the faith, rooted and grounded in the faith, committed to him though dark clouds circle your bedroom and your house. Hold on to his hand. Stay there in faith. Ask God to help you hold on.

I'm going to try to trust him. I've seen some dark days, but I'm going to trust God. I've seen some mean and cruel things done, but I'm going to trust him. I've seen some mean and cruel people, but I'm going to trust him. I'm going to trust him because I know God is good. God is great, and I'm thankful that God is still on the throne.

El Shaddai are the Hebrew words meaning God can take care of any situation. I know my God can! Thank you, God, for your Almighty power in my life and in the life of your church. Let's trust him, Church! Let's trust him, as we launch out into the deep waters of tomorrow—not knowing what tomorrow will bring. Let us trust him.

There may be someone here who needs an anchor. I recommend God's Word and Jesus Christ. Hold onto God's unchanging hand, and trust in him every day and every hour. *Amen.*

THE TENDERIZER OF OUR HEARTS

Job 23:16a

The late Dr. Martin Luther King, Jr., wrote a sermon which he entitled "A Tough Mind and a Tender Heart." In that sermon he points out that what God wants in most in us is a tough mind and a tender heart, but most us have a tough mind and a tough heart. We are not able to deal with life because of our toughness and roughness and crudeness.

Job gives us an insight for dealing with the tough heart. Job, in chapter 23, verse 16, is arguing from a perspective most of us are not able to argue from. Job is arguing from a point of strength, and not weakness. We argue from a point of weakness and lowliness, for we are filled with imperfections. Job, however, is the paragon of virtue, righteousness, and spiritual maturity. The Bible says that Job was perfect and upright, one that feared God.

Nietzsche, the atheistic German philosopher, said that God invented Jesus to apologize for what he did to Job. If Job were perfect, then God had no right to do what he did to Job. So Jesus becomes the solution to the agony of Job, to the problem of Job. Job, in this passage, is in the midst of all kinds of problems. He has said some awful things of God. Those of you who say he was patient haven't read that book with enough profundity and depth. Job is not patient. He says "If I lift myself up, thou dost hunt me like a lion" (10:16). That's an awful thing for a man to say about God. In 7:14 he says to God, "Thou dost scare me with dreams and terrify me with visions." In 13:15 he refers to God as a murderer. And in 23:8 he says, "Behold, I go forward, but he is not there; and backward, but I cannot perceive him; on the left hand I seek him, but I cannot behold him; I turn to the right hand, but I cannot see him." Job is angry at God. He's not only sick, going through trials and tribulations, but also his anger has turned to human wrath. He's looking for God in order that he might shake his finger in God's face and raise the questions, "Why are you doing this to me? I could understand if it was someone else, but I'm Job. I live right. I walk right; I'm perfect. I don't understand what you're doing to me. You're the only one that can touch me and the quality of the life that I live. What's happening here?" God will ultimately answer him, as we look at further insights from Job.

Job then comes to some conclusions. He says, "Therefore I am terrified at his presence" (23:15). He says, "When I consider, I am in dread of him" (23:15). He hadn't been afraid of God before he got sick—there's something about sickness that will either drive us to God or drive us away from him. Pain will do that. Suffering will do that. Misery will do that; it'll either drive you to God or it'll drive you away from God. Job says, "I am afraid of him." When Adam violated God's command, Adam went and hid himself. He said "I was afraid." He hadn't been afraid before to walk with God and talk with him in the garden. It had been a tremendous experience, but after he disobeyed God, he became afraid.

Whenever we sin, sin does that. It makes us afraid. Even our shadow frightens us sometimes. "The wicked flee when no one pursues" (Proverbs 28:1). The tenderizer of our hearts—Job said, that God makes his heart soft; he makes it tender. He's arguing from strength, not from weakness. The tender heart is the heart that has experienced suffering at the deep levels of existence.

The tender heart. Job had lost everything he had—he lost his children, his cattle, his money. His wife started acting stupid and foolish. He friends came—they knew the integrity of Job; yet, they jumped on him and told him that he must have some hidden sins in his background, in his life. They said that all he has to do is to confess his sins and God will forgive him. Job would not do that. Job said, "I stand on my record, and my vindicator is in heaven. I'm not going to confess that I have sinned."

Now, don't you try that! Don't try to stand on your record. If you've got a record to stand on, it's Jesus Christ. Point to Jesus—that's the solution. The psalmist says, "I am poured out like water, and all my bones are out of joint; my heart is like wax, it is melted within my heart" (22:14). My heart, the tender heart, is able to understand what has happened. The tender heart recognizes that things are out of joint, things are not like they ought to be. I know that there is something wrong and that there is an antagonist somewhere.

Job comes to the conclusion that God is his antagonist. What an awful position to be in! When you look around, it's not your wife; it's not your child; it's not your friends; it's not your loss of money—it's God Almighty who is the antagonist. God is the

The Tenderizer of Our Hearts

one that has visited your life with misery, pain, and agony. Suffering is from God Almighty. What do you do then? What do you do when you can't find the cause?

The tender heart. The tender heart is the exporting heart. It exports all of one's thoughts heavenward. It is God-centered; all thoughts are centralized on God. That's what Job meant when he said, "Where is God? O, if I knew where I could find him." Haven't you been like that? I remember when I was in the hospital, I felt God ought not do this to me. I was in the prime of life and here I was in the hospital. Lord, where were you? Didn't you know I was there? Don't you understand who I am? I'm trying to preach the gospel! Where are you, God?" I was scheduled to go back a few months ago, and I was raising the question again, "Lord, I don't want to go back again to the hospital. I was just there five years ago; I don't want to go back! Where are you, Lord?" And the Lord told me that time, "Just be patient and wait on me. Don't rush me! Let me take my time." And I haven't been back yet. Like the man who was converted and every day at work he'd say, "Jesus, Johnny is here." Then he'd go on and do his work in the factory. Everybody else around him thought he was crazy. "Every time that ol' boy comes here, he's talking about Jesus." One day the factory caught on fire, a great conflagration. Johnny and other workers were trapped in it. This man who had been saying, "Jesus, Johnny is here," heard a voice out of the midst of the crackling flames, saying, "Johnny, Jesus is here." He was the only one that got out of those flames.

Now, don't ask me about the justice of it. Sometimes God has his eye on one sheep who has been faithful and loyal. God takes care of us in the midst of the crackling flames and fires of affliction. God will take care of us, especially as he seeks to tenderize our hearts and make us focus on him. *The tender heart.* Job says, "He makes my heart soft."

The tender heart is not only the exporting heart of our thoughts, but it is also the expecting heart. Job lived in hope. Psalm 9:18 says, "For the needy shall not always be forgotten, and the hope of the poor shall not perish for ever." Job expects to be vindicated. Job says, "I know that my Redeemer lives. I expect to be vindicated. God is going to vindicate me in this situation."

We who are yet alive are challenged to live expectantly. Most of us don't expect too much when we come to church. We don't expect any great spiritual explosion. We don't expect the Holy Spirit to come with all of its quickening power, to draw a tear, to put a song on our lips and praise in our hearts, or to warm our hearts. Most of us are just here because it's the custom to be here, but did you come here expecting anything? Did anybody come, saying "What must I do to be saved?" Did you come here expecting to get an insight, a thought that would guide you this week as you go back out there in the highways and the byways of life? Somebody ought to say a word that speaks to your heart. Somebody ought to say a word that says something to your pain, to your suffering, and to your misery.

I know you're there. You sit here, looking wise, but are otherwise. I know there is some anguish and agony out there. I know there's some child out there longing for a father; some woman out there longing for a good husband; some man longing for a good wife. I know you're there—faced with cancer, faced with bad kidneys, faced with a heart that won't act right, faced with alcoholism, strung out on dope. I know you're there. Your heart is just tough. Your mind is tough. Nothing moves you. Nothing gets close to you, not even suffering. You can take suffering like a Nazi soldier in the camps in Germany. You're never moved. But keep on living! Somewhere down the line there is an experience in life that will tenderize your heart. Somewhere down the line there is an event in your life that will tenderize your heart. When you get that experience, remember Job. Job held on in faith.

The tender heart is the ennobling heart. Job rose on that ashpile—out there on that garbage dump—to new heights of faith, hope, and love. This is one of the secrets in the Bible; it teaches us how to rise out of the quagmires of existence, human existence, to new levels of faith, hope, and love. The Apostle Paul is a classic example. He rose from the quagmires of religious bigotry to become a prince of the church. He walked across the undulating hills of Palestine, Asia Minor, and Rome, talking about faith, hope, and love.

Suffering will ennoble you, if you let it. Elie Wiesel, who protested President Reagan's visit to a German cemetary, saw his mother killed in a concentration camp. He saw his sister killed. He saw little children pitch-forked by German soldiers.

The Tenderizer of Our Hearts

He saw Jews placed into the ovens and burned; he smelled burning human flesh. In that ungodly situation, Elie Wiesel must have said, "Where is God in all of this? Where is the God I have been taught about? Where is God that my forefathers talked about, that helped them across the Red Sea? Where is that God that gave them Canaan? Where is that God that stood with Samuel and David and all of my ancestors? Where is that God now? We need him in these concentration camps." He must have lost his confidence in God. He must have imagined that his God was dead.

You and I have been through troubles in America. Our forefathers, too, walked through the valleys and the shadows of death in this land, but they never lost their faith. They kept their trust in God, and they bequeathed to us a noble heritage. Keep on trusting, though all the earth seems to be against you. Keep on believing. Keep on hoping. Keep on expecting that the God of Abraham, the God of Isaac, and the God of Jacob will hear your cry! Keep on believing! God has tenderized our hearts.

I've asked the Lord to tenderize my heart, to give me a kind heart, a clean heart, a good heart, a gentle heart, a merciful heart, a genuine heart, a gracious heart, a grateful heart, a large heart. Give me, O God, create in me, O God, a clean heart. Clean it as only God can, through the gift and power of the Holy Spirit. Tenderize our tough hearts. Make us whole, healthy, and worthy to serve him each and every day. "He makes my heart soft," says Job. And he does do that! He does that, through the gift of the Holy Spirit in our lives.

The doors of the church are open. *Amen.*

DIVINE TARGET PRACTICE

Job 6:1-4; 7:20; 16:12

Then Job answered:
"O that my vexation were weighed, and all my calamity laid in the balances!
Then it would be heavier than the sand of the sea;
therefore my words have been rash.
For the arrows of the Almighty are in me;
my spirit drinks their poison;
the terrors of God are arrayed against me." (6:1-4)

If I sin, what do I do to thee, thou watcher of men? Why hast thou made me thy mark? Why have I become a burden to thee? (7:20)

I was at ease, and he broke me asunder; he seized me by the neck and dashed me to pieces; he set me up as his target. (16:12)

As we watch the disintegration of God's perfect man, we see the battle lines drawn. What is at stake is the soul of Job. One writer has said that there are three votes in every man's life: God has one vote, and it is always for us; Satan has one vote, and that is always against us; and you and I have one vote, and that can go either way. Job is exercising his privilege as a perfect man to cast his vote on the side of God, but in doing so, Job is not averse to saying to God, "Why have you used me as a target to practice your skill as a marksman? Why have you taken me, a perfect man—upright and gentle, brave and strong—and used me as your target, your divine target?" Job cannot understand it—he just cannot understand it. In a commentary on Job, it is stated that the ultimate question raised by the book of Job is not "Why do the righteous suffer?" but it is "Do men serve God disinterestedly?" Do we love God without expecting something from him? Do you love your wife without expecting her to cook your food, wash your clothes, take care of your children, make up your bed, and bring you your slippers? Do you love your wife enough to let her bring the money home—all of it? Do you love her enough to be with her in the trials and tribulations of life? Do you love her enough to do for her even though she might not do for you? Do you love her disinterestedly? That's the problem.

Job says that God has a quiver full of arrows. To have a quiver

Divine Target Practice

full of arrows presupposes that there is a marksman; and it also presupposes that there is an object. All of you who were soldiers know that on the practice range there is a target. You go out there not skillful, but if you practice at it long enough, you will become a marksman. Job says that God has selected him as one to be shot at. Skill, distance, and the weapon determine accuracy. And Job here says, "I know it's from the Almighty. I know that he's shooting at me." And God had seven arrows in his quiver.

A little further on, Job shifts from God's shooting the arrows to say that divine archers were shooting at him. He wants to relieve God of the burden of what's happening to him. He does not want to accuse God of being the one that's really involved, but he's at the point of the beginning of his disintegration; so he's saying that it's God, that the arrows of the Almighty are not only shot at him, but also the arrows have penetrated his being and are now inside him.

God had seven arrows. The first arrow that God shot at Job hit his ox and ass. When the servant ran in and told him, "Job, all of your oxens and asses are gone," he said the Sebeans fell on them. Before this servant could get out of Job's sight, another came in and said, "Job, God shot another arrow, and the camels and servants are gone. The Chaldeans stole them and carried all of them away, and I am the only one left, Job." That was number three.

God had four more arrows to use. You and I must come to understand that sometimes God will use us as divine targets in the Christian community. Someone has said that Americans have a misunderstanding of suffering. Indeed we have. The two oceans have kept bombs from falling on our shores, but maybe God's going to fix that now with nuclear weapons and intercontinental ballistic missiles.

God, said Job, decided to shoot another arrow. He shot the fourth arrow and hit seven sons and three daughters, all at one time. The servants came and told him, "Job, the wind came—God's wind came and bowled over the house where your seven sons and three daughters were having a party. And, Job, all of them are dead. It could have been that a hurricane came, or a typhoon came, or a tornado. Anything that God has created out there, he will use sometimes in his permissive will. Before he could get out the door, God decided to shoot another arrow. Each time he shot an arrow, the barbs in the arrow, like those of the Indians and the Bantu in Africa, went deeper. They made those arrows so that when you tried to pull them out, the arrow would tear the flesh—the Bantus discovered that you could poison an arrow, and that's what Job intimates here. He says, "My spirit drinks their poison."

God shot another arrow and struck Mrs. Job, turned the woman who had been faithful and loyal at his side into an unbelieving woman. She instructed Job, in order to get relief, to "Curse God and die, Job. Curse him to his face. He's done too much to you, Job. Our children are gone. Curse him, Job. Our asses and oxen are gone. Curse him, Job. Our servants are dead. Curse him, Job. All of our piety is for nothing. Curse him, Job! Curse him to his face. Do not maintain your integrity. Curse God, Job, and die!"

Job remembers the words of the psalmist, "The fool says in his heart, 'There is no God' " (Psalm 14:1). Job says that though God slay him, he will trust God. Shoot again!

God picks up the bow and another arrow from his quiver, and shoots at Job's friends. They come in bold, brash, and daring, and jump all over Job. They tell Job that he is a sinner to his face. It's as if a person were accused of lying, when he knows he is telling the truth. It hurts more when the accuser is close to you, who does not believe in your integrity. They sat with him seven days and nights and never said a word, and when they did, they started accusing him.

But there is something about target practice that is quite amusing. If you have watched archers on a practice range, on the target there is always what they call the bull's-eye. Job is the bull's-eye. The main target ultimately is Job. The arrows were surrounding the bull's-eye, they were all around the bull's-eye, the main target. Not his material possessions, not the things that are around him—his support systems—the main bull's-eye is Job, himself. So Satan says to God, "A man will give all that he has in exchange for his own soul. Touch Job himself, and I'll make him curse you to your face. Let me have Job. Yes, he'll give up his wife and children. He'll give up his asses and his oxen. He'll give up his camels. He'll give up everything. But let me at Job. Let me have your perfect man!"

And God says, "Go down. I'll let you shoot an arrow at Job, or I'll shoot the arrow." And God removed the hedge from around Job and shot that last arrow in his quiver, arrow number seven.

Divine Target Practice

It hit Job, and he became sore from the top of his head to the soles of his feet; boils, blisters, and pus started running everywhere after a few days. Job was miserable, helpless, defenseless, and almost faithless. He ran to the outskirts of town and got on the trashpile—or the ashpile. And he was out there throwing up ashes, trying to get relief. There were no medical doctors that could help Job. There he sat, in the ashpile, but he had the faith to say, "Naked I came from my mother's womb, and naked I shall return" (1:21). He says, "When he has tried me, I shall come forth as gold" (23:10).

The arrows of the Almighty. "God is testing me. God is trying me. God is using me. The arrows of the Almighty are within me. The arrows of the Almighty poison my system. My spirit is about to be drained away from me. All of my hope, my power, my strength is ebbing from me. Though he slay me, yet will I trust him. Thy will, O Lord, not mine." However hard the battle goes, Job is a witness to faith that if we stay with God at difficult times, God will see us through. *Thy way and thy will, O Lord, not mine!* God wants to know if he can use you this morning. Has he ever shot some arrows at you? Has he ever shot some arrows in your direction that you couldn't understand, any problems and difficulties that you can't handle, you can't explain? What is your testimony this morning? Thy will, O Lord, not mine. Amen.

OVERWHELMING THE FATHERLESS

Job 6:24-30

Once more we try to look at some exciting, but lesser-known, passages in the book of Job. In the sixth chapter of Job, starting with verse twenty-four, Job says in response to Eliphaz's statement in the fifth chapter,

> Teach me, and I will be silent; make me understand how I have erred. How forcible are honest words! But what does reproof from you reprove?
> Do you think that you can reprove words, when the speech of a despairing man is wind?
> You would even cast lots over the fatherless, and bargain over a friend.
> But, now, be pleased to look at me; for I will not lie to your face.
> Turn, I pray, let no wrong be done. Turn now, my vindication is at stake.
> Is there any wrong on my tongue? Cannot my taste discern calamity? (6:24-30)

Job is arguing from the point of view that his friend Eliphaz overwhelms him by the force of his argument. But Job knew that his Father is the Father and Lord of all creation. He is aware that the songwriter was right when she wrote,

> My Father is rich in houses and lands;
> He holdest the wealth of the world in his hands!
> Of rubies and diamonds, of silver and gold,
> His coffers are full—He has riches untold.
> I'm a child of the King!
> My Father's own Son, the Savior of men,
> Once wandered o'er earth
> As the poorest of them;
> But now He is reigning forever on high,
> And will give me a home in heav'n by and by.
> I'm a child of the King! A child of the King!
> With Jesus, my Savior,
> I'm a child of the King!
> "A Child of the King"

One of the great things about a father is that he's supposed to provide security for his children, his wife, and all his household. A father is supposed to be "the big, bad wolf." Many times boys will fight and say, "You wait until my father comes home." The father is supposed to provide certain protections for the daughter. Sometimes people are brutal when they know that a girl doesn't have a father. But if they know she has a father, and she will tell her father, it might go a little easier with her. Sometimes we overwhelm people because they don't have a father; we take advantage of people when we know that they don't have a father.

Job said to Eliphaz, "You're overwhelming me because you are aware that I don't have a father. You think I don't have a father. You have accused me with your tongue. You have battered and shattered me with words because you know everything has been taken from me. I am left alone here on this ashpile, and I don't have anyone to protect me, so you think." God shot seven arrows at Job, and each one hit a bull's-eye. The major bull's-eye was Job himself.

Eliphaz argues that God will deliver Job after six troubles, that a seventh trouble will not touch him. That's what Eliphaz had argued with Job; yet, we see that God has shot seven arrows at Job, and Job is still not delivered. Job is still on that trashpile. He says that Eliphaz makes a pit for his friend, Job. Sometimes the words of our friends are the harshest words we have to endure. They crush us; they shatter us; they batter us; they bruise us. Our friends are close to us, and their words can hurt more than the words of an enemy.

So Job, while sitting out here on his garbage pile, on his trash heap, experiences several things from his friends. One, when they come to visit Job, they sit there seven days and seven nights and never say a word—the profoundness of silence. They could have said a comforting word in that seven days and seven nights. They could have asked Job, "Is it possible for me to get you a drink of water? Are you broke? Do you need some money? Job, what can we do to help assuage the sorrow that has gripped your heart? What can we do to lift the burden from your brow? Everybody has deserted you. Everybody now looks down on you. We are your friends: Zophar, Bildad, and Eliphaz." They sat out there seven days and nights, but they never advanced a single word of hope and consolation to their friend in trouble.

The profoundness of their silence—how difficult it is to feel that someone is your friend, and when you're going through the valley of the shadow of death, that friend is not there, has no word of hope. The friend has no word of comfort, no consoling statement to make, as you walk across the charred valleys of disaster. As you walk across the valley that is deserted by every living thing, you walk alone. You stand there in the midst of the valley, alone, with no one to say a kind word to you, to extend a helping hand.

Thank God all of the story is not yet over, for there is a friend who sticks closer than a brother.

Job was treading the winepress alone. "You overwhelm the fatherless," said Job. They overwhelm Job when they did start speaking with a profusion of words. They just mouth off one word after another. And Job says, "How forceful are right words! Your words are wrong. You have examined me and you have scrutinized me, and you have evaluated me, but your words are wrong. I know I am upright. I know I'm a solid citizen. I know I am a man of honesty. I know I am a man whose integrity is intact. I live upright; I have followed the precepts and commandments of God, the testimonies of God. I know I have followed the statutes of God. I know I have lived a good life. Your words are wrong. You don't know all of the facts."

Most of us don't know all of the facts, but we draw our conclusions from partial data. The strange thing is that most of us don't want the facts, we prefer to have partial data before we draw our conclusions—a profusion of words. Over and over again in that conversation of Job and Eliphaz, Zophar, and Bildad, the friends keep piling onto this fatherless, pitiful man out there on the garbage pile. They just keep talking on and on; they just keep saying things that are not true.

One writer has said that these three friends argued from three points of view: traditionalism, conservatism, and dogmatism. All three of them, in all of their arguments, vary the theme of traditionalism just a little—and conservatism, just a little—and dogmatism, just a little. All three of them thought that they spoke for God.

May times in the church we have to make a distinction between what one great scholar calls tradition and what is traditionalism. There are great traditions in the church that should be carried on and are important—like reading the Bible, preaching the sermon, singing the old hymns. These are great traditions which must be carried on. But traditionalism—which door we'll come in, which door we'll go out—that's traditionalism. So what if you came in that door? You don't have to go back out that door. That's traditionalism. We get caught up in traditionalism, and think that it is sacred. It is not sacred. It's traditionalism that we start worship at eleven o'clock, but it is not fundamental to the kingdom. The pure in heart can worship at any hour, any time, any place, not just here! Jesus said, "For where two or three are gathered in my name, there am I in the midst of them [especially if they are agreeing and touching upon the same thing]" (Matthew 18:20).

They kept right on overwhelming this fatherless child, out there on that garbage dump. People can be so hard when you get down in the ditch. When you get down, people can just pile it on you.

Then Job says, "You overwhelm me by your presumptuous accusations." God said he was perfect. But they said he was a sinner. They came along and said the opposite of what God said, and that they thought they were speaking in the name of God. They made a presumption, what we call in theology a *presupposition*. They made a presupposition, "Job, you are a sinner." But God said that he was perfect. They thought they had more sense than God had.

Often, we spend our time also making accusations that we do not know anything about. We make certain presuppositions and draw certain conclusions as soon as we see somebody. We haven't even met the person. We form a judgment prior to knowing the person. That's what they did to Job. When you make a presupposition like that, you can treat a person any way you want to treat him or her.

Job said, "You're overwhelming me with your presuppositions—your presumptions—that I am a sinner." And then they weren't satisfied with making those presuppositions; they went one step further and had a proliferation of opinions. If you read those conversations and the monologue sections of Eliphaz, Bildad, and Zophar, you will see that they raise several questions that are philosophical, theological, and profound. But their opinions are wrong! This is one of the things that we have to be careful about in religion, that we don't have opinions that are wrong. That's why we ought to read our Bibles carefully, and prayerfully, and daily in order that when we form an opinion it will be the right one.

Men formed opinions about Jesus, and they did not know Jesus, did not want to know him. They'd go out of their way to sit at his feet, to hear him, to understand him, to see him in action, to recognize that here, indeed, was one in whom there was no guile. Here was one sent from God. Here was one whose heart was in tune with God's heart. Here was one whose mind was stayed on God. Here was one whose hands were God's hands. Here was one whose spirit was God's spirit. Here was one whose mind was wrapped in the mantle of God's unchanging hand. They did not want to know Jesus—that he walked and talked with God, that he was God, for he said, "When you have seen me, you have seen the Father."

You overwhelm the fatherless—but Job was sure that this was just his earthly father—but you cannot overwhelm the heavenly Father. That's why Job, throughout the book, is a paragon of stability in faith. Throughout the book we see him wrestling at the depths of his soul with faith, non-faith, and more faith. Job moves deeper into more faith as we follow the tracks of this bloody, bruised, and battered son of God. We see him wrestling, reaching out, and remembering what Jesus said, "Call man on earth 'father,' for one is your master. These are earthly manifestations of one who is to protect us, but there is a Father who reigns on high, who ultimately has the whole world in his hands." So Jesus says that when your father on earth forsakes you, lets you down, doesn't provide for you, and doesn't give you the security that you need, there is One on high who looks down and watches over all of his children. Not a sparrow falls from the sky but your Heavenly Father knows all about it. "Every strand of hair on your head," says Jesus, "is known by your Father in heaven."

You do have one, Job. You do have one, Fred. You do have one, God, who takes care of his own. My father is rich in houses and lands. When the world forsakes me, I've got a Father. I followed Jesus to Calvary, and out there on Calvary they came and told him one day, "Your mother, brother, and sisters are out here looking for you." And he raised the question, "Who is my mother and my brother and my sister? Whoever does the will of my Father in heaven is my mother, my brother, my sister, and my father. My Father in heaven watches over me, takes care of me." He takes care of all of us. We are his; we belong to him. Stay in there when life throws the cloak of misery about you and the agony of pain closes in on you. Stay there, for God takes care of his own. God takes care of us.

I followed him to Calvary. The first words from the lips of my dying Lord were "Father, lay not this sin to their charge. Not Joseph, my earthly father, but Father in heaven, lay not this sin to their charge. They don't know what they are doing. They don't know who they are crucifying. Father, lay not this sin to their charge." Just before he died, his head fell into his shoulders. Out there on Calvary, he said a prayer that every Jewish boy or child learns at his mother's knee, "Father, into thy hands I commend my spirit."

When life closes in around you and around me, there is an old song we might sing,

> Father, I stretch my hands to Thee;
> No other help I know:
> If Thou withdraw Thyself from me,
> Ah! whither shall I go?

Let's stretch our hands to our Father in heaven. In the crucibles of life's experiences, God will hold our hands until the storms of life are over. *Amen.*

Fred C. Lofton
Metropolitan Baptist Church
Memphis, Tennessee

APPENDIXES

A. HIGHLIGHT DATES OF THE CHURCH YEAR

FIVE YEAR
CHURCH YEAR CALENDAR

	1987 Series A	1988 Series B	1989 Series C	1990 Series A	1991 Series B
Epiphany	Jan. 6	Jan. 6	Jan. 6	Jan. 6	Jan. 6
Ash Wednesday	March 4	Feb. 17	Feb. 8	Feb. 28	Feb. 13
Palm Sunday	April 12	March 27	March 19	April 8	March 24
Good Friday	April 17	April 1	March 24	April 13	March 29
Easter	April 19	April 3	March 26	April 15	March 31
Ascension Day	May 28	May 12	May 4	May 24	May 9
Pentecost	June 7	May 22	May 14	June 3	May 19
Trinity Sunday	June 14	May 29	May 21	June 10	May 26
Thanksgiving	Nov. 26	Nov. 24	Nov. 23	Nov. 22	Nov. 21
Advent Sunday	Nov. 29	Nov. 27	Dec. 3	Dec. 2	Dec. 1

B. CALENDARS

THIS YEAR

1987 CALENDAR 1987

JAN.
```
S  M  T  W  T  F  S
            1  2  3
 4  5  6  7  8  9 10
11 12 13 14 15 16 17
18 19 20 21 22 23 24
25 26 27 28 29 30 31
```

FEB.
```
 1  2  3  4  5  6  7
 8  9 10 11 12 13 14
15 16 17 18 19 20 21
22 23 24 25 26 27 28
```

MAR.
```
 1  2  3  4  5  6  7
 8  9 10 11 12 13 14
15 16 17 18 19 20 21
22 23 24 25 26 27 28
29 30 31
```

APR.
```
          1  2  3  4
 5  6  7  8  9 10 11
12 13 14 15 16 17 18
19 20 21 22 23 24 25
26 27 28 29 30
```

MAY
```
                1  2
 3  4  5  6  7  8  9
10 11 12 13 14 15 16
17 18 19 20 21 22 23
24 25 26 27 28 29 30
31
```

JUNE
```
    1  2  3  4  5  6
 7  8  9 10 11 12 13
14 15 16 17 18 19 20
21 22 23 24 25 26 27
28 29 30
```

JULY
```
S  M  T  W  T  F  S
          1  2  3  4
 5  6  7  8  9 10 11
12 13 14 15 16 17 18
19 20 21 22 23 24 25
26 27 28 29 30 31
```

AUG.
```
                   1
 2  3  4  5  6  7  8
 9 10 11 12 13 14 15
16 17 18 19 20 21 22
23 24 25 26 27 28 29
30 31
```

SEPT.
```
       1  2  3  4  5
 6  7  8  9 10 11 12
13 14 15 16 17 18 19
20 21 22 23 24 25 26
27 28 29 30
```

OCT.
```
             1  2  3
 4  5  6  7  8  9 10
11 12 13 14 15 16 17
18 19 20 21 22 23 24
25 26 27 28 29 30 31
```

NOV.
```
 1  2  3  4  5  6  7
 8  9 10 11 12 13 14
15 16 17 18 19 20 21
22 23 24 25 26 27 28
29 30
```

DEC.
```
    1  2  3  4  5
 6  7  8  9 10 11 12
13 14 15 16 17 18 19
20 21 22 23 24 25 26
27 28 29 30 31
```

1988 Calendar on following page.

NEXT YEAR

1988 CALENDAR 1988

JAN.
```
S  M  T  W  T  F  S
            1  2
3  4  5  6  7  8  9
10 11 12 13 14 15 16
17 18 19 20 21 22 23
24 25 26 27 28 29 30
31
```

FEB.
```
   1  2  3  4  5  6
7  8  9 10 11 12 13
14 15 16 17 18 19 20
21 22 23 24 25 26 27
28 29
```

MAR.
```
      1  2  3  4  5
6  7  8  9 10 11 12
13 14 15 16 17 18 19
20 21 22 23 24 25 26
27 28 29 30 31
```

APR.
```
               1  2
3  4  5  6  7  8  9
10 11 12 13 14 15 16
17 18 19 20 21 22 23
24 25 26 27 28 29 30
```

MAY
```
1  2  3  4  5  6  7
8  9 10 11 12 13 14
15 16 17 18 19 20 21
22 23 24 25 26 27 28
29 30 31
```

JUNE
```
         1  2  3  4
5  6  7  8  9 10 11
12 13 14 15 16 17 18
19 20 21 22 23 24 25
26 27 28 29 30
```

JULY
```
S  M  T  W  T  F  S
            1  2
3  4  5  6  7  8  9
10 11 12 13 14 15 16
17 18 19 20 21 22 23
24 25 26 27 28 29 30
31
```

AUG.
```
   1  2  3  4  5  6
7  8  9 10 11 12 13
14 15 16 17 18 19 20
21 22 23 24 25 26 27
28 29 30 31
```

SEPT.
```
            1  2  3
4  5  6  7  8  9 10
11 12 13 14 15 16 17
18 19 20 21 22 23 24
25 26 27 28 29 30
```

OCT.
```
                  1
2  3  4  5  6  7  8
9 10 11 12 13 14 15
16 17 18 19 20 21 22
23 24 25 26 27 28 29
30 31
```

NOV.
```
      1  2  3  4  5
6  7  8  9 10 11 12
13 14 15 16 17 18 19
20 21 22 23 24 25 26
27 28 29 30
```

DEC.
```
            1  2  3
4  5  6  7  8  9 10
11 12 13 14 15 16 17
18 19 20 21 22 23 24
25 26 27 28 29 30 31
```

C. COLORS OF THE CHURCH SEASONS

White:	Christmas and Easter Seasons; Ascension Day; Trinity Sunday; All Saints' Day; Weddings
Red:	Day of Pentecost
Purple:	Seasons of Advent and Lent
Green:	Season after Epiphany; Thanksgiving
Black:	Good Friday; Funerals (Funerals optional White or Green)

D. LECTIONARY SERIES FOR 1987

Christmas Season

January 4—Second Sunday after Christmas—Psalm 147:12-20; Jeremiah 31:7-14 *or* Ecclesiastes 24:1-4, 12-16; Ephesians 1:3-6, 15-18; John 1:1-18

Epiphany Season

January 11—First Sunday after Epiphany (The Baptism of the Lord)—Psalm 29; Isaiah 42:1-9; Acts 10:34-43; Matthew 3:13-17

January 18—Second Sunday after Epiphany—Psalm 40:1-11; Isaiah 49:1-7; I Corinthians 1:1-9; John 1:29-34

January 25—Third Sunday after Epiphany—Psalm 27:1-6; Isaiah 9:1-4; I Corinthians 1:10-17; Matthew 4:12-23

February 1—Fourth Sunday after Epiphany—Psalm 37:1-11; Micah 6:1-8; I Corinthians 1:18-31; Matthew 5:1-12

February 8—Fifth Sunday after Epiphany—Psalm 112:4-9; Isaiah 58:5-9*a*; I Corinthians 2:1-11; Matthew 5:13-16

February 15—Sixth Sunday after Epiphany—Psalm 119:1-8; Deuteronomy 30:15-20 *or* Ecclesiastes 15:15-20; I Corinthians 3:1-9; Matthew 5:17-26

February 22—Seventh Sunday after Epiphany—Psalm 62:5-12; Isaiah 49:8-13; I Corinthians 3:10-11, 16-23; Matthew 27-37

March 1—Last Sunday after Epiphany (Transfiguration of the Lord)—Psalm 2:6-11; Exodus 24:12-18; II Peter 1:16-21; Matthew 17:1-9

Lent

March 8—First Sunday of Lent—Psalm 130; Genesis 2:4*b*-9, 15-17, 25–3:7; Romans 5:12-19; Matthew 4:1-11

March 15—Second Sunday of Lent—Psalm 33:18-22; Genesis 12:1-4*a* (4*b*-8); Romans 4:1-5, (6-12), 13-17; John 3:1-17 *or* Matthew 17:1-9

March 22—Third Sunday of Lent—Psalm 95; Exodus 17:3-7; Romans 5:1-11; John 4:5-26 (27-42)

March 29—Fourth Sunday of Lent—Psalm 23; I Samuel 16:1-13; Ephesians 5:8-14; John 9:1-41

April 5—Fifth Sunday of Lent—Psalm 116:1-9; Ezekiel 37:1-14; Romans 8:6-11; John 11:(1-16), 17-45

Appendix

April 12—Palm/Passion Sunday—Matthew 21:1-11; Psalm 118:19-29; Isaiah 50:4-9*a*; Philippians 2:5-11

Easter Season

April 19—Easter—Psalm 118:14-24; Acts 10:34-43 *or* Jeremiah 31:1-6; Colossians 3:1-4 *or* Acts 10:34-43; John 20:1-18 *or* Matthew 28:1-10

April 26—Second Sunday of Easter—Psalm 16:5-11; Acts 2:14*a*, 22-23; I Peter 1:3-9; John 20:19-31

May 3—Third Sunday of Easter—Psalm 161:12-19; Acts 2:14*a*, 36-41; I Peter 1:17-23; Luke 24:13-35

May 10—Fourth Sunday of Easter—Psalm 23; Acts 2:42-47; I Peter 2:19-25; John 10:1-10

May 17—Fifth Sunday of Easter—Psalm 23; Acts 2:42-47; I Peter 2:19-25; John 10:1-10

May 24—Sixth Sunday of Easter—Psalm 66:8-20; Acts 17:22-31; I Peter 3:13-22; John 14:15-21

May 31—Seventh Sunday of Easter—Psalm 68:1-10; Acts 1:6-14; I Peter 4:12-14, 5:6-11; John 17:1-11

Season of Pentecost

June 7—Pentecost—Psalm 104:24-34; Isaiah 44:1-8 *or* Acts 2:1-21; I Corinthians 12:3*b*-13 *or* Acts 2:1-21; John 20:19-23 *or* John 7:37-39

June 14—First Sunday after Pentecost (Trinity Sunday)—Psalm 33:1-12; Deuteronomy 4:32-40; II Corinthians 13:5-14; Matt. 28:16-20

June 21—Second Sunday after Pentecost—Psalm 91:1-10; Genesis 28:10-17; Romans 5:12-19; Matthew 10:24-33

June 28—Third Sunday after Pentecost—Psalm 17:1-7, 15; Genesis 32:22-32; Romans 6:3-11; Matthew 10:34-42

July 5—Fourth Sunday after Pentecost—Psalm 124; Exodus 1:6-14; 22–2:10; Romans 7:14-25*a*; Matthew 11:25-30

July 12—Fifth Sunday after Pentecost—Psalm 69:6-15; Exodus 2:11-22; Psalm 69:6-15; Exodus 2:11-22; Romans 9:17; Matthew 13:1-9, 18-23

July 19—Sixth Sunday after Pentecost—Psalm 103:1-13; Exodus 3:1-12; Psalm 103:1-13; Exodus 3:1-12; Romans 8:18-25; matthew 13:24-30, 36-43

July 26—Seventh Sunday after Pentecost—Psalm 105:1-11; Exodus 3:13-20; Romans 8:26-30; Matthew 13:44-52

August 2—Eighth Sunday after Pentecost—Psalm 143:1-10; Exodus 3:13-20; Romans 8:26-30; Matthew 13:44-52

August 9—Ninth Sunday after Pentecost—Psalm 106:4-12; Exodus 14:19-31; Romans 3:1-5; Matthew 14:22-33

August 16—Tenth Sunday after Pentecost—Psalm 106:4-12; Exodus 14:19-31; Romans 3:1-5; Matthew 14:22-33

August 16—Tenth Sunday after Pentecost—Psalm 78:1-3, 10-20; Exodus 16:2-15; Romans 11:13-16, 29-32; Matthew 15:21-28

August 23—Eleventh Sunday after Pentecost—Psalm 95; Exodus 17:1-7; Romans 11:33-36; Matthew 16:13-20

August 30—Twelfth Sunday after Pentecost—Psalm 114; Exodus 19:1-9; Romans 12:1-13; Matthew 16:21-28

September 6—Thirteenth Sunday after Pentecost—Psalm 115:1-11; Exodus 19:16-24; Romans 13:1-10; Matthew 18:15-20

September 13—Fourteenth Sunday after Pentecost—Psalm 19:7-14; Exodus 20:1-20; Romans 14:5-12; Matthew 18:21-35

September 20—Fifteenth Sunday after Pentecost—Psalm 106:7-8, 19-23; Exodus 32:1-4; Philippians 1:21-27; Matthew 20:1-16

September 27—Sixteenth Sunday after Pentecost—Psalm 99; Exodus 33:12-23; Philippians 2:1-13; Matthew 21:28-32

October 4—Seventeenth Sunday after Pentecost—Psalm 81:1-10; Numbers 27:12-23; Philippians 3:12-21; Matthew 21:33-43

October 11—Eighteenth Sunday after Pentecost—Psalm 135:1-14; Deuteronomy 34:1-12; Philippians 4:1-9; Matthew 22:1-14

October 19—Nineteenth Sunday after Pentecost—Psalm 146; Ruth 1:1-19*a*; I Thessalonians 1:1-10; Matthew 22:15-22

October 25—Twentieth Sunday after Pentecost—Psalm 128; Ruth 2:1-13; I Thessalonians 2:1-8; Matthew 22:34-46

November 1—Twenty-first Sunday after Pentecost—Psalm 127; Ruth 4:7-17; I Thessalonians 2:9-13, 17-20; Matthew 23:1-12

November 8—Twenty-second Sunday after Pentecost—Psalm 50:7-15; Amos 5:18-24; I Thessalonians 4:13-18; Matthew 25:1-13

November 15—Twenty-third Sunday after Pentecost—Psalm 76; Zephaniah 1:7, 12-18; I Thessalonians 5:1-11; Matthew 25:14-30

November 22—Last Sunday after Pentecost (Christ the King)—Psalm 23; Ezekiel 34:11-16, 20-24; I Corinthians 15:20-28; Matthew 25:31-46

Appendix

Advent

November 29—First Sunday of Advent—Psalm 80:1-7; Isaiah 63:16–64:8; I Corinthians 1:3-9; Mark 13:32-37
December 6—Second Sunday of Advent—Psalm 85:8-13; Isaiah 40:1-11; II Peter 3:8-15*a*; Mark 1:1-8
December 13—Third Sunday of Advent—Isaiah 61:1-4, 8-11; Luke 1:46*b*-55; I Thessalonians 5:16-24; John 1:6-8, 19-28
December 20—Fourth Sunday of Advent—Psalm 89:1-4, 19-24; II Samuel 7:8-16; Romans 16:25-27; Luke 1:26-38

Christmas Season

December 27—First Sunday after Christmas—Psalm 111; Isaiah 61:10–62:3; Galatians 4:4-7; Luke 2:22-40

E. BLESSINGS AND BENEDICTIONS

But this I call to mind, and therefore I have hope: The steadfast love of the Lord never ceases, his mercies never come to an end; they are new every morning; great is thy faithfulness. (Lamentations 3:21-23)

My son, do not despise the Lord's discipline or be weary of his reproof, for the Lord reproves him whom he loves, as a father the son in whom he delights. (Proverbs 3:11-12)

Know therefore that the Lord your God is God, the faithful God who keeps covenant and steadfast love with those who love him and keep his commandments, to a thousand generations. (Deuteronomy 7:9)

And it shall come to pass afterward, that I will pour out my spirit on all flesh; your sons and your daughters shall prophesy, your old men shall dream dreams, and your young men shall see visions. (Joel 2:28)

The Lord is my rock, and my fortress, and my deliverer, my God, my rock, in whom I take refuge, my shield, and the horn of my salvation, my stronghold. (Psalm 18:2)

Trust in the Lord, and do good; so you will dwell in the land, and enjoy security. Take delight in the Lord, and he will give you the desires of your heart. Commit your way to the Lord; trust in him, and he will act. (Psalm 37:3-5)

[We] who by God's power are guarded through faith for a salvation ready to be revealed in the last time. (I Peter 1:5)

So we are ambassadors for Christ, God making his appeal through us. We beseech you on behalf of Christ, be reconciled to God. For our sake he made him to be sin who knew no sin, so that in him we might become the righteousness of God. (II Corinthians 5:20-21)

Beloved, do not be surprised at the fiery ordeal which comes upon you to prove you, as though something strange were happening to you. But rejoice in so far as you share Christ's sufferings, that you may also rejoice and be glad when his glory is revealed. (I Peter 4:12-13)

For if while we were enemies we were reconciled to God by the death of his Son, much more, now that we are reconciled, shall we be saved by his life. (Romans 5:10)

If we live, we live to the Lord, and if we die, we die to the Lord; so then, whether we live or whether we die, we are the Lord's. For to this end Christ died and lived again, that he might be Lord both of the dead and of the living. (Romans 14:8-9)

And now, little children, abide in him, so that when he appears we may have confidence and not shrink from him in shame at his coming. (I John 2:28)

Beloved, if our hearts do not condemn us, we have confidence before God. (I John 3:21)

Blessed is the man who endures trial, for when he has stood the test he will receive the crown of life which God has promised to those who love him. (James 1:12)

No temptation has overtaken you that is not common to man. God is faithful, and he will not let you be tempted beyond your strength, but with the temptation will also provide the way of escape, that you may be able to endure it. (I Corinthians 10:13)

For he says to Moses, "I will have mercy on whom I have mercy, and I will have compassion on whom I have compassion." So it depends not upon man's will or exertion, but upon God's mercy. (Romans 9:15-16)

You did not choose me, but I chose you and appointed you that you should go and bear fruit and that your fruit should abide. (John 15:16*a*)

But you are a chosen race, a royal priesthood, a holy nation, God's own people, that you may declare the wonderful deeds of him who called you out of darkness into his marvelous light. (I Peter 2:9)

I am the vine, you are the branches. He who abides in me, and I in him, he it is that bears much fruit, for apart from me you can do nothing. . . . As the Father has loved me, so have I loved you; abide in my love. (John 15:5, 9)

And now I am no more in the world, but they are in the world, and I am coming to thee. Holy Father, keep them in thy name, which thou hast given me, that they may be one, even as we are one. (John 17:11)

Take heed to yourselves and to all the flock, in which the Holy Spirit has made you overseers, to care for the church of God which he obtained with the blood of his own Son. (Acts 20:28)

Let us draw near with a true heart in full assurance of faith, with our hearts sprinkled clean from an evil conscience and our bodies washed with pure water. (Hebrews 10:22)

He said to me, "My grace is sufficient for you, for my power is made perfect in weakness." I will all the more gladly boast of my weaknesses, that the power of Christ may rest upon me. (II Corinthians 12:9)

Go therefore and make disciples of all nations, baptizing them in the name of the Father and of the Son and of the Holy Spirit, teaching them to observe all that I have commanded you; and lo, I am with you always, to the close of the age. (Matthew 28:19-20)

These [signs] are written that you may believe that Jesus is the Christ, the Son of God, and that believing you may have life in his name. (John 20:31)

And Jesus answered them, "Have faith in God. . . . I tell you, whatever you ask in prayer, believe that you have received it, and it will be yours." (Mark 11:22, 24)

This is the covenant that I will make with the house of Israel after those days, says the Lord: I will put my laws into their minds, and write them on their hearts, and I will be their God, and they shall be my people. (Hebrews 8:10)

SERMON CONTRIBUTORS

Ahlers, Rolf
Russell Sage College
Troy, New York 12180
   December 13   The Presence of Jesus: Symbol or Reality?   341

Anderson, Virgil R.
Wallingford Lutheran Church
Wallingford, Iowa 51365
   March 22   He Loves Me . . . He Loves Me Not . . . He Loves Me!   87
   August 23   God's Gambling Grace   236

Beattie, Linda C.
Post Office Box 1117
Longview, Washington 98632
   July 26   Teach Me to Pray   209

Beckstrom, Edward A.
Route 1, Box 134A
Equality, Alabama 36026
   January 4   Dreamers and Producers   15
   May 3   Bolted Doors   127

Belles, Robert M.
St. Mark's Lutheran Church
2911 North Main Street at Vista Parkway
Roswell, New Mexico 88201
   Special   The City of God (Confirmation)   390

Borreson, Glenn L.
First Lutheran Church
604 West Broadway
Decorah, Iowa 52101
   March 1   How Much Energy Do You Have?   68
   September 13   You Want to Take It with You?   255

Chakour, Charles M.
North Illinois Conference of The United Methodist Church
77 West Washington Street, Suite 1806
Chicago, Illinois 60602
   Special   A Mixed or Ecumenical Marriage   380
   Special   The Lord Bless You and Keep You   382

Chrisman, Richard A.
First United Methodist Church
100 East Pine
Mason City, Illinois 62664
   February 22   The Sin That Couches at the Door   62
   August 9   Meeting God's Demands   223

Colvin, Roger O.
St. Mark's United Methodist Church
Mount Joy, Pennsylvania 17552
   January 18   The Power of Forgiveness   29

Deal, Harold G.
Luther Place Memorial Church
1226 Vermont Avenue, N.W.
Washington, D.C. 20005
   July 19   Harried into Hope   202
   November 29   In Praise of Unlikely Apostles   327

Gibson, Raymond W., Jr.
Kentucky Conference of The United Methodist Church
1387 New Circle Road, Post Office Box 5107
Lexington, Kentucky 40555
   March 29   You Can Too!   93
   June 21   How Big Is Your God, Daddy?   176

Hardt, Peter D.
4809 Mancini Drive
Castro Valley, California 94546
   May 17   Jesus, the Good Shepherd   140
   October 11   Grace   281

Hubbel, Marie
567 East Lassen #602
Chico, California 95926
   April 19   A Pharisee Speaks   114

Kern, Charles W.
Grace United Methodist Church
471 Main Street
Haverhill, Massachusetts 01830
   June 28   Has Christianity Failed?   183
   August 30   Religion and Justice   242

Appendix

Kidd, James L.
Asylum Hill Congregational Church
814 Asylum Avenue
Hartford, Connecticut 06105
   January 25   The Natural   36
   September 6   What Is the Meaning of Life?   249
   Special   Let It Be (Christmas)   372

Kindt, Karl M., III
Trinity United Church of Christ
1312 Franklin Avenue
Lexington, Missouri 64067
   May 31   My Peace I Give to You   155
   Special   The Christmas Star (Short Christmas
      Message)   376

Lindekugel, Jon
Christ the King Lutheran Church
1040 South Grade Road
Hutchinson, Minnesota 55350
   March 15   Jesus, Lord of All   81

Lofton, Fred C.
Metropolitan Baptist Church
767 Walker At McDowell
Memphis, Tennessee 38126
   Special   Series of four Old Testament sermons on the
      book of Job   406

Logan, James M.
Catalina Baptist Church
1900 North Country Club Drive
Tucson, Arizona 85716
   April 5   Who Holds the Title?   101
   December 27   A Boy, A Baby, and Bethlehem   356

McCurdy, Thomas W.
Village Meadows Baptist Church
1100 El Camino Real
Sierra Vista, Arizona 85635
   May 24   The Head of the Church   147

McEachern, Alton H.
First Baptist Church
1000 Friendly Avenue
Greensboro, North Carolina 27403
  Special John Calvin—Servant of the Word 393
  Special Christians and Government 400

Malchow, Bruce V.
Sacred Heart School of Theology
7335 South Lovers Lane Road
Hales Corners, Wisconsin 53130
  February 8 Live Religion 49
  October 18 The Leap in the Dark 287

Nelson, David C.
Mount Pleasant Lutheran Church
5000 Graceland Boulevard
Racine, Wisconsin 53406
  June 14 Forth in Thy Name 170
  July 12 Clay Feet 196

Nyberg, Warren A.
13910 Hill Ridge Drive
Minnetonka, Minnesota 55343
  September 20 To Your Advantage 261
  November 22 On Dealing With Our Anger 321
  December 6 The Good Thief 334

O'Neill, Terrence M.
First United Methodist Church
Wicker Street
Ticonderoga, New York 12883
  December 20 Surprise 349
  Special Give Thanks—The Tithe (Stewardship) 386

Phipps, Dan
Westwood Baptist Church
Post Office Box 183
Roxboro, North Carolina 27573
  October 4 God Promises No Rose Gardens 274
  November 8 Making Yourself Miserable 307
  Special Monetary Messiahs (Electronic Preachers) 397

Appendix

Richards, Thomas E., Jr.
St. Paul's Lutheran Church
Post Office Box 139, Route 611
Tannersville, Pennsylvania 18372
   April 12 To Be A Spectator 107
   July 5 Let Freedom Ring 190
   Special Death Is the Beginning (Ash Wednesday) 366
   Special A Funeral Sermon 384

Ring, D. Z., III
St. Mark's United Methodist Church
5005 Love Road
El Paso, Texas 79922
   April 26 Don't Leave Now—The Party's Just Starting 121
   May 10 Biblical Images of Women 133

Robinson, D. Timothy
St. Mark's Lutheran Church
300 Palm Boulevard
Isle of Palms, South Carolina 29451
   February 15 It's the Real Thing 55
   September 27 On Being Different 267

Schmalenberger, Jerry L.
St. John's Lutheran Church
Sixth and Keosauqua
Des Moines, Iowa 50309
   March 8 The Near Kingdom 74
   October 25 Raising a Tudor Rose 293

Showalter, Douglas K.
The First Church in Belfast (United Church of Christ)
6 Court Street, Post Office Box 234
Belfast, Maine 04915
   August 2 Believe in Yourself! 215
   November 15 Faith Without Love 313

Strom, John
St. Mark's Lutheran Church
1121 Linden Street, Post Office Box 33216
Indianapolis, Indiana 46203
   February 1 You Can Have Peace Within 44

Viehe, Carl Armin
United Church of Christ
54 Lorfield Drive
Buffalo, New York 14226
   January 11   A More Excellent Way   21
   August 16   On Knowing What To Do   229

Vuocolo, James S.
Wyoming Ministries in Higher Education
1115 Grand Avenue
Laramie, Wyoming 82070
   June 7   Hearing God in One Another   163
   November 1   The Politics of Faith   300
   Special   Complicity (Good Friday)   369